WASSERSTROM
10.00
SUF

Faith and Practice of Islam

D0939495

SUNY Series in Islam
Edited by Seyyed Hossein Nasr

Faith and Practice of Islam

Three Thirteenth Century Sufi Texts

Translated, Introduced, and Annotated by

William C. Chittick

State University of New York Press • Albany

Published by
State University of New York Press, Albany

Printed in the United States of America

For information, address State University of New York Press,
State University Plaza, Albany, N.Y., 12246

Production by Cathleen Collins
Marketing by Dana Yanulavich

Library of Congress Cataloging in Publication Data

Faith and practice of Islam : three thirteenth century Sufi texts /
translated, introduced, and annotated by William C. Chittick.
p. cm. — (SUNY series in Islam)
Includes bibliographical references and indexes.
ISBN 0-7914-1367-5 — ISBN 0-7914-1368-3 (pbk.)
1. Sufism—Early works to 1800. I. Series.
BP188.9.F35 1992
297'.4—dc20 92-6106
CIP

10 9 8 7 6 5 4 3 2 1

Contents

A Note on Dates and Koranic References

All dates are indicated according to both the Islamic hijrah calendar (A.H.) and the Common Era, with the two dates separated by a slash. Citations from the Koran are italicized, with the number of sura and verse indicated in parentheses or brackets.

Introduction

Most premodern Islamic texts are very long or highly specialized. It is easy to find heavy tomes on Koran commentary, Hadith, jurisprudence, theology, philosophy, and Sufism, or short works on the fine points of these sciences. But concise overviews of the essentials of Islamic faith and practice are rare. In what follows, I translate three Persian texts written from a Sufi perspective about the year 650/1252. They present their author's understanding of basic Islamic teachings succinctly, clearly, and simply. They may have been written by Ṣadr al-Dīn Qūnawī (d. 673/1274), the step-son of the "greatest master" (*al-shaykh al-akbar*), Ibn al-ʿArabī (d. 638/1240), and a good friend of the foremost Sufi poet, Jalāl al-Dīn Rūmī (d. 672/1273). It is more likely that they were composed by one Naṣīr (or Nāṣir) al-Dīn Qūnawī. The texts were almost certainly written in Konya or its environs at about the time when Rūmī and Qūnawī were beginning their careers. Whoever may be the author, he presents the teachings of Ibn al-ʿArabī and his school in a simplified and straightforward manner. Thus, these are perhaps the earliest examples of a genre that has continued to be written until modern times.[1]

I was originally attracted to these three treatises because of research on Qūnawī, but my interest in them did not diminish when I realized that he is probably not the author. The treatises provide a perspective on Islam that is rarely met in modern works and that may also help provide a corrective to the simplistic classifying that goes on in the secondary literature. Their content will be valuable to anyone interested in the history of Sufism and its place in the Islamic tradition.

The first treatise, *The Rising Places of Faith,* deals primarily with explaining the objects of faith, which are presented in terms of Islam's "three principles": *tawḥīd* (the assertion of God's unity), prophecy (*nubuwwa*), and eschatology (*maʿād*).

The second treatise, *Clarifications for Beginners and Reminders for the Advanced,* presents the same three principles in considerably more detail.

The third treatise, *The Easy Roads of Sayf al-Dīn,* is addressed to a person who knew little about the religion—Sayf al-Dīn Ṭughril, a government official apparently employed at one of the Seljuk courts of Anatolia. His name suggests that he was a Turk. He seems to have recently converted to Islam or, if he was a born Muslim, he had decided to take his religion seriously. The author sets out to tell Sayf al-Dīn about Islam's essential teachings. Hence, he divides the work into two main sections: what Sayf al-Dīn needs to understand about God and the world, and what he needs to do. The first section provides a bare outline of the three principles, while the second goes into some detail on the practices that every Muslim must perform. This text is especially interesting in that it suggests what might be called the "lowest common denominator" of Sufi practice in the thirteenth century, and at other times as well.

The three treatises share a warmth and joy that are typical for Sufi works but, as a rule, are absent from books on sciences such as jurisprudence, Kalām, Koran commentary, and philosophy. The author quotes poetry constantly and makes no attempt to enter the nit-picking discussions and debates, the interminable *in qultas* ("If you say. . .then I will say") of the specialized treatises. Like Ghazālī in *Iḥyā' 'ulūm al-dīn* and *Kīmiyā-yi sa'ādat,* he strives to bring out the spiritual essence of the religious teachings, but unlike Ghazālī, he avoids detailed proofs and arguments, maintaining a light touch throughout. The first two texts and parts of the third are written with a beauty and fluency that make them comparable with classics of Persian prose such as Aḥmad Ghazālī's *Sawāniḥ,* Fakhr al-Dīn 'Irāqī's *Lama'āt,* or Suhrawardī's visionary treatises. In contrast to these authors, however, the author structures his works clearly and logically in a way that is reminiscent of technical texts in philosophy or theology.

The author says that his aim in composing these treatises was to "call attention and incite desire." He definitely did not write them for the general run of Muslims who, like the general run of people anywhere, consider religion—if they take it seriously at all—as a transaction: If you follow the rules, you avoid punishment and receive a reward. The author speaks to those few who have ceased being satisfied with the constraints of temporal existence and yearn for the Infinite. One is reminded of Rūmī's line.

> What is Love? Perfect thirst.
> So let me explain the water of life.[2]

The significance of the works lies on several levels. From the point of view of the history of religious ideas, they provide insight into the thinking of a century that is a watershed in Islamic history. They offer a rare bird's-eye view of Islam in an era when detailed and rambling expositions were the rule. Thus, for example, while much is known about the author's contemporaries, Ibn al-'Arabī and Rūmī, they never wrote introductory works of this sort, so their basic views on faith and practice can hardly be expressed in a few words without entering into the domain of speculation.

The texts can help dispel a myth that is still prevalent in religious studies in general and Islamic studies in particular. This is the idea that Sufis had little concern for the Shariah (Islamic law), or that they considered it to be a preliminary stage of human development—that is, a stage that one can pass beyond. In other words, it is thought that Sufis were free of the constraints of Islamic "orthodoxy." It is not surprising that Sufi texts are sometimes read in this manner, since many

Sufis set up their teachings in contradistinction to those of the jurists (*fuqahā'*) or the dogmatic theologians (the specialists in Kalām). Hence, they are critical of the juridical and theological perspectives, and it is easy to assume that they themselves wanted to have nothing to do with these "exoteric" sciences. But the issue was rather one of establishing the right sort of priorities. Sufis did not deny the legitimacy of these sciences, merely the exaggerated claims for authority made by many of their practitioners.

A second important source for the myth of Sufism's unconcern for the Shariah is the wishful thinking of Westerners who see Sufism as congenial but Islam as oppressive, or who find Islam's spiritual teachings exciting but its attention to ritual details tiring. In fact, Islam has taken both these dimensions of religion seriously from the beginning, and the peculiar genius of Sufism has to do with finding a happy balance between works and spirituality.

The translated texts have a direct bearing on a question that is of concern to everyone interested in the history of Islam: what exactly is Sufism, and how does it relate to Islam as a whole? Studies of Sufism usually make no serious attempt to answer this question—and with good reason. It would be practically impossible to provide an answer that would satisfy all who are concerned. Most scholars draw a sharp line between mainstream Islam and Sufism. This is rather easy to do when one is dealing with figures such as al-Ḥallāj, Ibn al-ʿArabī, and Rūmī. But the teachings of such masters do not necessarily focus on what Sufism actually meant for the vast majority of the members of Sufi orders, or for the vast majority of Muslims. The three texts translated here illustrate why it is often impossible to distinguish between Islam and Sufism, or between "exoteric" and "esoteric" Islam. They may help show that such labels can never be anything more than pointers and that the actual situation is always infinitely more complex than scholarly theories suggest.[3]

The three works will be useful to those who are curious about Islam as a living religion, not as a by-gone historical phenomenon to be classified with other dead artifacts. As a general rule, modern scholars pay a disproportionately large amount of attention to the Shariah and Islam's social and political teachings, and not nearly enough to the internal logic of the Islamic world view. Analysis of external phenomena provides no insight into the religion's driving power. It does not help us understand why Islamic teachings are convincing for Muslims. The general tendency is to attribute Islam's hold on people to social and economic factors, if not to fanaticism and "fundamentalism." Only ignorance of the internal coherence of Islamic theology, cosmology, and anthropology could lead to this sort of conclusion. However, there are relatively few works in English that demonstrate this coherence—largely because most Western scholars have had other interests and priorities, while most Muslim authors have had only tenuous connections with their own intellectual traditions. These works have much to offer here, not because of their provenance, but because they make sense.

Finally, the works will be of interest to those concerned with the general field of spirituality in world religions. They speak to everyone interested in the deeper questions posed by religion in all its forms, in spite of what may be unfamiliar modes of expression. The language is Islamic, but the style and approach of the treatises—especially the first and second—have a universal appeal. The linguistic and cultural veils can easily be lifted by the wind of personal interest.

I have intended to publish translations of these texts for several years. I first became familiar with one of them more than twenty years ago when I was working on my doctoral dissertation. By 1978, I had edited and translated two of the texts and was preparing them for publication in Iran, but the revolution brought an end to those plans. At that time, I had only a single manuscript of the third treatise, *Easy Roads*, and did not feel that it was sufficient for an edition or translation.

Once back in America, I continued working on a book that included translations of two of the treatises, but I had to put it aside as other projects arose.[4] However, the more I taught introductory courses on Islam and Sufism, the more I realized that the texts would be useful for beginning students. In 1990, I learned that *Easy Roads* had been published, and I was able to obtain a copy. I translated that and revised the two earlier translations thoroughly, mainly with a view toward style. Although it is impossible to reproduce the delightful flow of the originals in English, I have tried my best to do so.

Part One serves as an introduction to the texts, suggesting the role of faith and practice in Islam and the way in which Sufism fits into Islamic religiosity.

Part Two contains the two texts on faith, and Part Three the text on practice. I have written introductions to both parts, but the translations can practically stand on their own. Because they were written for beginners and not for specialists, they are remarkably straightforward and clear. I have provided annotations in order to help situate the teachings within the context of Islamic lore and, where possible, to provide sources for the quotations.

Part Four continues the discussion begun in Part One on the role of Sufism in Islam. If Part One deals with issues that need to be grasped before the texts can be situated within the broad context of Islamic teachings, then Part Four suggests some of the implications of these texts for Islamic studies as a subdiscipline of religious studies.

In the first appendix, I have discussed all the evidence that I have been able to find concerning the author of the works.

I have followed the published editions in the translations, making corrections to the Persian texts where necessary. These corrections are listed in the second appendix.[5]

I am grateful to David Buchman, who volunteered to type the original version of the book into a word processor, thus making it possible, in this era of technological dependence, for me to carry out extensive revisions.

NOTES

1. On the importance of this school in Islamic thought, see Chittick, "Ibn ʿArabī and His School." I am not implying here that Rūmī was a follower of Ibn al-ʿArabī. Cf. Chittick, "Rūmī and *Waḥdat al-Wujūd.*"

2. Rūmī, *Dīwān* 17361 (quoted in Chittick, *Sufi Path of Love* 195).

3. I have suggested one way to deal with this extremely complex issue of the relationship among different varieties of Islam in my article, "Spectrums of Islamic Thought." See the fine study by Mark Woodward, *Islam in Java*, which suggests that even in contemporary Islam, the clear demarcations that people want to find between, for example, "Sufism" and "Orthodoxy," are completely misleading.

4. I mention this work since I referred to it in some of the footnotes of ʿIrāqī, *Fakhruddin ʿIraqi: Divine Flashes*, and a number of people have asked me over the years when it was coming out. The present book includes the two texts I promised, but not the glossary. Important terms that were included in the glossary of that work are explained in the annotations of this book, and, in any case, far more information is available today on many of the technical terms because of more recent publications, including my own *Sufi Path of Knowledge.*

5. Qūnawī (ascribed), *Maṭāliʿ-i īmān*, edited by W.C. Chittick, *Sophia Perennis* 4/1 (1978) 57–80; idem, *Tabṣirat al-mubtadī*, edited by Najafʿalī Ḥabībī, *Maʿārif* 1 (1364/1985) 69–128; Juwaynī (ascribed), *Manāhij-i sayfī*, edited by Najīb Māʾil Hirawī, Tehran: Mawlā, 1363/1984.

Part One *Islam in Three Dimensions*

As stated in the introduction, two of the three texts translated in this book focus on the contents of Islamic faith, while the third concentrates on the details of practice—that is, the works that Muslims should perform in order to observe the Shariah. Faith is an issue frequently discussed by the proponents of Kalām (dogmatic theology), while the details of practice are the specialty of the jurists. But these are "Sufi" texts, which is to say that they are written from a viewpoint that is neither theological nor juridical. Specialists in Islamic studies are well aware that Islamic thought has different perspectives, but others may be confused by the distinctions. It may be useful here to suggest the nature of these distinctions in order to clarify the role played in Islam by Sufi writings.

WORKS, FAITH, AND PERFECTION

When we talk about "Islam" today, our understanding of the term is shaped by a host of historical and social factors. Not the least of these is the way in which journalists, politicians, and television announcers understand the term. Contemporary opinions and ideologies—themselves based on presuppositions that are far from self-evident—instill in us certain views about what has significance in human life. Given our own assumptions about reality, it is not easy to grasp how Muslim authors of the thirteenth century looked upon their religion. But the translated texts will make it obvious that our author has a very different idea of Islam than that which is met with today, not only in the media but also in the works of specialists.

By twentieth-century lights, we expect an introductory study of Islam to give us information about such things as historical background, events surrounding the foundation of the religion, important personalities, the political and social implications of the establishment of the new community, the significance and role of the important constitutive elements of the religious self-consciousness—such as the Koran, Hadith, common law, local customs, and the heritage from previous civilizations—and the historical development of various sects and belief systems. But none of this is discussed in the present treatises, even though the author is clearly concerned with explaining the nature of the Islamic religion.

In order to grasp the significance of these texts in their own context, we need a definition of Islam that would make sense to our author and that can also be understood in modern terms. This demands looking beyond many contemporary ideas of what is significant in human history in order to investigate the presuppositions of Muslim thinkers concerning the nature of religion and how it relates with human beings. My goal in Part One of this book is thus to bring out the perspective of our author and others like him on the religion that they follow. What does "Islam" mean, and what does "Sufism" have to do with Islam?

It is self-evident, even in modern terms, that human affairs have different foci. Some are centered in bodily activity, some in the life of the mind, and some in the heart. One possible means of classifying these domains is to speak of three basic dimensions of human existence, such as acting, knowing, and willing, or activity, intellectuality, and spirituality. Such a tripartite division is commonly met in Islamic texts. One of its earliest formulations is found in a famous hadith (a saying of the Prophet) called the "Hadith of Gabriel," in which the Prophet divides "the religion"[1]—that is, Islam—into three basic dimensions that I will call *works, faith*, and *perfection*.[2]

In naming these three dimensions, the Prophet employed words that have played important roles in Islamic intellectual history: *islām* (submission), *īmān* (faith), and *iḥsān* (virtue). In order to understand the religion of Islam as a reality possessing these three dimensions, one must grasp some of the implications of these words in the Koran, the Hadith, and the tradition.

Already, in the Koran, the word *islām* or "submission" has at least four senses, all of which have to do with the relationship between God and His creatures. In the broadest sense, *islām* is used to indicate that every creature, by the fact of being God's handiwork, is controlled by Him. *To Him "submits" everything in the heavens and the earth* (3:83).

In a narrower sense, *islām* means voluntary submission to God's will by following His revealed messages. The Koran mentions among the "Muslims"—that is, those who have freely submitted to God—Abraham (2:131, 3:67), Joseph (12:101), Noah (10:72), Lot and his family (51:36), the apostles of Jesus (5:111), and other pre-Islamic figures. Even Pharoah claims to be a Muslim when he realizes that he is going to be drowned (10:90), and a Sufi such as Ibn al-ʿArabī could stir up a controversy by suggesting that Pharoah's Islam was sufficient for salvation.

In a third and still narrower meaning, *islām* designates the religion revealed to Muhammad through the Koran. The most obvious Koranic example of this usage is the verse revealed at the Prophet's farewell pilgrimage. *Today I have perfected your religion for you, and I have completed My blessing upon you, and I have approved Islam for you as a religion* (5:3). It is this meaning of the term which I want to clarify here and for which I will be employing the term "Islam" without italics.

In the fourth and narrowest sense, *islām* refers to the outward works of the religion as distinguished from an inner something that makes the religion genuine and sincere. One verse is especially significant, since it differentiates between *islām* and *īmān*, submission and faith. *The Bedouins say, "We have faith." Say [O Muhammad!]: "You do not have faith; rather, say, 'We have submitted;' for faith has not yet entered your hearts"* (49:14). In this fourth sense, *islām* corresponds to one of the three dimensions of Islam, and hence its meaning needs to be clarified if we are to understand the meaning of *islām* in the third sense.

The Hadith of Gabriel differentiates even more clearly than this Koranic verse between *islām* in this fourth sense and *īmān*. (It is true that some Koranic verses and hadiths use the two terms as synonyms, but this does not prevent the texts from drawing distinctions in other contexts.) According to this hadith, *islām* consists of the "Five Pillars": saying the double Shahadah or testimony (bearing witness that there is no god but God and that Muhammad is His messenger), performing the ritual prayer, fasting during the month of Ramadan, paying the alms-tax, and making the hajj if one has the means to do so.

Once the Islamic community moves beyond the earliest period and becomes differentiated into a variety of schools and approaches, *islām* in the fourth sense refers to the domain in which the science of jurisprudence exercises its authority. The jurists are those of the ulama who are experts in the five pillars and the other activities prescribed by the Shariah. If people want to know how to make an ablution or draw up a will or a marriage contract, they ask a jurist.

A jurist as jurist can have nothing to say about faith or perfection, since these belong to other dimensions of the religion. As Ghazālī puts it, "The jurist speaks about what is correct and corrupt in *islām* and about its preconditions, but in this he pays no attention to anything but the tongue. As for the heart, that is outside the jurist's authority [*wilāyat al-faqīh*]."[3] If the jurist also happens to be a theologian, then, as theologian, he can speak about faith, since faith is one of theology's concerns. One might object that the Shahadah—the gist of Islam's theology—is one of the five pillars and is therefore part of the first dimension. However, this is Shahadah as work, not as theory. *Islām* in the sense of submitting to the five pillars demands simply that a Muslim voice the Shahadah in order to bear witness to submission. Whether or not a person believes in or understands the Shahadah—and more importantly, *how* a person understands the Shahadah—are different issues, dealt with in theology and other parallel sciences, not in jurisprudence.

The second dimension of Islam is *īmān* (faith). The Koran frequently employs the term and various derived words, especially the plural of the active participle, *mu'minūn* (those who have faith, the faithful). Although translators normally render *īmān* as "faith" or "belief," such translations leave out an important connotation, because the word derives from a root that means to be secure, safe, and tranquil. Hence, the literal sense of *īmān* is to render secure, safe, calm, and free from fear. The implication is that, through faith in God, one becomes secure from error and rooted in the truth. Faith has a cognitive dimension that is a step in the direction of certainty.

In a number of verses the Koran provides a list of the objects of faith. For example, *True piety is this: To have faith in God, the Last Day, the angels, the Book, and the prophets* (2:177). In the Hadith of Gabriel, the Prophet gives a formulaic expression to these objects by defining faith as "having faith in God, His angels, His scriptures, His messengers, the Last Day, and the measuring out [*qadar*] of good and evil."[4] Notice that the Prophet repeats the word faith in the definition itself, which indicates that here—in contrast to certain other hadiths—the *meaning* of faith is not at issue, but rather the *objects* of faith. These objects later become systematized into the three principles of the religion already mentioned in the introduction of this book—*tawḥīd* (the assertion of God's unity), Prophecy (*nubuwwa*), and the Return to God, (*maʿād*, commonly translated as "eschatology"). All the objects mentioned in the hadith are studied in the Islamic sciences. Muslim scholars did not approach them as articles of belief, in the modern sense of this term. They did not suppose that these objects may or may not be true and real. On the contrary, they accepted them as objective realities to be found in the nature of things.

If the first dimension of Islam becomes the specialty of the jurists, the second dimension becomes the object of study of three main groups of scholars—the proponents of Kalām, Sufis who were concerned with theoretical issues such as theology and cosmology, and philosophers. These three broad schools of thought—each having several branches—can be distinguished in many ways. Elsewhere, I have suggested that one way in which to understand their differing approaches is to notice the stress that they place upon various forms of knowledge.[5] By and large, philosophers claim that reason (*ʿaql*) is a sufficient means to understand the nature of things. No prophetic intervention is necessary—at least not for philosophers. The proponents of Kalām stress the primacy of revelation, although they interpret it in rational terms and hence, on the question of reason's role, can be placed rather close to the philosophers. In contrast to both philosophers and Kalām authorities, the Sufis maintain that reason has clearly defined limits. They agree with the Kalām specialists that revelation has a primary role to play, but they hold that interpretation of the revealed texts by the sole means of reason prevents a full understanding. Reason must be supplemented by direct knowledge given by God. This knowledge is called by many names, including "unveiling" (*kashf*), "tasting" (*dhawq*), "witnessing" (*shuhūd*), and "insight" (*baṣīra*).

In the dimension of faith, divergence of opinion is much more pronounced than in the first dimension, and naturally so. The jurists are concerned with outward works, which can be seen with the eye and analyzed in concrete detail. But the specialists in faith are concerned mainly with invisible realities that require the full application of human intelligence, if not direct divine aid, in order to be grasped to any extent. Differences of opinion abound, even though there is a surprising unanimity on certain fundamental issues.

The third dimension of Islam is perfection or virtue. The Prophet employed the word *iḥsān*, which is the most difficult of the three terms to translate. It is an active form from the root *ḥ.s.n.*, which means beautiful and good. Hence, the word *iḥsān* means to accomplish what is beautiful and good, to do something well, to do something perfectly, to gain perfect and virtuous qualities. The standard by which the good, the beautiful, and the virtuous are judged cannot be an individual's opinion, because at issue here is what the religion teaches. In the Hadith of Gabriel, the Prophet defines *iḥsān* as "serving [or worshiping] God as if you see Him, because if you do not see Him, He nonetheless sees you." In other words, this third dimension of Islam is concerned with depth, or the inner attitudes that accompany activity and thought. One must be aware of God's presence in everything one does—which is to say that one must have a state of soul in conformity with works and faith.

If people fail to deepen the first two dimensions of the religion, they are left with meaningless activity and verbal definitions. But everyone knows that the worth of activity is intimately bound up with the intention that animates it, while verbal definitions are useless without understanding. All those who take religion seriously must ask how to go below the surface and enter into the depths. Naturally, there are degrees. Most Muslim thinkers hold that human beings will ultimately be differentiated in accordance with the extent to which they live up to the standard of perfection in works and faith.[6] This is one of the meanings of the traditional teaching that both paradise and hell embrace many levels.

Just as the first two dimensions of Islam have their specialists, so also the third dimension has scholars and sages who dedicate their lives to explicating its nature. Most of these have been called "Sufis," although many of the ulama known as philosophers or theologians also investigated this dimension of the religion. And just as the dimension of faith leads to more debate and disagreement than does the dimension of works, so also, for analogous reasons, the dimension of perfection is more controversial than that of faith.

In short, Islam, as defined by the Prophet in the Hadith of Gabriel, consists of works, faith, and perfection. One can classify many of the scholarly disciplines that become established in Islam on the basis of the respective emphasis placed on one or more of these dimensions. What is of immediate relevance here is that the translated treatises focus on all three dimensions, even though the author does not refer to this hadith, nor does he clearly separate the dimension of perfection from the other two. However, there is no need to make a clear differentiation. This tripartite division serves simply to provide an overview, not a hard and fast rule. Moreover, when Islam's dimensions are embodied in the actuality of being human, they become different aspects of a single whole. The more harmoniously the three dimensions are integrated, the closer the person approaches to a perfected human personality and to the nature of the Real itself, which is utter harmony and pure oneness.

FAITH AND KNOWLEDGE

In Islamic texts, faith is discussed from two basic points of view: its subjective impact and its objective content. The first type of discussion deals with the definition of the word and its implications for the person who possesses it.[7] The second type addresses the objects of faith—God, the angels, and so on.

The locus of faith is the heart (*qalb*), which is the center or essence of the human being.[8] The heart is the place of intelligence, understanding, and every positive human quality. The heart's deviation and illness lead to ignorance, unbelief, and negative character traits. Its faith is inseparable from knowledge and noble character traits. Many Koranic verses and hadiths mention the good qualities of the faithful or the bad qualities that cannot dwell in the same heart with faith.

Specialists in Kalām were especially interested in the cognitive dimension of faith and its implications for putting the Shariah into practice. Sufi theoreticians were more interested in the moral and spiritual dimension of faith, and their explanations of the nature of faith in the heart coalesce with explanations of *iḥsān* and its near-synonym, *ikhlāṣ* (sincerity).

If both the Koran and the hadith literature make clear that faith is intimately related to positive character traits, they also bring out the cognitive dimension implicit in the word itself. Some hadiths connect faith with knowledge in a way that fits into the concerns of the Kalām specialists. For example, the Prophet said, "Faith is a knowledge [*ma'rifa*] in the heart, a voicing with the tongue, and an activity with the limbs."[9] Abū Ḥanīfa followed up on this approach by defining faith as "confessing with the tongue, recognizing the truth [of something, *taṣdīq*] with the mind, and knowing with the heart."[10] Ghazālī expresses the basic position of the Ash'arite theologians when he defines faith as "recognizing the truth [of something] in the heart, voicing [that truth] with the tongue, and acting [on its basis] with the limbs."[11]

Notice that Ghazālī's definition—like the just-cited hadith—includes activity and works (that is, *islām*) as part of *īmān*. For most authorities, faith includes works, but works do not necessarily imply faith. One cannot judge from a person's observance of the Shariah that faith is the motive. No suggestion is made that the domains of the Shariah and faith are equal, and a clear distinction is drawn between the two. Faith transcends works and includes them, whereas works without faith have no value.[12] One can have the first dimension of Islam without the second, works without faith, but one cannot have faith without works.

The cognitive and moral dimensions of faith are affirmed by its opposite, *kufr*, a word that is normally translated as "unbelief" or "infidelity." However, the root meaning of the term is "to cover over, to conceal." By extension, it means to cover over something that one knows. In the Koranic sense, it means to cover over the truth that God has revealed through the prophets and to conceal the blessings that God has given to His creatures. The Koran frequently uses the term *kufr* as the opposite of *shukr* (gratitude). Hence, the *kuffār* (plural of *kāfir*) are at once those who are ungrateful and those who cover over the truth that they know.

As Muhammad Asad has pointed out, the term *kāfir* "cannot be simply equated, as many Muslim theologians of post-classical times and practically all Western translators of the Qur'ān have done, with 'unbeliever' or 'infidel' in the specific, restricted sense of one who rejects the system of doctrine and law promulgated in the Qur'ān and amplified by the teachings of the Prophet,"[13] since the term is already present in the earliest verses of the Koran to be revealed. The truth that people cover over is the self-evident reality of God. They conceal it while knowing in their hearts that it is true. Wilfred Cantwell Smith has brought out clearly the stubborn willfulness implied by the Koranic term *kufr*.[14] In order to keep this cognitive implication of *īmān* and *kufr* in the forefront, I will be translating the term *kufr* as "concealing the truth" or "truth-concealing."

To come back to the word *īmān* itself, one of the most common terms employed in Kalām to define it is *taṣdīq*, which means to recognize or affirm the truth of something. The essence of faith is to know that something is true and to acknowledge its truth in word and deed. As Smith has remarked, to say that faith is *taṣdīq* means that "Faith is the ability to trust, and to act in terms of, what one knows to be true."[15] What one knows to be true is the objects of faith—God, the angels, the scriptures, and so on.

In English, "faith" is normally understood as volitional rather than cognitive. People think of faith as related to supposition and opinion rather than to knowledge and certainty. In contrast, faith in Islam pertains primarily to knowledge and the commitments that people make on the basis of knowledge. It stands above knowledge, not below it. It adds to knowledge a dimension of personal commitment, an engagement with the truth that one knows. As Smith puts it, "The object of faith being thought of as pellucid and incontrovertible, the issue is, what does one do about what one knows?"[16]

Most authors who discuss the objects of faith do not discuss the subjective side of faith, any more than contemporary biologists or astronomers analyze the assumption that they are dealing with real things. Muslim scholars were interested in the objects of faith because they knew them to be components of the real configuration of existence. They often do not even bother reminding us, because it is self-evident, that discussion of God, the angels, or eschatology pertains to one of the three principles of faith—principles which, as suggested above, simply classify the objects of faith into convenient categories.

As already mentioned, there are three basic approaches to understanding the objects of faith: philosophy, Kalām, and theoretical Sufism. Accepting the articles of faith on the basis of imitation or following authority (*taqlīd*) was the business of the common people or the beginners—those who have no real grasp of the creed. In contrast, the theological, philosophical, and Sufi sciences brought out what could be known—with various degrees of certainty—about faith's objects.

In short, discussion of the three principles and their ramifications fills up most texts on philosophy and Kalām, and many texts on Sufism.

That the discussion of the contents of faith occupies the philosophers may be less obvious than in the case of Kalām. Indeed, many contemporary scholars, having applauded the philosophers' open-mindedness, might object to the use of the word "faith." But this is to fall into the trap of understanding faith in our terms, in which it has little cognitive content. In Islamic terms, the contents of faith are objects of real knowledge, and the philosophers analyze the same objects as do the theologians and Sufis. After all, the object of philosophical study is *wujūd* (existence or being), and *wujūd* is the underlying stuff of reality. For most philosophers, it is ultimately the Real itself—God—while it is also present in some mode through the things of experience. In effect, by studying *wujūd*, the philosophers investigate the first of the three principles of faith: *tawḥīd*, or the relationship of the many (which they like to call "the possible things," *mumkināt*) to the One (the "Necessary Being," *wājib al-wujūd*). Most philosophers also discuss prophecy and eschatology.

No one is claiming that the philosophers always come to the same conclusions as do the Sufis and Kalām authorities. Far from it. But they study the same realities, and they have faith in them, which is to say that they know them to be objectively true and live their lives accordingly.

Sufis join the theoretical discussions of the three principles of faith at a relatively late date in Islamic history. There were detailed books on philosophy and Kalām long before the Sufis began systematic discussions of the theoretical—rather than the practical and applied—dimensions of their science. Almost all early Sufis deal primarily with the deepening of faith and works and the nature of the various human qualities that can be achieved through imitating the Prophet. To the extent that the early Sufis address the contents of faith, they prefer enigmatic or gnomic sayings.

In all sophisticated studies of faith's principles, epistemology is a central issue. How do we know what we know? What can we know for certain? In what sense can we know God? In what sense can we know anything other than God? Such questions—with tremendous variety and nuance amplified by the different perspectives of diverse schools of thought—fill up countless volumes.

The authorities in all these sciences differentiate between the common people (*ʿāmma*) and the elect (*khāṣṣa*). The first imitate the faith of others and follow authority (*taqlīd*), while the second verify the truth of what they know (*taḥqīq*). In the context of Sufism, these terms refer to the Sufis as opposed to the general run of Muslims who are not Sufis. The implication is that what Sufis understand is beyond the understanding of the common people. This "elitism" of Sufism has sometimes been criticized, but the perspective is far from being exclusive to Sufism or to the various schools that deal with faith. The Koran itself supplies the principle in the verse, *Above everyone who has knowledge is one who knows*

(12:76). No one objects when Muslim grammarians or mathematicians talk about the elect and the common people, meaning thereby those who know their science and those who do not. Ghazālī points out that all scholars consider their own domain as God's chosen realm (and this seems to be no less true today). He says that each of more than twenty schools of thought claims that its own science is what the Prophet meant when he said that the search for knowledge is incumbent on every Muslim.[17]

The fact that the Sufis—like other possessors of knowledge in Islam—consider themselves to be an elect helps explain the often encountered description of Sufism as "Islamic esoterism." One cannot object to this expression, so long as it is kept within bounds. It does not mean that the Sufis jealously guarded certain teachings and practices from the majority. Rather, Sufi knowledge and practice remained relatively hidden because the majority were either uninterested or incapable of understanding. In this respect, grammar and mathematics are also esoteric. What stands out in Sufi esoterism is that it relates to the domain of Islam's faith and works, and it is contrasted with an exoterism that relates to the same domain. But here again, the first thing one should understand from this distinction is that the majority of people—the "common people" as opposed to the "elect"—had no interest in Sufism, or considered it to be suspect and dangerous if not heretical. Most people are satisfied to remain with works and faith as defined in simple terms. They do not want subtleties and complications, nor do they like to be told that they are not good people and that they should try to change themselves.

This is not to say that Sufism has no connection with esoterism in the sense of knowledge of the mysteries, the unseen things, the occult, the mysterious, the mystical. All this is implied in the attention which the Sufis pay to unveiling as a valid source of knowledge, a topic that will come up again in several places within this book.

IḤSĀN, IKHLĀṢ, AND *TAQWĀ*

The Prophet referred to Islam's third dimension with the term *iḥsān*, which he defined in the Hadith of Gabriel as "worshiping God as if you see Him, because if you do not see Him, He nonetheless sees you." The Koran employs the word *iḥsān* and its active participle, *muḥsin* (the person who has *iḥsān*), more than seventy times. Sometimes, the subject of the verb is God, and *al-muḥsin* is usually found in the lists of the divine names. As a human quality, *iḥsān* is always praiseworthy. Verses such as the following illustrate that human *iḥsān* is closely connected to divine *iḥsān*. *Who is better in religion than the one who submits his face to God, being a* muḥsin? (4:125). *Have* iḥsān. *God loves those who have* iḥsān (2:195). *God's mercy is near to the* muḥsins (7:56). *God is with the* muḥsins (29:69).

Literally, *iḥsān* means putting the good and the beautiful into practice. The Koranic usage makes clear that this is not only an external and ethical good, but also an internal, moral, and spiritual good. Hence, "virtue" may suggest some of what it involves. The Prophet's definition stresses the internal dimensions of the quality, tying it to an attitude of soul. For the Sufi sages, the internal and spiritual dimensions of *iḥsān* are, in any case, obvious.

Among the Koranic evidence that Sufis cite to show the spiritual dimensions of *iḥsān* is that the Book describes God's own qualities with the superlative adjective from the same root. In four verses it speaks of God's "most beautiful names" (*al-asmā' al-ḥusnā*). As the first Shahadah makes clear, everything good belongs essentially to God, and accidentally—if at all—to the creatures. "There is no god but God" means that all the qualities denoted by the most beautiful names belong to God in a true sense, and to other things in some other sense. It follows logically that "There is no good but the divine good," "There is no mercy but the divine mercy," and ultimately, "There is nothing truly real but the Real." *Iḥsān*, putting the good and the beautiful into practice, implies bringing God's goodness and beauty—real goodness and beauty—into the soul and the world.

One of the many ways of describing the process of achieving human perfection is to say that it involves "assuming the character traits of God" (*al-takhalluq bi akhlāq Allāh*). God's character traits are identical with His most beautiful names. The biblical and prophetic saying, "God created human beings in His own image" or "form" (*ṣūra*) was interpreted to mean that the innate disposition (*fiṭra*) of human beings embraces all the qualities designated by God's names.

To become perfect is to bring the latent divine qualities within oneself into full actuality. It is to act, know, and be as God would act, know, and be, were He to assume human form.

The acting is the easiest, since it can be described and delineated in exact terms. Hence, everyone is told to act. This is the Shariah, incumbent upon all.

The knowing is much more difficult. Although "The search for knowledge is incumbent upon every Muslim," the extent to which a person seeks and actualizes knowledge will depend upon personal qualifications.

Finally, to be as God would be is by far the most difficult, since it involves an utter transformation of the personality. This is Sufism's primary concern, and relatively few people attempt to achieve it.

On the level of seeking knowledge, a person might take any of several routes. The minimum knowledge that is incumbent upon every Muslim, as Ghazālī points out, is what allows a person to know the creed and perform the required practices.[18] People who feel themselves to be drawn to a broader and deeper knowledge of the religion will not follow the same paths. Some will become experts in jurisprudence, others in Kalām or philosophy, and still others in various other fields of learning. Both philosophy and theoretical Sufism have described the possibilities of human knowledge and awareness in terms that make it clear that these are unlimited, since the ultimate degree of knowing involves a lifting of many of the barriers that separate the finite from the Infinite.

It needs to be kept in mind that this seeking of knowledge—to the extent that it pertains to knowledge of the objects of faith—helps in the deepening and perfecting of faith. One cannot have faith in something about which one has no knowledge. In the same way, the more knowledge one gains of the nature of things—that is, the things dealt with under the heading of Islam's three principles—the firmer becomes one's commitment to what one knows.

The process of deepening one's knowledge is inseparable from that of knowing the most beautiful names of God, which are the archetypes of all that exists. To the extent that one knows these names and their implications, one becomes committed to and engaged in the human goodness and beauty that they demand. To "worship God as if you see Him" is to serve Him through becoming His vicegerent (*khalīfa*) and manifesting His qualities within oneself and the world.

A number of Koranic terms have semantic fields that overlap with *iḥsān* and are used in similar senses in the literature. Two are of particular interest: *ikhlāṣ* and *taqwā*.

Ikhlāṣ derives from a root having to do with purity, cleanliness, and freedom from admixture. Frequently translated as "sincerity," it means to purify, or to free something from extraneous elements or factors. The Koran employs the verb in the sentence, *akhlaṣū dīnahum li'llāh* (4:146): "They freed their religion from admixture for God," or "They purified their religion for God." Koran translators have rendered this sentence in a variety of ways: "They are sincere in their religion to God" (Palmer); "They make their religion pure for Allah (only)" (Pickthall); "They make their religion sincerely God's" (Arberry); "They are sincere in their devotion to God" (Dawood); "They grow sincere in their faith in God alone" (Asad); "They dedicate their religion solely to God" (Irving). In eleven more verses, the Koran speaks approvingly of "the *mukhliṣūn* [those who have *ikhlāṣ*] for God in their religion."

The hadith literature employs the term *ikhlāṣ* in suggestive ways, such as "purifying works for God" and "purifying the heart for faith." Hadiths sometimes mention the "sentence of *ikhlāṣ*," meaning the first Shahadah, which turns the mind and heart away from everything other than God. *Ikhlāṣ* is often taken as the antonym for *shirk* (associating others with God), which is the only unforgivable sin, and as a synonym for *tawḥīd*, which is also defined by the first Shahadah. Sura 112 of the Koran, which begins, *Say: He is God, One*, is called both the "Sura of *Tawḥīd*" and the "Sura of *Ikhlāṣ*." In short, the hadith literature makes explicit what the Koran implies—sincerity is a deepening of works and faith such that one's only motive in acting and thinking is God. If *tawḥīd* can be understood to mean the voicing of the sentence, "There is no god but God," *ikhlāṣ* implies that *tawḥīd* is internalized so that it becomes the determining factor in thought and action.

The word *taqwā* is especially significant in the present context because the author of the three treatises discusses it in some detail. It and related terms from the same root are employed far more frequently in the Koran than either *iḥsān* or *ikhlāṣ* and their derivatives. The term is especially difficult to translate and, with some trepidation, I have chosen "god-wariness."

The root of the word *taqwā* has two interwoven senses: to fear and to protect oneself. The basic meaning in the Koranic context is to stand in awe of God, to fear the consequences of acting against His will, and to do everything in one's power to protect oneself from these consequences. The term implies observing the religion meticulously, sincerely, and with full presence of mind. In the verbal form of *ittaqā*, the word often takes God as object, and I translate, "to be wary of God." That *taqwā* is a human quality established in relationship to God is clear in any case, whether or not God is mentioned in the immediate context.

The Koran always mentions the god-wary in positive terms. They have taken God's message to heart, have put it into practice completely, and will inhabit the Garden. In contrast, both those who have submitted (*muslimūn*) and those who have faith (*mu'minūn*) are sometimes criticized, whether explicitly or implicitly. Most of the Koran's commandments are addressed to those who have faith—that is, those who have recognized the truth of the message and are attempting to put it into practice. The Koran frequently tells the faithful that they must have *taqwā*, so it is a goal toward which they should be striving. Several verses say that the god-wary are the ones whom God loves and has guided. In effect, it is they who have perfected their works and faith.[19] The hadith literature employs the term *kalimat al-taqwā* (the sentence of god-wariness) as a synonym for the sentence of *ikhlāṣ* or *tawḥīd*—that is, the first Shahadah.

The Koran provides a great deal of evidence for suggesting that *taqwā* expresses in a single word the sum total of all good and beautiful human attributes, or the perfect human embodiment of Islam in its deepest sense. This is particularly clear in the verse, *The noblest of you in God's eyes is the one among you who has the most* taqwā (49:13). Translators have tried in various ways to bring out the fundamental importance of this term for Koranic religiosity. Each of the following translations reflects the translator's idea of the key virtue in Islam.

"The most honourable of you in the sight of God is the most pious of you" (Palmer). "The noblest among you with Allāh is the most dutiful of you" (Muhammad Ali). "The noblest of you, in the sight of Allah, is the best in conduct" (Pickthall). "The noblest among you in the sight of God is the most godfearing of you" (Arberry). "The most honourable of you with Allah is the one among you most careful (of his duty)" (Habib). "The noblest of you in God's sight is he who is most righteous" (Dawood). "The noblest of you in the sight of God is the one who is most deeply conscious of Him" (Asad). "The noblest among you with God is that one of you who best performs his duty" (Irving).

The term "god-wariness" makes *taqwā*'s orientation toward God explicit, brings out the implication of being aware and mindful, and avoids the negative and sentimental undertones of words such as "piety," "dutifulness," and "righteousness."

FELICITY

The goal of observing Islam's three dimensions is to gain salvation. The term most commonly employed for salvation in Islamic texts is *sa'āda*, which means happiness. I will be translating it with the Latinate word "felicity" in order to remind the reader that this happiness pertains fundamentally to life after death. The opposite of felicity is "wretchedness" (*shaqā'*).

The tradition locates felicity in paradise and wretchedness in hell, even though both have foretastes in this world. But Sufis stress *tawḥīd* and *ikhlāṣ*. In their view, perfecting works and faith involves relating all things back to God as well as purifying activity, thought, and will from service to anything other than God. If a person worships God with the intention of avoiding hell and gaining paradise, an ulterior motive has crept in, a concern for oneself rather than God. Since a god is anything that one serves, some authorities maintain that this is a subtle form of associating other gods with God (*shirk khafī*), and hence it prevents complete *ikhlāṣ*.

In Sufi literature one commonly meets the theme of desiring God alone and rejecting paradise. Many Muslim authors divide human beings into three major groups on the basis of Sura 56. The "Companions of the Left" will inhabit hell. The "Companions of the Right" will live in paradise, and "those brought near to God" (*al-muqarrabūn*) actualize full *tawḥīd* and *ikhlāṣ*. In the Sufi view, the members of this last group have erased both paradise and hell from their vision. We will meet this theme in all three texts translated below,

To reach felicity is to dwell in paradise or to live with God. But felicity has many levels. The Koran implies—and the tradition affirms—that the greatest felicity is the encounter (*liqā'*) with God, a term our author frequently mentions. This encounter means that people have a vision (*ru'ya*) of God. Theological debates about the nature of this vision—and whether it was attainable in this world—were common. If a distinction can be drawn here between the perspective of the Sufis and the theologians, it is that the Sufis held that one can encounter God already in this world, while the theologians maintained that the encounter will not occur until after death. Our author refers to the encounter in this world as the "arrival" (*wuṣūl*).

Although Sufis maintain that God can be encountered in this world, many—if not most—give an ambiguous answer to the question of actually seeing Him, whether here or in paradise. Usually they maintain that God *in Himself* cannot be seen, although He can be seen in the form in which He chooses to disclose Himself. Moreover, He discloses Himself in keeping with the receptacle. From here it is only one step to the position that God discloses Himself to all things—in this world as well as the next—in keeping with their capacities or preparednesses (*isti'dād*). God is never absent from His creatures. God is *nearer than the jugular vein* (50:16) and *with you wherever you are* (57:4). However, people are absent from God. He is there to be seen, but seeing Him takes a special kind of eye. Gaining that eye depends on actualizing *tawḥīd* and *ikhlāṣ*.

To encounter God is to encounter the object of one's faith. Here again, the importance of faith's cognitive dimension comes to the forefront. If Islam's third dimension stresses the deepening of faith, this implies that the object of one's faith comes to coincide more and more exactly with the Real. Ibn al-ʿArabī among others insists that the "god of belief" is always distinct from God in Himself, since a finite receptacle can never grasp the Infinite.[20] But the knowledge achieved through deepened faith is far beyond that which depends on rational arguments and conclusions. As our author often remarks, through god-wariness, faith can be transmuted into unveiling or the direct vision of the realities of things.

Unveiling allows people to "see God," since their faith and knowledge are transmuted into witnessing God's self-disclosures. This vision of God brings us back to *iḥsān*, which is "to worship God as if you see Him." As the Sufis like to point out, the highest degree of *iḥsān* is to worship God without the "as if"—that is, while actually seeing and recognizing Him through His self-disclosures. This is how many of them interpret the saying of the Prophet's cousin and son-in-law ʿAlī, "I would not worship a God whom I did not see."

In sum, Islam's third dimension completes the first two. Its characteristics confirm the hierarchical relationship that was mentioned in connection with works and faith. There can be works without faith, but no faith without works. In the same way, there can be faith without perfection, but no perfection without faith and the works that are a part of faith.

Hence Islam and being a Muslim have three basic degrees. The first and most superficial degree is defined as "voicing the Shahadah," the first of the five pillars. Within the first degree, there are, of course, many subdegrees that jurisprudence is able to differentiate. This explains the debates over issues such as whether simply voicing the Shahadah is sufficient to be a Muslim, or whether a person also has to observe the other pillars.

On the second level, people are Muslim if, being Muslim in the first sense, their beliefs are correct. This is the domain in which theologians set up their catechisms and creeds.

On the third and final level, the issues of sincerity, virtue, and human worth are discussed. On every level, there is a different understanding as to what "Islam" implies. Different schools of thought offer different interpretations. If anything differentiates the Sufis from other Muslims here, it is not only that they consider all three dimensions worthy of attention, but also that they view the third dimension as the proper fruition and completion of the first two.

PRIORITIES

The Sufi authorities along with other ulama take the first Shahadah as the fundamental truth in terms of which all other things must be understood. Hence their primary concern is God. But Sufi texts have a way of bringing out God-centeredness more clearly than do, let us say, texts on jurisprudence, Kalām, or philosophy.

The jurists soon ignore God by devoting all their attention to the details of the Shariah. The proponents of Kalām are interested in God, but primarily as an object of rational thought and cold analysis. They keep Him at arm's length, stressing His inaccessibility and incomparability. God becomes largely an abstraction—an "It"—of interest only inasmuch as He reveals certain laws and principles through the prophets. The philosophers usually put the religious language of Islam into the background, and they often seem careful to avoid mentioning the Koranic names of God. They prefer an approach that today we would call "objective" and "academic." Hence they like to refer to God with terms such as "necessary being" or "first principle."

The Sufis agree with the Kalām authorities that God is inaccessible. But they add that, just as He is ever-absent, so also He is ever-present. Inasmuch as He is present, He is eminently desirable and lovable. The God that Sufis keep at the center of their concerns is the God whom people want to have around, not the God who instills terror in the heart and plays a dominant role in jurisprudence and Kalām. Awareness of God's presence gives birth to joy and delight. This helps explain why Sufi texts are characterized by a stylistic lightness not found in writings from other branches of religious learning. It also suggests why most of the great poets of Islamic civilization are rooted in the Sufi tradition.

Scholars have often pointed out that "post-axial" religions are concerned mainly with salvation, and Islam is no exception. Although the religion is all about God, it is also totally anthropocentric, because knowledge of God is oriented toward the ultimate concern of every human being—one's personal destiny. The Koran and the Hadith focus all of their attention, directly or indirectly, on the question of what the reality of God implies for human beings.

In the Sufi reading, human felicity is inseparable from God Himself. This is implied in the saying, "God created Adam in His own form." The human being is a form (*ṣūra*), and every form demands an inner reality, a "meaning" (*maʿnā*). In some mysterious fashion, this inner reality is God Himself. Understanding this, and fully experiencing and living all its consequences, is the ultimate goal of *tawḥīd*. Through *iḥsān*—the perfection of what is good and beautiful in human beings—people come to embody and manifest the most beautiful names of God, or the reality of God Himself. Then they become worthy of the honor that God accords to Adam in the Koran, that of being God's vicegerent on earth.

In general, the Muslim authorities—and this is especially true of Sufis—put first things first (*al-ahamm fa'l-ahamm*). The Prophet said, "I seek refuge in God from a knowledge that has no profit." Profitable knowledge is knowledge that leads people to felicity. Any knowledge that does not pertain directly to the achievement of felicity must be placed in the background. Hence, these three treatises—in the manner of other traditional writings on Islamic faith and works—are oriented toward eschatology, life after death, avoiding wretchedness (*shaqā'*), and achieving permanent happiness. If our author is concerned only with works, the contents of faith, and perfection, it is because he sees these alone as immediately relevant to felicity. These dimensions of human existence must be addressed if people are to situate themselves correctly in relation to ultimate reality.

The accent on achieving felicity demands a strict hierarchy of values. This hierarchy is defined in terms of God, the ultimate value. Secondary values are those that come directly from God, such as the Koran and the Prophet. Third-level values—such as the Hadith and the Shariah—come from God through the intermediary of the second-level values. In this hierarchical way of looking at things, what is nearer to God is better. What brings about nearness to God (*qurb*, a term that is practically synonymous with felicity) is better than what brings about separation from Him. Any knowledge that helps bring about nearness is profitable, and any knowledge that works against nearness is unprofitable and should be avoided. That is why Ghazālī can write, alluding to the saying of the Prophet just cited,

> "Profitable" knowledge is what increases your fear of God, your ability to see your own faults, and your knowledge of how to serve your Lord. It decreases your desire for this world and increases your desire for the next. It opens your eyes to the defects of your own works so that you guard against these defects.[21]

To the extent that the Islamic sciences are oriented toward goals other than human felicity, they do not deal with profitable knowledge. Hence, they do not pertain directly to Islam but to what Marshall Hodgson calls "Islamdom." Of course, I am speaking in relatives, not absolutes. I would not remove from the category of Islamic knowledge any specific science cultivated by Muslims. But some sciences are closer to the salvific ideals of the religion, while some are further away. All of them can have their profit. The criterion of "Islamicity" here is much more subjective than objective. For some people, knowledge of the natural world may be a barrier to faith in the unseen reality of God, for others it may be a necessity for the same faith. The differing perceptions of the soteriological relevance of the sciences help explain the differing opinions of the Muslim intellectuals—such as jurists and philosophers—on what sort of knowledge needs to be acquired.

THE SCIENCES OF UNVEILING AND PRACTICE

At the beginning of *Easy Roads*, our author divides religious knowledge into two types: the science of faith and the science of god-wariness. He identifies these with the sciences of unveiling and those of practice—terms which, he tells us, are employed by the ulama. He certainly has Ghazālī in mind as one of these ulama, since Ghazālī goes to great length in the first book of the *Iḥyā'* to explain the nature of knowledge and of these two types of knowledge in particular. Ghazālī's major point is that the knowledge incumbent on every Muslim is the science of practice.

Note the distinction between the word *ʿamal*, which I translate as "works," and *muʿāmala* (practice), which is the third-form *maṣdar* from the same root. *ʿAmal* means working, doing or making something, something done, an activity, a work. The third-form *maṣdar* implies interaction. According to Lane's *Lexicon*, *muʿāmala* means "he worked, laboured, served, acted, or transacted business with him." Hence, "practice" is a work that keeps God in view, whereas works do not necessarily involve God. However, they *should*—and this is precisely the point. One can perform works that do not follow the Shariah, or works that observe the Shariite rules but are contradicted by the intention or the attitude. Ghazālī repeatedly reminds his readers that the competence of the jurists extends only to activity—the works themselves—not to the intention behind the activity. Their jurisdiction is the Shariah alone. As he remarks about the ritual prayer (*ṣalāt*),

> The jurist rules that a person's ritual prayer is correct if it exhibits the form of the acts along with the outward preconditions, even if the person is negligent throughout the whole prayer, from its beginning to its end, thinking instead about the calculation of his transactions in the market.[22]

For Ghazālī, in short, the science of practice deals with the deepening of works. In contrast, the science of unveiling pertains to the deepening of faith. *Mukāshafa* (unveiling), is a third-form *maṣdar* from *kashf*, which I also translate as unveiling. Most Sufi texts employ *kashf* and *mukāshafa* interchangeably. If there is a difference in nuance, it has to do with the interpersonality implied by the third-form *maṣdar*. Unveiling is not one-sided, since it pertains to a relationship between the human being and God.

It should be kept in mind that, although the knowledge gained through unveiling is different from that gained through reason, it is not irrational. Rather, unveiling is suprarational in the sense that it is inaccessible to reason without God's direct help.

One of the classic tales told to illustrate the difference between rational knowledge and unveiling concerns the Sufi shaykh Abū Saʿīd Abi'l-Khayr (d. 440/1049) and the great philosopher Avicenna (428/1037), who is mentioned in a similar context in a poem quoted by our author. The story, of course, comes from Sufi sources, since unveiling is pictured as superior to reason. It is noteworthy that no contradiction is seen between the two types of knowledge, because it is recognized that they have the same objects. I tell the story as I remember it, without reference to a source. In any case, the point of the story does not lie in its historical accuracy.

Avicenna went to Maymana with his train of students to visit the great shaykh Abū Saʿīd, who lived there surrounded by many disciples. The two immediately took a liking to each other, and Abū Saʿīd led Avicenna into his private chamber, where they sat together for three days and three nights. No one interrupted them, except to take in food and refreshments. After three days, Avicenna mounted his horse and rode off, his students following. After a respectful lapse of time, the eldest student asked Avicenna, "O great master, how did you find that man Abū Sa'īd? His disciples make extravagant claims about him." Avicenna replied, "Well, everything I know, he sees."

Back in Maymana, one of Abū Sa'īd's close disciples was delegated by the others to inquire about this philosopher, whose disciples were so cocksure about his knowledge of everything under the sun. Abū Sa'īd replied, "Well, it's true. Everything I see, he knows."

Sufis and philosophers frequently distinguish between suprarational and rational knowledge by calling one of them *ma'rifa* (gnosis) and the other *'ilm* (knowledge or learning). One of my favorite aphorisms is cited anonymously by Qushayrī. "The gnostic is above what he says, but the possessor of learning [*'ālim*] is below what he says."[23]

The ulama are below what they say because they understand only the surface implications of the words that they quote from the Koran, the Sunnah, and the traditional authorities. If the Sufi shaykhs are above what they say, this is because their words express only dimly the realities that they have seen and verified. Rūmī makes the same point in a slightly different fashion.

> Those people who have studied or are now studying imagine that if they attend faithfully here they will forget and abandon all their knowledge. On the contrary, when they come here their sciences all acquire a spirit. The sciences are all paintings. When they gain spirits, it is as if a lifeless body receives a spirit.[24]

The description of Sufism as Islamic "esoterism" relates directly to the type of knowledge gained through unveiling and gnosis, since it cannot be expressed in terms completely accessible to the ulama and the common people. The Sufi shaykhs do not necessarily conceal their knowledge, but people who have not verified it are "below" it.

Ghazālī points out that all Muslims have the obligation to deepen their works through understanding the sciences of practice, but he stresses that the sciences of unveiling are of a different sort. Everyone must know a certain amount about practice in order to be able to establish a correct relationship with God. But Ghazālī makes clear that unveiling, by its very nature, pertains to an elect—those whose hearts have been opened up to knowledge by God. Hence Ghazālī makes no attempt to explain the sciences of unveiling in the *Iḥyā'*, a book which, he tells us, deals specifically with practice. He defines and describes unveiling as follows:

> Unveiling is knowledge of the nonmanifest domain [*al-bāṭin*] and the goal of all the sciences. One of the gnostics says, "I fear that if a person has no share in this knowledge, he will come to an evil end." The least

share of it is that you acknowledge its truth and concede its existence in those who are worthy of it.

Another gnostic said, "If a person has two traits—innovation [*bid'a*] and pride [*kibr*]—nothing of this knowledge will be opened up to him."

It has been said that whoever loves this world and insists on following caprice [*hawā*] will never reach the reality of this science, even though he may reach the reality of the other sciences. . . .

The science of unveiling is the knowledge of the sincere devotees [*ṣiddīqūn*] and those brought near to God [*muqarrabūn*]. It consists of a light that becomes manifest within the heart when the heart is cleansed and purified of blameworthy attributes. Many things are unveiled by means of this light. Earlier the person had been hearing the names of these things and imagining vague and unclear meanings. Now they become clarified.

The person gains true knowledge of God's Essence, His perfect and subsistent attributes, His acts, His wisdom in creating this world and the next world, and the manner in which He makes the next world the consequence of this world; the true knowledge of the meaning of prophecy and the prophets, the meaning of revelation, the meaning of Satan, the meaning of the words "angels" and "satans," how the satans have enmity toward human beings, how the angel becomes manifest to the prophets, and how revelation reaches them; the true knowledge of the dominion of the heavens and the earth; the true knowledge of the heart and how the hosts of the angels and the satans confront each other within it; the true knowledge of the difference between the suggestion of the angel and the suggestion of the satan; the true knowledge of the next world, the Garden, the Fire, the chastisement of the grave, the Path, the scales, and the accounting; the meaning of God's words, *Read your book! Your soul suffices you this day as an accounter against you* [17:14]; the meaning of His words, *Surely the abode of the next world is life, did they but know* [29:64]; the meaning of the encounter with God and looking upon His generous Face; the meaning of nearness to Him and alighting in His neighborhood; the meaning of achieving felicity through the companionship of the higher plenum and connection to the angels and the prophets; the meaning of the disparity of degrees of the people of the Gardens, such that some of them see others as if they were shining stars in the middle of heaven; and so on.[25]

Our author provides similar lists of the sciences of unveiling, as in the introduction to *Clarifications,* and he devotes most of his attention to elucidating what this knowledge entails. In contrast, Ghazālī keeps his descriptions of these sciences to a minimum and emphasizes god-wariness and practice much more than the author of these three treatises.

The title of this book recalls Montgomery Watt's *The Faith and Practice of al-Ghazālī*, and it might be asked why I did not call it, "The Faith and Practice of a Thirteenth-Century Sufi." My answer is that the three works translated here have a much broader relevance and appeal than do the two works translated by Watt.

The second section of Watt's work translates Ghazālī's *Beginning of Guidance*, which is a relatively detailed introduction to the practice of the Shariah. The first section contains *Deliverance from Error*, Ghazālī's fascinating account of his own intellectual and spiritual journey. It is fair to call this a description of Ghazālī's faith—and not anyone else's—because it is a personal work that tells us much more about Ghazālī's intellectual background and milieu than about the concerns of most Muslims of his or other times. Moreover, Ghazālī wrote the work with clear polemical aims in the style of a Kalām treatise. He wants to warn the ulama—because no one else could have understood all the references and technical terms—to avoid certain dangerous heresies and to recognize the necessity of Sufism for the full manifestation of Islamic virtues. However, he makes little attempt to describe or explain the contents of Islamic faith.

If the three texts translated here deserve to be attributed to Islam rather than to a specific person, it is because they provide a systematic overview of the three principles of faith along with an outline of practice in terms which, I think, would be recognizable and largely acceptable to most intelligent Muslims from the author's lifetime to the dawn of modern times. If the text's provenance were unknown, little more than stylistic peculiarities would make us attribute it to the thirteenth rather than, for example, to the eighteenth century, or to Turkey rather than to Iran or India.

Ghazālī's approach is different from that of our author in the relative weight that he gives to faith and practice. In his best known works and as presented in Watt's *Faith and Practice*, Ghazālī pays a great deal more attention to practice and to the inner attitudes that should accompany it than he does to the actual contents of faith. In contrast, the three works translated here, taken together, stress the contents of faith far more than practice. This is not only because of the peculiarities of these three texts. Rather, it reflects a change in emphasis in Sufi writing that occurs in the 150 or so years that separate the two figures. Ibn al-ʿArabī, of course, is the major milestone here, since no one before him (or after him) discussed the contents of faith in such exhaustive detail.

Practically every scholar who has written in broad terms about the history of Sufism has remarked on this shift of emphasis in Sufi writings. Various theories have been proposed as to what took place.[26] Let me simply suggest here that one of the many reasons for this shift has to do with a principle expressed in a famous aphorism by the fourth/tenth-century Sufi Būshanjī. "Today Sufism is a name without a reality, whereas before it was a reality without a name." In earlier periods, the reality of Sufism to which Būshanjī is alluding was the full actualization of Islam on all three dimensions of works, faith, and perfection. By Būshanjī's time, the transformative power present in the initial period was already being lost. What had been the living reality of sincerity and god-wariness was turning into a topic for academic discussion or a means to deceive the simple-minded. Given that the essentials of Islam were becoming more and more inaccessible with the passage of time, Sufi authors found it necessary to go into greater detail than before. They felt that people needed more detailed explanation in order to understand what was at issue in being human.

Ghazālī represents a widespread opinion when he says that it is incumbent upon people to learn as much as the science of faith as is necessary to keep their faith firm.[27] When their faith starts to waver, they have need of greater explanation. Certainly the historical circumstances between the eleventh and thirteenth centuries—a period that witnessed among other things the serious decline of the caliphate—provided people with reasons to question their presuppositions about the meaning of life. It is perhaps a sign of our own times that many people today recognize a greater need than ever before for the elucidation of the internal logic of religious world views.

NOTES

1. *Al-dīn*, for which "religion" is the most common translation. The root meaning of the term is to become obedient and submissive, to be obedient to God, to follow a way. For present purposes, it is sufficient to know that the term is differentiated from "Islam" by the fact that a person can follow any path as a religion, including a false belief or deviant way of doing things, whereas Islam denotes submission and obedience to God on the basis of the Koranic revelation.

2. In the hadith, which is found in several versions in the standard sources, Gabriel comes to the Prophet in the appearance of a bedouin and asks him questions about the religion. For a translation of the text from Bukhārī and Muslim, see Tabrīzī, *Mishkāt al-maṣābīḥ* 5. A number of modern scholars have used this hadith as a model for understanding Islam's concerns. One of the earliest was Martin Lings, *A Moslem Saint of the Twentieth Century* 44–45.

3. *Iḥyā'* 1:14 (1.1.2.3); see also the translation of the passage in its context by Faris (Ghazālī, *Book of Knowledge* 42).

4. The word *qadar* is commonly translated as "predestination" or "destiny," but these terms have too much theological baggage to suggest *qadar*'s Koranic meaning. In Sufi writings, such as the books of Ibn al-'Arabī or the three translated texts, the Koranic context is kept firmly in view.

5. See Chittick, "Mysticism vs. Philosophy in Earlier Islamic History."

6. One could interject a theological criticism here by saying that divine grace is being ignored. However, divine grace is implicit in all Islamic theology—when it is not explicit—because human activity is overshadowed by God's activity.

Rūmī often points out that grace and works are simply two sides of the same coin. Typical are the following verses from the *Mathnawī*: "Everyone sees the Unseen in proportion to the clarity of his heart, and that depends upon how much he has polished it. . . . If you say, 'Purity is God's bounty,' well, this success in polishing the heart also derives from His bestowal. . . . God alone bestows aspiration—no wretched beggar aspires to be king" (4:2909-2913; quoted in SPL 162).

7. See L. Gardet, "Īmān."

8. See S. Murata's detailed study of the heart in *Tao of Islam*, chapter 10.

9. Ibn Māja, Muqaddima 9.

10. See Wensinck, *Muslim Creed* 125.

11. Gardet, "Īmān" 1171.

12. In sixteen verses, the Koran employs the root *ḥ.b.ṭ.* (to become null, to fail, to be fruitless) to explain the uselessness of activity without faith. For example, *Those who cry lies to Our signs and the encounter [with God] in the next world—their works are fruitless* (7:147). *They do not have faith, so God has rendered their works fruitless* (33:19).

13. Asad, *The Message of the Qur'ān* 907.

14. Smith, *Faith and Belief* 39–41; see also Asad, *Message* 4, n. 6.

15. Smith, "Faith as *Taṣdīq*" 107.

16. Ibid. 109.

17. Ghazālī, *Iḥyā' 'ulūm al-dīn* 1:19; idem, *Book of Knowledge* 30. Rūmī (*Mathnawī* 1:2835ff) makes fun of the pretensions of the ulama in the story of the grammarian and the boatman. Having gotten in the boat, the grammarian asks the boatman,

> "Have you studied any grammar?" "No," he replied.
> "Well, half your life has gone to waste."
> The boatman felt sorry for himself,
> but for the moment made no reply.
> Then the wind threw the boat into a whirlpool
> and the boatman shouted out to the man,
> "Do you know how to swim? Tell me!"
> "No," he said, "O you with good answers and fine face."
> He said, "Then your whole life has gone to waste,
> since this boat will soon be going down."

Rūmī's conclusion is the same as that of Ghazālī. None of the sciences have any use unless they serve the fundamental science, which is that of practice. As Rūmī puts it, you do not need grammar (*naḥw*), but rather obliteration (*maḥw*), which is the dissolution of human limitations achieved by following the prophetic model. Then you will not be drowned when the boat goes down.

18. Ghazālī, *Iḥyā'* 1:11; idem, *Book of Knowledge* 31–32.

19. Among the many hadiths that connect god-wariness to perfected faith is the following, which refers to all three dimensions of Islam, but makes faith and god-wariness more or less identical: "The Prophet said, '*Islām* is public (*'alāniya*), while faith is in the heart.' Then he pointed to his breast three times and said, 'God-wariness is here, god-wariness is here' " (Aḥmad 3:153).

20. See SPK, chapter 19.

21. Ghazālī, *Bidāyat al-hidāya* 14; also translated in Watt, *Faith and Practice* 107.

22. Ghazālī, *Iḥyā'* 1:14 (1.1.2).

23. *Al-'ārif fawqa mā yaqūl wa'l-'ālim dūna mā yaqūl*. Qushayrī, *Risāla* 607.

24. Rūmī, *Fīhi mā fīhi* 156; translated in SPL 25–26 (see also Rūmī, *Discourses* 163–164).

25. Ghazālī, *Iḥyā'* 1:15 (1.1.2); also translated in Ghazālī, *Book of Knowledge* 46–48.

26. Many historians of Sufism have not had much sympathy with Ibn al-'Arabī's theoretical orientation, preferring instead the apparent simplicity of earlier expressions. I say "apparent" because, as soon as one tries to analyze the early Sufi writings and sayings within the religious and cultural context, one finds them packed with nuances and allusions. To make them anything more than "nice sayings" for nonspecialists, one must take on Ibn al-'Arabī's mantle oneself, explaining in detail all sorts of background information, ranging from theology and metaphysics to psychology, sociology, and grammar.

27. Ghazālī, *Iḥyā'* 11–12; idem, *Book of Knowledge* 34–35.

Part Two *Faith*

STYLE AND CONTENT

Rising Places and *Clarifications* are structured almost identically, with an introduction, three main chapters, and a conclusion. The introductions and conclusions point out the relevance of the text to the religious life of the reader. The three main chapters explain Islam's three principles. In the first section of the third work, *The Easy Roads of Sayf al-Dīn*, the author discusses the three principles in basically the same way. The difference between the three texts lies mainly in degree of detail.

Easy Roads provides a thumbnail sketch. The text is so brief, in fact, that it often takes on the tone of a theologian's catechism, making statements without any attempt to bring out nuances of understanding. *Rising Places* provides a much more detailed outline of the contents of faith, but it is still brief in comparison with *Clarifications*, which discusses the topics in the most detail. Although the subject matter is the same in all three texts, the material is not especially repetitive, because the author provides a fresh look in each case.

The author did not set out to write works that are in any sense original. His concern was to bring out the essential teachings of Islam in a familiar and attractive way. He prefers brevity, aphorisms, poetry, and citation of authorities to detailed explanation. He has in view readers who are intelligent, sensitive to literature, and appreciative of beauty. He assumes that they are Muslims who feel that their faith and practice need deepening. His intended readership would have had to possess the basics of Islamic learning, since he quotes repeatedly from the Koran, the Hadith, and other Arabic sources without translating them into Persian.

In the title of the second work, *Clarifications for Beginners and Reminders for the Advanced*, the author alludes to the fact that even learned beginners would not be able to follow some of the Arabic passages. Thus, for example, he quotes twice from *al-Ishārāt wa'l-tanbīhāt* of Avicenna. Only advanced scholars would have studied this work, and no beginner would have been able to decipher these passages without receiving help from a teacher or studying them in the original context. But no beginner would have any idea of what the original context was, since the author does not mention the source, and the works of Avicenna are not the usual place in which one goes looking for statements of Sufi teaching.

The basic goal of all three treatises is the same. The author wants to stir up the reader's desire to follow the path of deepening his or her Islam. At the beginning of *Rising Places*, the author makes explicit the audience that he has in mind, and his remarks there certainly apply to all three treatises. It goes without saying that he is not writing for those who are skeptical of Islam or any of its basic teachings—that would be the approach of a Kalām apologist. Instead, he addresses his words to a single group among the verifiers. Here he defines the word *verifier* in a broad sense to include three groups: the faithful in general, the ulama, and the friends of God (*awliya'*). The faithful are praiseworthy in their faith, and the ulama in their learning. But the friends of God have been called by God to deepen their Islam through following its third dimension. In describing this third group, the author explains that they combine faith with god-wariness and follow the Sunnah of the Prophet with full sincerity. It is they who will understand what he is talking about. They will take it as a timely reminder and an aid in their quest.

In the first two treatises, the author sets out to provide a map of faith's territory. In contrast to texts on Kalām or philosophy, he provides few rational demonstrations. Instead, he draws his map by pointing to what is self-evident to the intelligence, by citing basic teachings derived from the Koran, the Hadith, and the consensus of the ulama, and by calling to witness the unveiling of the great Sufis. Just as often as he quotes from the Koran and Hadith, he cites poetry, usually Persian but sometimes Arabic. Many of the verses would have been known to his readers. Few arguments are more satisfying for those with taste (*dhawq*) than bringing out a fresh nuance in a familiar verse.

One might be tempted to read these texts as patchworks of quotations, but this would be to ignore the strong organizing principles and the integrating passages. The quotations merely serve to illustrate the points being made. The argument lies in the vision that infuses the work, producing a new tapestry woven with familiar designs. Despite the quotations and borrowings, most of the text belongs to the author himself, as is proven by the uniform style and the obvious mastery of the overall scheme.

Those familiar with the Islamic sciences that emphasize following authority (*taqlīd*) rather than verification (*taḥqīq*)—transmission rather than personal realization—will notice that the author has little concern for the principles of Hadith scholarship. Whether or not he knew that some of the hadiths he cites are of questionable authenticity, his approach here—typical for many Sufi writings—makes the authenticity of the sayings irrelevant. The author is not a compiler, a historian, a *muḥaddith* (an authority in the science of Hadith), or a scholar in the ordinary sense. He is a *muḥaqqiq* (verifier) and an *'ārif* (gnostic), which is to say that he has established the truth of the teachings through unveiling and direct experience. He is, if you insist, a "mystic."[1] He does not want to prove anything, either to himself or to others, since he has tasted. As the Arabic proverb puts it, "He who has not tasted does not know," but our author knows. From this perspective, what is significant about a given saying ascribed to the Prophet is whether or not it makes the point. If it expresses the truth tasted through unveiling, it is an authentic saying. The historical soundness (*ṣiḥḥa*) of the hadith is another question that the *muḥaddith*s can work out among themselves.[2]

It is perhaps worth noting that, after the Koran and the Hadith, the most common source for the author's quotations is the poet Sanā'ī of Ghazna (d. 525/1131). Sanā'ī is the first in a series of great Sufi poets of the Persian language who include the author's contemporary 'Aṭṭār (d. 618/1221), also quoted on occasion, and Rūmī, none of whose verses is cited for certain.[3] In only two of the citations from Sanā'ī is the poet's identity made clear, but many readers would have recognized the other verses or assumed that they were by Sanā'ī because of the style.

After Sanā'ī, the author seems to quote most frequently from Awḥad al-Dīn Kirmānī (d. 635/1238), a friend of Ibn al-'Arabī and a well-known Sufi shaykh who wrote a large number of Persian quatrains. He is the only contemporary authority mentioned by name, in three places. As pointed out in the first appendix to this book, the author seems to have been Kirmānī's disciple. Another important source—especially for the third treatise—is Ghazālī's *Iḥyā'*. For the most part, passages cited from it are translated into Persian or summarized and given the author's own stylistic peculiarities in the process. His translations bear little resemblance to those of his contemporary, Mu'ayyid al-Dīn Muḥammad Khwārazmī (who completed his translation of the whole *Iḥyā'* in 620/1223), but they are no less accurate.

THE THREE PRINCIPLES

It may be useful at this point to provide a certain amount of background material to prepare the reader for what may be unfamiliar concepts and terminology in the author's discussion of faith.

The three principles of faith are *tawḥīd*, prophecy (*nubuwwa*), and the Return (*ma'ād*). For Sufi authors, *tawḥīd*—which is expressed most succinctly in the first Shahadah, "There is no god but God"—follows necessarily from the self-evident reality of God. Implications can be derived from *tawḥīd* on many levels. As mentioned earlier, the concept is closely connected with sincerity and god-wariness. But the word itself means to assert or to profess the unity of God. This does not mean simply that there is one God and not two or three, but rather that everything must be related back to God in definite ways.

To understand the implications of *tawḥīd*, we need a concept of God. Muslim thinkers have held almost unanimously that, on the one hand, God is beyond our understanding and that, on the other, He is more evident than the sun. The history of God-talk in Islam can be written as the story of the differing stress placed on these two positions. God is inward or nonmanifest (*bāṭin*), just as He is outward or manifest (*ẓāhir*). Proponents of Kalām stress God's hiddenness and inaccessibility. Sufis usually stress His evidence and omnipresence, while recognizing that God is both far (*ba'īd*) and near (*qarīb*).

For Ibn al-'Arabī and his followers, correct understanding of *tawḥīd* depends upon maintaining a delicate balance between these two ways of conceptualizing God. Inasmuch as God is nonmanifest and far, He is declared to be "incomparable" (*tanzīh*) with all things. Inasmuch as He is manifest and near, He is declared to be "similar" (*tashbīh*) with all things. The fact that the author employs these two terms in explaining how one gains a balanced understanding of *tawḥīd* is one of many indications that he was familiar with Ibn al-'Arabī's teachings.

Prophecy, the second principle of faith, is almost as self-evident for Muslims as is the reality of God. The essential function of the prophets is guidance (*hidāya*). Guidance has a personal relevance for every human being, because the fruit of following it is felicity, while the result of rejecting it is wretchedness.

Tawḥīd draws a relatively static picture of the whole of reality, with God situated at both the center and the periphery, both the beginning and the end. But one obvious corollary is that everything comes from God and returns to Him. Prophecy is then a divine movement of mercy and guidance directed toward human beings, who by nature are forgetful of the realities of things. Although they can attempt on their own—usually without much success—to sort out this world's happiness and misery, they have no knowledge of felicity and wretchedness, unless God should provide it.

The third principle, the Return, deals with the destiny of human beings in the light of *tawḥīd* and prophecy. In a broad sense, it answers two basic questions, because there are two types of return—compulsory and voluntary. What are the stages of the return to God after death? How can one speed up the return to God and encounter Him in the present life? Both questions call for a knowledge of the human soul and the various forms which it can take. Central to the Return are issues of psychology (the science of the soul) as well as ethics and morality, which relate the soul's development both to God and to other human beings.[4]

THE COSMOLOGY OF *TAWḤĪD*

In terms of modern categories, we can say that the author's discussion of *tawḥīd* focuses on theology, cosmology, and anthropology. In other words, he is answering three basic questions. What is God? What is the cosmos (defined as "everything other than God")? And how does the human being fit into the picture? In discussing the nature of the human being, the author touches on the nature of the soul, which takes us into the domain of psychology. However, none of these modern terms is really appropriate—except perhaps theology—because the concerns of the modern disciplines that go by these names are so radically different.

On the level of theology, the author explains three standard concepts that are also employed in Kalām and philosophy: God's Essence (*dhāt*), His attributes (*ṣifāt*) or names (*asmā'*), and His acts (*af'āl*).

The Essence is God in Himself inasmuch as He is incomparable, inaccessible, and unknowable.

The attributes delineate the rough outline of what can be known about God inasmuch as He chooses to make Himself known. The fundamental attributes are the most beautiful names mentioned in the Koran. Thus God is named "Compassionate," which is to say that He possesses the attribute of compassion. He is "Wrathful," so He has the attribute of wrath.

The acts are what God produces through the attributes. As Creator, for example, God performs a single basic act: He creates the universe. Hence, the universe is His act, as is every individual thing within the universe, because each is born from His activity.

The acts or creatures are divided into two basic kinds: unseen (*ghayb*) or spiritual (*rūḥānī*), and visible (*shahāda*) or corporeal (*jismānī*). These correlate with the two basic worlds—the world of spirits and the world of bodies, also called the "dominion" (*malakūt*) and the "kingdom" (*mulk*). Here we enter into the domain of cosmology, or knowledge of the structure of the universe.

It should be kept in mind that Islamic cosmological teachings have little to do with the type of knowledge that is gained through modern science or the theories that are proposed in modern cosmology. Although many of the Muslim cosmologists claim that they have verified the truth of their teachings through experience, these teachings are not based primarily on experimentation or observation of the visible world. Rather, they are rooted in deductions from certain theological principles and certain givens concerning the human situation. The first and most fundamental of these principles is *tawḥīd*: God alone is truly real, while the cosmos is relatively real. But the exact degree of the reality or unreality of cosmic things must be clarified as no two things fit into the same niche. Everything in the universe reflects God's attributes in differing degrees. The more a thing reflects the divine, the more real it is.

In reading texts on cosmology, one should not think that the terms employed are synonymous with the identical terms employed in today's everyday language, the meaning of which is thoroughly shaped by the scientific world view. The thrust of Islamic cosmology is to explain *tawḥīd* in terms of the nature of the relationship between human beings and God. The major issues in this relationship have to do with invisible realities. Although the unseen domains are the fundamental concern, the terminology employed to discuss them is grounded in the visible domain—the world of language and experience. Hence the terms are no more than allusions (*ishāra*) to something that escapes language. To use the Zen expression, they are "fingers pointing at the moon." One must have a modicum of "tasting" (*dhawq*) to be able to look beyond the finger. If one insists on focusing on the finger—the language—one is bound to miss the point.

As Sachiko Murata has demonstrated in *The Tao of Islam*, in reading cosmological texts one should consider the attributes or qualities that are associated with the words. For example, two of the most common terms that come up are light (*nūr*) and darkness (*ẓulma*), especially because they play an important role in the Koran. One must leave aside the physical definitions and descriptions of light that dominate modern understandings. Instead, one must grasp the qualities that are associated with the terms in Islamic thought. Light is fundamentally a divine attribute and, secondarily, a quality found in creation. Light removes darkness, which is defined as the absence of light. Light discloses, divulges, unveils, reveals, illuminates, irradiates, clarifies, makes known, makes obvious, proves, demonstrates. Light takes away darkness, obfuscation, ignorance, unconsciousness, stupidity, dullness. It is inherent to God and to the great revelations of God, which are precisely illuminations, bestowals of knowledge, reminders, and means whereby intelligence is awakened and brought to life. Light is intelligence, consciousness, awakening, life. The Koran is light, as it often reminds us, and the Prophet is *a light-giving lamp* (33:46).

Notice that true light is not a physical reality, because life, awareness, and consciousness are its intrinsic attributes. According to a hadith, God created the angels from light. They are the nearest beings to God, so they share most intensely in His inherent luminosity. In contrast, bodily things are made of clay. They lack the qualities of light—not absolutely so, but for all practical purposes.

Hence, we have two worlds—the world of light and the world of clay or darkness. The world of light is invisible, because it is too bright to be seen with eyes made of clay. The world of darkness is visible, because organs molded of clay are able to perceive things made of their own substance. Again, one needs to take words such as "clay" and "light" here as allusions or symbols. At issue are the qualities associated with these realities in the world view of the people to whom the texts are speaking, not the light or clay that we analyze today in a laboratory.

The first axiom of Islamic cosmology is the distinction between the Real and the unreal, God and the cosmos, Light and darkness. The second axiom is that the qualitative difference set up between God and cosmos is reproduced within the cosmos itself. Just as the Real is distinguished from the unreal, so also, within the confines of the cosmos, the more real is distinguished from the less real, the higher from the lower, the luminous from the dark, the spiritual from the corporeal. But on closer analysis, this dichotomy is seen to be an indefinite hierarchy, ranging from the brightest (the nearest to God) to the darkest (the least bright, or the furthest from God). Hence, many intermediate domains between the unseen and the visible can also be taken into account.

Self-evident to Islamic thought is that the inner is more real and the things that we perceive are proof of the existence of some unseen reality that is made manifest. Every phenomenon demands a noumenon.

I said in Part One that Islamic teachings are both theocentric and anthropocentric. *Tawḥīd* is the foundation, tying everything back to God. But the real issue is what this means for human beings, because the revelation is addressed to people with the aim of guiding them to felicity. Muslim thinkers discuss the divine acts and cosmology in order to explain why human beings are singled out for revelation. The answer has to do with the all-comprehensiveness (*jamʿiyya*) of human beings. They contain in themselves something of all the worlds—the unseen and the visible, light and darkness, and everything in between.

The reason for human all-comprehensiveness is not difficult to find. The cosmos represents "everything other than God" (*mā siwā Allāh*). It is the sum total of God's creative acts. God displays all His names and attributes through the acts. Hence, the cosmos as a whole is a divine form. In the same way, human beings are made in the form of God, because all the divine qualities are found within them. Here we have the doctrine, standard in texts on Sufism and philosophy, that the microcosm (the human being) corresponds to the macrocosm (the cosmos as a whole).

The special place of human beings has to do with the fact that they can gather the properties of all the divine names in a conscious, active whole, whereas the cosmos merely reflects the divine names in indefinite diversity and dispersion and in a relatively unconscious and passive manner. In contrast to human beings, the individual things of the cosmos are incomplete images of God. Human beings, in short, were created to be God's vicegerents or representatives. They were given charge of the whole universe through their central, all-comprehensive, and active nature. However, in order to rule the universe on God's behalf, they must submit (*islām*) to His will. They must first be servants (*ʿabd*), then vicegerents. Before all else, the true vicegerent is a perfect servant. The false vicegerent is a human being who has not submitted his or her will to God's will. Not submitting to God is to corrupt the vicegerent's domain, which is, first, one's own internal world; second, the immediate world with which one has everyday contact; and third, the whole cosmos.

The Islamic approach to cosmology is especially relevant to modern concerns in its refusal to reduce visible reality to dead matter, unconscious forces, or energy bereft of intelligence, love, and compassion. The universe is the locus in which God discloses His own nature. Hence all the divine qualities are present, although they become manifest in differing degrees according to diverse creaturely capacities. The essential nature of reality itself is *wujūd* (being or existence or finding), but this is not an inanimate, unconscious, and indifferent *wujūd*. It is a *wujūd* that is identical with the life, love, and gentleness of a personal God. We will see that the author of the three treatises identifies *wujūd* with God's mercy (*raḥma*), as did Ibn al-ʿArabī and others. The cosmos, in short, is full of the traces of God's most beautiful names. Hence, human interaction with the cosmos must be rooted in human interaction with God. True knowledge of the cosmos is inseparable from the perception of a moral and spiritual dimension to all things. There are no "objects" to be treated with indifference or strictly for our own ends.

In contrast to Islamic cosmology, modern science and cosmology root out personal dimensions from external reality, in effect freeing science and technology from moral constraints. From the perspective of the Islamic cosmologists, the fact that the vast majority of Muslims educated in the modern school systems have been trained in Western scientific thinking has deep repercussions within the objective universe, not only within their subjective perception of the universe. If *Corruption has appeared in the land and the sea because of what the hands of human beings have earned* (30:41), it can only increase when people fail to perceive the personal dimension of reality and, as a result, *tawḥīd* becomes an abstraction, signifying simply that "God is one," and, for the rest, we can think and do as we see fit.

NOTES

1. I explain my reticence in using this word in Part Four.

2. For Ibn al-ʿArabī, unveiling becomes the method of proving or disproving the historical truth of the hadiths, but few would be bold enough to take his position. See SPK 250–252.

3. I say "for certain" because several quatrains cited by the author are found in Rūmī's *Dīwān*. This is not strong evidence for their ascription to Rūmī, however. In fact, their presence in these treatises provides evidence that they are not by him.

Scholars of Persian literature have often discussed the problem of the "wandering quatrains" that have been ascribed to many authors. The quatrain was an extremely popular form of poetry. In a civilization in which poetry and taste carry at least as much weight as do philosophy and rational demonstration, citing an appropriate verse or two was—and still is in many parts of the Islamic world—one of the most common ways of making a point. The popularity of the quatrain stems largely from its ability to make points succinctly and powerfully. People quote them constantly, and poets had nothing against quoting the poetry of others. One must remember that poetry was primarily recited, and reading was secondary. Disciples wrote down the poetry they heard their master recite and, if no one knew any better, it could easily be added to his *dīwān* (collected poetry)—especially if the latter was put together after the poet's death.

There were several other reasons that led to the inflation of poets' collections of quatrains, among them the fact that people were not primarily interested in the author of poetry, but rather in the content and the point being made. "Criticism" was directed not at who composed the poem, but at the theme being expressed. Those who devoted their attention to writing histories of literature wanted to come up with entertaining and edifying anthologies. If a quatrain seemed to reflect ʿUmar Khayyām's major themes, then it might as well be by him, so it was placed under his name.

In short, for these and other reasons, the quatrain presents contemporary scholars with particularly intractable problems in trying to determine authorship.

4. For a fine example of a Sufi text dealing with these issues, see Najm al-Dīn Rāzī, *Mirṣād al-ʿibād min al-mabdaʾ ilaʾl-maʿād*, translated by H. Algar as *The Path of God's Bondsmen from the Origin to the Return*. The most detailed study in English is Sachiko Murata, *The Tao of Islam*.

The Rising Places of Faith

In the Name of God, the Merciful, the Compassionate

Gratitude is due to Him who lifts the veils and guides upon the paths, that Loving King who made discipline and god-wariness the means to dispel the darknesses of the sensory realm and who made faith in the unseen the key to the treasuries of holy unveiling. Through these two premises—faith and god-wariness—He takes the knowers of the majesty of His unity and the lovers of the beauty of His eternity to the conclusion—the paradise of encounter—and He spreads the carpet of nearness in the highest garden.

Blessings be upon those who dwell in the pavilions of the dominion, the veil-keepers of the court of the invincibility—not least upon the confidant of the retreat of "Two Bows' Length" and the mystery and epitome of the two engendered worlds, Muhammad Mustafa, and upon his household, partisans, companions, and followers, who are the custodians of the Kaaba of unity and the keepers of the mysteries of divinity.

To come to the point: With the remoteness of the era of prophecy, God's carpet was rolled up and the foundation of religion destroyed. Hence, the sun of faith turned toward eclipse, the light of Islam hid in the corner of exile, and the truth of the allusion of the Shariah-bringer became manifest. "Islam began as an exile and will become again as it was, an exile. How happy are the exiles!" The fog of error filled every direction and the darkness of innovation and sectarian caprice spread to all the regions of East and West. A cry from the unseen voiced the situation with the words, *Corruption has appeared in the land and the sea* [30:41].

If you want enemies, Mahdī,
  come down from the sky!
If you want helpers, Antichrist,
  show yourself at once!

But the truthful master—upon him be peace—has reported and promised that "A group among my community will never cease to support the Truth until resurrection day." Hence, as long as heaven and earth remain and the resurrection is held back, the blessing of those with living hearts and Jesus' breath—those who guard the treasury of the Presence of Lordship—will remain in the earthly world. "They are God's vicegerents in the earth and His elect creatures; it is they who call to His religion." Therefore, in an era like the present, to bring dead souls to life and to incite seeking spirits with the desire to follow this group can be one of the best of works.

These words were written in the spirit of this introduction. They include an explanation of the three principles upon which the primordial religion is based and from which the creed of Mustafa is derived: faith in God, in prophecy, and in the Last Day. These principles will be explained in a manner that accords with the Book of God, agrees with the Sunnah of the Messenger, corresponds with the consensus of the Community, and is attested to by the tasting of the masters of unveiling and the leaders of the path.

I have named this brief treatise "The Rising Places of Faith." My goal in these pages will be expressed in an opening, a conclusion, and three rising places. From God I seek aid, and from Him come guidance and success. "There is no power and no strength but in God, the High, the Tremendous."

THE OPENING

You should know that those who uphold the truth of the Origin and the Return and who, in brief, know that the possible things have a Support and that human beings will subsist after the annihilation of this body are divided into two groups. Either they have borrowed illumination from the niche of prophecy and learned from the revelation and sending down of God, or they have traveled with the mental faculty and caught a scent through rational deductions. The first group is called the "people of the creeds," the second the "companions of the schools."

As for the companions of the schools, their views and proofs conflict in the extreme, and their steps toward the station of verification are as shaky as can be imagined. *Most of them follow only surmise, and surmise avails naught against the Truth* [10:36].

I wandered in all those places
  and cast my glance in all those regions—
I saw only the hand of perplexity on the chin,
  or teeth gnashing in regret.

Let your natural reason go
  before your soul assumes
the form of every heretic's imaginings
  through logical proofs.

"How evil a steed is man's opinion!" What a great loss it is for the determined and well-prepared seeker to follow contradictory views blindly and become a truth-concealer through imitation!

If you want to fly to Mount Sinai,
  why weaken your wings with Avicenna?
Fix your heart on Muhammad's words, O Son of ʿAlī!
  How long will you listen to the Father of ʿAlī?
If you have no eye that sees the Way,
  better a leader from Quraysh than Bukhara!

As for the people of the creeds, they follow the prophets step by step. They acknowledge the Ocean of the Unseen through the Shariahs of the messengers, hobbling their rational faculties with the cord of commands and prohibitions. And now of those Shariahs, only the authority of our own Prophet's Shariah—which has abrogated the other Shariahs—remains on the face of the earth.

The verifiers in this creed are limited to three groups.

The first group comprises the people of faith in the unseen. They accept the truth of everything that the prophets and messengers have brought to the creatures from the Presence of Lordship by means of the Holy Spirit. They say, "We have faith in God and what has come from God as He has meant it; and we have faith in the Messenger of God and what has come from the Messenger of God as he has meant it." In this faith, they make no attempt to travel the path of investigation and consideration. Rather, they dismiss their rational faculties from meddlesome behavior and set out on the path of safety. *And if he be a Companion of the Right, "Peace be upon you, Companion of the Right!"* [56:90–91].

The second group includes the ulama and the people of heedfulness and consideration. Made restless by the mystery of *Those—He has written faith upon their hearts* [58:22], they adopt true beliefs with unquestioning approval on the basis of the principles of the Book, the Sunnah, and the consensus of the Community. They turn their gaze to the details of the Shariah and the wondrous signs of the engendered things, giving this verse its due. *Say: "Consider what is in the heaven and in the earth!"* [10:101]. They gain knowledge of unknown things through what they know. They nurture their reflective journey with the light of faith and the support of good works. They arrive at the vast expanse of the world of the knowledge of certainty. *God will raise up in degrees those of you who have faith and have been given knowledge* [58:11].

The third group includes the friends of God and the possessors of unveiling. They drank the wine of *He loves them* [5:54] at the banquet of Alast. "Then He sprinkled some of His light on them."

We came from the Ruins of Love,
  drunk with Alast.
How could we say "Yes"?
  We all came drunk.

They came to this nest of darkness at the cry of *Get down out of it!* [2:36], putting on the clothing of composition within the four walls of human-nature.

I think the soul forgot covenants through fever
and homes it really did not want to leave.

Then they read for a while from the tablet of faith in the unseen. For a long lifetime, they walked with the foot of god-wariness on the road of *Say [O Muhammad!]: "If you love God, follow me, and God will love you"* [3:31]. Finally, they completely cleansed the rust of the possible things and the darkness of the engendered things from the mirror of the heart with the polish of faith and god-wariness. They became worthy to receive divine self-disclosures and holy illuminations. *Those who have faith and do good deeds—their Lord will guide them because of their faith* [10:9]. Once again, they witnessed the beauty of their own original disposition. They found their lost falcon. They heard this voice from the sky-light of the dominion: *Peace be upon you! Well have you fared; enter in, to dwell forever!* [39:73].

Solomon has found his missing ring!
Lost Joseph has come back to Canaan!

The distraught lover from Khorasan has given a sign of their state in this verse:

The pain that we heard about
from the people
came from knowledge to actuality,
from ear to breast.

I have written these hurried lines for the sake of this last group. Let them learn these words at the outset and conceive a rough idea of their meaning. When they overcome difficult obstacles in their wayfaring, leave behind the darkness of human nature, reach the Fountain of Life and, in the company of Khizr, drink their fill from the spring of *We taught him knowledge from Us* [18:65], they will see everything they have been told about and know everything they have imagined. The tongue of their state will keep on saying,

We are the sun, the crescent, the full moon of meanings.
We are the goal of the secret, "Be, and it was!"
Having passed beyond the darkness of water and clay,
we are Khizr and the Water of Life.

Now let us enter our subject and seek nearness to the Presence of Unity by means of "There is no power and no strength but in God." *Exalter of ranks is He, Possessor of the Throne, He casts the Spirit of His command upon whomsoever He will of His servants* [40:15].

THE FIRST RISING PLACE

On the Realities of the First Principle, Faith in God

This section contains three stars: the first star, giving true knowledge of the Essence; the second star, giving true knowledge of the attributes; and the third star, giving true knowledge of the acts.

THE FIRST STAR

Giving True Knowledge of the Essence

Know that He through whom existence subsists—greatly exalted is He!—is nondelimited Being. Nothingness has no approach to the magnificence and inaccessibility of His Being. He is God, the Unique, the Everlasting Refuge. He was, and no one was with Him. He will be, and no one will be with Him. And, in reality, He is, and no one is with Him. *There is no god but He. Everything is perishing except His Face* [28:88].

With God
  "others" are inconceivable.
Gate, court, sentinel—
  all are naught.

"Glory be to Him who discloses Himself from every direction and is empty of every direction."

No matter how much you look
  before and behind,
on every side
  you see but One.

To the majesty of His unseen He-ness—which is called the "Presence of the Essence"—no angel brought near or prophet sent out has access. Glory be to Him! Glory be to Him! *They measured not God with His true measure!* [6:91]. All those marked with the sign of possible existence and the brand of temporal origination—whether knowledgeable or ignorant, high or low—are equal in their lack of knowledge of the inmost center of the Essence. "All creatures are fools before the Essence of God."

O Thou who bringest forth the world!
  Who knows Thee as Thou art?

May God be pleased with Abū Bakr—how well he made allusion to this place of witnessing. "Glory be to Him who has set down no path for His creatures to know Him save the incapacity to know Him!" Whatever fits into the fancies, thoughts, and rational faculties of the creatures—He is more than that, higher than that, and different from that. *High exalted then is God, the King, the Real!* [20:114].

No heart has a way
to His inmost center—
reason and soul know nothing
of His perfection.

One of the great possessors of true knowledge was asked, "What is true knowledge?" He answered, "The existence of a reverence within you that prevents you from declaring Him similar to things or disconnected from them." The people of witnessing have said that one side of true knowledge lies in the declaration of similarity and the other side in the declaration of incomparability. The mystery of incomparability is turned toward the name Nonmanifest, while the mystery of similarity is one of the properties of the name Manifest.

If I speak,
I declare Him similar—
but if I speak not,
I have no religion.

He is the First and the Last, the Manifest and the Nonmanifest [57:3].

Because of hiddenness
He is totally apparent,
because of apparentness
He is totally hidden.

Eyes perceive Him not [6:103] and *Thou shalt not see Me* [7:143] allude to the properties of the name Nonmanifest. This is called the "position of asserting incomparability." But *Upon that day faces shall be radiant, gazing upon their Lord* [75:22–23] and "I saw my Lord in the most beautiful form" allude to the properties of the name Manifest. This is called the "position of asserting similarity." "Glory be to God above similarity and incomparability!"

Since you call Him manifest and hidden,
know for certain that He is neither this nor that!

He shows His inaccessibility and tremendousness to His servants in the manner that He desires. The people of faith and true knowledge see Him with the eyes of their head. But here tears flow forth! One of the greatest of the Prophet's companions said, "Verily the Messenger of God saw the Lord of the worlds in a green meadow of paradise."

If love makes your heart want to see,
you can easily see the Beloved.
But beware! Content yourself with a shadow.
Think it not proper to see more than His shadow!

"Glory be to Him who is high in His lowness, low in His highness, nonmanifest in His manifestation, and manifest in His nonmanifestation."

It is He that is He, and the he-ness of all things derives from Him. *Nothing is like Him, and He is the Seeing, the Hearing* [42:11]. This place of witnessing is exceedingly tremendous. The perfect human beings and those brought near to God have not the courage or strength to speak of it more than this. Great is the One, the Unique!

The heart knows only the temporal,
  the lips speak only words—
How can I know Thee in my heart,
  how can I call Thee with my tongue?

Glory be to your Lord, the Lord of inaccessibility, above what they describe! And peace be upon the messengers, and praise belongs to God, the Lord of the worlds! [37:180–182].

THE SECOND STAR

Giving True Knowledge of the Attributes

Know—may God confirm you with His help and make you one of those who possess certainty—that the Loving God is described and designated by perfect attributes and the most beautiful names. *To God belong the most beautiful names, so call Him by them* [7:180]. In the eyes of the possessors of spiritual ascents and intimate prayer, *names* and *attributes* are two words with one meaning.

Just as His undefiled Essence is unlike the essences of creatures, so also His holy attributes are unlike the attributes of creatures. One of the greatest of the masters of true knowledge was asked, "What is *tawḥīd*?" He replied, "To affirm that the Essence is not similar to essences and not disconnected from attributes."

In the eyes of the pillars of true knowledge, it is obligatory to affirm the attributes of His majesty and beauty. The tasting of the perfect prophets and messengers testifies that He possesses these attributes immutably.

He is Alive, and anything alive perceives and acts. He always was and always will be. Disappearance and annihilation have no access to His everlasting magnificence. *He is Alive, there is no god but He. So call on Him, being sincere to Him in religion. Praise belongs to God, Lord of the worlds* [40:65].

He is Knowing. All things that were, are, and will be—both the undifferentiated and the differentiated, the universal and the particular—are one in His eternal knowledge. There past, present, and future have but a single color. *With Him are the keys to the Unseen—none knows them but He. He knows what is in the land and the sea. Not a leaf falls, but He knows it. There is not a grain in the earth's shadows, not a thing, fresh or withered, unless in a Manifest Book* [6:59].

He is Desiring. Whatever He desires is, and whatever He does not desire is not. Faith and truth-concealing, acknowledgement and denial, good and evil, benefit and loss, worship and ungodliness, disobedience and obedience—all occur according to His desire and decree. "None repels His decree, *None holds back His judgment* [13:41]." Although He is displeased with the truth-concealing and disobedient acts of the servants—*Verily God...is not pleased with the truth-concealing of His servants* [39:7]—desire is different from good-pleasure. This question is one of the difficult problems of true knowledge. It can only be completely unveiled after the mystery of the measuring out becomes manifest, but every soul does not have access to perception of that mystery's beauty.

When the fire takes Gabriel's wings as fuel,
  how can Satan's friends find room in the kitchen?

Those who have been shown the way to the ocean depths of the mystery of God's measuring out have forbidden that it be divulged. They say, "Measuring out is God's mystery, so divulge it not!"

In short, everything happens in accordance with His desire and will. *You will not will unless God wills* [76:30].

What Thou willest will be,
  though I will it not.
And what I will will not be,
  if Thou dost not will it.

He is Powerful. He produces the existent from the nonexistent and things from not-things. This is one of the characteristics of His power's majesty. He has no associate in that—glory be to the King, the Alive! *Is there any creator, apart from God?* [35:3]. Heaven, earth, Throne, Footstool, jinn, mankind, satans, angels—all come forth moment by moment through His perfect power. If He desired, in one instant He would take everything back to its root—which is sheer nonexistence—and then bring a new creation into existence. *If He will, He will put you away and bring a new creation; that is surely no great matter for God* [14:19–20].

He is Hearing. He hears the movements of His servants' passing thoughts on a dark night beneath the seventh layer of the earth just as well as He hears the voicing of glorifications by Seraphiel and Gabriel beneath the heavens.

He is Seeing. He sees the Kaaba, the monastery, the mosque, and the tavern. He witnesses the obedience of the obedient in that place and the disobedience of the disobedient in this place. *God knows the unseen of the heavens and the earth, and God sees what you do* [49:18].

He is Speaking. He speaks to the angels, the prophets, and His friends. *And unto Moses God spoke directly* [4:164]. The Torah, the Gospel, the Psalms, and the Furqān are all His speech. As long as His speech was in the heart—*The*

Faithful Spirit has brought it down upon thy heart [26:193–194]—it was incomparable with the form of letter and sound. But when the Holy Spirit personified it and cast it as a locus of manifestation into the pure ears of Mustafa, it put on the clothing of letters and sounds. However, the perfection of this tasting comes only in the school of "My Lord taught me courtesy." A soul is needed that is holy, that sees with the light of unity, and that has escaped from the blindness of ignorance. Then it can know the wondrous mysteries of the Koran and rend the veils formed by the patterns of letters and words.

The Koran-bride will keep on her veil
  until she sees faith's dominion free of strife.
No wonder if the only thing you find in her is patterns!
  A blind eye sees nothing of the sun but warmth.

In spite of all this, the Koran is memorized by hearts, recited by tongues, and written on pages. The writing and the form of the letters and sounds originate in time, but what is written and recited is eternal. *And behold, it is with Us in the Mother of the Book, sublime indeed, wise* [43:3].

The Book of Realities has no end,
  no chapters are found in it, no verses.
All these unrolled scriptures are nothing
  but one of its letters reported by Gabriel.

Though all the trees in the earth were pens, and the sea [were ink]—seven seas after it to replenish it, yet would the words of God not be spent [31:27].

His names and attributes are beyond count. It is impossible for anyone but God to know them in all their differentiation. The possessors of minds learn some of them from the side of Lordship in this world, and some in the next. But some remain unknown in both this world and the next world. "[Those names Thou hast] kept for Thyself in the knowledge of the Unseen" refers to these. A rational faculty anointed with the light of faith sees them all as summarized in four types: positive, correlative, negative, and report-derived. Within the configuration of the present world, the amount that is important for wayfarers to know has been explained at the end of the Sura al-Hashr: *He is God, there is no god but He. He is the Knower of the unseen and the visible; He is the Merciful, the Compassionate. He is God, there is no god but He. He is the King, the Holy, the Peaceable, the Faithful, the Preserver, the Inaccessible, the Invincible, the Magnificent. Glory be to God, above what they associate with Him! He is God, the Creator, the Author, the Form-giver. To Him belong the most beautiful names. All that is in the heavens and the earth magnifies Him; He is the Inaccessible, the Wise* [59:22–24].

THE THIRD STAR

Giving True Knowledge of the Acts

Know—may God confirm you with success and guide you to wayfaring on the path—that all existent things seen with the eye of your head or perceived with the eye of your reason are creatures and acts of God, but He is beyond all of them. He is not similar to anything of His handiwork. *Is He who creates like him who does not create?* [16:17]. In sum, His acts are purely spiritual, purely corporeal, or intermediary between the world of spirits and the world of bodies.

[A] That which is purely spiritual is called the "world of the dominion." It can be seen only with the eye of the spirit. It cannot be described in the world of the kingdom, which is called the "world of bodies." "Surely in that are signs for the possessors of minds!"

If you don't want reason to laugh at you,
  don't take Khwarazm's cash to Iraq.

Thus We showed Abraham the dominion of the heavens and the earth, that he might be one of those having certainty [6:75]. Unless one dies to corporeal life through supraformal reality, one will not come alive through spiritual life. And until one comes alive through spiritual life, one will not understand the meanings of the dominion's signs.

In the world of reason and faith,
  the body's death is the spirit's life.

Jesus said, "None will enter the dominion of the heavens unless he is born twice."

Now, however, my intention is to explain briefly the different levels of the inhabitants of the dominion, in order that the seeker might have faith in them and make them his own belief. *Perhaps after that God will bring something new to pass* [65:1].

Know, O friend—may God strengthen you with true knowledge of the holy enigmas—that those who live in the dominion are of three kinds:

[1] The first are the cherubim, who are also called the "inhabitants of the invincibility." They are secluded within the palisades of holiness and enraptured by the splendors of the Essence's lights.

[2] The second are the spirituals, who are divided into two kinds: [a] Some are the bearers of the Glorious Throne, and others the custodians of the Spacious Footstool. *None of us there is, but has a known station; we are the rangers, we are those that give glory* [37:164–166]. Some populate the seven heavens, and others take care of the Gardens and the Fires. *None knows the hosts of your Lord but He* [74:31]. Their ranks come to an end at the first heaven. They are the inhabitants of the higher dominion. [b] Among the second kind, some are given charge of the simple elements, and others of compound things—minerals, plants, and animals—and of thunder, lightning, clouds, mist, mountains, seas, and deserts.

Or rather, an angel has been given charge of every single thing. Mustafa alluded to this when he said, "An angel comes down with every drop of rain." In the same way, some of them have been made guardians of and given charge over the human species. But only the eternal knowledge of the Creator encompasses the details of their number. *None knows the hosts of your Lord but He* [74:31]. These are the inhabitants of the lower dominion. *To God belong the hosts of the heavens and the earth* [48:4].

[3] Since the jinn and satans also cannot be seen with the eye of the head, they are inhabitants of the lower dominion. Some of them have faith, and some do not. Iblis is their lord and leader. Until the resurrection, God has given him and his offspring mastery over mankind, *except for God's sincere servants* [37:40]. Their mastery over human beings is one of the branches of the mystery of the measuring out. "None knows it but God, and those firmly rooted in knowledge."

For those on the path, faith in all this is obligatory, until *God brings opening, or some commandment from Him* [5:52].

[B] As for the purely corporeal acts—which are called the "world of the kingdom"—they are of two kinds: the heavenly things and the earthly things. The heavenly things include the Throne, the Footstool, the fixed stars, the planets, and the seven heavens. The earthly things include the simple elements, the compound things—the minerals, plants, and animals—and the effects of the higher realm, such as clouds, lightning, thunder, wind, and rain.

Only the elect are aware of the world of the dominion, so it was mentioned only briefly in the Koran. But all creatures constantly witness the sensory bodies with their sensory eyes, so the Koran mentions these in detail; and, based on these, proofs are offered as guidance toward the Eternal Essence. *Surely in the creation of the heavens and the earth and the alternation of night and day and the ship that runs in the sea with profit for people, and the water God sends down from heaven therewith reviving the earth after it is dead, and His scattering abroad in it all manner of crawling things, and the turning about of the winds and the clouds subjected between heaven and earth—surely there are signs for a people having intelligence* [2:164].

[C] As for what is intermediate between the world of the spirits and the world of bodies, that is called the "world of images and semblances." The revealed religion refers to it as the "barzakh." The ulama who have insight and the possessors of unveilings see the spirits of angels and prophets personified in this world. Also the forms and semblances that are seen in dreams and visions are found in this world. The wonders of this world have no end.

But the most marvelous, wonderful, mighty, and perfect divine act is the human being, who is compounded of all the worlds. Everything that is scattered throughout the two engendered worlds is brought together within him. He is the vicegerent of God, the shadow of the divinity, and the epitome and quintessence of the engendered things. Everything created was created to perfect his level. When he attains completion and returns to his own world, the heavens will be rolled up. On that day the bodies will be lost within the spirits, just as today the spirits are lost within the bodies. *On the day when We shall roll up heaven as a scroll is rolled up for the writings. As We originated the first creation, so We shall bring it back again—a promise binding on Us; so We shall do* [21:104].

The complete explanation of these questions would lead to divulging the mystery of the measuring out and the true knowledge of the ends of God's affairs. "But God dislikes you to make complete expositions," even though the possessors of eyes see this meaning more manifest than the sun in the Book of God. ʿAlī alluded to this point when he said, "The Messenger of God never confided any secret to me that he kept hidden from the people which God has not explained to an understanding servant in His Book." In the following Koranic verse, the explanation of the beginnings and the ends is contained, but

A *man* is needed to catch the scent—
after all,
the world is full
of the east wind's fragrance.

Surely in the creation of the heavens and earth and in the alternation of night and day there are signs for the possessors of minds, those who remember God, standing and sitting and on their sides, and reflect upon the creation of the heavens and the earth: "Our Lord, Thou hast not created this in vain. Glory be to Thee! Guard us against the chastisement of the Fire" [3:190–191].

To return to what we were busy with: The human being and all his outward and inward acts, movements, thoughts, and steps appear in keeping with the divine desire—moment by moment, in accordance with a previous measuring out and an appended power. *Surely We have created everything according to a measuring out* [54:49], and *No affliction befalls in the earth or in yourselves, but it is in a Book before We create it; that is easy for God* [57:22] are references to the previous measuring out. *God created you and what you do* [37:96], and *Is there any creator, apart from God?* [35:3] refer to the appended power, which produces creation minute by minute. *Every day He is upon some task* [55:29]. However, the human being is the channel for the divine acts, so they are attributed to him metaphorically. *You did not throw when you threw, but God threw* [8:17].

Though the act is not mine,
it cannot occur without me.
The soul does the acting,
but not without the body.

The act issues from the human being, but in reality he is not the agent. If someone says, "This line on the paper has issued from the pen," he is right. But if he says, "In reality it did not issue from the pen," he is also right. For there are two different points of view. Here the waves of the seas of compulsion and free will are in collision. Nor is anyone delivered from their blows but the perfect and those firmly rooted in knowledge.

Faith in the measuring out is incumbent, but courtesy demands that you witness your own lapses and insufficiencies. No power prevents disobeying God save God's protection, and no strength brings about obeying Him but His giving success. Everything follows His decree and measuring out. From God help is sought, in Him refuge is taken from Him, and in Him trust is placed. "What He wills will be, and what He does not will will not be." He is the Judge, the Just, the Subtle, the Aware—*An excellent Protector, an excellent Helper!* [8:40].

THE SECOND RISING PLACE

On the Realities of the Second Principle: Faith in Prophecy

This section contains two stars.

THE FIRST STAR

Giving True Knowledge of the Initial Characteristics of the Stage of Prophecy and its Particularities and Wonders

Know—may God make you qualified for His wondrous mysteries and give you success in taking illumination from His marvelous lights—that the human being possesses stages, and in each stage there are specific perceptions, for the perceptions of the coming stage are absent from the present stage. For example, the embryo has specific perceptions, and in relation to its perceptions the suckling infant's objects of perception are "unseen." Hence the stage of the suckling infant is beyond that of the embryo. Likewise, the stage of the child who can discriminate is related to that of the suckling infant in the same way that the stage of the suckling infant is related to that of the embryo. Then, the stage of the person in control of reason is beyond that of the discriminating child, the stage of being God's friend is beyond that of reason, the stage of prophecy is beyond that of being a friend, *and above everyone who has knowledge is one who knows* [12:76].

You should know that it is impossible for the embryo to perceive anything of the child's objects of perception, for the embryo is bound by the constricting limits of the womb and has not yet reached the open space of the world. And so it is in the other cases as well: Whoever resides in a determined human stage is incapable of grasping the objects of perception of the stages beyond his own.

Take for example the Mujassima. They are bound by the chains of imitation to the stage of fancy and imagination and its narrow confines. In no sense can they understand the objects of perception of the stage of reason. But if they are released from the bottom of the well of fancy and imagination and attain to the open space of the world of reason, they will come to know where they have been.

When the dust clears
  you will know
if you are sitting on a horse,
  or a donkey.

When morning comes
  you will see
to whom you made love
  in the black night.

In a similar way, those rational thinkers who are confined to the stage of reason are related to the stage of being a friend of God just as the Mujassima are related to the stage of reason. In the stage of friendship there are specific objects of perception that rational thinkers are incapable of grasping. In the world of reason and imagination, only declaring similarity and coining likenesses can tell of these objects. *Those likenesses—We coin them for the people, but no one understands them save those who have knowledge* [29:43].

Meanings are there
  that cannot fit into fancy—
reason grasps nothing
  but a fable.

Whenever human beings reach any stage, they must consider "faith in the unseen" as their ready cash in relation to the stages beyond them. If not, arrival at the coming stage will be impossible. One of the duties deriving from faith in the unseen is that they should make no judgments about the coming stage through deduction. They must consider themselves similar to someone born blind in relation to the perception of colors, because before attaining the sense of sight, any judgment made by such a person concerning colors will be deductions based on smell and hearing. All will be mistaken.

The blind man knows
  he has a mother,
but he cannot imagine
  what she looks like.

Unless human beings are delivered from the stomach of mother nature, leave the womb of mortality, and reach the world of the dominion, they will not be able to understand the stage beyond reason through witnessing and tasting. They can only have faith in the unseen. *When you were embryos in your mothers' wombs—therefore hold not yourselves purified* [53:32].

Heart, how long in this prison,
  deceived by this and that?
Just once leave this dark well
  and see the world!

After these introductory remarks, it is necessary to know that the final stages of the rational thinkers are the beginning stages of God's friends, and the final stages of the friends are the beginning stages of the prophets. *God has preferred some of you over others* [16:71]. *Those messengers—some We have preferred over others* [2:253]. The saying related from Ibn ʿAbbās is an allusion to something like this: "The possessors of knowledge have degrees beyond the possessors of faith. Between every two degrees is a journey of five hundred years."

Only the prophets understand the wondrous objects perceived in prophecy's stage in all their detail. But a few trickles of what they perceive—some of which have reached the stage of reason and some the stage of friendship and about which something can be said on the basis of the interpretation of reason and learning—are as follows: From the horizon of the unseen the prophets are given all the details of the origin and the return in the most complete manner without any human instruction or study. They gain knowledge of a universal law upon which the order of the formal world is based. All the unseen things that ordinary people perceive clothed in images while dreaming are shown to them while they are fully awake. They are given a power through which, with God's permission, they can exercise governing control over anything they desire in the heaven and the earth. When any act issues from a human being in this world, they know its fruit in the barzakh, the resurrection, and the next world. They know definitely and through verification the measures of reward and punishment for actions. In addition, they are commanded through the intermediary and mediation of the Holy Spirit to guide human spirits and to perfect mortal souls. Thereby they give human beings the good news of endless felicity and warn them of everlasting wretchedness. *We do not send the messengers, except good tidings to bear, and warning* [6:48].

THE SECOND STAR

On the Prophecy of Muhammad with an Allusion to the Mystery of his Lordship

Know—may God expand your breast with the light of the gnostic sciences—that just as the stage of prophecy is the furthest limit of the human stages, so also the tasting of Muhammad Mustafa is the furthest limit of the tastings of the prophets and messengers, and he is the most perfect and most excellent of creatures. On the day of resurrection, when all the perfect human beings will be present upon the plain, he will be the lord and epitome of the ancients and the later folk. In the highest degrees of the supreme paradise is found a degree beyond which is no other. It is called the "praiseworthy station." *And as for the night, keep a vigil for part of it, as a work of supererogation for thee; it may be that thy Lord will raise thee up to a praiseworthy station* [17:79]. This station is fitting only for one person, and it is set apart. His Shariah abrogates all other shariahs, his religion is the most perfect religion, and he is the seal of the prophets, the lord of the messengers, and the most eminent of the supreme masters—God bless him and give him peace. *Muhammad is not the father of any one of your men, but the messenger of God, and the seal of the prophets* [33:40].

Ever since being's night gave birth to day,
  no sun like him is remembered.
Anyone not like dust at his door—
  even an angel—dust be on his head!

Glory be to Him who sent him with the truth to all creatures, giving good tidings and warning, *calling unto God by His leave, and as a light-giving lamp* [33:46]. With him He sealed prophecy and perfected messengerhood. To imagine prophecy after him is ignorance and insolence, since adding to perfection is to bring about imperfection.

THE THIRD RISING PLACE

On the Realities of the Third Principle:
Faith in the Last Day

This section contains two stars.

THE FIRST STAR

On Faith in Human Subsistence after the
Annihilation of the Mortal Form

Know—may God help you and purify you from the darkness of mortality—that human spirits were created for everlasting subsistence and eternal life. According to the revelation of God, the testimony of the prophets, the witnessing of God's friends, and the elucidations of the ulama and the sages, disappearance and annihilation have no access to the spirits. *Count not those who were slain in God's way as dead, but rather living with their Lord* [3:169].

The force of death reaches
  the world of the body—
death has no path
  to the world of the spirit.

"You were created for eternity without end; you will only be transferred from one abode to another." "The grave is one of the plots of the Garden or one of the pits of the Fire."

In that house
the people of soul and breath
will see the death of death,
then none will die.

"On the day of resurrection, death will be brought in the form of a salt-colored ram and slaughtered between the Garden and the Fire."

To perceive this question and similar matters by setting up logical premises—like those agreed upon by the rational thinkers and written about in their books—is impossible. *So come to houses by their doors* [2:189]. The morning of certainty will dawn from the east of the world of the dominion only on the basis of faith and god-wariness. *Had the people of the cities had faith and been god-wary, We would have opened upon them blessings from heaven and earth* [7:96]. One must have a soul cleansed from the wrappings of nature's darkness and transformed for a time into a receptacle for the reflection of the rays of the beginningless Sun. Then one can understand the subsistence of mortal souls with a certainty that erases doubt and an unveiling that burns away darkness. *It is He who sent down tranquility into the hearts of the faithful, that they might add faith to their faith* [48:4]. It is obvious what two or three perplexed skeptics can understand about the states of the next world through the forms of imagination. *They follow nothing but surmise, only conjecturing* [10:66].

Men down the wine of gnosis eagerly—
should they,
like the ignorant, drink the dregs
of ambiguity?
Every time you understand
through proofs
you are drawing water from a well
with a sieve.

O God, make me a member of Muhammad's community through Thy bounty and Thy spacious mercy, O Self-subsistent, O Guide!

THE SECOND STAR

On Faith in the Barzakh, the Mustering, the Resurrection, and all the States of the Next World

Know—may God lift the wrapping of mortality from your insight—that when human beings break their attachment with the sensory body through physical death, the first world in their path is one of the marvelous worlds of God, called the "barzakh." The eternal Koran tells of it as follows: *Before them is a barzakh until the day they shall be raised up* [23:100]. The questioning by Munkar and

Nakīr, which the Prophet of God spoke about, takes place in this world in bodily form. Among the wonders of the barzakh is that the good or evil that human beings have done in this world will be seen there once again in appropriate form. *The day every soul shall find what it has done of good brought forward, and what it has done of evil; it will wish there were a far space between it and that day* [3:30]. The marvels of the barzakh are beyond count. The property of its configuration will remain until the day of the mustering of the bodies. *And the Trumpet shall be blown; then behold, they are hastening from their tombs unto their Lord* [36:51]. This is the day of the greater resurrection. *Say: "The ancients and the later folk shall be gathered to the appointed time of a known day"* [56:49-50]. Human spirits will once again be given governing control over bodies. The heavens will be rolled up, and this earth will be changed into another earth. *Upon the day when the earth shall be changed to other than the earth, and the heavens, and they come forth unto God, the One, the Intensely Severe* [14:48]. The stars will be thrown down and the sun and moon made black. "The sun and the moon will be darkened in the Fire on the day of resurrection."

At the resurrection the sun will turn black
to show that it is Thy black slave.

The Throne will be lifted up by eight angels. *The angels shall stand upon its borders, and upon that day eight shall carry above them the Throne of your Lord* [69:17]. God will disclose Himself in a tremendous locus of manifestation, such that all the people of the plain will see Him, each according to his own belief. Thus it has been said,

When they gaze on your beautiful face,
looking upon it from every side,
They see nothing but their own faces—
hence the difference in indications.

Bounty will judge among the servants. *And We shall set up the just scales for the resurrection day, so that not one soul shall be wronged anything; even if it be the weight of a single mustard seed, We shall produce it, and sufficient are We for accounters* [21:48]. Scales appropriate to this task will be brought in keeping with that configuration's relationship with the creatures' perception.

Over the floor of hell a bridge will be erected called the "Path," sharper than a sword and thinner than a hair. In crossing over it, people will have different levels. "Whoever is a flier will fly, whoever is a walker will walk, whoever is a crawler will crawl, and whoever is a faller will fall into the crushers of the deepest Burning." Any person whose foot was more firmly fixed on the straight path of the Shariah in the abode of this world will fly and travel there more perfectly.

The felicitous and the people of insight will be given access to the watering pool called "Kawthar," and there they will drink their fill. The lord of the ancients and the later folk, Muhammad Mustafa, will be taken to the Praiseworthy Station, which is the opening of the gate of intercession. The Banner of Praise will be placed in his hand, and all the lords of the children of Adam—the prophets and friends—will stand in its shadow. First, he will intercede, then the prophets, then the friends, then the ulama, then the faithful, each in keeping with his own rank.

The godly will be taken to endless bliss, and the ungodly imprisoned in eternal hellfire. The chastisement of the disobedient of the Community will come to an end, but the wretchedness and the painful chastisement of the truth-concealers and those who associated others with God will last forever. In the descending degrees of hell there will be various types and varieties of corporeal and spiritual pains, but the greatest and most difficult pain will be to be veiled from witnessing the beauty of Lordship.

> We have no fear or dread of hell—
> our soul's calamity is the smoke of the Veil.

We seek refuge in God from the darkness of His veil! *No indeed; but upon that day they shall be veiled from their Lord* [83:15].

The ascending degrees and chambers of paradise will have many types and manners of spiritual and corporeal joys. But the most noble and tremendous joy will be the incomparable and ineffable encounter with the Creator, the Living, the Loving, the Lord of the worlds, *in a sitting place of strength, with a Powerful King* [54:55].

> When You showed us Your beauty,
> love for all these idols became foolish.
> Let them go, these heart-takers—
> none has any profit but You.

So let him who hopes for the encounter with his Lord work upright works and not associate anyone with his Lord's worship [18:110].

> O seeker of this world,
> you are a hireling.
> O lover of paradise,
> you are far from this truth.
> O happy with both worlds,
> you have stayed ignorant—
> Not having seen the joy of heartache for Him,
> you have an excuse.

More than this cannot fit into such a short work. But God's friends who undergo unveiling and those firmly rooted in knowledge know that the results of the tastings of those who travel in the land of holiness have been mentioned and recorded in these pages only briefly. Their meaning can be learned in detail only in the school of *We taught him knowledge from Us* [18:65]. The introductory lesson for entering that school is to wipe the impression of the two engendered worlds from the tablet of the heart with the eraser of faith and god-wariness.

When you wipe the two worlds
  from the tablet of the heart,
the Holy Spirit will come
  and gaze on your beauty.
One by one, your being's mysteries
  will be written—
none will be able
  to grasp your perfection.

Now, in conclusion, we will write a few words by way of reminder and friendly admonition. May God let us—and you—listen to advice, and may He give us success in what He loves and what pleases Him!

CONCLUSION

Know O friend—may God take you to the highest levels of the travelers—that, in its own field, each group among the ulama has certain technical terms, rules, and norms. By gaining a command of these and understanding them, one can become informed about all the details of their sciences. The present group—who are the people of witnessing and gnosis—also have their technical terms, rules, and norms, and to describe them briefly or in detail would require many long introductions. This short work cannot accomplish such a task.

But their norms are limited to four kinds: the Book of God, the Sunnah of the Messenger, the consensus of the Community, and the heart. By this heart is meant the heart described by God as related by the Prophet. "My heaven embraces Me not, nor My earth, but the heart of My faithful, gentle, and meek servant does embrace Me." No one can gain such a heart who has not completely cleansed the filth of nature and the darkness of engendered things from his inward self by following the Shariah and the Tariqah.

The heart is love's confidant,
  the treasury of mysteries,
in the garden of being,
  a rose without thorns.
The goal of all things
  is the heart, no doubt,
but to gain such a heart
  takes a great deal of heartache.

With this introduction, we continue: Whenever a gnostic or a traveler finds something shining down from the horizon of the dominion upon the tablet of his heart, he must compare it with the Book of God. If it agrees with the Book, he should accept it; if not, he should pay no attention to it. Then he should compare it with the Sunnah of the Messenger. If it corresponds to it, he should judge it to be true; if not, he should take no further action. In the same way he should also compare it with the consensus of the ulama and the shaykhs of the Community.

The following has been related from Shaykh Abū Sulaymān Dārānī: "It may happen that the Reality will knock at my heart for forty days, but I give it no permission to enter except with two witnesses: the Book and the Sunnah." The errors of this path have no end, because the signs on the horizons and in the souls become confused in formal and supraformal unveilings. No one is saved from the clashing waves of the oceans of the signs except the masters among His sincere servants—and how few they are!

Hence, except in rare and exceptional cases, one cannot avoid the need for a shaykh who is a wayfarer, a truth-teller, and a verifier. "He who has no shaykh has Satan for his shaykh" is the allusion of the king of the gnostics, Abū Yazīd Basṭāmī.

He who has no moon-like face to guide him on the Path
  stands in danger, but people do not understand.

God in His perfect bounty and benevolence has placed in the shaykh's soul and in the shadow of his companionship a light and a mystery that cannot be explained in words.

Do nothing without the command
  of the "old man"—
old through knowledge,
  not through time's wheel.

"The shaykh among his people is like the prophet in his community."

O you who have faith, be wary of God, seek the means to come to Him, and struggle in His way; perhaps you will prosper [5:35]. The verifiers say that *seek the means to come to Him* is a command to seek out a shaykh.

If you find a guide in His path,
  place your head at his feet.
Perhaps then
  you will get some place.
Those without pain
  see no color in this cup—
your own heart's pain
  will take you to the medicine.

When the seeker finds the shaykh, he must know that, as long as the Reality's ruling authority has not come and servanthood's perfection is not attained, perseverance in being the companion of the shaykh's slippers is the source of the greatest felicity. The seeker must welcome the shaykh's commands and prohibitions with his heart and soul. Then he will be nourished in the shadow of the shaykh's good fortune by the gusts of the gentleness and the blows of the severity of the divine beauty and majesty. He will be fully delivered from the errors and falsifications of fancy and imagination.

At the same time, the seeker should know with certainty that the celestial axis of wayfaring on the straight path has two poles: perseverance and opposition—opposition to caprice, and perseverance in the remembrance of God. The preliminaries and fruits of these two poles can be achieved through being the companion of a living-hearted Master of the Time in a way that is not possible by any other means.

In short, the essential prerequisite of this task is to empty the locus and cut off all attachments. The seeker must strive never to let his heart have intimacy with any but God, for at the resurrection only this will give deliverance—*the day when neither wealth nor sons will profit, [and none will be saved] except for him who comes to God with a wholesome heart* [26:88–89]. The ladder to the pavilions of *tawḥīd* is correct disengagement.

If caprice makes you want
  nothing but a needle,
you may be Jesus son of Mary,
  but they won't let you in.

The densest and thickest veil is a person's attachment to other human beings. The great ones have acknowledged that this is the most difficult of all the difficult obstacles. To be held back by it yields complete deprivation. *You have only taken to yourselves idols, apart from God, as a mark of mutual love between you in the life of this world; then on the day of resurrection you will deny one another* [29:25]. Attachment to people is of different types and to explain these would require some detail. Most of these types are harmful on the Path. The great ones have said, "One of the signs of ruin is to be intimate with people." The eternal Koran teaches how to avoid such intimacy as follows: *Remember the name of your Lord, and devote yourself to Him very devoutly—Lord of the East and West, there is no god but He, so take Him for a guardian* [73:8]. Someone spoke for the Unseen in the language of love as follows:

Put up with pain,
  for I am your medicine;
sit with no one,
  for I am your intimate.

In short, hindrances and difficult obstacles are many, and deliverance from them can only come by following the Shariah and obeying a shaykh.

The road has a thousand calamities—
sometimes a fall, sometimes a climb.

As long as manyness remains, the properties of the path will stay. When manyness goes, the traveler also disappears. *The Real has come, and the unreal has vanished away* [17:81].

All these deceptive tints
will be given one color
by the dying vat
of Oneness.

As long as an atom of the traveler remains, God will not lift the veil of inaccessibility's jealousy from the beauty of sheer Singularity.

As long as an atom of us remains,
Thy inaccessibility will not show Thy beauty.

He should know with certainty that wayfaring on God's path can be done only with God's solicitude. "Whoever supposes he can reach God through other than God has been deceived."

For a lifetime I have known for certain
that, without Thy help, none can reach Thee.

No one can reach Him through performing good works, but no one has ever reached Him without them.

What has not been allotted
cannot be gained through effort,
but unless you show your effort,
you will never reach your lot.

The end has the properties of what came before, and what existed at the first will exist at the last. The universal order is directed toward the good, and precedence belongs to mercy. "My mercy precedes My wrath." Having a good opinion of the Lord is one of the beautiful traits of servanthood. *God summons to the Abode of Peace, and He guides whomsoever He will to a straight path* [10:25]. *Remember God often, and glorify Him at dawn and in the evening* [33:41–42]. *And hold fast to God's cord, all of you together* [3:103]. *God commands justice, virtue, and giving to kinsmen; and He forbids indecency, dishonor, and insolence. He admonishes you—perhaps you will remember* [16:90].

Clarifications for Beginners and Reminders for the Advanced

In the Name of God, the Merciful, the Compassionate

Worthiness for praise belongs to the presence of unity's majesty, the loving God. The fruit of the preliminary work of His creativity was the spirits of those who carry the light of knowing Him, and the goal of bringing heaven and earth into existence was the essences of those who guard the mysteries of love for Him.

Fitness for blessings belongs to the holy Muhammadan threshold. Through the light of that master's messengerhood, the lands of the East and the West were lit up, and through the fragrance of the breeze of his friendship with God, the corners of the dominion and the kingdom turned into rose gardens.

Merit for salutations belongs to his inheritors and household—God bless them all—who are the lamps that shine in the darkness of error and the keys that open the treasuries of guidance.

To come to the point: These are a few words on the principles of the gnostic sciences and the foundations of the stage of friendship with God, words that have disclosed themselves from behind the curtain of the unseen and become manifest within the clothing of letters and words. By studying and gaining a command of them, the gnostic and seeker may reap the benefit of being reminded and finding the right path, and by that means he may aid me through an upright supplication. Perhaps through its blessing I may be delivered completely from the darkness of my own selfhood and reach the furthest limit of my heart's aspiration—arriving at the encounter with God and being consumed by the witnessing of His majesty and beauty. I have called these words "Clarifications for Beginners and Reminders for the Advanced." In brief, they will consist of an introduction, three lamps, and a conclusion. We seek recourse in God, and upon Him we depend.

INTRODUCTION

It should be known that the pillars of unveiling and the great masters of witnessing have seen with their penetrating insights and recognized with their God-knowing hearts that the Creator gave existence to the cosmos for the sake of the people of true knowledge—the angels, the prophets, and the friends of God (upon all of them be God's blessings!). David asked his Lord about this meaning after he had cast off the world of darknesses. "O Lord, why didst Thou create the creatures?" From behind the pavilions of inaccessibility came the call, "I was a Hidden Treasure and I loved to be known, so I created the creatures that I might be known."

In the same way, the following is related in the *Ṣaḥīḥ* of Muslim from the Messenger of God:

> Moses asked his Lord, "Which inhabitant of the Garden is lowest in level?"
>
> God replied, "A man who will come after the people of the Garden have been placed in the Garden. It will be said to him, 'Enter the Garden!' He will reply, 'My Lord, how can I? The people have settled in their stations and taken what they will take.' Then it will be said to him, 'Will you not be satisfied to receive the like of the kingdom possessed by a king of the lower world?' He will say, 'I will be satisfied, my Lord.' Then God will say, 'To you belongs that, and its like, and its like, and its like. . . '. When He says 'and its like' for the fifth time, the man will say, 'I am satisfied, my Lord.' Then God will say, 'This belongs to you, and the like of it ten times over. To you belongs what your soul desires and what refreshes your eye.' He will say, 'I am satisfied, my Lord.' "
>
> Then Moses asked, "My Lord, what about him whose station is highest?'
>
> God replied, "Those—they are the ones I desired. I planted their noble field with My own hand and sealed it. No eye has seen it, no ear has heard of it, and it has never passed into the heart of any mortal."
>
> Then the Prophet said, "This is corroborated by the Book of God: *So no soul knows what refreshment of the eyes is hidden away for them* [32:17]."

The point of relating this hadith is contained in the words, "Those—they are the ones I desired." From the top of the Throne to the earth beneath our feet, everything has been created for the sake of this group. All things are designed to give them advance and benefit, and all things are subjected to them. *Have you not seen how God has subjected to you everything in the heavens and the earth, and He has lavished on you blessings, outward and inward?* [30:20].

You think this emerald field is play,
  you think this glassy vault is folly.
If not for the Shariah, the turning wheel would stop;
  if not for religion, the Twins would quit the sky.

The true knowledge carried by those who are God's desire has details that the people of ascents and eyes call the "sciences of unveiling."

Among these sciences is:

[1] The true knowledge of God's Essence in the respect that He knows Himself and others know Him not. This Essence is called the "Unseen He-ness." No creature perceives anything of It. *God warns you about His Self* [3:28]. To admit the incapacity of perceiving that presence is the perfection of those brought near to God. "Glory be to Him who has set down no path for His creatures to know Him save the incapacity to know Him!"

Intellect of intellect is He,
  spirit of spirit,
And what is higher than that—
  that is He.

Thou shalt not see Me [7:143] and *Eyes perceive Him not* [6:103] are allusions to this.

[2] The witnessing of that Essence in respect of Its manifestation within the loci of manifestation. This is expressed in the sayings, "You will see your Lord just as you see the full moon—nothing will be mixed with His vision" and "I saw my Lord in the most beautiful form." He is *the Manifest and the Nonmanifest* [57:3].

Look! Everything marked
  by existence
is either His Light's shadow
  or He.

"There is nothing in existence but God." "None other than God inhabits the two worlds."

No one's in the village,
  they're all drunk—
let out a cry
  in the ruined village!

The mystery of Oneness and the annihilation of the kingdom and the dominion, and the mystery of *Everything is perishing except His Face* [28:88], both derive from this world. This is the most enigmatic and excellent science of unveiling. But none knows it fully and truly save the great ones and the perfect among those brought near to God.

[3] The true knowledge of His names and attributes in the respect that, from one point of view, they are identical with the Essence and, from another point of view, different from the Essence; the true knowledge of the universal names and the particular names under their scope; the true knowledge of the names whose knowledge can be attained by the gnostic; the true knowledge of the incapacity to know those names to which no creature has access. On this last point, the following allusion has been transmitted from the Messenger (God's blessings be

upon him). "I ask Thee by every name by which Thou hast named Thyself, or sent down in Thy Book, or taught to any of Thy creatures, or kept for Thyself in the knowledge of the Unseen."

[4] The true knowledge of His acts, which, in brief, can be divided into two kinds: command and creation, which are called "dominion" and "kingdom." The kingdom is the world of bodies, and the dominion is the world of spirits.

[5] The true knowledge of the inhabitants of the higher dominion and the lower dominion, and the levels of the cherubim, the spirituals, and the enraptured angels; the true knowledge of the satans and the jinn; the true knowledge of those worlds which are subordinate either to the world of spirits or to the world of bodies; and the true knowledge of other worlds that are intermediate between the world of spirits and the world of bodies.

[6] The true knowledge of the stage of friendship and prophecy and of revelation, inspiration, recurring thoughts, and satanic whisperings.

[7] The true knowledge of the mystery of the measuring out; the mystery of this world and the next, and of how the next world grows out of this world; how works become embodied and character traits, thoughts, and words become personified; the mystery of the world of the barzakh; and the mysteries of the resurrection, the Mustering, the Uprising, the Path, the Scales, paradise, and hell.

All these meanings pertain to the sciences of unveiling. The perfect gnostics must know all of them. But the tablet of these sciences will be inscribed only in the school of *We taught him knowledge from Us* [18:65]. This will not happen until the rust of possible things has been completely cleansed from the mirror of the heart with the polish of faith and god-wariness and until the wine of disengagement has been drunk down in the tavern of the annihilation of mortal attributes.

Not lately has meaning's kingdom
  come to an accomplished master
unless form's kingdom
  has first gone off to the side.

Had the people of the cities had faith and been god-wary, We would have opened upon them blessings from heaven and earth [7:96].

Hold back your tongue for a time
  from measuring words—
Silent outside, you will see nothing inside
  but tongue.

"Whoever entrusts himself sincerely to God for forty days will find the springs of wisdom welling forth from his heart onto his tongue."

He who is confirmed by the dominion of heaven in wayfaring on this path will be given success in that for which God created the creatures. *I have not created the jinn and mankind except to worship Me* [51:56].

Enter God's school—
  why be busy with creation's alphabet?
Become praised by God—
  why be praised by His creatures?
For an instant make present
  your absent heart:
Witness the Creator and let His creatures
  cite you as witness.

In composing this brief treatise I seek refuge in the Self-subsistent Being from satanic thoughts and dark inrushes. "There is no power and no strength but in God, the High, the Tremendous." Following the habit of God's friends and the Sufis, I will make no more than an allusion to each of the principles mentioned above, in the manner of a public address, for these types of sciences—in keeping with the eternal custom of God and the principles of verification—cannot fit into the robes of letters and words, because of their extreme inaccessibility and tremendousness. "When someone knows God, his tongue becomes dumb" means that the gnostic can find no expression to explain the inmost depth of what he knows. "He who has not tasted does not know."

O friend, the story of love is another,
  greater than the measure of words.
If you open your heart's eye for an instant,
  you will know how this story unfolds.

The aim of the great ones in speaking and writing about this science has never been more than to call attention and to incite desire. In them we have a beautiful model and an approved example.

Now let us enter into our subject. God gives success, and He protects from the evil of the enemy and his hosts.

THE FIRST LAMP

On the True Knowledge of the Creator

This lamp contains three gleams: the first gleam, on the true knowledge of the Essence; the second gleam, on the true knowledge of the attributes; and the third gleam, on the true knowledge of the acts. God inspires what is correct. *He casts the Spirit of His command upon whomsoever He will of His servants* [40:15].

THE FIRST GLEAM

On the True Knowledge of the Essence

Know—may God give you success to ascend to the highest heavens—that those who seek the presence of Self-subsistence and yearn for the beauty of the

Eternal Refuge, those who have been incited by the turmoil of yearning and seeking to climb out of the well of imitation with the help of yearning's ladder and seeking's rope and to reach the open space of the world of witnessing and direct vision, are of two kinds: the companions of investigation and reflective thought, and the possessors of unveiling and eyes. In striving for this goal, each kind has a specific path.

The people of investigation and consideration want to reach the utmost limit of their desires by setting up propositions and composing proofs and arguments. Their books are famous, and their paths well-known. From the existence of the possible things, they draw conclusions concerning the Necessary Being—great is His holiness! They go from the creature to the Creator and from the handiwork to the Maker. Although this way is praiseworthy, it is empty of the light of prophetic effusion. In the end, it yields nothing but blameworthy bewilderment.

Bewilderment is of two types: the bewilderment of the considerative thinkers and the bewilderment of the possessors of eyes. The bewilderment of the considerative thinkers is blameworthy. It rises up from the clashing of doubts and the mutual conflict of proofs. As Ḥusayn ibn Manṣūr [al-Ḥallāj] has said,

Whoever seeks Him
  taking reason as his guide
is made to wander
  bewildered and distracted.
Confused, he sullies
  his own awareness,
asking in his bewilderment,
  "Is that He?"

Seek not the path of *tawḥīd*
  with reason,
scratch not the spirit's eye
  with thorns.
The severity of "But God"
  has hung reason
from the two-branched gallows
  of "No" [لا].

The bewilderment of the possessors of eyes is praiseworthy. It derives from the continuous flux of self-disclosures and the constant flashing of illuminations during the witnessing of magnificence, unity's glory, and the wonders of Lordship's affairs and properties. The saying "My Lord, increase my bewilderment in Thee!" alludes to this station.

I am bewildered in Thee,
  take my hand,
O guide of everyone
  bewildered in Thee!

Why, O tress, do you take each moment
another form on the beloved's face?
Why are you now an ambergris rope,
now a musky polo stick?
Why weave so much chain mail?
Are you then David, the chain mail weaver?
Why cast so many spells?
Are you Harut, the great spell caster?

As for the people of unveiling and insight, they purify the inward center, empty the locus, perfect their devotion, and make their attentiveness constant. Thereby they reach the ultimate goal of their desires—arrival at the true knowledge of God and the encounter with Him. They call this "wayfaring on the straight path." It is the path of the 124,000 prophets—God bless them all. *He has laid down for you as religion what He charged Noah with, and what We revealed to thee, and what We charged Abraham with, Moses and Jesus: "Perform the religion"* [42:13]. But the noblest of these ways and the most perfect of these religions is the primordial creed, the religion of Mustafa—God bless him and his pure household—as divine revelation has explained. *Today I have perfected your religion for you, and I have completed My blessings upon you, and I have approved Islam for you as a religion* [5:3].

It is this group that has been given success in wayfaring on the straight path. Their names were written out one by one at the place and covenant of *Am I not your Lord?* [7:172] in the register of *He loves them* [5:54]. They are the beloved of Him who does not disappear and will never disappear. *God is well-pleased with them and they are well-pleased with Him* [5:119].

Those taken at Alast
are still drunk from that day's covenant.
They are foot-bound in the station of pain,
open-handed in throwing away their lives.
Quick they go and with one stride
they jump the river of time.
Annihilated from themselves and subsistent in the Friend,
this is strange: they are and are not.
These are the people who have reached *tawḥīd*—
the rest all worship themselves.

They have reached the depths of the Ocean of Unity and passed beyond the darknesses of temporal events. Whatever is unseen for all creatures is visible to them. Whatever people have heard talk about, they have seen with their insight. The tongue of their station keeps on reciting this verse.

Thy Face has lit up my night
  while night's shadows cover the people.
They stay in the shadows of night,
  we bask in the light of day.

They have remained in the purity of their original disposition. The darknesses of engendered things and the fluctuations of temporal events have no effect upon them.

I see the days' changing colors,
  but your love never leaves my heart.

Love cures the heart
  of every poor dervish,
but it can't be reached
  by those who serve caprice.
It filled my head
  in eternity without beginning,
it will keep me busy
  until eternity without end.

Those—He has written faith upon their hearts, and He has confirmed them with a spirit from Himself [58:22].

For certain, this group perceives the existence of the Creator without setting up logical premises. Far from that! How could the person with eyes have need for conclusions drawn by touch to perceive colors? *Is there any doubt concerning God?* [14:10].

Where is a heart to know for an instant
  His secret,
where an ear to hear for a moment
  His words?
The Beloved shows His beauty
  night and day.
Where is an eye to take enjoyment in
  His vision?

The original disposition of God, according to which He originated mankind—there is no changing God's creation. That is the right religion [30:30].

Junayd was asked, "What is the proof of the Maker's existence?" He replied, "Morning has freed me of need for a lamp."

Another possessor of true knowledge was asked, "Where is God?" He answered, "God take you away! In face of His plain presence, you ask 'Where'?"

But unless His light is found, He cannot be recognized. *Is he whose breast God has expanded unto Islam, so he walks in a light from his Lord...?* [39:22].

Shaykh al-Islām Anṣārī said, "My God, You were kind to Your friends, so they recognized You. If You had been kind to Your enemies, they would not have denied You."

The explanation of the principles of the true knowledge that is tasted by their spirits cannot fit into letters and words.

Not every well-kept secret
is divulged,
not every wink of the gazelle's eye
is reported.

However, we will write as much as the present moment allows, in the form of indications and summaries, seeking aid and guidance from God.

The wayfarer is delivered from the prison of caprice and the four pegs of nature, and the eye of his heart is anointed with the antimony of Unity's light. Then the might of the mystery of *God is the Light of the heavens and the earth* [24:35] removes its mask and lets him know the meaning of *We are nearer to him than the jugular vein* [50:16]. The majesty of *To God belong the East and the West—whithersoever you turn, there is the Face of God* [2:115] speaks to him in the private cell of *Everything is perishing except His Face* [28:88]. It says,

With God
"others" are inconceivable.
Gate, court, sentinel—
all are naught.

That is because God—He is the Real, and what they call upon apart from Him—that is unreal [22:62].

All these deceptive tints
will be given one color
by the dying vat
of Oneness.

Is it Thou or I, this entity in the eye?
Far be it from Thee, far be it from me, to affirm two!
A He-ness is Thine in the midst of my not-ness forever:
each is confused with each in two respects.

Don't think this thread is two-ply!
The root and branch are one—look closely!
All is He, but appearing in me;
all is I, no doubt, but in Him.

Here, the solicitude mentioned in *God confirms those who have faith with the firm word* [14:27] must gently nudge the gnostic, or else he will perish. *God warns you about His Self* [3:28].

I have killed two thousand lovers like you
with heartache—
my finger has never been tainted
by blood.

God is independent of the worlds [29:6].

Thousands of wayfarers have fallen from the path at this station, having been overcome by corrupt doctrines, such as incarnationism, unificationism, and so on. God is exalted high above what those who have deviated imagine!

One of the people of true knowledge said, "The science of annihilation and subsistence revolves around freeing Unity from admixture and being a true servant. Anything else is blatant error and heresy."

"Glory be to the King, the Holy—to whom nothing is connected, from whom nothing is separate, and with whom nothing is!"

The light is not cut off from the sun—
The defect's in the mirror and the eye.
Anyone caught in the everlasting veil
is an owl looking at the sun.

No one meddles in this question but him
who cannot tell self-disclosure from incarnation.
The more your heart's face is polished,
the more prepared it is for self-disclosure.

"God discloses Himself to people in general and to Abū Bakr in particular."

Here one comes to know the mystery of oneness and the true knowledge of the immutable entities—which are called "creatures"—and their annihilation and nonexistence when they are considered in themselves. Here the gnostic recognizes the infinite Essence of the Real in Its attribute of being the Eternal Refuge, and he comes to know the realities and mysteries of majesty and generous giving.

When the gnostic contemplates the Unseen He-ness, he sees nothing but nonmanifestation and majesty, which is the Presence of the Essence. *He is God, the One, the Intensely Severe* [39:4]. *Eyes perceive Him not, but He perceives the eyes; He is the Subtle, the Aware* [6:103]. "Glory be to Him who alone knows what He is!"

The gnostic sees that those in the higher plenum brought near to God are like himself—deprived and incapable of perceiving the inaccessibility of His He-ness. *Glory be to your Lord, the Lord of inaccessibility, above what they describe!* [37:180].

But when the gnostic looks at the manifest dimension of the existent things, he sees nothing but manifestation and generous giving, for that is the presence of self-disclosure and the court of descent. "Glory be to Him who is manifest in His nonmanifestation and nonmanifest in His manifestation!" Here the gnostic comes to know the meaning of *Upon that day faces shall be radiant, gazing upon their Lord* [75:22–23] and the sense of "I saw my Lord in the most beautiful form."

Here the mystery of the veil of inaccessibility and the cloak of magnificence will become known in its entirety. It will be verified that God can only be seen through the intermediary of the cloak of magnificence. "Nothing stands between the creatures and their gazing upon their Lord except the cloak of magnificence upon His Face in the Garden of Eden."

My head's eye gazed on that meaning
  and I saw form, but my spirit saw meaning.
I look with the eye of the head at form
  since meaning can be seen in no other way.

To Him belongs the magnificence in the heavens and the earth [45:37]. God bless the one who said, "I have never seen anything without seeing God within it."

In Thy world is found
  no rose or stone
without a hint of the fragrance
  of union with Thee.

Once the gnostic comes to know all the realities and properties of the names Manifest and Nonmanifest, he will know in what respect God can be seen and in what respect He cannot be seen. He will know what the Prophet meant when Abū Dharr Ghifārī asked him, "O Messenger of God, have you seen your Lord?" He replied, "He is a light. How should I see Him?" But in another place he said, "I saw my Lord in the most beautiful form."

If love makes your heart want to see,
  you can easily see the Beloved.
But beware! Content yourself with a shadow.
  Think it not proper to see more than His shadow.

When the eye of the heart comes to see with the light of true knowledge, these meanings will become more manifest than the perception of self-evident principles. But I dare not say and write more, for this is an awesome locus of witnessing and a tremendous station. "What does dust have to do with the Lord of lords?" From the unseen direction they keep on saying,

Do not boldly fly so high, for in this path
  the scissors of "No" [لا]
snipped a hundred thousand feathers
  from Gabriel's wing.

Even those of the higher plenum brought near to God and the holy ones of the sublime invincibility admit their complete incapacity to witness God's magnificence and inaccessibility. "Glory be to Thee—we have not truly known Thee!" On the contrary,

When Eternity's magnificence makes itself manifest,
  our *tawḥīd* is utter polytheism.

"None recognizes God but God. None says God but God. He who supposes that he has expressed *tawḥīd* has associated others with God."

Does anyone exist to whom reason may say, "O He,"
  other than Thou?
Does any have grandeur and power
  other than Thou?
What should I say about Thee?
  What can I say?
Thou speakest, Thou hearest—where is a thou-ness
  other than Thou?

"Glory be to Him who expresses His own *tawḥīd* with the tongue of His servant!" Praise belongs to God, and peace be upon His servants whom He has chosen.

THE SECOND GLEAM

On the True Knowledge of the Attributes

Know that the Self-subsistent Being says as follows in His mighty word: *To God belong the most beautiful names, so call Him by them* [7:180]. In the eyes of the leaders of unveiling and the pillars of witnessing, *names* and *attributes* are two words with one meaning. But, in the Book and the Sunnah, they have been described mainly by the word *names*. In this station, the duty of the well-prepared, verifying seeker is, first, to learn God's names and attributes from the prophets and friends by way of faith. Then he must go forward in their path and through the light of following them become aware of the realities of the names. *Be wary of God, and God will teach you* [2:282].

Follow God's good pleasure
  all day until night—
sleep as a Kurd,
  wake as an Arab!

Nothing can be learned by argumentation and discussion. May God be well pleased with the unique Shaykh, Awḥad al-Dīn Kirmānī. How well he has spoken!

The mysteries of the path cannot be solved
  by asking,
nor by throwing away dignity
  and wealth.
Unless your heart and eyes shed blood
  for fifty years,
you will not be shown the way
  from words to states.

The station of knowing the names and attributes is of the utmost tremendousness and majesty. Only the people of true purity and sincere love are made aware of it. How can quoting all sorts of sayings, transmitting different doctrines, and memorizing volumes of Kalām and philosophy make a person into a receptacle for the reflection of the luminous rays of God's names and attributes?

Go, say to him who claims
  knowledge of philosophy,
"You've learned a little something,
  but much has passed you by!"

Let your natural learning go
  before your soul assumes
the form of every heretic's imaginings
  through logical proofs.

Not everyone who knows the technical terms of the scholars and the sages is a scholar and a sage. Nor does everyone who cultivates renunciation and worship have the eyes to see the majesty and beauty of Eternity without beginning. Far from it! *All the people know their own drinking places* [2:60]. Only a holy soul knows the meanings of His names and attributes.

Sahl Tustarī said, "The ulama, the renouncers, and the worshipers departed from this world, their hearts locked. Only the hearts of the witnessers and sincere devotees have been opened." Then he recited, *With Him are the keys to the Unseen; none knows them but He* [6:59].

Not everyone who comes from a mountain
  has the message of Moses,
not every child of an old man
  has the strength of Dastān!

Not every heart can hold the light of His mysteries' inaccessibility, and not every ear can bear the sound of the assaults of His gnostic sciences' majesty.

First you'd better find a listener—
  the Indians don't know Arabic.

You two came to ask the secret
  of my beloved—
you will find me stingy
  with her secret.

Those who have taken these realities in hand with their own tools—overelegant reason, bob-tailed cleverness, cross-eyed insight—have never gained anything but concealing the truth, misguidance, bewilderment, and ignorance. Some of them negate attributes, but the tasting of the prophets and friends gives witness to the contrary. Some of them affirm attributes, but in a manner that utterly contradicts the Essence. From here, pure truth-concealing and unmixed associating others with God are the necessary consequences. Still others consider His Essence the locus of temporal events. High indeed is God exalted above what the wrongdoers say!

But the masters of the path and the guardians of the mysteries of Oneness—those who have taken illumination from the niche of prophecy—have come to see and know through God's teaching and instruction that His attributes are, in one respect, identical with the Essence and, in another respect, different from the Essence, for His names are all meanings, standpoints, relationships, and attributions. They are identical with the Essence inasmuch as no existent thing can be found there other than the Essence. But they are different from the Essence inasmuch as what is understood from them is certainly diverse. The manyness of the names stems from the diversity of the existent things and the mutual opposition of meanings and standpoints. But here there are enigmatic mysteries.

Alive, Knowing, Desiring, and Powerful are among the names whose meanings subsist through the eternal Essence. For the people of insight, the names are, in reality, those eternal meanings, while these words are the "names of the names." Names such as these are called "positive attributes." These four names are the "four pillars of the Divinity."

As for Exalter and Abaser, Life-giver and Slayer, Bestower and Preventer, Benefitter and Harmer—these all arise from relationships and are called "correlative attributes."

Peace, Holy, and Independent negate defects, imperfections, and need, and are called "negative attributes."

All the names are included in these three categories.

As for God [*Allāh*], it is an all-comprehensive name of the eternal Essence inasmuch as It is described by all names and attributes, both in respect of Its manifestation and Its nonmanifestation. No other name has the tremendousness of this name. Most of the ulama hold that this name is not derived and that it is for Him what a proper name is for others.

Merciful is a name of that eternal, undefiled Essence inasmuch as the lights of existence radiate out from the presence of His majesty upon the entities of the possible things. This name has no relationship with the Unseen He-ness in respect of the fact that It is the Unseen He-ness. Rather, it pertains to the presence of manifestation—in contrast to the name God, which embraces the unseen and the visible, manifestation and nonmanifestation. These two names possess the utmost inaccessibility and majesty. *Say: "Call upon God, or call upon the Merciful. Whichever you call upon, to Him belong the most beautiful names"* [17:110].

As for the other names that human beings can perceive, their properties are perceived by the gnostic through tasting moment by moment. In this station, I will allude to a few names and present a general rule that, for the possessor of a wholesome original disposition, can act as a key to the true knowledge of the other names. It is God who inspires.

Know that, when the gnostic comes to understand the mystery of the Throne and grasps its affinity with the presence of mercifulness, he will know the meaning of *The Merciful sat Himself upon the Throne* [20:50]. In the same way, when he comes to know the configuration of the angels and grasps their holiness and purity, he will understand their affinity with the two names Glorified and Holy, in keeping with which they say, *We glorify Thee through praise and call Thee holy* [2:30]. When he comes to know the meaning of satanity and grasps the mystery of Iblis, he will understand what mysteries exist between Iblis and the Inaccessible, so that he is led to say, *Now, by Thy inaccessibility, I shall lead them all astray* [38:82]. When he comes to know the configuration of the human being, discerns in detail the composition of his faculties and constitution, and understands each faculty's affinity with a name—and with all this the mystery of *He loves them and they love Him* [5:54] winks at him—then he will know why the Forgiving and Loving pertain exclusively to Adam and his descendants. Glory be to the King, the Loving!

Love's dew made clay of Adam's earth,
  discord rose, tumult spread;
Love's lancet reached the spirit's vein,
  a drop fell out, they called it "heart."

It has been reported that the ready cash of each heaven and each angel is a specific name, from which it derives its power for all eternity. The one that knows the Subtle does not know the Intensely Severe, and the one that says "Tremendous" does not say "All-covering." *He taught Adam the names, all of them* [2:31] is the specific characteristic of God's vicegerent. The locus of manifestation for the name of Divinity is Adam the pure.

When We sent Adam out,
  We placed Our own beauty in the desert.

In this station there are tremendous mysteries, but the loss that people would suffer from hearing them is greater than the gain. Hence it is better to pull in the reins of exposition. I fear that, if the bridle of free choice slips from my hands, things will be written down such that a murmur will be heard in protest from the sky-light of the Unseen:

The nightingale told the rose
  a thousand tales—
the candle's burning heart,
  the secret of the moth.

Losing his senses,
  the mad nightingale
told a secret
  to which no one was party.

What has been said up to this point is enough. A short work like this cannot carry more. No one can encompass the names of God, and He alone knows them in detail. This is the meaning of "[Those names Thou hast] kept for Thyself in the knowledge of the Unseen." *Though all the trees in the earth were pens, and the sea [were ink]—seven seas after it to replenish it, yet would the words of God not be spent* [31:27]. Concerning the names, we have preferred brevity. God's peace be upon Muhammad and his household, the good!

THE THIRD GLEAM

On the True Knowledge of the Acts

Know that the Maker of the cosmos swears by His acts in a summary manner in His eternal Speech. He says, *No! I swear by what you see and what you do not see* [69:38–39].

His acts are of two kinds: the unseen and the visible. In the mighty Word He calls these "command" and "creation" where He says, *Verily, His are the creation and the command* [7:54].

The world of creation is a world to which sensory indications have access. It is called the "world of the visible," the "world of the kingdom," the "world of bodies," and the "low world." All these terms are applied synonymously to this single meaning.

The world of command is a world to which sensory indications have no access. It is called the "world of the unseen," the "world of the dominion," the "world of spirits," and the "high world." All these expressions are likewise synonymous.

No! I swear by what you see [69:38] alludes to the world of bodies, while *what you do not see* [69:39] refers to the world of spirits. In the eternal Book, the world of bodies is mentioned in detail, but the world of spirits is mentioned only briefly, for anyone with a verified understanding of the states of the dominion has reached the dominion. But unless a human being has in hand the ready cash of a second birth, he cannot reach the dominion. Jesus said, "None will enter the dominion of the heavens unless he is born twice."

Unless God wills, all the world's inhabitants have the characteristics of embryos in the womb of their mother, the low world. *When you were yet unborn in your mothers' wombs—therefore hold not yourselves purified* [53:32]. When the key of *When comes the help of God, and opening* [90:1] is sent from the presence of *With Him are the keys to the unseen—none knows them but He* [6:59], and the lock of mortality—*Or are there locks on the hearts?* [47:24]—is removed, the human being will be given access to the no-place of the dominion. "My essence has become distinct where there is no 'where.' "

We have another tongue
  apart from this,
another place,
  apart from hell and paradise.

Thus We showed Abraham the dominion of the heavens and the earth, that he might be one of those having certainty [6:75].

Having passed beyond the darkness of water and clay,
  we are Khizr and the Water of Life.

When he arrives at the dominion, he will eliminate his need for reports through seeing directly. "Reports are not like seeing face to face."

The pain that we heard about
  from the people
came from knowledge to actuality,
  from ear to breast.

The states of the dominion cannot be expressed in the kingdom. Nevertheless, I will follow the dictation of the present moment, emulating the custom of the perfect human beings and the gnostics, and allude briefly to the enraptured spirits, the inhabitants of the higher and lower dominions, and the distinction between the cherubim and the spirituals. God gives success, and from Him come guidance and preservation from error. "There is no power and no strength but in God."

Know—may God take you to the highest stations of the gnostics—that the existent things of the dominion are of two kinds:

[A] The first kind have no governance or control over the world of bodies. They are called the "cherubim" and are of two kinds:

[1] The first kind have no news whatsoever of the world and its inhabitants. "They have been enraptured in the majesty and beauty of God since He created them." They are called the "enraptured angels." The Prophet reported about them as follows: "God has a white earth, in which the sun takes thirty days to cross the sky. Each day is thirty times longer than the days of this world. This earth is filled with creatures who do not know that God is disobeyed in the earth or that He has created Adam and Iblis."

[2] The second kind have no care for the world of bodies and are enthralled and bewildered by the witnessing of the Self-subsistent. They are the veil-keepers of the court of Divinity and the intermediaries for the effusion of Lordship. The technical term for these angels is the "inhabitants of the invincibility," and their lord and master is the greatest spirit. There is no spirit greater than he in the higher plenum. In one respect he is called the "Supreme Pen," for "The first thing God created was the Pen." In another respect he is called the "First

Intellect,'' for ''The first thing God created was the Intellect. God said to it, 'Come forward,' so it came forward. Then He said, 'Turn away,' so it turned away. Then He said, 'By My inaccessibility and majesty, I have created no creature more honored in My eyes than you. With you I shall give, with you I shall take, with you I shall reward, and with you I shall punish.' '' The Greatest Spirit stands in the first row of this group, and the Holy Spirit—who is called ''Gabriel''—in the last. *None of us there is, but has a known station* [37:164].

[B] The second kind [of existent things in the dominion] govern and control the world of bodies. They are called ''spirituals'' and are of two kinds:

[1] The first kind are spirits that exercise control over the heavenly things. These are the inhabitants of the higher dominion.

[2] The second kind are spirits that exercise control over the earthly things. These are the inhabitants of the lower dominion. Many thousands of them are given charge over the human species, and many thousands over minerals, plants, and animals. Or rather, an angel has been given charge over every single thing. Among the sayings of the past prophets that have come down to us are the words, ''Everything has an angel.'' And from him who brought our own Shariah has been transmitted the saying, ''An angel comes down with every drop of rain.'' The people of unveiling say that unless there are seven angels, a leaf will not be created on a tree. Thus has been the custom of God, *And you shall never find any changing in the custom of God* [35:43].

In a similar way, other hadiths have mentioned the ''angel of the mountains,'' the ''angel of the wind,'' the ''angel of thunder,'' and the ''angel of lightning.'' But unless the beauty of *So glory be to Him in whose hand is the dominion of each thing* [36:83] throws off its veil, the meaning of all this cannot be known through verification.

Consider the body a shadow,
  the spirit its source—
How can there be a shadow
  without a source?

Unless something exists in the dominion, the existence of the body cannot be imagined. This is one of the great mysteries, but how few there are on the face of the earth who understand it!

My words have risen high—
  I fear
something will jump
  from my tongue.
The horse of exposition
  runs so fast—
I fear its reins
  will slip from my hands.

As for the human reality—which is called the "lordly subtle reality"—it is the quintessence and mystery of the world of the dominion. The human being is compounded of both worlds—the spiritual and the corporeal—and is the most perfect existent thing. In the view of the people of insight, no intermediary stands between him and God. The goal of all the acts is he—save for those among the higher plenum brought near to God, who are excepted. The mystery of "But for you, I would not have created the spheres"—voiced by God concerning the master of the ancients and the later folk (God's blessings be upon him!)—has been verified for the possessors of eyes and verification. He was singled out because, in the unanimous opinion of the people of unveiling and the great masters of witnessing, he is the most excellent and most perfect of the ancients and the later folk. Otherwise, the people of true knowledge—whoever they might be—are the sought and beloved of the side of Eternity without beginning. "I was a Hidden Treasure and I loved to be known."

> Know for certain that We sent out all these wonders
> for the sake of a single seeing heart.

In the same way God revealed these words to David: "O David, I created Muhammad for Myself, I created the children of Adam for Muhammad, and I created what I created for the children of Adam. When people occupy themselves with Me, I send to them what I created for them. But when they occupy themselves with what I created for them, I veil them from Myself."

> You were brought up from the two worlds,
> you were nurtured by many intermediaries.
> The first in thought, the last to be counted
> is you—take not yourself in play.

Here, when the morning light of friendship rises from the horizon of eternity without beginning, its illuminating radiance will make known the mystery of the bestowal of existence on the engendered universe and the mystery of the measuring out. The meaning of "My mercy precedes My wrath" will be understood, as well as the sense of "God created Gehenna from an excess of mercy as a whip to drive His servants to the Garden." But if one enters into the explanation of this meaning, it will lead to divulging the mystery of the measuring out, and that is forbidden in the eyes of the great ones of the path and the ulama of *tawḥīd*, for "Measuring out is God's mystery, so divulge it not!"

> When the saints seize the mystery
> of the measuring out,
> all this vain talk
> is trampled under foot.
> The liver of the Shariah's mufti
> fills with blood,
> the tongue of reason's dignity
> is struck down dumb.

Here the meaning of these words will become known. *As for the truth-concealers, alike it is to them whether you have warned them or have not warned them, they will not have faith* [2:6]. In the same way, the mystery of *Truly God was gracious to those who have faith when He raised up among them a Messenger* [3:164] will come out from behind the veil, and it will be known through verification why the Prophet said, "The good, all of it, is in Thy hands, while the evil does not return to Thee"—even though his tasting gives witness that "There is no agent but God," or rather, "There is nothing in existence but God."

In the two worlds
  there is nothing but Thou—
Everything is perishing
  except His Face [28:88].

How could something come into existence without His desire and power? Why have the pillars of wisdom said that no evil occurs in existence and that things that appear as evil to the imperfect occur accidentally within the divine decree and measuring out, not essentially? Why did Idris say, "God is praiseworthy in all His acts"?

Far be it from Thee! Far be it from Thee—
  O Thou before whom my spirit is sacrificed—
How couldst Thou perform an ugly act
  that would mar Thy lovely Face?

Everything He does to my heart and soul
  is justice and religion—
And were He to do injustice, I would see it
  as justice, since it was done by Him.

When He created hell, He created it in perfect tenderness and mercy. Wait until the beauty of "the Merciful, the Compassionate" comes out from the pavilion of inaccessibility and tells you without the tongue of flesh and skin what mystery is hidden in the allusion, "A time will come when watercress will grow from the deepest pit of hell."

If wind takes the dust of Thy lane
  to hell,
hell's fire will become
  the Water of Life.

The wrath of a generous man,
  even if its fire flares up,
is like smoke from incense—
  it has no substance.

The assaults of the severity of Eternity's desire are taking the reins of free choice from my hands—*And God prevails over His affair* [12:21], that is, over His servants. What was not in my mind to write is being written. I return to the subject at hand—and my confidence is in the Living, the Self-subsistent.

Once you come to know that the human being is the quintessence and mystery of the world of the dominion, that the goal of creating the two engendered worlds is he, and that he is compounded of both worlds, you will also know that his spiritual thoughts and corporeal movements are all acts of God. *God created you and what you do* [37:96]. God's power and desire create the human essence along with its accidents and states moment by moment. *He inspired the soul in its wickedness and its god-wariness* [91:8].

You are the instrument of an act,
  nothing else.
Of the act's Agent,
  you are nothing but a sign.
You are a world,
  and the goal of the world is you.
But look carefully—
  in the midst of all this you are nothing.

However, since the human being is the channel through which these acts and states flow, they are attributed to him. He acts, but he does not act. He speaks, but he does not speak. In truth the agent is God, but the human being undergoes change and becomes the locus of activity. *You did not throw when you threw, but God threw* [8:17].

Though the act is not mine,
  it cannot occur without me.
The soul does the acting,
  but not without the body.

Here the oceans of compulsion and free will are in collision, and the isthmus of the Shariah is a barrier between the two. *He let forth the two seas that meet together, between them an isthmus they do not overpass* [55:19]. If a person should attribute the act to himself, he believes in free will, and "Those who believe in free will are the fire worshipers of this Community." But if he should dismiss his own self in every respect, the eagle of the Shariah will leave the nest of *He guides whomsoever He will to a straight path* [10:25] and cry out with the tongue of its state, "Perform works, for everyone will be eased to that for which he was created."

You will know the perfection of this mystery after the unveiling of the true knowledge of the immutable entities, the mystery of *tawḥīd*, and the mystery of the measuring out. But these realities are the reality of the Koran. The Koran's beauty cannot be seen unmasked in the mirror of the heart without the rays of the Self-subsistent's light. It can never be reached through the mind's reflection or the guidance of reason. *Surely in that there is a reminder for him who has a heart* [50:37].

How can the partial intellect grasp the Koran?
  How can a spider hunt a phoenix?

The allusions made thus far in these introductory remarks have been enough to call attention and incite desire. To say or write more than this would be to throw the world into tumult. "But let evil pass."

I cannot voice Thy mystery
  with the spirit's tongue,
I cannot say a word
  in two hundred mornings.

How many the pearls of knowledge!
  Were I to disclose but one,
they would say to me, "You are one
  of those who worship idols."
Muslim warriors would count
  my blood as lawful
and they would see their ugliest act
  as beautiful.

At every moment destiny keeps on taking the reins of free choice from my hands. *But you will not will unless God wills* [76:30]. Let us return to what we were busy with by mentioning the rest of the acts.

In a similar way the fiery spirits—who are called "jinn" and "satans"—can be classified generally as part of the lower dominion. Some of them have been given mastery over the human species, and Iblis is their lord and chief. Knowing the mystery of their mastery over mankind is a branch of the mystery of the measuring out. Some of them are capable of having religion prescribed for them and are addressed by divine revelation, just as the true religion has mentioned.

In brief, there is much disagreement among the leaders of the path and the masters of verification concerning how the realities of the jinn and satans should be understood. Each of these leaders and masters has given a report from his own station. To explain these views would take too long and cannot fit into such a short work. "O God, show us things as they are, guide us, lead us, and busy us with Thee rather than with what is other than Thee."

As for the world of bodies, it is of two types: the heavenly things and the earthly things. The heavenly things include the Throne, the Footstool, the seven heavens, the fixed stars, and the planets. The earthly things include the simple elemental things and the high effects—such as thunder, lightning, clouds, and rain—and the compound things, such as minerals, plants, animals, and the human body, which is the noblest part of the elemental world. In the eternal Book, these meanings are mentioned in many places, because both the common people and the elect share in the perception of most of these bodies. But as for the realities of the dominion, only the elect are aware of them.

In the same way there are other worlds subordinate to the essences of the bodies, such as movement and rest, heaviness and lightness, subtlety and density, colors and lights, sounds, smells, and their various types and classes. Each of these types is another world. Then there are other similar worlds subordinate to the world of spirits.

In the same way there are other worlds intermediary between the world of spirits and the world of bodies. A group of those learned in wisdom have called their totality the "world of images," and, in the eyes of the verifiers, this world has many details. One part of it is called "contiguous imagination," and the mental faculties are the precondition for perceiving it. Dreams and their marvels take place in this world. Another part, which has no such precondition, is called "discontiguous imagination." Embodiment of spirits, spiritualization of bodies, personification of character traits and works, manifestation of meanings in appropriate forms, and the witnessing of the essences of disengaged realities in corporeal forms and semblances all take place in this world. In this world the Prophet used to see Gabriel in the form of Diḥya Kalbī. The spirits of past prophets and friends that are witnessed in forms and semblances by shaykhs and masters of the path exist in this world. Khizr is also seen in this world. Here there are wondrous mysteries.

The ocean of the acts has no end, and its wonders cannot be counted—*There is no thing whose treasuries are not with Us, but We send it down only with a known measuring out* [15:21]. But the basic kinds of acts have been included in what was mentioned. *Praise belongs to God, who guided us to this; had God not guided us, we had surely never been guided* [7:43]. Blessings be upon Muhammad and his household, the pure.

THE SECOND LAMP

Concerning the Properties and Peculiarities of the Stages of Friendship and Prophecy

It contains two gleams.

THE FIRST GLEAM

Concerning the Reality and Properties of the Stage of Friendship

Know—may God make you verify true knowledge and witnessing of Him—that those who guard the mysteries of the psalms of love are called the "Folk of Allah.'' They have come to see and know through the light of Lordship and the confirmation of the Holy Spirit that the final stages of the rational thinkers are the beginning stages of the friends, and the final stages of the friends are the beginning stages of the prophets. At the utmost limit of the world of reason is a point where the stage of friendship begins. It is a light in the spacious plain of dominion's world that shines from the Right Side of the Valley upon the soul of him who has cleansed the billowing darkness of nature's vapors from the mirror of the rational faculty by following Mustafa. Thus he has come out from under the cover of illusion and imagination. The smallest sign of this light's manifestation is that the person becomes disengaged from and casts off the world of deceit and delusion. Mustafa alluded to this with his words, ''When light enters the heart, it expands and dilates.'' He was asked, ''O Messenger of God, does that have a mark?'' He answered, ''Yes, shunning the abode of delusion and turning toward the abode of everlasting life.''

When greed leaves you,
  Gabriel comes in at once;
when Gabriel comes,
  Ahriman goes.

The stage of friendship lies beyond the stage of reason. Within it are found specific objects of perception that reason cannot perceive. Reason's inability to perceive them is similar to the inability of fancy to perceive reason's objects.

Reason the tailor
  sewed many thought-stitches,
but never a garment
  worthy of love.

One of the properties of the objects of perception within the stage of friendship is that the person perceives the existence of God without stringing together rational premises and understands the mystery of God's nearness to each existent thing.

The concept of nearness has four levels, but reason has access only to three: temporal, spatial, and rational. Temporal nearness is like saying, ''The time of Mustafa is nearer to us than the time of Jesus.'' Spatial nearness is like saying, ''The moon is nearer to us than Jupiter, since the moon shines from the first heaven, while Jupiter shines from the sixth heaven.'' As for rational nearness, that is like saying, ''Abū Yazīd Basṭāmī and Abu'l-Hasan Kharaqānī were nearer to Mustafa than 'Utba and Shayba,'' even though the latter two were nearer to him in time and space. In this case, nearness and distance are qualities connected to the dominion.

As for the nearness of the Creator to each creature and the mystery of *He is with you wherever you are* [57:4], that is understood only by the gnostic possessor of insight. This is the fourth level of nearness. The words related from Ḥusayn ibn Manṣūr al-Ḥallāj at the time of his crucifixion allude to the witnessing of such a nearness.

> O God, Thou art empty of every direction and Thou disclosest Thyself from every direction, for Thou standest up for my rights and I stand up for Thy rights. My standing up for Thy rights is at the human level, while Thy standing up for my rights is at the divine level, even though my human level is consumed by Thy divine level without being mixed with it, and Thy divine level dominates over my human level without touching it.

When the majesty of this nearness casts its shadow upon the gnostic, he sees that Mustafa, Gabriel, the Lote Tree, the person of faith, the truth-concealer, an ant, and a gnat are all equally near to the Self-subsistent Being. This is the meaning of *You see no disparity in the creation of the Merciful* [67:3]. *To God belong the East and the West—whithersoever you turn, there is the Face of God. God is All-embracing, All-knowing* [2:115].

His Face in every direction—
  wherever I look a moon!

By day I praised Thee
  but did not know,
by night I slept with Thee
  but did not know.
I kept on thinking
  that I was I—
I was all Thou
  but did not know.

Everyone drawn to a beloved
  is subject to her:
all are subject to Thee
  but unaware.

In the same way, one of the characteristics of the stage of friendship is leaving the narrow confines of time and the constricting limits of space. Unless one leaves time and space, one can never fly to eternity without beginning. Here the beginning of the world of no-time is called "eternity without beginning." In such a vision, past and future disappear, the mystery of "With your Lord is neither morning nor evening" comes out from the mask of inaccessibility, and this verse shows its beauty. *O tribe of jinn and men, if you are able to pass through the confines of heaven and earth, pass through them! You shall not pass through except with an authority* [55:33].

Better to leap on the piebald stallion of time,
then with one jump to pass beyond heaven.
With heaven under foot,
he will fly to the city of no-place.
When he reaches the land of nowhere,
he will jump in secret out of self.

Among the characteristics of this stage are perceiving the rolling up of time and space and the mystery of the resurrection and mustering of the bodies, understanding the realities and states of the second configuration, having perfect faith in the stage of prophecy, and acknowledging one's incapacity to perceive the enigmas of the true sciences and to understand all the prophetic hints and allusions. In the same way the manifestation of the ruling authority of love, the glory of its states, and the wonders of its sweetness and bitterness in union and separation are among this stage's characteristics.

Reason can find no way to love's lane—
expect nothing from that blind fellow!

The level of friendship pertains exclusively to human beings. Angels have no share in it, since the words *He loves them, and they love Him* [5:54] are addressed to humans. It has been reported that the angels do not know the meaning of the name Loving.

This path cannot be walked with reason's feet—
The earth trod by love lies beyond reason.
A secret of which the angels know nothing—
O you without reason, how could that belong to reason?

The path of reason and learning extends only to the shore of love's ocean. After that are bewilderment and tracelessness.

No one gives a trace of Thee—
This is the trace of tracelessness.

It is here that temporality departs. This station is called the "station of arrival."

He hides him in the secret center
of His signs.

No created thing has love—
only the one who has arrived is a lover.

It has been said, "The journeys are two: a journey to God, and a journey in God." Here the journey to God comes to an end, and the journey in God remains. Until now, the lover traveled by means of the Beloved, but from now on, the Beloved will travel in the lover.

Can someone reach You
  without walking with Your feet?
Can a heart be Your bird
  not flying with Your wings?

The properties of his own he-ness disappear, *The Real comes, and the unreal vanishes away* [17:81].

Keep traveling this road
  till duality leaves you—
if duality stays,
  you can leave it through travel.
You won't become Him,
  but if you strive,
you will reach a place
  where your you-ness will leave.

The wonders of this stage have no end, but its states can be known only through wayfaring. And, in keeping with the custom of eternity without beginning, the seeker's wayfaring must be preceded by attraction. It is not true that everyone who seeks will certainly find, nor that everyone who wayfares on the path will reach the goal. Far from it!

My friend, those who cross the desert to safety
  are many,
but those who reach the goal
  are few.
Did you hope for union with Salmā
  and not find it?
By my soul! When did the greedy
  ever reach union?

Although the divers have no fear,
  every shell does not contain a precious pearl.
That happens rarely in a lifetime,
  nor is it just any wretch's luck.

Supplement to the Gleam

Know—may God exalt you through wayfaring on the straight path—that each spiritual and corporeal faculty of the human being was created for specific objects of perception. For example, vision was created to perceive objects of sight, and hearing to perceive sounds. Hearing cannot perform the task of sight, nor can sight perceive the objects of hearing. In the same way, reason was created to perceive self-evident concepts. The perception of the enigmas of rational consideration lies outside its fundamental nature. So also, writing is by nature a characteristic of the hand. If someone were to write with his foot, it could only be done with great effort, it would not look beautiful, and it would be outside the foot's fundamental nature. Hence the realities and meanings to which allusion has been made cannot be perceived by reason. True knowledge of them depends on the manifestation of friendship's light.

In the stage of reason, objects of perception are of two types: self-evident concepts, which can be grasped without the need for setting up premises; and considerative concepts, whose perception demands setting up premises. Likewise, certain objects of perception are related to the stage of friendship in the same way that self-evident concepts are related to the stage of reason, while other objects are related to it just as considerative questions are related to the stage of reason. But unless this light's morning dawns from the horizon of the invincibility, these realities and meanings cannot be verified. And this is not found on the page of free choice, since it depends on attraction. "A single attraction of God equals all the works of jinn and men."

They found, but did not seek—
how can they be compared
with those who sought,
but did not find?

For the most part, the properties of this stage lie beyond the limits of learning and reason.

Thy beauty is greater than my sight,
Thy mystery hidden from my knowledge.

Before the shining light of this dawn breaks, meanings of this type appear to most people—except those confirmed by the Unseen—as *fairy tales of the ancients* [6:25].

Voicing Sanā'ī's subtleties and symbols
for the ignorant
is like playing a lute for the deaf
or holding a mirror for the blind.

"If someone hears of it and recoils from it, let him suspect his soul of not having an affinity for it." Beware! Every craw has a capacity, and every soul a drinking place. *All the people know their own drinking places* [2:60].

Caress each one and give
according to his excellence—
to the lovers give a cup of wine
equal to the vat!

His lovers keep on saying,

> Then there happened what happened—
> what I cannot mention.
> Think only the good,
> and ask for no news.

What wonderful words!

> A *man* is needed to catch the scent.
> After all,
> the world is full
> of the east wind's fragrance.

The eternal Koran says, *Say: "It is a mighty tiding from which you are turning away"* [37:67]. But they have an excuse. Seeking depends upon perception. Since they have not perceived, how can they recognize the truth?

> Nothing can be found
> unless you seek—
> except the Friend: until you find,
> you will not seek.

"In the gnostic's view, people's faith and truth-concealing are the same."

> Put aside your blame—
> no dog's barking
> holds back the caravan
> from passing in the night.

Surely in that there is a reminder for him who has a heart, or will give an ear while he is a witness [50:37]. Either one must have a heart, or give an ear. The veracious heart belongs to the possessor of unveiling, the trustworthy ear to the possessor of faith. In order to become a lover, one first must hear.

> Sometimes the ear falls in love
> before the eye.

Then one must wayfare in order to become a possessor of the heart. *What, have they not traveled in the earth in order that they might have hearts?* [22:46]. When a person finds the heart, the howdah of love's magnificence will be set down within him.

> Had I no heart,
> I would not remember Thee.
> The heart is my good fortune—
> bravo to the heart!

Then he will remember his past stages and realize how he had been deprived during the time he was veiled. Though he is still held in the cage of the human form by the fetter of the fixed term, and though he hears this call from the side of the Lord—*We have now removed from you your covering, so your sight today is piercing* [50:22]—his state will keep on saying,

And I, when people spoke of love,
  was laughing,
but they kept on letting flow
  their tears.
Then it happened that they said,
  "He's a lover,"
and I answered them with weeping
  and with sighs.

Praise belongs to God, and blessings be upon His servants, the pure.

THE SECOND GLEAM

On the True Knowledge of the Stage of Prophecy, its Properties, and its Characteristics

Know—may God ennoble you with seeing Him and witnessing Him—that the furthest limit of the stage of friendship is the beginning of the stage of prophecy. Hence, all the sciences of unveiling bestowed upon the friend are known by the prophet, but not vice versa. The duty of the possessor of friendship when faced with the tastings of prophecy's stage is to have faith in the unseen, exactly like the duty of the possessor of reason when faced with the stage of friendship. *Above everyone who has knowledge is one who knows* [12:76]. In each stage the key to felicity and the source of benefits and generous gifts is to keep one's own arrogation and power of perception away from the perceptibles that pertain to the stage beyond oneself and to have faith in the unseen *until God brings His command* [2:109]. The verse *Question me not on anything until I myself introduce the mention of it to thee* [18:70] warns the wayfarer to have patience until the opening of the eye of his insight.

Your master is love—
  when you reach it,
it will tell you what to do
  with its own tongue.

"God have mercy on my brother Moses! If he had been patient with Khizr, he would have seen many wonders."

When serving kings,
  wear the strongest armor.
When you enter, enter blind.
  When you leave, leave dumb.

Among the characteristics and properties of the stage of prophecy are [1] knowledge of the Essence and attributes, of wayfaring on the straight path, and of the details of the states of the return to God; knowledge of the states of the prophets and the friends and of the various sorts of kindness that God has shown to them; knowledge of the states of the truth-concealers and those who associate others with God and of the wrath and vengeance of God that overtakes them; knowledge of the disputations of the truth-concealers and the quarrels of the people of falsehood; the unveiling of their scandals through a clear demonstration; the nullification of their corrupt imaginings and beliefs concerning things not seemly for God's majesty and tremendousness. These include their words, "The angels are His daughters," "He has a son" or "an associate," and "Truly He is the third of three"—high exalted is He above what the evildoers say! They also attribute sorcery, soothsaying, and insanity to the prophets. They deny the Uprising, the resurrection, the subsistence of spirits, and the mustering of bodies; and they reject reward and punishment. In a similar way, [the stage of prophecy includes] knowledge of the universal law upon which the order of the earthly world depends. This is called the "science of definitions and properties." All of this the prophet acquires through the teaching and confirmation of the spirit of holiness, without the intermediary of human teaching or study.

In the same way [among the characteristics and properties of the stage of prophecy are] [2] a power through which the prophet exercises control over the corporeal bodies of the cosmos by God's command as He desires, such as splitting the moon, bringing the dead to life, and changing the staff into a serpent.

Likewise [the prophet's characteristics include] [3] a faculty through which the prophet perceives in wakefulness the unseen things that the common people perceive only in sleep.

The ulama have a certain access to the perception of these three characteristics. But the possessors of unveilings know other characteristics as well. These include the mysteries of the rulings of the revealed laws, the results of works, and the way in which acts and character traits become personified. Thus, the Prophet knows how much reward is entailed by two cycles of ritual prayer; what is the result of one day's fasting; why " 'There is no power and no strength but in God, the High, the Tremendous' is one of the keys to the Garden"; why the sin of him who says "Glory be to God, and His is the praise" one hundred times is effaced; why five ritual prayers must be said each day; how much punishment is deserved by someone who misses two ritual prayers; why people have to fast for one month each year; why, after one year passes, half a dinar out of every twenty dinars must be spent for the needy; who the needy are, and why they are divided into eight classes; why the Night of Power is better than a thousand months; why fasting on the Day of ʿArafa expiates the sin of two years; what the wisdom in these amounts and periods is; how these specific works correspond with the felicity of the next world; what result each good and bad work has; and how it becomes personified.

Concerning the personification of works in the world of the dominion Mustafa—God bless him and give him peace—has spoken as follows: "In the Garden is a barren plain that is uncultivated, so multiply the Garden's seedlings in this world." He was asked, "O Messenger of God, what are the Garden's seedlings?" He answered, "Saying 'Glory be to God' and 'There is no god but God.'"

In the same way the Prophet reported, "In his grave the person of faith dwells in a luxuriant garden; his grave becomes seventy cubits wide and as radiant as the full moon." Then he said, "Do you know concerning what the verse, *His life shall be a life of narrowness* [20:124], was revealed?" They said, "God and His messenger know best." He said, "Concerning the chastisement of the truth-concealer in his grave: ninety-nine *tinnīns* will be given mastery over him. Do you know what a *tinnīn* is? It is a serpent. There will be ninety-nine serpents, each of which has nine heads: They will gnaw at him, eat at him, and blow into his body until the day he is raised up."

These gardens, castles, trees, ants, serpents, scorpions, pits, fires, and darknesses are nothing but his works and his character traits personified. "They are only your works given back to you." The properties of the next world are configured from this world. This world is the mother of the next world. But unless the bride of *We will configure you within what you know not* [56:61] throws off her mask, the mysteries and the detailed properties of the next world's configuration will not be unveiled.

The tremendous Koran alludes to each of these configurations. Concerning the barzakh configuration following the sensory configuration it makes the following allusion: *Before them is a barzakh until the day they shall be raised up* [23:100]. Concerning the configuration of the Mustering it says, *It will only be a single cry, and behold, they are at the Awakening* [79:13]. The Koran expresses the homecoming and place of return of the felicitous and the wretched as follows: *A party in the Garden, and a party in the Blaze* [42:7]. God willing, in the Third Gleam the properties of this configuration will be described to the extent possible through allusions. From God come guidance and success.

The mystery of the Market of the Garden also derives from this world. Mustafa—God's blessings be upon him—alluded to the Market of the Garden as follows: "The Garden has a market in which there is no selling or buying, only the forms of men and women. When a person desires a form, he enters into it."

The wonders of this stage are beyond count. They are among the most marvelous sciences of unveiling. One must not try to penetrate these meanings with the endowments of reason, since true knowledge of them depends upon another light, beyond reason.

What do you know
  of the birds' speech?
When did you sit for a night
  with Solomon?

One must receive illumination from the sun of the Muhammadan Presence. Otherwise it is obvious what the lamp of reason can perceive.

You need a star-consuming sun—
How can your lamp turn night into day?

Marvelous indeed are the Prophet's virtues and majesty! For the loving God Himself addresses him with the words, *He has taught thee what thou knewest not; God's bounty to thee is ever great* [4:113].

Mustafa in the world,
then someone says "reason"?
The sun in the sky,
then someone says "Alcor"?

A group of the perfect friends in the Muhammadan community have received a share of his stage's tastings—God bless him and give him peace. They are called the "prophets among the friends." In truth they are the vicegerents, inheritors, and brothers of Mustafa. "Oh, the yearning to encounter my brothers after me!" is a specific allusion to this group. "The ulama of my community are like the prophets of the Children of Israel" or "like the prophets of the other communities" also refers to them. *Of those We created are a community who guide by the Real, and through it act with justice* [7:181]. "It is they who, when they ascend, gain benefit, and when they descend, give benefit."

Here it should be known that the friends are of two types: the restored and perfected friends, who are the sober; and the consumed and perfect friends, who are the intoxicated.

When the consumed friends are taken from the narrow confines of human nature, drowned in the ocean of *tawḥīd*, and obliterated in the direct vision of the majesty and beauty of the Eternal Refuge, they have no awareness of their own selfhood. How could they concern themselves with others? How could they have the capacity to acquaint someone else with that Side? Their spirits' constant words of glorification are

O desire
of the desirous,
take me from myself
to Thyself!

Love for Thee took away
my we-ness and I-ness—
Thy love leaves
no choice but selflessness.

This group has no share in the tastings of prophecy, and they are not made to busy themselves with calling people to God.

As for the restored friends, they are taken from the darkness of the two engendered worlds and the obscurity of temporal existence. Time and space are rolled up for them, and they are stolen away from themselves. *Nay, but we hurl the Real against the unreal and it prevails over it, and behold, it vanishes away* [21:18].

When the face of my moon-face comes,
 who am I to be I?
I am happy only when
 I am without myself.
I am only someone when,
 in the domain of His decree,
I am neither heart, nor soul,
 nor head, nor body.

Then the controlling power of everlasting beauty gives them back to themselves. This station is called "affirmation after obliteration." They are given the robe of deputyship and placed upon the throne of vicegerency. Their judgment is put into effect in the empire. *We appointed them to be leaders guiding by Our command* [21:73]. Their station is as the poet says:

We are the radiance of glory's candle,
 we are the shadow of God's compassion,
We are the tablet of being's realities,
 we are the mirror displaying God.

Say: "This is my way. I call to God upon insight, I and whoever follows me" [21:108]

I am Jesus and my miracle
 is this breath of mine:
Every heart that catches its scent
 comes to life.

Who speaks better than he who calls to God and works upright deeds and says, "Surely I am one of those who submit"? [41:33].

The Commander of the Faithful, ʿAlī—God be pleased with him—reports about their station in a long sermon.

> The earth will never be empty of him who is supported by God with a true argument—whether he is manifest and uncovered, or fearful and vanquished—lest the arguments and clear signs of God be nullified. How many are they and where? They are the least in number, the greatest in worth. . . . They are not found in outward existence, but their likenesses exist in hearts.

They share in all the tastings and unveilings of the prophets except the prophecy of law-giving, which they do not possess, since that is a closed door—*Muhammad is not the father of any one of your men, but the messenger of God, and the seal of the prophets* [33:40]. "O Abū Bakr, there is no difference between me and you, except that I was sent forth by God." "O ʿUmar, if I had not been sent forth, you would have been sent forth."

God speaks the truth, and He guides on the way [33:4]. Praise belongs to God, the Lord of the worlds, and peace be upon His servants whom He chose.

THE THIRD LAMP

On the True Knowledge of This World and the Next World

It contains two gleams.

THE FIRST GLEAM

On the True Knowledge of the Reality of This World, its Profits and Benefits for one Group, and its Dangers and Disasters for Another

Know—may God protect you from relying upon the abode of delusion—that as long as human beings control this corporeal frame, the states that overtake them and that are turned toward passing pleasures and the properties of the world of nature are called "this world."

The pleasures of this world have three aspects: One aspect concerns the human being himself, the second the things through which pleasures are attained, and the third the person's occupation with cultivating and acquiring the things that are the stuff of his pleasures.

The things of this world are of four kinds: mineral, plant, animal, and human. Minerals are for adornment, coin, and containers. Plants are for nourishment, taking enjoyment, and medication. Animals are for food and mounts. As for human beings, some are for marriage and putting to use, and some for other things. The divine revelation explains all these meanings in this verse. *Decked out fair to people is love for passions—women, children, heaped-up heaps of gold and silver, horses of mark, cattle, and tillage. That is the enjoyment of this world's life* [3:14].

Concerning the aspect in which the pleasures of this world relate to the human being, the glorious Koran employs the word "caprice." *As for him who feared the station of his Lord and forbade the soul its caprice, surely the Garden shall be the refuge* [79:41].

As for the aspect that concerns a person's occupation with cultivating and acquiring the things that are the stuff of his pleasures, this is the various kinds and manners of trades and professions and the diverse classes and varieties of stratagems and snares with which people are busy and because of which they have forgotten their Origin and Return. *They forgot God, and so He caused them to forget their own souls; those—they are the ungodly* [59:19].

I think the soul forgot covenants through fever
and homes it really did not want to leave.

A tremendous loss
and terrible grief:
to sit on a dunghill
and forget the king's palace.

They are like pilgrims on the way to Mecca who busy themselves in the desert with collecting water and fodder for their mounts and forget the Kaaba, their original goal. The caravan moves on, and hunger and thirst make them perish in the wilderness. They become the prey of crawling things and wild beasts. *O you who have faith, what is amiss? When it is said to you, "Go forth in the way of God," you sink down heavily to the ground! Are you so content with the life of this world, rather than the next world?* [9:38].

Before you is a road
and you must get going.
If you do not reach the goal here,
the goal will be gone.
The body is the means
for you to get someplace.
If you become the body's means,
where can you go?

After this introduction, you should know that the things of this world are not blameworthy merely because they are things of this world. Rather, human attachment to them and love for them are blameworthy. Hence, the master of the revealed law has said, "Love for this world is at the head of every fault." After all, the things of this world can take people to the highest heaven, or drag them down to the lowest of the low.

Intelligence takes this one
to the high things,
caprice drags that one
down to the Blaze.

The reason for this is that some people make the things of this world a means for the path of religion. They detach their gaze from the enjoyment of corporeal pleasures. Whether in prosperity or adversity, they keep *They expend what We have provided them* [2:3] before their eyes. In their forms they dwell in this world, but in their hearts they dwell in the higher plenum. "God has servants whose bodies are in the world, but whose hearts are with God." They live for God, not for caprice. For such people, this world is a tremendous aid in wayfaring on the straight path. "How good is honest wealth for the honest man!"—so long as it is spent for His good-pleasure.

Whatever you have,
  give it to Him—
beggars are more elegant
  in bestowal.

Such people will necessarily return and go home to the higher dominion, *in a sitting place of strength, with a Powerful King* [54:55].

A world where every heart you find
  is king,
a world where every soul you see
  is joyful!

But there are others who make the things of this world a means to follow the path of the satans. They spend their time attaining the desires and pleasures of the soul that commands to evil. They recognize no other world beyond this pile of clods. *They know an outward of the life of this world, but of the next world they are heedless* [30:7]. The tongue of their level and preparedness says only this:

Should I abandon the pleasure of wine in the cup
  for the milk and honey they promise?
Life, then death, then a mustering?
  Fairy-tales, my dear!

Their place of return and overthrow will be the descending degrees of the Blaze, and their gain and revenue will be painful chastisement. The clasping darknesses of attachment to the bodily world will keep on dragging their hanging heads to the lowest Crushers. *Ah, if you could see the guilty, hanging their heads before their Lord!* [32:12].

Look at Jesus' renunciation
  and Korah's avarice—
concerning the two
  God says,
We made the earth swallow him down [28:81]
  from his greed's abode,
and *We raised him up* [4:158]
  by the ladder of his need.

In their use of this world, the likeness of the ulama and the friends as opposed to the ignorant and the rich is as follows: When a physician wants to prepare an antidote for the poison of vipers, he seeks help from the viper itself. In keeping with the requirements of his learning and great erudition, he catches the viper in a specific way, then cuts off a specific amount from its head and tail. Then he boils the remaining parts and, according to what is given by the principles of his science, prepares an antidote that can repel the harm of poisons.

When an ignorant fool happens to observe the states of the physician, he immediately sets out to catch a viper. But he does not know the details of how to catch it and is ignorant of the aim and goal of the person of learning. He imagines that the aim in catching it is to play with it and gaze upon the colors and patterns of its skin. He goes and blindly stretches out his hand toward the viper. With a single strike it destroys him such that he will never see bodily life again. Thus, it is said to most people, "Fear this world, for it is more enchanting than Harut and Marut."

My advice to you
  is only this:
you are a child,
  and the house is gaudily painted.

O people, God's promise is true. So let not the present life delude you, and let not the deluder delude you concerning God [35:5].

But as for the perfect, the possessors of insight, they have cast off the darkness of caprice and died a voluntary death before physical death. The state of "Whoever wants to look at a dead man walking on the face of the earth, let him look at Abū Bakr" has become the ready cash of their present moment. In whatever way they make use of this world, they will suffer no harm. One of the great companions of the Prophet said, "Wealth and poverty are two steeds. I care not which I mount."

Someone remarked to Aḥmad Ghazālī, "You spend the whole day blaming this world and encouraging people to cut off their attachments, but you have several tethers of horses, mules, and donkeys. How do you explain that?" He replied, "I have driven the tethers' pegs into the ground, not into my heart." "God looks not at your forms or your works, but He looks at your hearts."

In the heart
  keep no more than one.
In the house
  let there be a thousand.

May God give us success to guard ourselves against the abode of delusion and to climb to the world of light. Praise belongs to God, and His blessings be upon those He has chosen among His pure servants.

THE SECOND GLEAM

On the States of the Next World and the Subsistence of the Human Spirit, and on the Spirit's Need for a Locus of Manifestation in Whatever World it Resides; with an Allusion to the Universal Configuration

Know—may God inspire you with right guidance and guard you from the evil of your own soul—that after their attachment to the body is completely severed, human beings have diverse waystations and various configurations before them. But all the states that overtake them from the time they sever the bodily attachment until eternity without end are called the "next world."

All the prophets, friends, ulama, and sages have agreed, and all the revealed books have stated, that the human reality—which is called the "divine spirit," the "lordly subtle reality," and the "rational soul"—does not undergo extinction at the occurrence of physical death. "Dust does not eat the locus of faith and knowledge."

Human beings were created for the subsistence of eternity without end, and their outcome will be either endless felicity or everlasting wretchedness. Mustafa—God bless him—spoke briefly of this meaning as follows: "You were created for eternity without end; you will only be transferred from one abode to another."

He described the subsistence of the two parties in detail. Concerning the subsistence of the spirits of the felicitous he said, "The spirits of the martyrs are in the craws of green birds that live in lamps hanging from the Throne. They roam freely in the Garden wherever they wish, then they go back to the lamps."

Concerning the subsistence of the spirits of the wretched, he made the following allusion. On the day of the Battle of Badr, he called out one by one to the notables of Quraysh who had been killed. "O Abū Jahl ibn Hishām, O Umayya ibn Khalaf, O ʿUtba ibn Rabīʿa, O Shayba ibn Rabīʿa, have you not found what your Lord promised to be true? For verily, I have found what my Lord promised to be true!"

ʿUmar heard the words of the Prophet and said, "O Messenger of God! How can they hear and how can they answer? For they have become corpses."

He replied, "By Him whose hand holds my soul, you do not hear what I am saying better than they, but they are unable to answer."

When the reality of the spirits becomes known—either by way of argument and demonstration, or by way of unveiling and direct vision—it will be verified with certainty that God did not create them for annihilation and oblivion.

In that house
  the people of soul and breath
will see the death of death,
  then none will die.

People were created for subsistence—
misguided is that group
who thinks that they were made
for extinction!
They are merely transferred
from the house of works
to the house of wretchedness
or right conduct.

A person must first become aware of the spirit's reality through one of the two paths mentioned. Only then does the Shariah allow him to be told about the spirit's mystery. For the spirit is qualified by descriptions that most people do not accept as true for the Creator of the cosmos. How could they accept them as true for one of His creatures? The cause of this denial is that, within the narrow confines of mortality, people are veiled by the veils of fancy and imagination. They cannot understand an existent thing that is neither outside nor inside the world, neither connected to it nor separate from it. This meaning cannot easily be understood at the stage of reason. But, if today in the house of this world, a person does not vanquish the satan of fancy and imagination with the faculty of knowledge and reason, tomorrow upon the plain of the resurrection he will say, *Our Lord, show us those that have led us astray, both jinn and men, and we shall set them beneath our feet, that they may be among the lowest* [41:29].

When the mystery of the spirit is completely unveiled—though its perfect unveiling depends upon a stage beyond reason—it will be verified that the spirit possesses a locus of manifestation in each configuration and world appropriate for that configuration and world. This meaning can be explained through a sensory example. *Those similitudes—We coin them for the people, but no one understands them save those who have knowledge* [29:43].

In accordance with the custom of eternity without beginning, water cannot be held without a container, even though water is a substance independent in itself, and the container is another substance. In the same way the spirit must have a locus of manifestation, even though the spirit is a substance in itself, and the locus of manifestation is another substance. Of course, the spirit's meeting with its locus of manifestation is different from that of water with its container, because in the latter case, both are bodily things. But an example does not have to be analogous in every respect. The point is simply that spirits have need of loci of manifestation. One of the great ones has put this meaning into verse.

One is the spirit,
diverse the body's configurations.
This is the reality,
so pay close attention.
The diverse configurations
belong to the body—

depend on what I say in this
  and remember it well!
This is a knowledge
  that no doubt can touch.
The sun knows what we said,
  and the moon.

Since it has been verified that the spirit is one while its configurations and loci of manifestation are many, it should now be known that after the abode of Alast, human spirits have many configurations and homes. Some of these configurations belong exclusively to the spirits of the felicitous, and others are shared by both the felicitous and the wretched.

First is the sensory configuration, which is called "this world." It is where we are now. This configuration's ruling property extends from the time of birth to the hour of death.

Second is the configuration of the barzakh. Its ruling property extends from the moment the spirit leaves the body until the time of the Mustering. *Before them is a barzakh until the day they shall be raised up* [23:100]. This configuration's properties have many wonders, for human beings see all their states, works, and character traits personified in appropriate forms. *The day every soul shall find what it has done of good brought forward, and what it has done of evil; it will wish there were a far space between it and that day* [3:30].

Wait, till they lift up the covering!
  Wait, till they start talking to you—
"Which ones did you take in your arms?
  Which ones did you leave outside?"

Upon the day the secrets are put to the test [86:9].

When they take off the mask
  of sensory faculties,
If you're an infidel, you'll see scorching hell;
  if a believer, the Gardens.

The barzakh is a world where the outward becomes inward, and the inward outward. Every attribute that dominated over human beings in the house of this world will manifest itself to them in the barzakh in an appropriate form. If, for example, love of position dominated, the person will appear in the form of a leopard. If the faculty of appetite dominated over the other attributes, he will appear in the form of a pig. If the faculty of anger dominated, he will appear as a dog. This is the meaning of "People will be mustered on the day of resurrection in keeping with their intentions." There, wealth and position have no importance. Without the heart's wholesomeness and purity, the outward form of knowledge and works will have no benefit. *The day when neither wealth nor sons will profit, [and none will be saved] except for him who comes to God with a wholesome heart* [26:88–89].

On the outside, he has the banner of knowledge,
  on the inside, the underwear of ignorance.
What appears as underpants today
  will be the overpants of the Mustering.

There are many details to the properties of this configuration. The possessor of a wholesome original disposition can understand a sample of them through the properties of dreams and the science of their interpretation. For the human being can enter the barzakh in two ways—either through the lesser death, which is called "sleep," or the greater death. This greater death is of two kinds. The first is compulsory; it occurs through the dissolution of the natural constitution. The second is voluntary; it occurs for the people of purity when they cast off the world of darkness.

Between sleep and death there is only a small difference. "Sleep is the brother of death" alludes to this meaning. If the beauty of the following verse were to disclose itself to a person in the world of the dominion without the mask of letters and words, he would understand many mysteries. *God takes the souls at the time of their death, and that which has not died in its sleep. He withholds that against which He has decreed death, but sends back the other till a stated term. Surely in that are signs for people who reflect* [39:42]. Sleep is the mirror of the mystery of annihilation and *tawḥīd* and resembles the states of the next world. "As you sleep, so you shall die; and as you wake up, so you shall be raised up."

A person came before Ibn Sīrīn and said, "Last night I dreamt that, at the break of day, I had a signet ring on my hand and I was sealing the mouths and private parts of men and women." Ibn Sīrīn said, "You are a muezzin, and in the mornings of Ramadan you give the call to prayer."

Wonderful words! When sleep freed that man for a short time from the sensory world and he became disengaged from some of the attachments and opaqueness of the present world, he witnessed this meaning in the clothing of such an appropriate image! When at death, the attachment is completely severed, all states, works, beliefs and character traits will be personified. *O human being! Thou art laboring unto thy Lord laboriously, and thou shalt encounter Him* [84:6].

All this is with him in the abode of the present world. "By Him whose hand holds Muhammad's soul, verily the Garden and the Fire are nearer to each of you than his shoelace!"

Your paradise and hell are within you,
  look inside and find
blazing fires in your liver,
  blooming gardens in your heart!

However, the veils of nature and the covering of caprice blind the eye of the human heart from perceiving this. *We have put before them a barrier, and behind them a barrier; and We have covered them, so they do not see* [36:9].

When the night of life passes and the morning of the lesser resurrection dawns, the ready cash of the human being's inward dimension will become outward, and he will see once again everything that issued from him in the lower world. *We have now removed from you your covering, so your sight today is piercing* [50:22].

When morning comes
  you will see
to whom you made love
  in the black night.

The questioning by Nakīr and Munkar, the pit, and the garden plot are all in this world. But more than this cannot be discussed in such a short treatise. *God speaks the truth, and He guides on the way* [33:4].

Third is the configuration of the Mustering, which is an elemental configuration. Everything within it corresponds exactly and identically with the configuration of this world. The glorious Koran speaks of the certainty and sureness of this configuration and the manner in which people deny its occurrence as follows: *Has not the human being regarded how We created him of a sperm-drop? Then lo, he is a manifest adversary. And he has struck for Us a similitude and forgotten his creation. He says, "Who shall quicken the bones when they are decayed?" Say: "He shall quicken them, who configured them the first time; He knows all creation"* [36:77]. Among the properties of this configuration are many wonders and states, but reason is incapable of perceiving most of them. This abode's properties can be perceived either by the light of faith or the light of unveiling.

It will only be a single cry, and behold, they are at the Awakening [79:14]. The "Awakening" is the configuration of the Mustering. The "Terror" is the day of resurrection. *Then, on that day, the Terror shall come to pass, and heaven shall be split, for upon that day it shall be very frail, and the angels shall stand upon its borders, and upon that day eight shall carry above them the Throne of your Lord. On that day you shall be exposed, not one secret of yours concealed* [69:15–18].

Among the wonders of that day is that, in relation to one group, it will seem like fifty thousand years and, in relation to another, like a single instant. The problem of the objection made to the rolling up of time for Khizr—God's blessing be upon him—can be understood from this. This day is called the "greater resurrection," and all the prophets and friends agree on its occurrence. *Say: "The ancients and the later folk shall be gathered to the appointed time of a known day"* [56:49–50].

In the view of the possessors of insight, the word *resurrection* has several meanings. It is applied to this specific day, which is called the "greater resurrection.'' It is applied to the day of physical death, which is called the ''lesser resurrection.'' ''When someone dies, his resurrection comes'' alludes to this meaning. It is also applied to the state of arrival achieved by the gnostic, that hour when in his eyes the two engendered worlds are erased and obliterated in the light of unity, and nothing remains but the Living, the Self-subsistent.

A resurrection overcame me
  and I saw
your face was paradise,
  your lips the pool of Kawthar.

Upon the day when the earth shall be changed to other than the earth, and the heavens, and they come forth to God, the One, the Intensely Severe [14:48]. This is called the ''greatest resurrection.''

Here, however, we are concerned with the greater resurrection. It has been described in detail in the Book and the Sunnah, and the perception of its realities and wonders depends upon the lights of the stages of friendship and prophecy—may God make us worthy of its mysteries!

After this configuration the felicitous experience two more configurations—the configuration of paradise, and the unveiling of the vision of God. But their marvelous states, wonderful mysteries, and the explanation of their joys cannot be contained by the measures and weights of rational faculties and fancies. *No soul knows what refreshment of the eyes is hidden away for them, as a recompense for what they were doing* [32:17].

O heart, how long will this and that deceive you
  inside this prison?
Just once leave the dark well
  and see the world!

In the *Ṣaḥīḥ* of Muslim, it is related that the Messenger of God said, ''When the people of the Garden enter the Garden, a caller will call out, 'It belongs to you to live, so you will never die; it belongs to you to be healthy, so you will never be ill; it belongs to you to be young, so you will never grow old; it belongs to you to live in comfort, so you will never be miserable'.''

High up in His sky—
  no heart-hunting hawks.
Deep down in His sea—
  no soul-seizing sharks.

The felicitous are of two types—those brought near to God, and the companions of the right. The paradise of houris, castles, fowl, and sweetmeat belong to the companions of the right. The paradise of self-disclosure, gnosis, and encounter belong to those brought near. ''Most of the people of the Garden are simpletons, but the high things belong to the possessors of minds.''

In the paradise of the spheres,
  all the unripe,
in Thy paradise,
  hell-drinkers.

As for those who will be wretched truth-concealers forever, they have only one more configuration after the configuration of the Mustering, namely, the configuration of hell. They move around among different kinds of spiritual and corporeal chastisement, *therein dwelling forever, so long as the heavens and earth abide* [11:107]. *As often as their skins are wholly burned, We shall give them in exchange other skins, that they may taste the chastisement* [4:56]. We seek refuge in God from their states!

With the tongue of their level they constantly ask to borrow illumination from the lights of the spirits of the felicitous, but they, with the tongue of their state, refer them back to this world, which is the house of acquisition and works. *Upon the day when the hypocrites, men and women, shall say to those who have faith, "Wait for us, so that we may borrow your light!" It shall be said, "Return you back behind, and seek for a light!" And a wall shall be set up between them, having a door in the inward thereof is mercy, and against the outward thereof is chastisement. They shall be calling unto them, "Were we not with you?" They shall say, "Yes indeed: but you tempted yourselves, and you waited, and you were in doubt, and hopes deluded you, until God's commandment came, and the Deluder deluded you concerning God"* [57:13–14].

May God the High give aid through His bounty and mercy! May He bestow through His perfect generosity and kindness the perfections of the dominion! And may He give us in our actual state the ready cash of death before physical death and disengagement from the world of darknesses!

In such a short work no more need be said, since this is enough to call attention and incite desire. In several places allusion has already been made to the fact that the sciences of unveiling can only be grasped by way of wayfaring and tasting, not through investigation and reflection. Worthiness to perceive these meanings depends upon constant remembrance of God and perfect disengagement and devotion. *Remember the name of your Lord, and devote yourself to Him very devoutly—Lord of the East and the West, there is no god but He, so take Him for a guardian* [73:8].

If you drive nature's rabble
  out from your heart,
you will see nothing but God's mysteries
  expressed in your thoughts.

"O Children of Israel! Do not say, 'Knowledge is in heaven, who can bring it down?' or 'In the depths of the earth, who can bring it up?' or 'Behind the mountains, who can cross over them and bring it?' Knowledge is placed in your hearts. Model your conduct on the spirituals and assume the character traits of the sincere devotees until knowledge becomes manifest from your hearts, inundates you, and covers you."

Here, I will conclude the book with a few subtle points from the dominion which yearning spirits can take as an antidote against the poison of heedlessness. We ask God to provide us with attentiveness and give us success in what He loves and approves. In Him are power and strength, and from Him come guidance and preservation from sin.

CONCLUSION

Know, O refreshment of the world's eye—may God confirm you with the Holy Spirit—that you were created for a great task. The mystery of God's trust and the light of His vicegerency have been deposited in your sacred inward self. Beware of extinguishing and dissolving that holy mystery and divine light through the billowing darknesses of following caprice. *David, behold, We have appointed you a vicegerent in the earth; therefore give rulings among the people by the Real, and follow not caprice, lest it mislead you from the path of God* [38:26].

Through aspiration become a vicegerent
  in your substance—
bring your potential
  into actuality!
In value you are greater
  than the two worlds—
What can I do?
  You know not your own worth!

Your vicegerency and governing control appear first in your own specific empire, which is called the "mortal form" or the "human frame." First, you must fulfill the obligation of this vicegerency and maintain the law of equity within your own faculties. But you will not be able to maintain the law of equity unless you achieve a character rooted in justice. A character rooted in justice combines temperance, courage, and wisdom, which are the middle points of the principle character traits. Then, in keeping with God's promise, you will be worthy of the general vicegerency in all empires. *God has promised those who have faith and work upright deeds to make them vicegerents in the earth, even as He made those who were before them vicegerents* [24:55]. In the kingdom and the dominion you will be the successor of Adam the Pure. The ear of your spirit will hear the cry, *When your Lord said to the angels, "I am setting in the earth a vicegerent"* [2:30]. The eye of your heart will see the mystery of "When God wants to set a vicegerent in the land, He anoints his forehead with His right hand."

But to attain this character of justice, you must first keep water away from the noxious tree that drinks down the love of this world. You must weaken that tree for, without doubt, "Love for this world is at the head of every fault." With the scissors of god-wariness you must cut one by one the seams of the darknesses of mortal attachments. You must let the falcon of the lordly subtle reality fly with the wings of the sciences of certainty. You must stop obeying the rulings of fancy and imagination. You must kick away beastly and predatory enjoyments. With the broom of disengagement, you must sweep the filth of nature and the rubbish of temporal existence from the house of the heart—which is the locus wherein shine the lights of the inaccessibility of divinity's holiness. Then the Sultan of eternity without beginning and eternity without end may descend into the heart—which is His house—robed in the cloak of magnificence. "My heaven embraces Me not, nor My earth, but the heart of My faithful, gentle, and meek servant does embrace Me."

Though You can't fit into the world,
  You have a home in my narrow heart.

This self-disclosure is the paradise of the elect. "Within it is found what no eye has seen, no ear has heard, and no man's heart has imagined—not to speak of all I have told you of."

In the dominion's garden the lovers
  have no food but God's beauty.

"God has a Garden in which are no houris, no castles, no milk, no honey—within it Our Lord discloses Himself laughing."

If I can seize your tress in hell,
  I will scorn the state of those in paradise.
But if I am called to the plain of paradise without you,
  paradise's plain will be too tight for my heart.

"The person who considers it proper to make the Real a means partakes of mercy in a certain respect. Since he has not been given to taste the joy of bliss in Him, he does not seek to taste it. He is acquainted only with imperfect joys, so he yearns for them and remains heedless of what lies beyond them."

O seeker of this world,
  you are a hireling.
O lover of paradise,
  you are far from this truth.
O happy with both worlds,
  you have stayed ignorant—
Not having seen the joy of heartache for Him,
  you have an excuse.

What a great loss! Someone is worthy of being the boon companion and vicegerent of his King, but he pollutes himself with appetite's defilements in the dustbin of nature.

O high through noble spirit and intellect,
let not your high station be corrupted!
You have not seen your whole self—
you are nothing but a new Adam!

It is hardly a good transaction to sell the sultanate of eternity without end for a two-day service to the soul that commands to evil, or to trade the spaciousness of the World of Light for the narrow confines of the world of deceit. *Those are they that have bought error at the price of guidance; their transaction has not profited them, and they have not been guided* [2:16].

Is it not ugly to keep the Holy Spirit
waiting outside,
while you sit with Ahriman
in the abode of delusion?

The summons of beginningless kindness calls you to itself moment by moment, but you pretend not to hear. Beginningless beauty shows itself to you instant by instant, but you pretend not to see. True joy seeks for you, but you flee from it. False joys flee from you, but you cling to them. "O sinner, beauty seeks you, but you flee from it. You seek the ugly, but it flees from you."

It was revealed to one of the prophets, "O son of Adam, how low is your aspiration and how vile your soul! I seek you, but you flee from Me. Other things reject you, but you go after them."

In my whole life,
one night during prayer,
the image of my beloved
came to me.
She lifted the veil from her face
and whispered,
"See now from whom
you are being held back!"

If you do nothing today when the reins of aspiration and free choice are in your hands, tomorrow when the hand of the controlling majesty of *The command that day shall belong to God* [82:19] lifts the veil of imagined free choice from your acts and when the caller of inaccessibility calls out from the depths of magnificence, *"Whose is the kingdom today?" "God's, the One, the Intensely Severe"* [40:16], what use will be the cry, *Alas for me, that I neglected my duty to God* [39:56]?

How long will your heart weep
for a comforter?
Understand that your heart
has now become nothing!
If you find no cure
for your poor heart today,
who will cure your heart
when you reach tomorrow?

O you who have faith, expend of what We have provided for you, before there comes a day wherein shall be neither commerce, nor companionship, nor intercession; and the truth-concealers—they are the wrongdoers [2:254].

Before this excuse-offering soul
runs out of excuses,
before this admonition-seeing eye
fails in its task!

"Provide from your wealth for the day of your poverty, from your health for the day of your illness, from your youth for the day of your old age, and from everything in this world for your world to come. And beware of being one of those who put things off, for most of the wailing of the people of the Fire derives from 'I will, I will.' "

Did it ever occur to you, O heart,
to leave the soul behind?
To act like a man,
to give up loss and profit?
I fear that you have followed
the wind of fancy so much
that all at once, like dust,
you will be swept far away.

Through the immediate pleasures and false imaginings of this world, Satan pours the wine of hopes and expectations laced with the opium of heedlessness and delusion down the throat of the souls. *He promises them and fills them with hopes, but there is nothing Satan promises them except delusion* [4:120]. Beware, beware, O quintessence of the engendered things—may God confirm you with a spirit from Him! *Stretch not your eyes to what We have given pairs of them to enjoy—the flower of the present life—that We may try them therein. Your Lord's provision is better, and more enduring* [20:131].

Strive—if you can take advice—
for two or three days,
so you may die before death,
by two or three days.

This world's an old hag.
  So what if you're not close
to an old hag,
  for two or three days?

"Be in the world like a stranger or like a traveler on the road, and count yourself already in the grave." Until you become one of the possessors of minds, beware of the deception and trickery of this world. But you will not become one of the possessors of minds unless you witness the reality of this world in the mirror of the heart with the light of God's revelation so that you are no longer deceived by this world's glitter. The likeness of the reality of this world is explained by the eternal Koran. *The likeness of this present life is as water that We send down out of heaven, and the plants of the earth, whereof men and cattle eat, mingle with it till, when the earth has taken on its glitter and has decked itself fair, and its inhabitants think they have power over it, Our command comes upon it by night or day, and We make it stubble, as though yesterday it flourished not. Even so, We distinguish the signs for a people who reflect* [10:24].

If you have relaxed in ease
  all your life,
tasting this world's joys
  all your life,
Even for you the end
  will be death—
you will see the dream you have dreamed
  all your life.

One can only reach the pavilions of the dominion from the bottomless pit of this world with the cord of God. *And hold fast to God's cord, all of you together* [3:103]. Deliverance from the shadows of caprice comes only through following Mustafa—God's blessings be upon him. *You have a good example in God's Messenger* [33:21].

Seize the words of God and the Prophet
  and go!
What is not Koran and Hadith
  is idle talk and folly.
Do you know why the Koran begins with *b*
  and ends with *s*?
In religion the Koran
  is "sufficient" [*bas*] guide.

Know that the keys of the treasuries of endless felicity are contained in the hints and allusions of Mustafa—peace be upon him. Learn the following words—which Ibn ʿAbbās (God be pleased with him!) has related from that holy presence

(God's blessings be upon him!)—and constantly act in accordance with them. Through the power of their light, you will be granted constant victory and triumph over the darkness of Iblis.

Ibn ʿAbbās said, "I was seated on a camel with the Messenger of God—God bless him and give him peace—and he said to me, 'My boy, should I not teach you some words by which God will profit you?'

"I said, 'Please do, O Messenger of God!'

"He said, 'Be mindful of God, and He will be mindful of you. Be mindful of God, and you will find Him in front of you. Make yourself known to God at the time of ease, and He will know you in difficulties. When you ask, ask from God. When you seek aid, seek aid from God. For the Pen has dried concerning what will be. If all the creatures should desire to profit you with something that God has not decreed for you, they will not be able to do so. And if they desire to harm you through something that God has not decreed for you, they will not be able to do so. Perform works for God's sake on the basis of gratitude and certainty. And know that there is great good in being patient in what you dislike, that victory lies with patience, that relief resides in distress, and that *Truly with hardship comes ease* [94:6].' "

Constantly flee from yourself to God, *So flee unto God!* [51:50]. Ask Him to help you against Himself. With the tongue of your soul say, "I seek refuge in Thy pardon from Thy punishment, I seek refuge in Thy good pleasure from Thy anger, I seek refuge in Thee from Thee; I cannot count Thy praises, Thou art as Thou hast praised Thyself."

Belong to Him,
  so that you may be blessed
and your words may be heard
  like Yā Sīn and Tabārak.
Place your head in the dust at His door,
  and great men
will make the dust of your door
  their hat and crown.

Praise belongs to God, the Bestower, the Loving, the Effuser of munificence, the Originator of mercy and existence; and blessings be upon our master Muhammad and all his household.

Part Three *Practice*

As explained earlier, *The Easy Roads of Sayf al-Dīn* was written for one Sayf al-Dīn Ṭughril, who was apparently a recent convert to Islam. The author speaks as a Sufi teacher who wants to introduce Sayf al-Dīn to the essentials of faith and practice. What makes the work Sufi is the fact that all three dimensions of Islam are discussed explicitly. Most of what the author says about the Shariah can be found in manuals of Islamic practice that outline the basic duties of Muslims. Western readers unfamiliar with Islam perhaps should be told that these duties have not changed significantly from the earliest compilations of Islamic law. By and large, what is said here about practice could have been written at any time over the past one thousand years.

If these Shariite duties are usually not discussed in the classical works on Sufism, this is because the Sufi authors took it for granted that their readers already knew all these details and were putting them into practice in their daily life. What is unusual about this treatise is that it was written specifically for someone who apparently had not been practicing the Shariah. Hence it begins at the beginning.

Many readers may be surprised by what seems to be excessive detail in unimportant matters. However, it is sufficient to compare this work with, for example, Ghazālī's *Beginning of Guidance* (translated in Watt's *Faith and Practice of al-Ghazālī*), to realize that the treatise is in fact extremely brief. From the point of view of Islamic jurisprudence, what the author says is rather sketchy. He leaves out many of the fine points, especially in the sections on ritual prayer, and beginners could not use this work as a do-it-yourself manual unless they had someone to fill in the details. The author wants to set down what he feels are the most essential elements of everyday practice, knowing that Sayf al-Dīn would easily be able to find someone to explain anything that was not sufficiently clear.

In contrast to Ghazālī in *The Beginning of Guidance*, the author of this treatise pays little attention to the moral concomitants of the Shariite practices. Ghazālī's work is written for those who had more knowledge of Islam than Sayf al-Dīn, and hence he pays greater attention to the inner dimensions of the outward acts. Moreover, in keeping with his approach in the *Iḥyā'*, Ghazālī wants to avoid any suggestion that the Shariah is sufficient unto itself. Hence, he stresses the moral blemishes that need to be avoided. In other words, he focuses on reforming the heart, an endeavor which, as he frequently reminds us in his various works, is outside the competence of the jurists. The authorities he cites on this topic—after the Koran, the Prophet, and some of the Companions—are invariably figures who came to be known as Sufis.

Most of what our author says about purification, ritual prayer, and supplication is modeled on Ghazālī's *Iḥyā'* and has parallels in works such as *The Beginning of Guidance.* As in the *Iḥyā'*, the juridical details pertain to the Shāfiʿī *madhhab* (school of law), although they also seem to be sufficient for the Ḥanafī school, because the author points out a discrepancy in one instance. I have made no attempt to correlate the views expressed here with the positions of the various *madhhab*s except in one or two instances in which knowing the difference seemed to be helpful to understand what is being said. A detailed explication of the legal context of these teachings would demand a work far longer than the text itself. It is sufficient for the reader to know that *Easy Roads* is not the final word on how ablutions or ritual prayers should be performed or on what supplications should be said in which situations.

I included this treatise in this book only after a good deal of thought. I was tempted to follow the easy road simply by limiting this book to faith. Then I could have dropped *Easy Roads* and mentioned it as a work by the same author that adds nothing to the discussion. I finally concluded that I would not be doing justice either to the author or to the Sufi approach to Islam by following that course.

My doubts about translating this treatise were based on the negative reactions that some readers will have to parts of the text. By contemporary Christian and post-Christian standards, the work goes into far too much detail not only on ritualistic practices in general, but also on matters of personal hygiene not usually associated with religious observance—questions that today are not normally discussed outside a clinic. But this is standard procedure in any manual of the Shariah, and Ghazālī does the same in the *Iḥyā'* or *The Beginning of Guidance*. Neither Islam nor Sufism has ever disregarded the body or its functions. The body has its rules, just as the mind and the heart have their rules, and the former are as important for observing Islamic teachings as the latter. *Easy Roads* reminds us that Sufis such as our author—not to mention their disciples—observed the minor details of the Shariah in everyday life.

The negative reaction of contemporary readers to parts of this work—a reaction I felt myself the first time I read it—surely tells us something about ourselves and our expectations from "spiritual" writings. No one will have any problem in recognizing *Rising Places* and *Clarifications* as works on spirituality. Both fit nicely into the "sweetness and light" stereotype of Sufism. But *Easy Roads*, by dealing with matters that are not normally discussed in public, helps us realize that—to the extent we are repulsed—we still live in a romantic world that separates spirit from body and pretends that the spiritual life is exempt from anything but the beautiful and the angelic.[1]

This is not the place to explain why Islam stresses the importance of observing carefully prescribed rites. Among the world's religions, Islam is certainly not alone in this. In fact, it is mainly modern forms of Christianity that are the exceptions. From the Sufi point of view, the function of ritual is to sanctify life and integrate the many into the One. The initiative for this integration must come from God, the source of all guidance.

Given that *Easy Roads* recognizes explicitly the necessity for actualizing all three dimensions of Islam, it is highly instructive to see what the author thinks are the most important elements of Shariite practice. His position is, I suspect, normative for Sufism over much of its history.[2] He pays no attention to secondary matters such as social context. In his view, Muslims must begin with the reform of themselves, and this depends upon the most essential pillars of Islam. Like Ghazālī in *The Beginning of Guidance*, he discusses only two of the five pillars: ritual prayer and fasting. The first pillar—voicing the Shahadah—is taken for granted, so it is not discussed. (Of course, the discussion of the three principles of faith covers in broad terms the Shahadah's meaning and implications.)

If the author limits himself to ritual prayer and fasting, it is because both are unavoidable duties for every Muslim. Ritual prayer is more fundamental, not only because of explicit statements to this effect by the Prophet, but also because fasting is mandatory for only one month of the year—not every day—and there are many reasons, such as illness, that would exempt a person. The fourth pillar of Islam, *zakāt* or the alms-tax, depends utterly on circumstances. No one has to pay the tax who does not fulfill the requirements. Many of those—such as Sufi novices—who would end up reading a text like this should probably be receiving the alms-tax, not paying it. In a similar way, the explicit commandment concerning the fifth and last pillar, the hajj, is to "make the pilgrimage to the House of God if you have the means to do so." If you do not have the means, you are excused from the obligation. Hence, what is important in the first place is how to pray and how to fast, since these are things that every Muslim has an immediate need to know. And since the precondition for prayer is ritual purity, that also deserves explanation.

As in the two works on faith, attention to Islamic social and political teachings is totally absent. This is not because these teachings are unimportant. It is simply a question of priorities. What comes first is God and human felicity. The essence of the individual relationship with God is faith and practice as defined in the Koran and the Sunnah, and neither faith nor practice demands interrelationships with other people. There are all sorts of legitimate reasons for not concerning oneself with social and political situations. As Ghazālī says, a deaf and dumb person does not need to know what words he must avoid.[3]

People need enough knowledge of the religion and the world to ensure their felicity. Knowledge that does not aid in this goal is unprofitable and thus to be avoided if possible. The knowledge that is absolutely necessary for every individual (*farḍ 'ayn*) pertains strictly to faith and practice. As for knowledge in its other forms—such as medicine or politics—it is sufficient if some individuals assume the responsibility of learning it (*farḍ kifāya*), and there are always such people.[4]

After explaining purity, prayer, and fasting, the author devotes a section to remembrance of God (*dhikr*) and supplication (*du'ā'*), which are, as it were, voluntary extensions of the ritual prayer. His manner of explaining the necessity of *dhikr* proves without a doubt his Sufi affiliations. But his emphasis upon supplication may prove surprising to people with only a superficial familiarity with Sufism.

Supplication, after all, is basically personal or petitionary prayer, or asking God for what you want. The Koran commands it in several verses, such as *Supplicate Me, and I will answer you* (40:60). Elsewhere I have dealt with the significance of supplication as an expression of early forms of Islamic spirituality—Sufism in the broadest sense—and I will not repeat what I have already said.[5] Let me simply make two points.

The Prophet called supplication "the marrow of *worship*" (*mukhkh al-'ibāda*).[6] Islam's third dimension, *iḥsān*, is to "*worship* God as if you see Him." The word *'ibāda* (worship) is a term of fundamental importance for understanding the Islamic concept of the human being. It means to venerate, to serve, to be a servant (*'abd*). Ultimately, to be a creature is to be God's servant, and all creatures—except human beings (and the jinn)—serve God by nature. Human beings have the privilege of choosing whether or not to serve God.

Of course, careful theologians point out that there are two types of worship and servanthood—compulsory and voluntary—just as there are two types of return to God. Everything without exception serves and worships God by being the object of His creative power. But since human beings have a certain freedom, they can add a voluntary worship to their compulsory worship. Human perfection lies in this voluntary surrender of self to God.[7]

One accepts to be God's servant by following His guidance and "worshiping Him." In other words, people worship God by doing what He wants them to do. Again, careful theologians point out that God does not want people to do things for His sake—He is "independent of the worlds" and has no needs—but for their sakes. He wants them to reach felicity, but to reach it, they must choose to reach it. No one is surprised if parents want their child to be happy purely out of love, even if the child suffers certain strictures as a result. But the parents cannot impose happiness on the child. The child must achieve it, because that is the nature of happiness. Why should anyone be surprised that God has no self-interested motive in commanding worship, or that He cannot impose felicity upon us?

To become a perfect servant of God, one must act as if one is seeing God before one's eyes. *Iḥsān* is "to worship God as if you see Him." There can be no hypocrisy and double-dealing in such a relationship. Perfect worship is inseparable from sincerity and god-wariness. Moreover, it is a continuous state, not pertaining simply to the times of day that one sets aside for God. As the well-known saying has it, "The Sufi is the child of the present moment" (*al-ṣūfī ibn al-waqt*), which is to say that a true Sufi lives with the awareness of God's presence at every moment.

The word *du'ā'* (supplication) means literally "to call upon" God. It is to address one's attention to God by voicing one's personal situation. If it is "the marrow of worship," this is because sincere supplication demands an intense personal involvement with serving God, not heedlessness and indifference.

But a second point also needs to be made to bring out the importance of supplication. Those with knowledge of the spiritual teachings of the world's religions are aware that petitionary prayer is not given a high rank by most teachers, mainly because it involves an affirmation of the ego's desires, which are among the basic obstacles to spiritual perfection. But much of supplication in Islam is lifted beyond the concerns of the ego, first, because God Himself commands people to supplicate God, and second, because Muslims often *recite* the supplications of others, such as the Prophet or the friends of God. Through this second type of supplication—the type recommended in this treatise—people give up the desires of the ego and place themselves within the mold of the great human exemplars of the religion.

Repeated recitation of the received supplications can have the effect of gradually reshaping the soul in conformity with the models of human perfection. When supplication refers, as it does here, to recitation of received prayers, it plays an intermediary role between the relative impersonality of the ritual prayer or the remembrance of God and the excessive personal orientation of petitionary prayer when people are left to their own devices. It is essential to Sufi practice, and even the most advanced Sufi masters recite supplications and prescribe them for their disciples. Historically speaking, it is probably fair to say that most of the supplications that are commonly recited by Muslims derive from the Prophet, members of the Prophet's family, and Sufi shaykhs.

NOTES

1. It is perhaps not out of place to point out that the purification rites described here do not compare unfavorably with contemporary Western hygienic practices—remember that water is a much more thorough cleanser than paper. A little historical perspective can also be helpful in understanding the significance of these instructions. As is well known, Europeans considered water to be unhealthy over most of the past two thousand years. There were more baths, so it is said, in any city in Muslim Spain than in the whole of Christian Europe.

2. The author's priorities, both here and in the other two works, help explain why the Muslim reformers of the nineteenth century reacted not only against the deviated and decadent Sufi orders that were—and still are—sometimes found in the Islamic world, but also those orders that kept to the traditional norms. The priorities set down for personal practice in Sufi treatises do not provide the best foundation for modernization. All this attention to first things does not make

people into docile factory workers and eager consumers. Nor does it shape them into revolutionaries, which helps explain why some of the more recent political movements in the Islamic world have also been opposed to Sufism.

3. Ghazālī, *Iḥyā'* 1:13; idem, *Book of Knowledge* 33.

4. For Ghazālī's explanation of the distinction between these two types of knowledge, see *Book of Knowledge* 30–72. For a good summary, see M.A. Sherif, *Ghazali's Theory of Virtue* 12–14.

5. See my introduction to 'Alī ibn al-Ḥusayn, *The Psalms of Islam*.

6. Tirmidhī, Du'ā' 1.

7. Again, this is not quite exact, because there are two types of perfection. One pertains to compulsory servanthood, and the other to voluntary servanthood. See SPK, chapter 17.

The Easy Roads of Sayf Al-Dīn

In the Name of God, the Merciful, the Compassionate

I have no success but through God.

Glory be to Thee!
We know not save what Thou hast taught us.
Surely Thou art the Knowing, the Wise. [2:32]

Worthiness for praise belongs to the sacred threshold of the Divinity, the Nourisher who lifted the veil of nature from the insight of the people of purity by sending the winds of wisdom. He inscribed the patterns of the realities and the gnostic sciences on the tablets of their hearts with the pen of *And thy Lord is the Most Generous, who taught with the Pen* [96:3–4].

Fitness for blessings belongs to the purified presence of Mustafa. The sun of that master's messengerhood rose from the east of eternity without beginning, and the radiance of his sun's shining lit up the lands of East and West.

Merit for salutations belongs to his companions and household, who are the stars of the heaven of guidance.

To come to the point: It has been verified for the people of insight that human spirits become acquainted and familiar in the world of water and clay following their familiarity in the world of the dominion. The Muhammadan threshold has alluded to this meaning as follows: "Spirits are assembled troops. Those acquainted with one another become familiar, and those not acquainted keep apart."

Given this introduction, in the world of holiness I was connected and became familiar with the great commander, the master of the elect, the "sword of the empire and the religion" [Sayf al-Dawla wa'l-Dīn], the good fortune of Islam and the Muslims, the chosen of the great sultans, the beloved of God's friends and the sincere devotees, Ṭughril—God lengthen his duration and lead him on the path of His good pleasure! Hence, in the world of sense perception, my spirit has developed a great attachment to his spirit (God make us brothers in His religion and loving friends in Him!). So I desired that he should be my companion in the journey of *I am going to my Lord* [37:99]. I have set out to overcome difficult obstacles in wayfaring so that I may advance from the *lowest of the low* [95:5]—which is the station of beasts, predators, and satans—to the highest of the high—which is the station of the angels brought near to God, the holy beings of the higher plenum—along with *those whom God has blessed: the prophets, the sincere devotees, the witnesses, and the upright—good companions they!* [4:69].

Since his companionship with me depends on gaining command of a few preliminaries of the intellectual and practical pillars of Islam, the knowing of which is mandatory for the seeker, I write down—in keeping with my present state—a few short words. I will explain the preliminaries of the knowledge of religion that must be known by the wayfarer. I seek help from God—glory be to Him, and high exalted is He!—in completing this goal, for "There is no power and no strength but in Him."

My goal in all this will be confined to an introduction, five easy roads, and a conclusion. In order to seek an auspicious omen and good fortune, I have called this treatise by Ṭughril's blessed title, "The Easy Roads of Sayf al-Dīn." *And God's it is to show the path* [16:9].

INTRODUCTION

On the Manner and Goal of Perfecting One's Character

At the outset it should be known that God did not create human beings in play—*What, did you think that We created you only for sport, and that you would not be returned to Us?* [23:115]—for they will subsist forever, whether in endless felicity or everlasting wretchedness. Mustafa—God bless him and give him peace—expressed this meaning as follows: "You were created for eternity without end; you will only be transferred from one abode to another." "The grave is one of the plots of the Garden or one of the pits of the Fire." It is incumbent on intelligent people who have recognized the truth of the Shariahs of the prophets—God bless them all—to reflect and to try with complete seriousness to discover for what work their Creator has created them. What is the use of sending the prophets to them? Which road leads to felicity and which to wretchedness? Without doubt, such reflection is better than the worship of seventy years, just as Mustafa has said. "An hour's reflection is better than the worship of seventy years."

A PRELIMINARY REMARK AS PART OF THE INTRODUCTION

Know that all the prophets, the friends of God, the ulama, and the sages—God bless them all and sanctify their spirits—have agreed that God created human beings for the sake of true knowledge and obedience. He sent the prophets to teach people the science of acquiring true knowledge and the way to obey Him. *It is He who has raised up from among those without a scripture a messenger from among them, to recite His signs to them and to purify them, and to teach them the Book and the Wisdom, although before that they were in plain misguidance* [62:2].

The knowledge of religion has no more than these two parts: The first part is called the "science of faith," and the second the "science of god-wariness."

The science of faith in all its details is the ultimate goal of all the sciences, and the beauty of the friends and prophets derives from truly knowing it. It has many branches. These include the true knowledge of the Essence of God, His holy attributes, and His acts in the kingdom and the dominion; the true knowledge of the angels and the satans; discernment between inspiration and satanic whispering; the mystery of revelation, prophecy, and friendship with God; the true knowledge of this world and the next world; the mystery of the measuring out; and the mystery of the spirit. The duty of the common people is simply to have faith in the unseen. To see and know all this by way of unveiling and witnessing is the business of the prophets and the friends. The ulama call this type of knowledge the "sciences of unveiling."

As for the science of god-wariness, it is explained in the Koran in great detail, and every human being is obliged to learn it. Thus, the Prophet said, "The search for knowledge is incumbent upon every Muslim." The meaning of "god-wariness" is that a person should be obedient to God, not to caprice. For a person's movement and rest do not go outside two types. Either they follow the command of God or that of caprice. If they follow the command of God, this is called "obedience." If they follow the command of caprice, this is called "disobedience." Obedience and disobedience have two paths—felicity and wretchedness. This is the meaning of the verse, *We guided him on the two highways* [90:10]. The ulama call this kind of knowledge the "sciences of practice."

Whenever a person gives this type of knowledge—which is called "practice"—its due, God will effuse various kinds of knowledge upon him from the world of the unseen through unveiling without human teaching or learning. God has explained this in the glorious Book. *Had the people of the cities had faith and been god-wary, We would have opened upon them blessings from heaven and earth* [7:96]. In the same way He says, *Be wary of God, and God will teach you* [2:282]. The bringer of the Shariah said, "When someone acts in accordance with what he knows, God will make him an heir to the knowledge of what he does not know."

In this brief treatise, I will now set down that to which one must commit oneself according to the science of faith. After that, I will write what is appropriate to the situation and required by the present moment concerning the science of practice. God gives protection and success, and aid is sought from Him against the evil of the enemy and his soldiers.

THE FIRST EASY ROAD

On the Kinds of the Science of Faith

It contains five road-clearings.

THE FIRST ROAD-CLEARING

On the True Knowledge of the Essence of God—
Majestic is His Majesty!

Those learned in wisdom and the leaders in the principles [of faith] follow the path of affirming the Being of God—mighty is His authority—by composing rational propositions and setting up categorical proofs and demonstrations. The people of reason consider this path praiseworthy and high in level, but the pillars of unveiling and the great masters of witnessing—who have reached a stage beyond reason—do not consider it laudable. They call the method of argumentation and demonstration the "remedy of those who have corrupt constitutions." That is why Mustafa, who was the best and most perfect of creatures, did not command the community to follow this method. In the divine revelation, enough was sent down to alert intelligent people with wholesome original dispositions. Nothing can be added to God's explanation. *Surely in the creation of the heavens and the earth and the alternation of night and day and the ship that runs in the sea with profit for people, and the water God sends down from heaven, therewith reviving the earth after it is dead, and His scattering abroad in it all manner of crawling things, and the turning about of the winds and the clouds compelled between heaven and earth—surely there are signs for a people having intelligence* [2:164].

One of the great possessors of true knowledge has said that searching for God with proofs is like looking for the sun with a lamp. The majesty of Lordship is too manifest to have need of proofs. "Glory be to Him who is veiled from His creatures by the intensity of His manifestation." The original disposition [of human beings] bears witness to His existence.

The God of highness and lowness is Thou:
  I know not what Thou art—all being is Thou.

In each thing is found a sign
  showing that He is one.

He raised up this tremendous heaven, kept it hanging with perfect power, and adorned it with several thousand stars. He spread out this wide earth, kept it steady with firm mountains, and made many thousands of wonders appear upon it in the various kinds of minerals, plants, and animals. *He created the heavens without pillars you can see, and He cast on the earth firm mountains, lest it shake with you, and He scattered abroad in it all manner of crawling things. And We sent down out of heaven water, and caused to grow in it of every generous kind* [31:10].

What a pure Artisan! The dustmotes of heaven and earth bear witness to His existence, unity, magnificence, and tremendousness! *All that is in the heavens and the earth glorifies God, and He is the Inaccessible, the Wise* [57:1].

Ponder the plants of the earth,
look upon the effects of that King's making!
The emerald herbs bear witness
that God has no partner.

You should know that this all-knowing Nourisher is not similar to any created thing, nor is any created thing similar to Him. No creature, whether angel or prophet, has known Him as He is in Himself, nor will any creature ever know Him. "Glory be to Him who alone knows what He is!"

O you who are unable to know yourself,
when will you ever know God?
Since you are too weak to fathom yourself,
how can you grasp your Creator?

Those firmly rooted in knowledge agree that, in the row of the higher plenum brought near to God, no angel has greater knowledge than the Greatest Spirit. Nevertheless, his words of glorification are these: "Glory be to Thee wherever Thou art and wherever Thou mayest be!" Mustafa—God's blessings be upon him—who is the quintessence of creation and the most knowledgeable of the prophets and the friends, used to pray to God with these words: "Glory be to Thee—we have not truly known Thee!"

Intellect of intellect is He,
spirit of spirit,
and what is higher than that—
that is He.

He is nearer to the servants than the jugular vein, and further from them than any distance that comes to mind. His relationship of nearness to the majestic Throne is the same as His relationship with the bottom of the earth. He is hidden because of extreme evidence, and evident because of extreme hiddenness. *He is the First and the Last, the Manifest and the Nonmanifest, and He is knower of everything* [57:3].

Whatever may pass into the fancies, imaginations, and minds of human beings—He is not that, and He is not like that. On the contrary, He is its Creator. *Nothing is like Him, and He is the Hearing, the Seeing* [42:11].

He is One and has no associate or partner. *Your God is One God; there is no god but He, the Merciful, the Compassionate* [2:163]. For, were He to have an associate and partner—high indeed is God exalted above what the wrongdoers say!—the business of the cosmos would be disrupted and the universe would leave the confines of order. The same thing would happen if two people gave commands in a city, or if two sultans ruled a kingdom. The business of that city and that kingdom would break down and leave the confines of order. But the view of intelligence lets us see that the creation of the cosmos follows the best kind of order. Its temporal events become manifest in the mode of wisdom and justice. *Were there gods in earth and heaven other than God, these two would surely be corrupted* [21:22].

All the gnostics and faithful will see Him in the Abode of Permanence without how or why, just as they know Him in this world without how or why.

Majesty, tremendousness, and power belong to Him, and magnificence, invincibility, and inaccessibility befit Him. *Glory be to your Lord, the Lord of inaccessibility, above what they describe! And peace be upon the messengers, and praise belongs to God, Lord of the worlds* [37:180–182].

THE SECOND ROAD-CLEARING

On the True Knowledge of His Attributes—Mighty is His Authority!

He is Knowing. From the top of the Throne to the bottom of the earth, no dustmote stands outside His eternal knowledge. Whatever was, is, and will be is all one in His eternal knowledge. In His knowledge the days of Adam are not in the past, nor is the day of resurrection in the future. Wherever the servants seek Him, they find Him through His eternal knowledge and perfect power—whether they seek Him in the Throne, in the layers of heaven, upon the earth, or in the depths of the ocean. *To God belong the East and the West—whithersoever you turn, there is the Face of God; God is All-embracing, All-knowing* [2:115].

He is Alive. He has never died and will never die. He always was and always will be. He was, and the creatures were not. He is, and the creatures are not. He will be, and the creatures will not be. *Everything is perishing except His Face; to Him belongs the judgment, and to Him you shall be returned* [28:88].

He is Desiring. Whatever He desires is, and whatever He does not desire is not. "What God wills will be, and what He does not will will not be." The faith of the faithful, the obedience of the obedient, the truth-concealing of the truth-concealers, and the disobedience of the disobedient all occur through His desire and decree. No dustmote in heaven and earth moves or stands still without His desire. *But you will not will unless God wills* [76:30]. "None repels His decree, *None holds back His judgment* [13:41]."

He is Powerful. He can do whatever He desires. Angels, Throne, Footstool, sun, moon, heaven, earth—all subsist through the light of His power. *God holds the heavens and the earth, lest they disappear* [35:41]. "Self-subsistent" means that He subsists through Himself and others subsist through Him. *There is no god but God, the Alive, the Self-subsistent* [2:255]. If He desired, in one instant He would take all things to nonexistence, and if He desired, He would create a hundred thousand like them. *God is powerful over everything* [5:40]. *If He will, He will put you away and bring a new creation; that is surely no great matter for God* [14:19–20].

He is Hearing. He hears the sound of an ant's footsteps under the seventh layer of the earth just as well as He hears the glorifications of those among the higher plenum brought near to Him at the base of the Throne. Blessed is God whose hearing embraces all things!

If I call Thee from a wailing breast,
  Thou knowest.
If I hold my tongue and speak not,
  Thou knowest.

He is Seeing. If His servants obey, He sees, and if they disobey, He sees. *Does he not know that God sees?* [96:14]. He sees an ant and a gnat in a dark, black night on a black stone just as well as He sees Seraphiel and the Greatest Spirit on the ladders of holiness. *He knows what enters into the earth and what comes out of it, what comes down from heaven and what climbs up in it. He is with you wherever you are, and God sees what you do* [57:4].

He is Speaking. He speaks to the people of the dominion with beginningless, eternal speech. He spoke to Adam, He spoke to Moses at Mount Sinai, and He spoke to Mustafa on the night of the *miʿrāj*. His speech is incomparable with letter and sound. It is not similar to the speech of any created thing. The Torah, the Gospel, the Psalms, and the Koran are all His speech. His speech is His attribute, and His attribute is eternal, subsisting in His Essence. Therein His command and prohibition are true, and His promise and warning true. The Koran is memorized by hearts, recited by tongues, and written on pages. Memorization, recitation, and writing originate in time, but what is memorized, recited and written is eternal. *No! I swear by the falling of the stars—and indeed, that is a tremendous oath, did you but know—that it is a noble Koran in a hidden Book that none but the purified shall touch, a sending down from the Lord of the worlds* [56:75–80].

THE THIRD ROAD-CLEARING

On the True Knowledge of His Acts—Majestic is His Power!

The whole cosmos and everything that appears within it is the handiwork and ray of His power's light. Through His penetrating wisdom and perfect power, He created the cosmos in two kinds—spiritual, called the "world of the dominion"; and corporeal, called the "world of the kingdom." He has explained this in His eternal Book. *Verily, His are the creation and the command* [7:54]. The command is the spiritual world, and the creation the corporeal world.

He created the human being as a compound of both worlds. The human spirit comes from the spiritual world and the human body from the corporeal world.

He created everything that He created in the two worlds with wisdom and justice, so that nothing more perfect and more excellent than it can assume form. *Surely in the creation of the heavens and earth and in the alternation of night and day, there are signs for the possessors of minds, those who remember God, standing and sitting and on their sides, and who reflect upon the creation of the heavens and the earth. "Our Lord, Thou hast not created this in vain. Glory be to Thee! Guard us against the chastisement of the Fire"* [3:190–191]. The following verses were composed by Shaykh Awḥad al-Dīn—God be well pleased with him:

Worthy of giving decrees is no decreer
  other than God—
outside His decree stands nothing
  that exists.
Whatever exists must be
  the way it is,
and what should not be the way it is
  does not exist.

Whatever He causes to occur for the servants—poverty or wealth, sickness or health, felicity or wretchedness—follows the law of equity and the way of justice. Injustice from Him cannot be imagined, since injustice is to exercise control over the possessions of someone else. But heaven and earth, angel and celestial sphere, jinn and mankind, are all His possessions and handiwork. If He should place all the glorifiers of the higher plenum in hell forever and take all the truth-concealers and the disobedient to the gardens of paradise, that would be justice from Him, not injustice. *To God belongs what is in the heavens and what is in the earth. He forgives whom He will, and He chastises whom He will. God is Forgiving, Compassionate* [3:129]. All acts of the servants—whether they be good or evil, obedience or disobedience—are created by Him. *God created you and what you do* [37:96].

When God creates someone for felicity, He subjects him to the works of the felicitous, and when He creates someone for wretchedness, He subjects him to the works of the wretched. *As for him who gives and is god-wary and recognizes the most beautiful, We shall surely ease him to the Easing. But as for him who is a miser, and claims independence, and cries lies to the most beautiful, We shall surely ease him to the Hardship* [92:5–10].

Although the servant, the power of the servant, and those things over which the servant has power are all created by Him, the servant still has a certain acquisition and free choice. Were this not the case, there would be no accounting or book at the resurrection and God would not examine and question the servant. But this meaning is affirmed clearly in the Koran. *And every human being—We have fastened to him his bird of omen on his neck; and We shall bring forth for him, on the day of resurrection, a book he shall find spread wide open. "Read your book! Your soul suffices you this day as an accounter against you"* [17:13–14].

The people of insight agree that the pleasures and the pains of the Bliss and the Burning will be the fruits of human works. The divine revelation gives voice to this. *The human being shall have only as he has labored, and his laboring shall surely be seen. Then he shall be recompensed for it with sure recompense* [53:39–41].

It is extremely difficult to reconcile compulsion and free will, and this is a place where the feet of most people slip. God fix us and you upon the straight path! The unique shaykh Awḥad al-Dīn—God be pleased with him—has brought these two together beautifully in the following lines:

> You will not find honey's sweetness
>   without a bee's sting.
> You will not reach good fortune
>   without the soul's pain.
> What has not been allotted
>   cannot be gained through effort,
> but unless you show your effort,
>   you will never reach your lot.

THE FOURTH ROAD-CLEARING

On Prophecy

Know that in eternity without beginning, God—majestic is His power—established felicity and wretchedness for human beings. He ordained that this felicity and wretchedness would be the fruit of human works. Hence His overflowing mercy, complete solicitude, and eternal beneficence required that He should select a group of human beings and give them the robe of election, purity, and prophecy. Then by means of the angels brought near to Him—who are the trustees of His Presence and the keepers of His mysteries—He taught this group so that they could tell human beings which works yield felicity and which yield wretchedness. This group is called the "prophets"—God's blessings be upon them all—*messengers bearing good tidings and warning so that people should have no argument against God after the messengers* [4:165].

God sent our own prophet—God's blessings be upon him—after all of these, but He placed him above every one of them in rank. He sent him to the creatures with truth and rectitude and made His religion reach the extremity of perfection. Thus He says, *Today I have perfected your religion for you, and I have completed My blessings upon you, and I have approved Islam for you as a religion* [5:3]. He made him the seal of the prophets and the lord of the children of Adam—God bless him and give him peace!

Send greetings of peace, O people!
  Shower blessings upon the foremost, the trusted!
Mustafa—
  he came *only as a mercy for the worlds* [21:107].

God confirmed him with dazzling miracles and radiant signs, such as the moon's being split in the sky through his pointing, the pebbles' glorifying God in his hand, and the poisoned, roasted lamb's speaking to him. The greatest miracle is the Koran, for all the eloquent speakers of the Arabs and the erudite scholars of the non-Arabs were incapable of vying with it, and they will remain incapable until the resurrection. *Say: "If human beings and jinn band together to produce the like of this Koran, they will never produce its like, though they back one another"* [17:88].

After the Prophet, the leader of the people and the Prophet's rightful vicegerent was Abū Bakr al-Ṣiddīq, after him ʿUmar al-Khaṭṭāb, after him ʿUthmān al-ʿAffān, and after him ʿAlī al-Murtaḍā—God be pleased with them all! All of the Prophet's companions were able through his light to pass beyond the darknesses of nature to the lights of the heart. "My companions are like stars—no matter which one you follow, you will be guided."

THE FIFTH ROAD-CLEARING

On the States of the Next World

Know that after death human beings will subsist. Death consists of the cutting off of the spirit's control from the body. It is no more than a transferal from the world of the visible, which is called "this world," to the world of the unseen, which is called the "next world."

The first waystation of the next world is the grave. There the truth-concealers and the disobedient members of this community will be chastised. Mustafa—upon him be peace—sought refuge in God from the chastisement of the grave. "May God give us and you refuge from it, through His bounty and mercy."

The questioning of Munkar and Nakīr is true. They are two awesome angels whose eyes are like flashing lightning and whose voices like clattering thunder. They ask the servant, "Who is your Creator? Who is your prophet? What is your religion? What is your kiblah?" If he has faith and certainty, he will answer them in the best manner. If he is a deprived truth-concealer, he will be helpless.

In the same way, the resurrection, the mustering, and the uprising are true. On that day, the heavens will be split, the stars will fall down, the mountains will be naughted, and this earth will be changed into another earth. Bodies will be spurred forth, and spirits will once again be given control over them. On that day—whose measure is fifty thousand years—the creatures will be kept on the plains of the resurrection. Each person will be made to see his own works. Scales appropriate to this task will be set up, but these scales will not be similar to other scales. Through them, the creatures will know the measures of their own works, both the good and the bad. *Whoso has done an atom's weight of good shall see it, and whoso has done an atom's weight of evil shall see it* [99:7–8].

One group will be taken to paradise without the accounting, while another group will be questioned at the accounting. Then the creatures will be made to cross over the Path. This is something stretched over the floor of hell, sharper than a sword and thinner than a hair. The creatures will travel across in different ways. One group will fly like birds, another group will run like charging horses, and another group will fall on their heads into hell—*a party in the Garden, and a party in the Blaze* [42:7].

Likewise, paradise and hell are true. In hell are found descending degrees and various types of pains and punishments. The greatest punishment belongs to the truth-concealers, who will remain there forever and be veiled from the encounter with God. *No indeed, but upon that day they shall be veiled from their Lord* [83:15]. In the same way, ascending degrees and pleasures are found in paradise, but the greatest pleasure for its people is the encounter with God. *Upon that day faces shall be radiant, gazing upon their Lord* [75:22–23]. On that day the prophets will intercede, the friends of God will intercede, and every person with faith will have an intercession. May God preserve the whole community of Muhammad—upon him be blessings and peace—from the disgrace and humiliation of that day! May He give them the success to seek His good pleasure!

This amount is sufficient for the science of faith. After this, God willing, we will begin the science of practice. Reliance is upon the Alive, the Self-subsistent.

THE SECOND EASY ROAD

On the Rules of Ablution and Purity

It contains five road-clearings.

THE FIRST ROAD-CLEARING

On the Excellence of Purity, the Distinction between Outward and Inward Purity, and the Various Degrees of Purity

Know that God says in His uncreated Speech, *[Therein are] men who love to purify themselves—and God loves those who purify themselves* [9:108]. Mustafa said, "The religion is built upon cleanliness." He also said, "The key to the ritual prayer is purity, and the key to the Garden is the ritual prayer." What greater excellence could a thing have than that it be the key to everlasting felicity?

Here you should know that purity is of two types—purity of the body from defilements and filthiness, which is called "outward purity;" and purity of the soul from the darkness of disobedient acts, filthy beliefs, and blameworthy character traits, which is called "inward purity."

Outward purity without inward purity has a low degree, and no attention will be paid to it at the resurrection. On that day the property of the outward will become inward, and the property of the inward outward. Attention will be paid to [what is today] the inward. The divine revelation alludes to this point where it says, *Upon the day the secrets are put to the test* [86:9].

Wait till God lifts the coverings
from the hearts—
See a world of beauty,
in truth full of sorrow.

Know that in the view of the verifiers of this Community—the gnostics who know the mysteries of the Reality—purity has five levels.

The first level is purity of the outward body from defilements, filthiness, and excretions. The Shariah has prescribed it for both the common people and the elect of the Community. Achieving it depends upon water and earth.

The second level is purity of the seven organs from acts of disobedience and things to be avoided according to the Shariah. Achieving it depends upon abstinence and temperance. This is the furthest degree attained by the common people.

The third level is purity of the brain from corrupt imaginings and ruinous fancies. This is achieved through wisdom—not the wisdom that is well-known among the creatures, but rather the wisdom mentioned in the verse, *Whoso is given wisdom has been given much good* [2:269].

The fourth level is purity of the spirit from destructive attributes, blameworthy character traits, and false beliefs. This purity derives from the science of true knowledge and god-wariness. This is the furthest level of the elect.

The fifth level is purity of the heart from the darknesses of attending to anything other than God. This purity is achieved through *tawḥīd*, sincerity, and love. This is the level of the elect of the elect. Their attribute is this: *They desire His face* [6:52].

Many are the needy in this world—
I need nothing but Thy musky locks.

Say: "Surely my ritual prayer, my sacrifice, my life, and my death belong to God, the Lord of the worlds" [6:162].

Whatever holds you back from the way—
Let it be truth-concealing or faith!
Whatever keeps you back from the Friend—
Let it be ugly or beautiful!

They are called "those brought near." Their place is the highest of the high. *No indeed, the book of the pious is in the high things. And what shall teach you what the high things are? A book inscribed, witnessed by those brought near* [83:18–21].

Although these points are not appropriate for this brief work, I have written them to call attention and incite desire, so that the seeker may not be satisfied with the first level of purity.

Know also that outward purity is like the shell of inward purity, and a shell without a kernel is useless. O God, give us success in what Thou lovest and approvest!

THE SECOND ROAD-CLEARING

On the Rules of Relieving and Cleaning Oneself

If a person wants to sit and relieve himself in an open area, he must be hidden from people's eyes. He should not turn his back toward the kiblah, nor should he face the kiblah. He should not sit facing the sun or the moon. He should not urinate in standing water. He should not sit under a tree that has fruit. He should avoid urinating in a place where the ground is hard or the wind is blowing since—God protect us!—the disobedient of this community will suffer chastisement from that. Mustafa said, "The chastisement of the grave is three thirds: a third from urine, a third from backbiting, and a third from slander." The person should not bare his private parts before reaching the place of relieving himself. He should separate from himself anything that has the name of God on it.

If the person should be at home and go into the toilet, first he should put his left foot forward and say, "O God, I seek refuge in Thee from filth and filthy things." When he sits, he should lean on his left leg. When he finishes, he should take one or two steps forward and cough lightly two or three times. He should rub his penis with his left hand and clean himself with the wall or a stone. This is called *istibrā'* [cleansing oneself of urine].

When it is necessary to do *istinjā'* [cleansing oneself of excrement], the person must first make the stones ready. Then he should lift up a stone with the left hand and put it on a place that is not defiled. He takes it and moves it around, cleaning away the impurity from the beginning to the end of the anus. Then he should take a second stone and do the same thing from the end of the anus to the beginning. He should keep using stones until he is certain that no impurity remains. The number of the stones should be odd—three, or five, or seven. Mustafa—God's blessings be upon him—said, "He who cleans himself with stones should use an odd number."

If the person uses water, he should pour with his right hand and wash with his left, until he can feel that no trace of impurity remains.

When the person comes out of the place of purification, he should say, "Praise belongs to God, who has taken out from me what harms me and left within me what benefits me. O God, purify my heart from hypocrisy and protect my private parts from indecencies!"

If the person combines stones and water, that is better, for this verse was revealed concerning the people of the mosque of Qubā: *Men who love to purify themselves—and God loves those who purify themselves* [9:108]. Mustafa said to them, "What purity is this that God praises you for?" They replied, "We combine stones and water." If both are not available, the person limits himself to one of them. God is He from whom help is sought, and He it is who is relied upon!

THE THIRD ROAD-CLEARING

On the Rules of the Minor Ablution

When the person finishes purifying himself after going to the toilet, he makes the minor ablution. First he washes his hands three times and says, "In the name of God, the Merciful, the Compassionate," for it has been reported that when a person says "In the name of God" at the beginning of the ablution, his whole body will be cleansed of sin. Then he says,

> "In the name of God" be upon the water, and praise belongs to God for the religion of Islam. O God, I ask Thee good fortune and blessing, and I seek refuge in Thee from misfortune and destruction. *My Lord, I seek refuge in Thee from the goadings of the satans. I seek refuge in Thee, my Lord, lest they be present with me* [23:97–98].

Then he puts water in his mouth and washes it, three times. This is called *maḍmaḍa*. He does this vigorously unless he is fasting. He says, "O God, give me to drink from the pool of the Prophet, upon whom be peace. O God, help me recite Thy book and remember Thee much."

Then he takes water into his nose three times. This is called *istinshāq*. He says, "O God, refresh me with the fresh fragrance of the Garden, and from the smoke of the Fire—keep me far away!"

Then he makes this intention in his heart: "I will now cease speaking and make the ritual prayer permissible for myself." If he says this with his tongue, that is even better. Then he takes water to his face and washes it three times in its length and width. The length of the face is from the place where hair grows on the top of the head to the end of the chin; the width is from one ear to the other. If he has dense and thick whiskers, it is permissible to wet them only on the outside. But if they are sparse, he should run his fingers between them and make the water reach between the hairs. Then he says, "O God, whiten my face with Thy light on the day Thy friends' faces are whitened, and blacken not my face with Thy darknesses on the day Thy enemies' faces are blackened."

Then he washes his right hand as far as the elbow three times and says, "O God, give me my book in my right hand and call me to account with an easy accounting." In the same way he washes his left hand to the elbow three times and says, "O God, I seek refuge from Thee lest Thou givest me my book in my left hand or behind my back." If he washes to the upper arm, that is better, since a hadith says, "On the day of resurrection, the hands and feet of my community will be white from the effects of the ablution."

Then he touches his head. The minimum is that two or three hairs should become wet. The best is that he should join the tips of the fingers of the right hand with the tips of the fingers of the left hand and draw them from the front of the head to the end of the neck and then bring them back. He should do this three times. He says, "O God, wrap me in Thy mercy, send down upon me some of Thy blessings, and shade me under the shadow of Thy Throne on the day when there is no shadow but Thy shadow."

Then he rubs both ears, on the outside and inside, three times with new water, putting his forefingers inside the holes of his ears and turning his thumbs around the outside of his ears. He says, "O God, allow me to hear the caller to the pious." Then he rubs his neck and says, "O God, I seek refuge in Thee from the chains and the fetters."

Then he washes his right foot three times. He rubs between his toes with his left hand. He begins with the small toe on the right foot, and he ends with the small toe on the left foot. He says, "O God, fix my feet upon the Path on the day when the feet upon it shake." Then he washes his left foot three times and says, "O God, I seek refuge with Thee lest Thou makest my foot slip on the Path on the day when Thou makest the feet of the hypocrites slip." He brings the water to the middle of his shank, on the basis of the hadith that I have already related. "On the day of resurrection my community will be white in face and limbs from the effects of the ablution."

Then he looks toward the sky and says,

O God, I bear witness that
there is no god but God alone, who has no associate.
To Him belongs the kingdom
and to Him belongs the praise [64:1].
He gives life and He makes to die [7:158],
and He is Alive and does not die.
In His hand is the good,
and He is powerful over everything [5:120].
And I bear witness that Muhammad
is His servant and His messenger.
Glory be to Thee, O God,
and Thine is the praise.
There is no god but Thou.

I have done evil and I have wronged myself.
I ask forgiveness from Thee
and I turn to Thee,
so forgive me and turn toward me.
Surely Thou art the Turning, the Compassionate [2:128].
O God, make me one of those who turn,
make me one of those who purify themselves,
make me one of Thy upright servants,
make me patient and grateful,
and make me remember Thee much
and glorify Thee morning and evening.

It has been reported that, if a person makes an ablution in this manner and in this order, the eight doors of paradise will be opened for him and it will be said, "Enter from any door you like." A seal will be placed on his ablution and it will be taken to heaven as far as the lower side of the Throne. Until the resurrection, it will glorify God, declare Him one, and call Him holy. The reward for this will be written in his book.

It should be known that six things in all this are mandatory—making the intention, washing the face, washing the hands as far as the elbows, rubbing the head a little, washing the feet, and keeping the order. Several things are reprehensible and should be avoided—using a great deal of water, washing any part more than three times, speaking in the midst of the ablution, scattering water from the hands, slapping the face, and making an ablution with water that has been warmed by the sun. This last is reprehensible medically—and God knows best.

An Allusion in the Road-Clearing

When the person finishes the ablution and aims to say the ritual prayer, he should turn away from all things to the extent possible. He should make his heart present and be aware of the tremendousness and majesty of God. He should understand that he will be talking intimately with the Sultan of sultans. Since he has purified the parts of himself where the creatures look with outward water, he should also purify the place where God looks—which is called the "heart"—with the water of turning toward God, repenting, and asking forgiveness. If he does not do this, he is like someone who wants to bring the sultan into his home. He cleans the outside of the house, but he leaves the inside of the house—the place where the sultan will sit—full of filth. We seek refuge in God from that! "God looks not at your forms, nor at your works, but He looks at your hearts."

THE FOURTH ROAD-CLEARING

On the Rules and Method of the Major Ablution

When the person wants to make the major ablution, first he washes away any impurity that may be on his body. Then he performs the minor ablution in the manner explained. However, he refrains from washing his feet, so that water will not be wasted, and he washes them at the end. During the major ablution, he avoids touching his private part with his hand. If his hand touches it, he starts again with the minor ablution. He pours water three times on his right side, three times on his left side, and three times on his head. He rubs wherever his hand reaches so that the water will touch the space between every hair.

Only two things are mandatory in the major ablution—making the intention and wetting the whole body. For men, the ablution becomes obligatory for two things—the emergence of semen, whether in sleep or wakefulness, and the entrance of the head of the penis into the vulva. Other major ablutions, such as the major ablution of Friday or a festival, the major ablution of a truth-concealer who becomes a Muslim, the major ablution of a madman who comes back to himself, and so on, are all sunnah. And God knows best.

THE FIFTH ROAD-CLEARING

On the Tayammum *and the* Masḥ

When water is unavailable to the person because he looked for it but could not find it; some obstacle stands between him and the water, such as a wild animal or an enemy; someone is holding him back; his body has a wound such that he fears that if water touches it, he will be harmed; he is ill, and because of his great weakness and incapacity he cannot touch his body with water; water is nearby, but he fears that he himself or his companion will go thirsty; or there is water, but it belongs to someone who will not sell it except at more than its price—then he should wait until the time for the ritual prayer arrives. He looks for pure earth, such that dust rises up from it. He strikes his palms on the earth with his fingers joined together. He makes the intention, "I am making the prayers permissible to myself." In striking the earth, the dust of the earth should touch the skin. This is achieved through striking it once, for the width of the face is not greater than the width of the two hands. Then he wipes his whole face once with both hands. Then he takes the ring off his finger and strikes the earth once more, while joining together the ends of his thumbs and keeping his fingers apart. He places the back of the fingers of his right hand on the front of the fingers of his left hand such that the sides of the fingers do not extend beyond the width of the forefinger on either side. He passes the left hand from where he has placed it over the back of his forearm to the elbow. Then he passes the front of his left hand along the front of his forearm to the wrist. He passes the inside of his left thumb over the outside of his right thumb. Then he wipes the left hand in the same manner. Then he rubs his palms together while putting his fingers between each other.

The point of all this trouble is to take with one striking enough dust to reach the elbows. If the person is not able to do this, he may make two strikes or three.

Every obligatory ritual prayer needs a separate *tayammum*. Once he has performed an obligatory prayer with one *tayammum*, he can make as many supererogatory prayers as he likes.

It is permissible to wipe one's boots [with water instead of removing them] once in a full day, or, for three days and three nights on a journey. The person must wear boots that are perfectly pure. And God knows best.

THE THIRD EASY ROAD

On the Rules and Requirements of the Ritual Prayer

It contains four road-clearings.

THE FIRST ROAD-CLEARING

On the Excellence of the Obligatory Ritual Prayers, which are called the "Prescribed Ritual Prayers"

Know that Mustafa—God bless him and give him peace—said, "The ritual prayer is the foundation of the religion. If someone leaves it, he has destroyed the religion." He also said, "The first act of the servants that will be called to account is the ritual prayer. If a servant is found to have all of the prayers, they will be accepted along with all his works. If he is found not to have them all, they will be thrown in his face along with all his works."

Know that the ritual prayer is the foundation of being a Muslim. It is the master and leader of works. The Presence of Divinity loves no work more than it, for it has been reported that God has made obligatory for His servants nothing more beloved to Him after *tawḥīd* than the ritual prayer. If He loved something else more, He would make the higher plenum—who are those brought near to His Presence—busy themselves with it. But they are all busy with the ritual prayer—some are standing, some are bowing, some are prostrating themselves, and some are sitting in witness. May God place us and you among the people of the ritual prayer, and may He make us worthy of intimate discourse with Him! Surely He is Forgiving, Loving, Kind to the servants.

THE SECOND ROAD-CLEARING

On Determing the Number of Cycles of the Prescribed Ritual Prayers, and on Determining the Recommended Voluntary Prayers and their Excellence

Know that the Creator has brought together the five times for the ritual prayer in this verse of the eternal Koran. *So Glory be to God when you enter the night and you enter the morning; His is the praise in the heavens and the earth, alike in the afternoon and the noonday* [30:17–18].

The earliest time for the noon ritual prayer is when the sun passes the middle of the heaven. This is called "decline from the meridian." The latest time for it is when a thing's shadow is slightly longer than the thing itself, and this is also the first time for the afternoon ritual prayer. The latest time for the afternoon ritual prayer is when the sun sets, and this is also the earliest time for the sunset ritual prayer. Its latest time is when the evening glow disappears from the western horizon, and this is also the earliest time for the night prayer. Its latest time is dawn, and this is the earliest time for the morning prayer. Its latest time is when the sun rises.

The morning ritual prayer has two cycles, while the recommended voluntary prayer before the obligatory prayer also has two cycles. Its excellence is great, since Mustafa—God's blessings be upon him—said, "The two cycles of the dawn are better than this world and everything within it."

The number of cycles in the noon prayer is four. The recommended voluntary prayer has six cycles, four before the obligatory prayer and two after it. Concerning its excellence, Abū Hurayra (God be pleased with him!) relates that Mustafa (God's blessings be upon him!) said, "When someone performs four cycles of ritual prayer after the sun passes the meridian, with a good recitation, bowing, and prostration, seventy thousand angels perform the prayer along with him and ask forgiveness for him until night."

The obligatory cycles of the afternoon ritual prayer are four, while its recommended voluntary prayer is four cycles before the obligatory prayer. Abū Hurayra relates that Mustafa said, "God have mercy on a servant who prays four cycles before the afternoon ritual prayer."

The obligatory cycles of the sunset prayer are three. Its recommended voluntary prayer is two cycles after the obligatory prayer. Concerning its excellence, Ibn ʿAbbās commented on the verse *Glorify thy Lord at night and at the ends of the prostrations* [50:40] by saying that this means two cycles after the sunset prayer.

The obligatory cycles of the night prayer are four. Its recommended voluntary prayer is two cycles, according to one report, and four cycles, according to another.

As for the *witr* ritual prayer, that is a confirmed sunnah. Abū Hurayra relates, "Mustafa counselled me not to sleep without a *witr*." Anas ibn Mālik relates that Mustafa used to perform three cycles of the *witr* ritual prayer after the night ritual prayer. In the first cycle, he would recite the sura *Glorify the name of thy Lord the Most High* [87], in the second, *Say: O you truth-concealers* [sura 109], and in the third, *Say: He is God, One* [sura 111] and the two refuges [suras 113 and 114].

It is not appropriate to perform any ritual prayers after this. However, people who have undertaken the duty of *tahajjud* at night and want to say the *witr* at the beginning of the night must recite two cycles of prayer, while seated, after the *witr*. In the first cycle they should recite the sura *When the earth shakes with her shaking* [99] and in the second cycle *Say: O you truth-concealers* [sura 109]. Then, when they wake up from sleep, they can perform as many ritual prayers as they like. At the end, they should perform one cycle of *witr*. Mustafa used to perform these two [seated] cycles. And *praise belongs to God, Lord of the worlds* [1:1].

THE THIRD ROAD-CLEARING

On How to Perform the Outward Acts of the Ritual Prayer

Having finished with the preliminary steps—the minor ablution, purification from uncleanliness, purification of clothing and place, and covering the private parts from the navel to the knee—the person stands up straight. He turns toward the kiblah and keeps his feet apart to the space of four open fingers. He turns his head downward and looks at the place of prostration. If he closes his eyes, that is appropriate, since a group of the people of abstinence have done that. In order to fend off Satan, he recites the sura *I seek refuge in the Lord of mankind* [114]. Then he makes this intention in his heart, although if he wants to he can voice it with the tongue. "I make the intention to perform the obligatory noon ritual prayer at its proper time, for God's sake." He should keep this intention in his mind until he finishes with the *takbīr* [saying "God is greater" to begin the ritual prayer]. Then he lifts up his hands to his shoulders so that his palms are level with his shoulders, his thumbs are level with the lobes of his ears, and the tips of his fingers are level with the holes of his ears. Thus he will have combined all the different reports. When his hands are settled in this place, he says, "*Allāhu akbar*" ["God is greater"]. He should not draw this out, such that he adds a *wāw* to the name Allāh [pronouncing it *Allāhū*] or an *alif* [to *akbar*], as if it were *akbār*.

Then he places his right hand on top of his left hand above the navel and below the chest. He places his right index and middle fingers on the back of his left forearm and holds his left wrist with the ring and little fingers of his right hand.

After "God is greater" he should say, "Greatly, and praise belongs to God fully, and glory be to God in the morning and the evening." Then he should say,

> *I have turned my face to Him who originated the heavens and the earth, having pure faith, submitted, and I am not one of those who associate others with God* [6:79]. *Surely my ritual prayer, my sacrifice, my life, and my death belong to God, the Lord of the worlds. No associate has He, and I am the first of those who submit* [6:162–63].

Then he says, "I seek refuge in God from Satan the accursed," and he recites the Fatiha [sura 1]. He should take care in its letters and its double consonants. He should preserve the difference between *ḍād* and *ẓā'*. Then he says, "Amen." He should not join the "amen" to the "and not those who are astray" [at the end of the Fatiha]. Then he recites another sura or another verse.

In the morning ritual prayer and the first two cycles of the sunset and night prayer, he recites all this aloud, unless he is praying behind an imam. In all the other cycles, he recites silently.

In the morning prayer, he should recite a sura from among the long *mufaṣṣal* chapters, such as Qāf [50] or Tabārak [67], and in the sunset prayer from the short *mufaṣṣal* chapters. In the noon prayer [he should recite short passages] such as *By the heaven, possessor of constellations* [sura 85] or the Footstool Verse [2:254].

Then he bows and says "*Allāhu akbar*," drawing out the saying of this until he is fully bowed. He places his two hands on his knees. He extends his fingers on his shins so that they face the kiblah and are spread apart. He flattens his back as if his neck, his back, and his head were a single board. He keeps his elbows away from his sides and says three times, "Glory be to my Lord the Tremendous." After the bowing he stands up straight, becomes still, and says, "God hears the one who praises Him. Our Lord, to Thee belongs a praise that fills the heavens and fills the earth and fills everything else that Thou willest."

Then he says "*Allāhu akbar*" and prostrates himself, pulling out the saying of this until he is fully prostrated. He places his knees, his palms, and his bare forehead on the ground. He must first put his knees on the ground, then his hands, then his nose and forehead. He keeps his elbows away from his sides and says three times, "Glory be to my Lord the Highest." Then he says "*Allāhu akbar*" and comes up from the prostration, sitting on his left foot. He places his hands on his thighs and says, "My Lord, forgive me, have mercy on me, provide for me, guide me, give me well-being, and pardon me." Then he makes a second prostration just like the one mentioned.

After the prostration he sits back lightly. This is called the "sitting of rest." Then he stands up and performs another cycle, like the first cycle. When he finishes the second prostration of this cycle, he sits and makes the witnessing. He places his hands on his thighs and, if his juridical school is Shāfiʿī, he makes the fingers of his right hand into a ball, except for the index finger, which he extends. If his juridical school is Ḥanafī, he extends all his fingers. When he reaches the expression of *tawḥīd* [the words, "There is no god but God"], at "but God" he points with the index finger while he continues reciting the greetings until the formula, "Bless Muhammad."

During the second recitation of the greetings, he brings his two feet out from under him and sits on his left buttock. He blesses Muhammad and his household. Then he says, "Just as Thou hast blessed Abraham and the household of Abraham. And give benedictions to Muhammad and the household of Muhammad just as Thou hast given benedictions to Abraham and the household of Abraham. Surely Thou art Praiseworthy, Glorious."

Then, at the end of the greetings, he recites the supplications that are related from Mustafa—God bless him and give him peace. He should recite regularly the supplication that Mustafa taught Abū Bakr Ṣiddīq to say at the end of the greetings. "O God, I have wronged myself with much wrong, and none forgives sins but Thou. So forgive me with a forgiveness from Thee and show compassion toward me. Surely Thou art the Forgiving, the Compassionate."

Then he says, "Peace be upon you, and God's mercy and blessings," and he turns his face to the right so that someone behind him would see half his face. In the same way he gives peace to the left. He makes the intention of completing the ritual prayer, and he makes the intention of giving peace to the angels and the faithful who are on his right and his left sides.

A Hint that Comprehends Many Benefits

The person should avoid those things that are forbidden and reprehensible in the ritual prayer. He should not make for the ritual prayer at the time of hunger, thirst, anger, the need to go to the toilet, or an occupation of the heart that prevents presence. He should not put his two feet together [while standing in the ritual prayer], an act that is called *ṣafd*. He should not lift up one leg, an act called *ṣafn*. A report tells us, "The Messenger of God forbade *ṣafd* and *ṣafn*."

He should not look around, scratch his body, yawn, or play with his hair or his beard. He should not blow on the earth at the time of prostration. He should not cross his fingers. He should not lean back against anything. In short, he should observe courtesy—after all, in whose presence is he standing? "If the one in prayer knew with whom he is discoursing intimately, he would not become distracted."

In the form of the ritual prayer just described, only twelve things are obligatory—the intention, the first *takbīr*, standing, reciting the Fatiha, bowing, prostrating oneself, becoming still in the prostration, straightening up after it, witnessing at the end, sitting during the witnessing, blessing Mustafa, and giving peace. When the person has put this form into practice, his ritual prayer is considered by the exoteric jurists to be correct, in the sense that he is protected from the sword. But, in the view of the verifiers and the wayfarers, this amount is not sufficient. On the contrary, they hold that a correct ritual prayer must be acceptable to the Presence of Divinity and take the person to felicity after death. God gives success, and from Him help is sought.

THE FOURTH ROAD-CLEARING

On the Mysteries and Conditions of the Inward Dimensions of the Ritual Prayer

Know that the ritual prayer has a spirit and a body. The body of the ritual prayer is the outward activity made up of pillars and sensory form. The spirit of the ritual prayer is presence and humility. Just as a body without a spirit has no value, so also a ritual prayer without presence and humility has no worth. The fruit of a ritual prayer with humility and meekness is prosperity, just as the Koran says, *Prosperous are those who have faith, those who have humility in their ritual prayer* [23:2]. The fruit of a ritual prayer with forgetfulness and without presence and collectedness is woe, just as the divine revelation has explained. *Woe to those who perform the ritual prayer and in the prayer are heedless* [107:4]. Mustafa said, "If a heart is not present in a ritual prayer, God does not look at the prayer." He also said, "Many are the servants who perform the ritual prayer, but for them no more than one-sixth or one-tenth of it is written. As much of the servant's prayer is written down as he grasps"—that is, as much of it as is done with presence. Ḥasan Baṣrī said, "When the heart is not present in a ritual prayer, that prayer is closer to hastening punishment [than to yielding reward]."

In short, every fortunate and prosperous person whose spirit has caught a scent of the severity of *We shall advance upon what work they have done and make it scattered dust* [25:23] will want his ritual prayer to be taken to heaven, to be looked upon with the gaze of God's acceptance, and to be personified as a luminous condition in the world of the dominion. Hence, he will dedicate his whole self to establishing presence and, to the extent possible, free himself from the dominating power of Satan. With the pegs of god-wariness and the lock of self-examination, he will shut the doors of his heart to satanic whispering.

As soon as a person hears the call to prayer, he should think of the blast on the Trumpet and the call at the resurrection. He should leave aside whatever he is busy with, rise up in happiness, and put on the belt of servanthood. He should know for certain that, on the Day of the Presentation [in the next world], the group that heard the call [to prayer] in this world with happiness and joy will hear the call of mercy and rejoicing.

Then he sets out to purify himself. He should know that outward purity is like the skin and sheath for inward purity. He removes defilement and filth from the outward dimension, which is the place where creatures look, with earth and water. At the same time, he must wash the opacity and darkness of disobedient acts and base character traits from the inward dimension, which is the locus of Lordship's gaze, with the water of repentance and asking forgiveness.

Then he covers his private parts. The meaning of covering the private parts is that he should conceal what is ugly and blameworthy in himself from the view of people. The spirit and mystery of this meaning is that he should conceal the ugly qualities and disgraceful attributes of his inward dimension from the view of God. But how can anything be hidden from Him, since *He knows the thoughts within the breasts* [57:6]? Hence, the way is to make a curtain through repentance, fear, embarrassment, and shame and to let that down over one's own disgraceful qualities. The person must stand before that Presence like a runaway servant who is embarrassed and ashamed before his master.

O you who are fed up with yourself—
  that is "hunger"!
O you who are bent double in regret—
  that is "bowing in prayer"!

O faithful, turn to God in sincere repentance. It may be that your Lord will acquit you of your evil deeds [66:8].

Then he turns his face toward the kiblah and away from all other directions. The meaning of this is that he turns away from both worlds. He is saying farewell to his own soul and his own caprice—or rather, to every engendered thing. Say a prayer in farewell, and look at the beauty of this verse. *Whoever denies false gods and has faith in God has laid hold of the firmest handle* [2:256].

With two kiblahs, you can't walk straight
  on *tawḥīd*'s path—
Choose either the Friend's approval
  or your own caprice.

Then he says *Allāhu akbar*. The meaning of *Allāhu akbar* is that God is greater than anything that enters into the fancy and imagination and anything that fits into the creature's rational faculty. "Glory be to Him who alone knows His tremendousness!"

Whatever you set up
  with the senses, imagination, and reason,
the stone of futility knocks down,
  thrown by His magnificence.

Here he should search within his inward self—*Your soul suffices you today as an accounter against you* [17:14]—to find anything greater than God. If God is greater in his view than all things, the mark of this is that he obeys God the most. But if he obeys caprice—God forbid!—then caprice is greater in his view. Hence, he has lied in saying "God is greater." *Have you seen him who has taken his caprice to be his god?* [45:23].

O you whose caprices have stirred up caprice!
O you whose gods have displeased God!

Here, there is tremendous danger unless God should support him through His mercy.

Then he says, *I have turned my face to Him who originated the heavens and the earth* [6:79]. The meaning is the same as was said about turning toward the kiblah. He must exert effort so that the face of his heart is turned only toward the threshold of the holiness of Divinity. Otherwise, he will have uttered a lie. A prayer that begins with a lie will have no worth or weight at the plain of the resurrection. *On the day of resurrection, We shall not assign to their deeds any weight* [18:105]. Many a deluded worshiper will suffer loss on the day when the curtain is lifted from works!

Then he says, "I seek refuge in God from the accursed Satan." Here he seeks refuge in God from Satan, who is his enemy and is constantly looking for opportunities to hold him back in some way from the threshold of the Eternal Refuge.

Then, by way of seeking good fortune and an auspicious omen through the name of God, he says, "In the name of God, the Merciful, the Compassionate." From the name, he should understand the Named. He should know that everything is from Him and in Him.

Then he says, *Praise belongs to God* [1:1] in gratitude for His boundless blessings. In *Lord of the worlds* [1:1], he should see all creatures in need of Him at every instant for existence, subsistence, and order. Once again, in *the Merciful, the Compassionate* [1:2], he should witness the varieties of His kindness and mercy toward the servants so that the motivation of hope appears in his heart. In *Master of the Day of Judgment* [1:3] he makes present the magnificence, inaccessibility, and independence of God so that the motivation of fear shows its head. Through this fear and hope he will be delivered from the severity of God on the day of accounting and recompense.

In *Thee alone we worship* [1:4], he should renew his sincerity and seek to be free of [taking] *his caprice to be his god* [45:23]. *O my people, surely I am free of everything that you associate with God* [6:78]. In *From Thee alone we seek help* [1:4], he should seek help and assistance from Him in his own worship and sincerity. He should know for certain that there is no power against disobeying God without God's protecting him, and no strength to obey God without God's giving him success.

When he finishes declaring God's unity, praising Him, calling Him holy, renewing his sincerity, and seeking help, he is in the presence of the Most Generous of the generous. Then he makes a request through *Guide us on the straight path* [1:5]. He asks for his most important need. What is that? Wayfaring on a path that brings about the arrival at God. He remembers the prophets and friends of

God who were singled out for this blessing and honor. He asks for their companionship—*The path of those whom Thou hast blessed* [1:6]. He seeks refuge from the companionship of the outsiders who were deprived of this blessing—like Jews, Christians, and other truth-concealers—*not those against whom Thou art wrathful, nor those who are astray* [1:7]. Then he asks that his supplication be answered by saying "Amen."

In the bowing and prostration, he calls to mind his own lowliness, contemptibleness, and abasement before God's magnificence and tremendousness.

In the same way, in each pillar [of the ritual prayer] and in every glorification and word, he should understand what is appropriate. He should not become neglectful of the kernel and spirit and should not be satisfied with the shell and form. For the profit of the form of the ritual prayer is simply that it keeps the sword away from the neck. But the ritual prayer that is worthy of being a key to paradise—since "The key to the Garden is the ritual prayer"—stands beyond these specific pillars and conditions. An example of this was given to call attention and incite desire, but this brief treatise cannot carry more than this. *God speaks the truth, and He guides on the way* [33:4].

THE FOURTH EASY ROAD

On the Rules and Secrets of Fasting

It contains three road-clearings.

THE FIRST ROAD-CLEARING

On the Excellence of Fasting

Know that Mustafa—God bless him and give him peace—related that God says, "Every good deed will be rewarded with from ten to seven hundred the like of it, except fasting, since it belongs to Me and I will recompense it." He also said, "By that God in whose hand is my soul! God finds the odor of the mouth of the fasting person sweeter than you find the fragrance of musk." The person who keeps the fast has been promised the encounter with God, which is the greatest of felicities. It is well known that the Prophet said, "The fasting person has two joys—a joy when he breaks his fast and a joy when he encounters his Lord." It has also been reported that when the month of Ramadan arrives, the doors of paradise are opened and the doors of hell are closed. The satans are put in chains, and a caller calls out, "O seeker of good, hurry, since this is your time! O seeker of evil, stay back, since this is not your place!"

THE SECOND ROAD-CLEARING

On the Secret of Fasting
and the Explanation of its Degrees

Know that the goal in fasting is for the veil of appetite and anger to be lifted from the heart's eye so that the heart may see the mystery of the dominion of heaven and earth. For the human spirit comes from the world of dominion, while the satans keep it back from union with the spirits of the higher plenum, conversation with the inhabitants of the palisades of holiness, and intimate whispering with the Presence of Eternity. Mustafa expressed this meaning as follows: "If the satans did not swarm around the hearts of the children of Adam, they would look at the dominion of the heavens." The instruments used by the satans in leading astray and misguiding human beings are anger and appetite.

Could Adam have been brought down
  from the Garden
had the peacock and serpent
  not guided Iblis?
Your anger and appetite
  are peacock and serpent—
The first helps the devil,
  the second the soul.

Through hunger the substance of anger and appetite is weakened. Thereby Satan becomes thin, since "The satan of the person of faith is emaciated." When Satan has no instrument or weapon left, he cannot whisper. The Seal of the Prophets—the Merciful's blessings be upon him—explained this meaning as follows: "Satan runs in the child of Adam like blood. So constrict his running places through hunger and thirst." Hence Jesus—God's blessings be upon him—counseled his apostles by saying, "Keep your bellies hungry, your bodies naked, and your livers thirsty, so that perhaps your hearts may see God."

The cause of anger and appetite
  is a bite of bread,
the blight of mind and wisdom
  is a bite of bread.

However, excessive hunger also causes harm. It carries the danger of madness, corruption of the brain, and other illnesses. In short, a middle course is desirable in all things. The seeker must always keep "The best of affairs is their middlemost" before his eyes. "Both sides of moderation in affairs are blameworthy." This alerts you to a universal law. And from God, aid is sought.

Know that, in the view of the verifiers, fasting has three degrees.

The common people fast by refraining from food, drink, and sexual intercourse from morning to the sunset prayer.

The elect fast by preserving the seven bodily members from sins and acts of disobedience. They prevent the tongue from lying, obscenity, and backbiting; the eye from looking with caprice and appetite; the ear from listening to nonsense, obscenity, idle talk, and their like; and the hand, foot, and other members from acts made unlawful and forbidden by the Shariah. The divine revelation gives news of this meaning. *The hearing, the sight, the heart—all these shall be questioned* [17:36]. Mustafa—God bless him—said, "Five things break the fast of the faster—lying, backbiting, slander, ungodly oaths, and looking with appetite."

The elect of the elect fast by examining their thoughts and preventing their innermost consciousness from paying attention to anything other than God. These are the people of poverty, and their capital and provisions for wayfaring on the path to God are nothingness.

God's Being inclines
  only toward not-being—
In this path, take not-being
  as your provision.

God has bought from the faithful their selves and their possessions in order that they should have the Garden [9:111]. I have sold myself at the auction of "I don't care" and bought Thee! As long as an atom of them remains, they will not have bestowed the degree of beauty upon the perfection of fasting.

A man of perfection
  walked the path of annihilation
and departed from existence
  like dust.
A thread of his being
  went along with him—
in poverty's eye,
  that thread was an infidel's belt.

When the perfection of annihilation becomes their ready cash and no name or mark remains for them, the secret of "When the poor man is complete, he is God" comes out from behind the curtain of inaccessibility. "When someone is destroyed in God, God has to give him a substitute."

THE THIRD ROAD-CLEARING

On the Obligations and Prophetic Customs of Fasting

Know that fasting in the month of Ramadan has six obligations.

[The first is] observation of and looking for the moon, so that it becomes known whether the month is twenty-nine or thirty days. Mustafa—God bless him and give him peace—said, "Fast, having seen [the moon], and break the fast, having seen. If you are prevented from seeing, then count thirty days." In seeing the moon of Ramadan, it is permissible to rely on the word of a single just person. In contrast, for seeing the crescent moon of Shawwal [marking the end of the fast], two just people must have been heard to give witness, or else precaution demands that the fast be performed. If a person hears from someone whom he considers a reliable truth-teller that he has seen the moon, then the fast is obligatory for him, even if the Shariite judge does not rule it so.

The second obligation is the intention. Each night the person must make the intention and remember that this is the fasting of the month of Ramadan and that it is an incumbent obligation. It is not allowable to make the intention to perform the obligatory fast during the daytime, unless it be as a supererogatory act. Mustafa used to go into the house and ask, "Is there anything for me to eat?" If there was, they would bring it for him. If not, he would say, "Then I am fasting."

The third obligation is that he must not allow anything to go inside him intentionally. If something goes inside unintentionally, such as an insect that flies in, or the dust of the road, or the water of rinsing [the mouth during the ablution] that splashes into the throat, that does no harm. In the same way, bloodletting, cupping, anointing the eyes with collyrium, and putting a cleaning rod in the ear do not nullify the fast. If the person should eat something in the morning or evening in doubt, and later it becomes apparent that he did so after the beginning of the morning or before the setting of the sun, then he has to make up for the fast.

The fourth obligation is that he should avoid sexual intercourse. This is defined as the head of the penis being covered by the vulva. If he should perform sexual intercourse in forgetfulness, his fast is not nullified. If he should have intercourse at night or have a wet dream and then make the major ablution during the day, that is permissible.

The fifth obligation is that he must not aim in any way to have semen come out from him. He should avoid kissing and embracing, unless he is someone who has control over the soul that commands to evil, or is old or weak.

The sixth obligation is that he must not intentionally vomit. If he should vomit unintentionally, the fast is not nullified.

The prophetic customs of fasting are also six—delaying the morning meal [until the last moment], hurrying to break the fast [at sunset] with a date or water before the ritual prayer, refraining from brushing the teeth after the sun passes the meridian, being generous by giving alms and food, reciting the Koran a great deal, and secluding oneself in the mosque, especially during the last ten days, during which is the Night of Power. Mustafa used to fold up his sleeping clothes during these ten days, and he and his family did not rest from worship, because of watching out for the Night of Power.

The ulama have disagreed on determining the date of the Night of Power. The choice of Imam Shāfiʿī—God be pleased with him—is the night of the twenty-first. The choice of Ibn ʿAbbās—God be pleased with him and his father—is the night of the twenty-seventh. In brief, all the odd nights of the last ten days are likely. Another group among the people of learning hold that the Night of Power is hidden in the whole year. "He who knows and He who tells is God."

The seeker of everlasting felicity must not be satisfied simply with fasting during the month of Ramadan. He must watch over the noble days of the year, such as ʿArafa, ʿĀshūrā, the first ten days of Dhu'l-Hijja, the first ten days of Muharram, the whole of Rajab and Shaʿban, the white days of each month, and Monday and Thursday of each week.

The ulama of the next world's affairs and the possessors of insight say that constantly breaking one's fast, and especially eating twice in the daytime, brings hardness of heart, opens the doors of appetite, and gives birth to bad habits. Hence, at all times one must open the gates to acts of worship and collectedness with the help of fasting, so that its effects may be witnessed in religion and this world. And God bless Muhammad and his pure household.

THE FIFTH EASY ROAD

On Remembrance and Traditional Supplications

It contains three road-clearings.

THE FIRST ROAD-CLEARING

On the Secret of Imparting Remembrance and the Excellence of "There is no god but God"

Know that Mustafa—God's blessings be upon him—said, "The best that I and the prophets before me have said is 'There is no god but God.' " He related that God says, " 'There is no god but God' is My fortress—he who enters it is secure from My chastisement."

The firmly rooted friends of God and those among the ulama who undergo unveiling—God sanctify their spirits—have agreed that these words have a tremendous virtue in lifting veils. They are the lamp in the darkness of human nature, the key to the treasuries of the dominion, and the ladder that arrives at Unity's magnificence. The people of purity have taken the fire of this lamp from the holy soul of Muhammad—God bless him and his household—by means of the spirit of the Commander of the Faithful and the sultan of the gnostics, the lion and friend of God, ʿAlī ibn Abī Ṭālib—God ennoble his face. Because of this secret Mustafa said, "I am the city of knowledge, and ʿAlī is its gate." In the view of the leaders of the path and the masters of wayfaring—God be pleased with them all—it is better known than the breaking of dawn that one day the Commander of the Faithful, ʿAlī ibn Abī Ṭālib, came before Mustafa and said, "O Messenger of God! Show me the nearest path to God, the easiest for God's servants, and the most excellent in God's eyes."

Mustafa said, " 'Alī, you must cling to that which I have reached through the blessing of prophecy."

'Alī said, "What is that, O Messenger of God?"

Mustafa said, "Constant remembrance of God in seclusion."

'Alī said, "Does remembrance have such an excellence, when all people are rememberers?"

Mustafa said, "But 'Alī, the Hour will not come as long as someone on the face of the earth is saying 'Allah, Allah.' "

Then 'Alī asked, "O Messenger of God, how should I remember?"

Mustafa said, "Close your eyes and hear [this sentence] from me three times. Then repeat it, so that I may hear it from you three times."

The shaykhs—God's blessings be upon them—impart remembrance in this same fashion, following the Sunnah of the Messenger of God—God bless him and give him peace.

In reality, through imparting remembrance, the soul of the shaykh exercises governing control from the Eternal Side on the soul of the disciple. To use an example, imparting remembrance resembles a spirit being blown into a body or a sperm drop being cast into a womb. But, in the view of the verifiers, the root of imparting remembrance is the exercise of governing control. As for the form of the remembrance, that is like a container for this meaning. *It belongs not to any mortal that God should speak to him, except by revelation, or from behind a veil, or that He should send a messenger and he reveal whatsoever He will, by His leave; surely He is High, Wise* [42:51].

A remembrance voiced by oneself without its having been imparted by a shaykh who is a possessor of governing control does not have the same profit and benefit as that which is learned from the breath of a living-hearted possessor of governing control. The likeness of this is as follows:

A king takes out of his own quiver a special arrow and gives it to a person in order to guard and honor him. Any subject or servant of the king who meets this person considers it necessary to respect him and does not have the courage to trouble or harm him. Then another person acquires an arrow from the shop of an arrow maker and expects the same thing. By my life, he will be the laughing stock of the intelligent! This pertains to the path of the gnostics and the verifiers.

"The good deeds of the pious are the evil deeds of those brought near to God." The common people of the community have no access to the highest degrees simply by pronouncing the sentence, "There is no god but God," even if they have heard it from a shaykh who is the possessor of governing control. But if they say it out of an untainted conviction, it will give many benefits at the resurrection and will take them to a felicity appropriate to their level.

Nonetheless, the work of the gnostics has another way. Their states cannot be perceived with the weights and measures of rational faculties and fancies. They are called the "Folk of Allah," and their station is God's paradise, where there are no houris, palaces, or honey. "God has a Garden in which are no houris, no castles, no milk, no honey—within it Our Lord discloses Himself laughing."

O seeker of this world,
  you are a hireling.
O lover of paradise,
  you are far from this truth.
O happy with both worlds,
  you have stayed ignorant—
Not having seen the joy of heartache for Him,
  you have an excuse.

The first group are called the "People of the Garden." Their ready cash in heaven's paradise will be the rivers, trees, houris, and castles. Mustafa—God's blessings be upon him—reported about both groups with these words: "Most of the people of the Garden are simpletons, but the high things belong to the possessors of minds."

In the paradise of the spheres,
  all the unripe,
in Thy paradise,
  hell-drinkers.
At Thy door what will I do
  with beautiful and ugly?
When Thou art there,
  what will I do with paradise?

My Lord, apportion for me that I be thankful for Thy blessing wherewith Thou hast blessed me [27:19]!

THE SECOND ROAD-CLEARING

On Transmitted and Traditional Supplications

I begin with the supplication of Mustafa—God's blessings be upon him. He used to recite this in the morning between the obligatory and recommended ritual prayers. Perseverance in it yields and necessitates blessings and felicities in religion and this world. This is the supplication.

O God, I ask Thee for a mercy from Thee
  through which Thou wilt
    guide my heart,
    gather my scattered affairs,
    set straight my disorderly occupations,
    increase my familiarity,
    set right my religion,
    protect my unseen self,
    uplift my visible self,

purify my works,
whiten my face,
inspire me with right conduct,
and guard me from every evil.
O God, I ask Thee for
a faith that will take my heart in hand
and a true certainty,
so that
I may know that nothing afflicts me
but what Thou hast written against me
and I may be satisfied
with what Thou hast apportioned for me.
O God, I ask Thee for
a true faith and a certainty
after which there will be no truth-concealing,
and a mercy
through which I may reach the height of Thy generosity
in this world and the next.
O God, I ask Thee for
the triumph at Thy decree,
the life of the felicitous,
help against enemies,
and companionship with the prophets.
O God, I set down before Thee my need:
My view is weak,
my works fall short,
and I require Thy mercy.
So I ask Thee, O Decreer of affairs and O Healer of breasts!
Just as Thou keepest the seas apart,
keep me apart from
the chastisement of the Burning,
the call for destruction,
and the trial of the grave.
O God,
when there is a good
before which my view falls short,
in which my works are weak,
and which my intention or hope fails to reach—
a good that Thou hast promised to one of Thy creatures,
or a good that Thou art giving to one of Thy servants—
then I beseech Thee for it and I ask Thee for it,
O Lord of the worlds!

O God, make us
guides and guided,
not misguided or misguiders,
a war against Thy enemies
and a peace for Thy friends.
Allow us to love people with Thy love
and have enmity through Thy enmity
toward those of Thy creatures who oppose Thee.
O God, this is my supplication,
and it is Thine to answer.
This is my effort,
and in Thee is trust.
Surely we belong to God
and surely we return to Him [2:156].
There is no power and no strength,
except in God, the High, the Tremendous,
the Master of intense affliction and right command.
We ask Thee for
security on the threatened day
and the Garden on the day of everlastingness
along with
those brought near through witnessing,
those who bow and prostrate themselves,
and those who fulfill the covenants.
Surely Thou art Compassionate and Loving,
and Thou dost what Thou wilt.
Glory be to Him who has clad Himself in might
and has thereby overcome.
Glory be to Him who has put on majesty
and through it given generously.
Glory be to Him other than whom
none is worthy of glorification.
Glory to the Possessor of power
and generosity.
Glory be to the Possessor of munificence
and blessings.
Glory be to Him who counts all things
in His knowledge.
O God, appoint for me
a light in my heart,
a light in my grave,
a light in my hearing,
a light in my sight,

a light in my hair,
a light in my skin,
a light in my beard,
a light in my blood,
a light in my bones,
a light before me,
a light behind me,
a light on my right side,
a light on my left side,
a light above me,
and a light beneath me.
O God, increase me in light,
give me a light,
and appoint for me a light,
through Thy mercy,
O Most Merciful of the merciful!

The following is also a supplication of Mustafa—God bless him. Within it are found the greatest names of God.

O God, I supplicate Thee
with Thy concealed, hidden name—
Peace, Revealer,
Holy, Sanctified,
Pure, Undefiled!
O Time, O Eternal, O Maker of time!
O Endless, O Beginningless!
O He who remains forever He!
O He! O He! O "There is no god but He"!
O He other than whom none knows what He is!
O He other than whom none knows where He is!
O Being! O Existence-giver! O Spirit!
O He who is before every existent thing!
O He who gives existence to every existent thing!
Ihyā ashar ihyā!
Adūnay ṣabā'ūth!
O He who discloses tremendous affairs,
glory be to Thee for Thy pardon after Thy power!
So if they turn their backs, say: "God is enough for me.
There is no god but He,
in Him I have put my trust.
He is the Lord of the tremendous Throne [9:129].
Nothing is like Him,
and He is the Hearing, the Seeing [42:11].

O God, bless Muhammad and the household of Muhammad
as Thou blessed Abraham
and the household of Abraham.
Give benedictions to Muhammad and the household of Muhammad
as Thou gave benedictions to Abraham
and the household of Abraham.
Surely Thou art Laudable, Glorious.

Mustafa—upon him be peace—taught the following supplication to Abū Bakr al-Ṣiddīq:

O God, I ask Thee by
Muhammad, Thy prophet,
Abraham, Thy intimate friend,
Moses, Thy confidant,
and Jesus, Thy word and Thy spirit,
and by the Word of Moses,
the Gospel of Jesus,
the Psalms of David,
and the Furqān of Muhammad
—God bless him and give him peace—
and by every revelation Thou hast revealed,
every decree Thou hast decreed,
every supplicant whom Thou hast answered,
every rich man whom Thou hast made indigent,
every poor man whom Thou hast made rich,
and every misguided man whom Thou hast guided!
I ask Thee by Thy name which
Thou sent down upon Moses;
I ask Thee by Thy name through which
Thou hast made provision steady for the servants;
I ask Thee by Thy name which
Thou placed upon the heavens,
so they rose up;
I ask Thee by Thy name through which
Thy Throne rose up;
I ask Thee by Thy name which is
undefiled, pure, one, everlasting, unique,
and sent down in Thy Book, the Manifest Light;
I ask Thee by
Thy name which Thou placed upon the day
and it became bright
and upon the night,
and it became dark,

and by Thy tremendousness and magnificence,
and by the light of Thy face,
that Thou givest me the provision
of the Koran and knowledge,
that Thou makest it blend with
my flesh, my blood,
my hearing, and my sight,
and that Thou puttest my body to work through it,
by Thy power and Thy strength,
for surely there is no power and no strength
except in Thee,
O Most Merciful of the merciful!

The next supplication was transmitted from Mustafa—God bless him—by the Commander of the Faithful, ʿAlī ibn Abī Ṭālib—God ennoble his face. It should be recited at the beginning of the ritual prayer after *I have turned my face to Him who originated the heavens and the earth* [6:79].

O God, Thou art the King
and other than Thou there is no god.
Thou art my Lord, and I am Thy servant.
I have wronged myself, and I confess my sin,
so forgive all my sins,
for none forgives sins but Thou.
Guide me to the best of character traits,
for none guides to the best of them but Thou.
Turn evil character traits away from me,
for none turns them away from me but Thou.
I am at Thy service and disposal.
The good, all of it, is in Thy hands,
while evil does not go back to Thee.
The guided is he whom Thou hast guided,
and I am in Thee and through Thee.
Thou art blessed and high exalted;
I ask forgiveness from Thee
and I turn myself to Thee.

The next supplication is that of ʿĀ'isha—God be pleased with her. Mustafa—God bless him—taught her this prayer, saying, "O ʿĀ'isha, you should recite the all-comprehensive words, which are these words of mine:"

O God, I ask Thee for the good,
all of it,
the immediate and the deferred,
what I know of it and what I know not,

and I seek refuge in Thee from the evil,
all of it,
the immediate and the deferred,
what I know of it and what I know not.
I ask Thee for the Garden
and every word and deed that brings near to it,
and I seek refuge in Thee from the Fire,
and every word and deed that brings near to it.
I ask Thee for what
Thy servant and prophet, Muhammad
—God bless him and give him peace—
asked from Thee
and I seek refuge in Thee from what
Thy servant and prophet, Muhammad
—God bless him and give him peace—
sought refuge in Thee.
I ask Thee that Thou makest the outcome
of everything that Thou hast decreed for me
right guidance,
by Thy mercy,
O Most Merciful of the merciful!

The next is the supplication of Fāṭima—God be pleased with her. She learned this supplication from Mustafa—God bless him and give him peace.

O Alive, O Self-subsistent,
in Thy mercy I seek aid!
Entrust me not to myself for the blink of an eye,
and set right my situation, all of it.

The supplication of Abraham, God's intimate friend—God's blessings be upon him.

This supplication should be recited every morning, and one should persevere in it.

O God,
this is a new creation,
so open it for me
in obedience to Thee
and close it for me
with Thy forgiveness and good pleasure.
Provide for me within it a good deed
that Thou acceptest from me,
then purify it
and multiply it for me;

and whatever I work of evil within it
  forgive me for it.
Surely Thou art the Forgiving,
  the Compassionate,
  the Loving,
  the Generous.

The supplication of Jesus—God's blessings be upon him:

O God,
  I wake in the morning
    not able to fend off what I dislike
    and not owning the benefit of what I hope for.
  The affair is in the hands of others,
    and I awake as a pawn to my works.
  There is no poor man poorer than I.
O God,
  let not my enemy gloat over me
    and let not my friend suffer evil from me.
  Place not my affliction in my religion,
    make not this world my greatest concern,
    and give no power over me
      to him who will not have mercy upon me.

The supplication of Adam—God's blessings be upon him.

It was through the blessing of this supplication that God accepted his repentance.

O God,
  Thou knowest my secret and my open,
    so accept my excuse,
  and Thou knowest my need,
    so give me
      a faith that will take my heart in hand
      and a true certainty
    so that I may know that nothing afflicts me
      but what Thou hast written for me
    and I may be satisfied
      with Thy decree.

The prayer of 'Utbat al-Ghulām.

Someone saw him in a dream after his death and he said, "I entered paradise through these words:"

O God,
  O Guide of those who are astray,
  O Merciful toward the sinners,
  O Annuller of the stumbles of the stumblers!

Have mercy upon
Thy servant, overcome by great peril,
and all the Muslims, every one.
Place us among the chosen, the provided for,
and muster us with those whom Thou hast blessed—
the prophets, the sincere, the martyrs, and the upright.
Amen, O Lord of the worlds!

The next is an excellent supplication called the "supplication of the bird." One of the great ones of religion was imprisoned in a well in a city of Anatolia. Suddenly, a bird recited this supplication before him, and he learned it. Through its blessing, he was released.

O God, I ask of Thee.
O He
whom eyes do not see,
with whom opinions do not mix,
whom describers cannot describe,
whom events and years do not change!
He knows
the measures of the seas,
the number of the raindrops,
the number of the trees' leaves,
what the night covers over with darkness,
what the day illuminates with light.
Not hidden from Him is
any heaven by a heaven,
any earth by an earth,
any mountain and what is in its rubble,
any ocean and what is in its depths.
It is Thou before whom prostrates itself
the darkness of the night,
the brightness of the day,
the shining of the sun,
the whistling of the wind,
the rippling of the water,
the crackling of the fire,
the rustling of the trees.
It is Thou who
saved Noah from drowning,
forgave David his sin,
lifted harm from Job,
relieved Jonah of his distress in the belly of the fish,
returned Moses to his mother,
turned evil and indecency away from Joseph.

It is Thou who split the sea for the Children of Israel:
When Moses struck it with his staff,
it split, and each part of it
was as a mighty mountain [26:63],
so Moses and his tribe walked across it.
It is Thou who turned the hearts of Pharoah's sorcerers
toward faith in the prophecy of Moses, until
they said, "We have faith in the Lord of the worlds,
the Lord of Moses and Aaron" [7:121–122].
It is Thou who made the fire
coolness and safety for Abraham
when Thou ennobled him with Thy call and said,
O fire, be coolness and safety for Abraham!
They desired to outwit him,
so We made them the worse losers [21:69–70].
I ask Thee to make
the best of my life its end
and the best of my days the day of encounter with Thee,
O Kind Companion!
O Loving Friend!
O my Neighbor close at hand!
O my Protector in truth!
Relieve me of constriction
and burden me not with what I cannot endure.
Surely Thou art the Manifest Truth,
O saver of the drowning,
O deliverer of the perishing,
O sitting companion of every stranger,
O intimate of everyone alone.
Relieve me at this moment,
for I have no patience.
Surely Thou art powerful over everything [3:26],
an excellent Protector, an excellent Helper [8:40]!

THE THIRD ROAD-CLEARING

On Traditional Supplications for Every Time and Every Event

In morning upon waking up, a person should say,

Praise belongs to God
who brought us to life after making us die,
and to Him is the Uprising.

O God,
  through Thee we enter the morning,
  through Thee we die,
  through Thee we live.
We rise up in the morning
  and all rise up,
    the kingdom belonging to God,
    the tremendousness belonging to God,
    the power belonging to God,
    the light belonging to God,
    the proof belonging to God,
    the authority belonging to God,
    the argument belonging to God,
    the might belonging to God,
    the magnificence belonging to God,
      the One, the Intensely Severe.
We rise up with the original disposition of Islam
    and the word of sincerity,
  in the religion of our prophet, Muhammad
    —God bless him—
  in the creed of our father, Abraham,
  who submitted himself
    having pure faith;
  he was not of one of those
    who associate others with God [3:67].
O God, I ask Thee for
    the good of this day
    and the good of what is in it
  and I seek refuge in Thee from
    the evil of this day
    and the evil of what is in it.

When someone begins to do something, he should say,

Our Lord,
  give us from Thee mercy
    and prepare right guidance for us in our task.
  My Lord, open my breast,
    ease for me my task,
    and loose the knot upon my tongue
    so that they will understand my words [20:26].

When someone sees something that he does not consider to be auspicious, he should say,

O God, nothing brings us good things but Thou.
There is no power and no strength except in God.

When someone gives alms, he should say,

Our Lord, receive this from us;
Thou art the Hearing, the Knowing [2:127].

If—God forbid—some harm should reach him, he should say,

It may be that our Lord will give us better than it in exchange;
we beseech our Lord [68:32].

When someone looks at heaven, he should say,

Our Lord, Thou hast not created this in vain.
Glory be to Thee!
Guard us against the chastisement of the Fire [3:191].
Blessed is He who set in heaven constellations,
and set among them a lamp
and an illuminating moon [25:61].

When the wind blows, he should say,

O God, I ask Thee for
the good of this wind,
the good of what is in it,
and the good of what Thou sendest through it
and I seek refuge in Thee from
its evil,
the evil of what is in it,
and the evil of what Thou sendest through it.

When he hears the sound of thunder, he should say,

Glory be to Him—
the thunder glorifies Him in praise,
and the angels too, in awe of Him [13:13].

When he sees the new moon, he should say *Allāhu akbar* three times. Then he should recite this supplication, which is related from the Commander of the Faithful, ʿAlī—God ennoble his face.

My Lord and your Lord is God, O illuminating crescent,
frequenter of the sphere of revolution,
moving about in the stations of determination.
I have faith in Him who
lights up the darknesses with you,
illuminates the jet-black shadows with you,

appointed you one of the signs of His kingdom
and one of the marks of His authority,
and tried you with increase and decrease,
rising and setting,
illumination and eclipse.
In all this you are obedient to Him,
prompt toward His desire.
Glory be to Him!
How wonderful is what He has arranged!
How subtle your task!
God has made you the key
to a new month
for a new situation.
God has appointed you
a crescent of
blessings not effaced by days
and purity not sullied by sins;
a crescent of security and faith,
mercy and submission,
satisfaction and forgiveness.
O God,
place me among
the purest of those over whom it rises
and the most felicitous of those who look upon it.
Give me success during the month to repent,
and turn misdeeds away from me,
by Thy mercy,
O Most Merciful of the merciful.

When someone goes to the market, he should say,

There is no god but God alone,
who has no associate.
To Him belongs the kingdom
and to Him belongs the praise [64:1].
He gives life and He makes to die [7:158],
and He is Alive and does not die.
In His hand is the good,
and He is powerful over everything [5:120].
O God, I ask Thee for
the good of this market
and the good of what is in it.
O God, I seek refuge in Thee
lest I be afflicted by an ungodly oath
or a losing handshake.

If someone—God forbid—should have a debt, he should say,

O God, spare me what Thou hast made unlawful
through the lawful,
and remove my need for anyone other than Thou
through Thy bounty.

When he puts on new clothing, he should say,

O God, Thou hast clothed me in this garment,
so to Thee belongs the praise.
I ask Thee for its good
and the good of that for which it was made
and I seek refuge in Thee from its evil
and the evil of that for which it was made.

When he looks in a mirror, he should say,

Praise belongs to God who has
proportioned my creation,
then balanced it,
ennobled the form of my face
and made it beautiful,
and made me one of the Muslims.

When it is time to go to sleep, he should recite this supplication.

In Thy name, my Lord,
I put down my side.
So forgive me my sins.
O God, this is my soul that Thou takest.
Its death and its life belong to Thee.
If Thou withholdest it,
forgive it,
and if Thou sendest it back,
protect it with that through which Thou protectest
Thy upright servants.

CONCLUSION

On the Nature of the Journey from the Origin to the Return

Know, dear friend—may God exalt you with wayfaring on the straight path—that the human being is a traveler. The origin of his journey is his mother's belly, and his goal is the next world. Each year is a waystation, each month a parasang, each day a mile, each breath a step. This meaning is exceedingly clear and apparent in the mirror of reason. At every instant, a person moves closer to death in a nonsensory journey. "No day passes us by without destroying our waystations."

> Take an example from the house of delusion:
> the vendor of ice in Nishapur town.
> In the month of July he put ice on his tray—
> no one bought, and he a poor man.
> The heat caused the ice to melt and he,
> with painful heart and icy breath,
> Kept saying these words and weeping,
> "The ice is gone, and no one has bought."

With all this, people have gone to the well of nature with the rope of delusion, thinking that the wine of enjoyments and the ornaments of this sensory world are pure water. *The present life is nothing but the joy of delusion* [3:185].

> In this world's delusion
> rich man and poor
> are as happy as imagination
> dwelling on a treasure.

Reason sometimes reads to him from the book of revelation. *Let not the present life delude you, and let not the Deluder delude you concerning God* [31:33]. Sometimes with the pen of loving kindness it writes on the tablet of good counsel and shows its words to him.

> My advice to you
> is only this:
> you are a child,
> and the house is gaudily painted.

Love for this dark world has made him so blind and deaf that he does not see or hear. "Your love for a thing makes you blind and deaf."

> Why be kind to that unkind companion
> who killed the great Alexander?
> Why make love to that untrue friend
> who stole the kingdom of Darius?

So struggle, dear friend, and consider these two days of passing life as a godsend,

> For the present moment is a cutting sword,
> life an army, and youth a commander.

You must earn through these few breaths the felicity to which these words allude: *No soul knows what refreshment of the eyes is hidden away for them, as a recompense for what they were doing* [32:17]. *O you who have faith, be wary of God, seek the means to come to Him, and struggle in His way; perhaps you will prosper* [5:35].

Seek the knowledge
  that unties knots!
Before the soul
  departs from the body—seek!
Leave aside this nothing
  that seems to be something
and seek that something
  that appears to be nothing.

What a great loss—to give up such felicity for these passing enjoyments and false imaginings!

In my whole life,
  one night during prayer,
the image of my beloved
  came to me.
She lifted the veil from her face
  and whispered,
"See now from whom
  you are being held back!"

Know that the key to this felicity is to serve a possessor of the heart. This is the meaning of *seek the means to come to Him* [5:35].

Do you want to find favor like the Men?
  Entrust yourself to those with favor.

They are the ones "whose sitting companion will never be wretched."

He who has no moon-like face to guide him on the Path
  stands in danger, but people do not understand.

"He who has no shaykh has no religion."

In order to attain to this felicity without delay, practice obedience as much as you can and avoid disobedience. *So be wary of God as far as you are able, and listen, and obey, and expend the good for yourselves. Whosoever is guarded against the avarice of his own soul, those—they are the prosperous* [64:16]. Avoid as much as you can the companionship of evil comrades, who are the vicegerents of Iblis, since companionship has a tremendous power to exercise influence, and spirits are easily influenced by one another.

In this path, observe a hundred thousand Iblises
  with the face of Adam—
Be careful, don't consider everyone with Adam's face
  a human being!

To the extent possible, drink down hell, for "Wrath is a flame of the fire of Gehenna." Every time you swallow your anger, you will be called a "hell-drinker" in the dominion of heaven. Every time you leave aside an appetitive impulse, sincerely desiring the face of God, you should consider that a key to paradise. *As for him who feared the station of his Lord and forbade the soul its caprice, surely the Garden shall be the refuge* [79:40]. Keep "Alms in secret extinguish God's wrath" before your eyes. Remember God constantly. *Perhaps after that God will bring something new to pass* [65:1]. Know for certain that the effects of the blessings of remembrance will quickly show themselves. And remember me with an upright supplication!

Praise belongs to God, whose favor brings upright needs to completion. Blessings be upon the master of mankind, the quintessence of the engendered things, Muhammad Mustafa, and upon his household, the good, and his wives, the pure.

Part Four *Sufism and Islam*

The subtitle of this book and the introductory material declare that the three translated works belong to the genre of Sufi writing. In Part One I suggested what this characterization means in general terms. In what follows, I examine more carefully what the term *Sufism* implies. There is little agreement among specialists, not to mention generalists, as to how the word should be employed. However, it seems that many of the ideas that are commonly associated with Sufism have little basis in the original texts.

ORTHODOX ISLAM

The three translated works provide examples of a genre of writing that has been common in Islamic languages for the past six or seven hundred years. One way to reach the conclusion that they are Sufi works is by a process of elimination. They do not deal with jurisprudence, Kalām, philosophy, Koran commentary, and so forth.

One might say that these are general works on Islam. However, which perspective in Islamic thought allows one to have a general overview of all of the branches of strictly Islamic learning, including concepts such as *iḥsān, ikhlāṣ,* and *taqwā*? The answer is Sufism. It is true that some later philosophers also have a broad view of things, but their style and language make their works accessible only to the ulama. And typically, these philosophers were involved with practices that are associated with Sufism.

If one grants that Sufism does coincide, by and large, with what I have called "Islam's third dimension," this makes it easy to understand why Sufi authors alone are able to provide an overview of all dimensions of Islam. To repeat what was said in Part One, faith includes works, but works do not include faith. As a result, the perspective of jurisprudence is not wide enough to take the principles of faith into consideration. So also, faith does not provide a wide enough perspective to grasp the nature of human perfection. Another dimension of learning must be added, and that dimension will by its nature have an overview of both faith and works. Hence Sufism, by being anchored in Islam's third dimension, is correctly situated to see all three dimensions. In contrast, a theologian, as theologian, has no way to gain the same outlook on Islam, because his learning is simply not situated in the right place.

Western secondary sources commonly tell us that Sufism came into existence in the second or third century of Islam. One cannot object to this viewpoint, so long as those who hold it acknowledge that sciences such as jurisprudence and Kalām also came into existence at more or less the same time. The great Muslims, beginning with the Prophet, lived all three of Islam's dimensions, although some were recognized as especially knowledgeable in one field or another. The need to develop and systematize the teachings of the Koran and the Sunnah arose gradually and, along with systematization, came specialization and fragmentation. By the third or fourth century, it is often easy to say that scholar "X" is a jurist, scholar "Y" a follower of Kalām, and scholar "Z" a Sufi—in other words, that the first had specialized in the science of works, the second in faith, and the third in the way to achieve perfection. However, all three domains were present in Islam from the beginning. Given the multidimensional nature of human affairs and the all-embracing concerns of religion, they had to be present.[1]

Although Sufism, according to a certain definition, was no more present in early Islam than was jurisprudence or Kalām or philosophy, its subject matter was a living reality from the beginning, as was the subject matter of the other two dimensions. Thus it is surprising that certain scholars have been happy to recognize Islam's juridical dimension (the Shariah) or Ash'arite theology as "orthodoxy," thereby suggesting that Sufism is not really Islamic, but was added later on. Other scholars have objected to this imposition of an alien category on Islamic institutions, but one commonly meets with the word, even in sources written over the past few years.[2]

It may be that use of the term "orthodoxy" has simply become a habit for some scholars, and that they use it without reflecting on its implications, especially because so many of the great orientalists have used it. It also may be that scholars who continue to use the term after having studied Islam are revealing something about their own attitudes to the subject that they would be reluctant to express in so many words. The term "orthodoxy," after all, implies that everything that does not fit under its umbrella—typically, a very small umbrella—is not "right doctrine." Rather, it is heterodox or heretical and, hence, does not properly belong within the Islamic tradition. To call the Shariah "orthodoxy"—even though the Shariah is concerned strictly with orthopraxy—is to imply that "right religion" for Muslims lies only in activity, and anything else is "wrong religion" and must have come from deviation or outside influences. Even some who have ceased referring to orthodoxy still exhibit this attitude by insisting that certain fundamental currents in Islam have been borrowed from earlier religions.

As for the application of the word *orthodoxy* to Ash'arite theology, this is no doubt done because Ash'arism came to be looked upon as the dominant form of Kalām—for many reasons not necessarily having to do with "right doctrine." One of the most important of these reasons is simply that modern scholars have taken the claims of the Kalām specialists seriously, perhaps because they were looking for some authority analogous to the Catholic church. Moreover, the more spiritual understanding of Islamic teachings found in the writings of the Sufis sounds like "mysticism"—and everyone knows that mysticism has been peripheral to most forms of Christianity and Judaism. Hence, it must be peripheral to Islam as well.

In fact, Kalām as a science—as has often been pointed out—cannot be said to play a role analogous to theology in Christianity. There is little doubt that theoretical Sufism has been far more pervasive as an intellectual force in Islamic civilization than either Kalām or philosophy. As W. C. Smith rightly remarks, Kalām "has been not even a secondary expression of Islamic faith, but takes at best a tertiary place after the moral-legal (*sharī'ah*) and the mystic Ṣūfī."[3] Ghazālī tells us that one specialist in Kalām is plenty for a town, just as one physician is sufficient, since theologians are like physicians in employing medicine to cure people of disease. But Ghazālī adds that Kalām is dangerous because a self-interested theologian can inflict deeper damage than can a quack. Everyone is required to have a minimal knowledge of Islam, but Ghazālī, at least, does not include Kalām in what most people should know about, because it will do them more harm than good.

Kalām is a mental exercise aimed at intellectuals with a particular type of mind-set. There are many other ways to gain sufficient knowledge of God to be a good Muslim, beginning with studying the Koran and the Hadith. Kalām has been able to gain a certain preeminence because it approaches the religion defensively and even stridently. The word *Kalām* often simply means "dispute." It fits in nicely with the legalistic mind-set of jurists, who, in turn, tended to congregate in centers of power. If one gives the jurists' motives the benefit of the doubt, one can say that they were concerned with seeing that governments put the Shariah into effect. If one follows a Ghazālī or an Ibn al-'Arabī and thinks ill of jurists, one suspects that most of them were simply ambitious in the worst sense of the term. Nevertheless, their opinions attracted attention because they voiced them loudly, and often with the support of a king or a caliph.

In short, the type of religiosity that comes to be associated with the word Sufism was present in Islam from the beginning. True, specifically Sufi teachings and approaches appear later, but so also do specifically juridical, theological, and philosophical approaches. On the basis of historical beginnings, there is no current of Islamic learning—certainly not jurisprudence or Kalām—that can call itself the original Islam, from which other currents have deviated.[4]

Some Muslims, recognizing that all expressions of Islam are precisely expressions and nothing more, make the claim that the Koran is enough, or the Koran and the Hadith are enough. But this is an empty claim, because the way in which the Koran and the Hadith are understood and interpreted depends on intellectual and spiritual predispositions, not to mention historical, cultural, and linguistic factors. By ignoring the problems of understanding and interpretation, people ensure that they will take their own intellectual limitations as the norm for everyone else. Those oriented toward works will see commandments and prohibitions. Those oriented toward thinking and theorizing will see theology or philosophy. Those oriented toward spirituality will find Sufism, and those oriented toward historical contexts will see influences.

MYSTICISM AND DISCIPLINE

I have suggested that Sufism, in the broadest sense of the term, is Islam's third and innermost dimension. It is primarily concerned with perfecting works and faith, or with sincerity and god-wariness. Providing a narrower and more specific definition of Sufism is much more difficult. It is sufficient to look at the definitions that have been offered—not only in modern studies, but also in the early texts—to realize that there has never been any consensus concerning the word, any more than there is a consensus in modern scholarship as to how the word *religion* should be defined.

In classical Sufi texts, scores of definitions for the words *Sufism* (*taṣawwuf*) and *Sufi* have been proposed.[5] However, the definitions here are not logical, historical, or sociological. Instead, they are "allusions" (*ishāra*) designed to alert people to what Sufis achieve or what Sufi practice demands. Such allusions have the spiritual profit of the listener in view. In other words, they are given with the aim of helping the listener gain felicity.

The many modern scholarly definitions of Sufism have clearly not been offered with a view toward human felicity. More recently, most specialists have ceased trying to define Sufism in any narrow sense, offering instead a working description such as "Islamic mysticism."[6] Then they focus on certain interesting, attractive, peculiar, or "mystical" characteristics that are found in some of those who have applied the name Sufi to themselves or have had it applied to them. This approach has the advantage of avoiding methodological complications, and I would be wise to follow it myself. However, since I have already proposed a broad definition of Sufism, I will attempt to narrow this definition down a bit and, in the process, suggest why some of the terminology commonly employed in discussing Sufism can be misleading.

Mysticism is a good word with which to begin, because Sufism is so commonly associated with it. The word does not really help the uninformed reader because, first, it is far from clear what mysticism is. For many people, the term itself implies an aberration from the human norm. Others, thinking mysticism is a good thing, may well find that most of what is discussed in classical Sufism is too humdrum for their tastes. Frequently people of the second type assume that anything in Sufi texts not having a "mystical" ring to it must be a sop for the exoterically minded, who always, it is supposed, were hostile toward the Sufis.

In the case of specialists in the field of religious and Islamic studies, Sufism's association with mysticism has unfortunate consequences. Those who work in the field of Sufism are well aware that the term *mysticism* is problematic, but other scholars are likely to take it as the general reader would take it. I have witnessed dismissive reactions from scholars to the mention of Sufism. "That's just mysticism," they have told me. And mysticism, as everyone knows, is peripheral to the concerns of serious and sane people.

It is true that the word *Sufism* has been applied to a wide range of phenomena in Islamic history and that some of these phenomena represent concerns peripheral to Islam—and to serious and sane people. But the word has many other applications, and before one dismisses Sufism's role in Islam, one had better consider these as well. For example, if Sufism does indeed coincide with Islam's third dimension, then Sufism is Islam's life-blood and, without it, little is left but juridical nit-picking and theological bickering.

According to a dictionary definition, mystics are those who have "direct or intimate knowledge of or communion with God (as through contemplation, vision, an inner light)." Mysticism is associated with the experience of supranormal phenomena, if not abnormal mental states. Without question, direct and intimate knowledge of God plays an important role in Sufism. We have seen how often our author and others appeal to "unveiling" as a source for authentic knowledge. But there is no guarantee that a person who enters the Sufi way will gain such knowledge. It is probably fair to say that most people who consider themselves to be Sufis or who are disciples of Sufi masters have not experienced unveiling, although they certainly respect its existence in the prophets and the great friends of God. Relatively few Sufi authors claim such privileged knowledge for themselves, but they never deny its existence in others. On the contrary, like Ghazālī, they consider the acknowledgement of its existence in others as a necessary prerequisite for sound faith.[7]

According to one traditional understanding, a Sufi is someone who has achieved direct and intimate knowledge of God in a way that has transmuted the person's human substance. His or her "copper" has become gold, to use one of Rūmī's favorite images. But such people are exceedingly rare, so, by this definition, the vast majority of people affiliated with Sufism are not Sufis. Rather, they are seekers of God. In actual fact, few practitioners of Sufism in Islamic countries call themselves Sufis. Members of Sufi orders refer to themselves by a variety of names, such as "one of the poor" (fakir, from the Arabic *faqīr*; or dervish, from the Persian *darwīsh*). This refusal to apply the term *Sufi* to oneself recognizes that, strictly speaking, the Sufi is the one who has arrived.

In order to embrace all the phenomena in Islamic history that have gone by the name Sufism or been labelled as Sufism, we need a broad definition of the term. The association with direct and intimate knowledge of God is helpful, but it leaves out most of what Sufism involves. If we do define Sufism as the intimate knowledge of God possessed by those who have arrived at the goal, then we will ignore most of what is taught in the texts. These books were not written for perfect human beings, but for those who desire to achieve perfection. They are guidebooks for becoming Sufis, if we take this term to mean those who have reached the goal. The main focus of such guidebooks is the deepening of works and faith.

Another problem with the word *mysticism* is that it is usually associated with a certain psychic extravagance or passivity before fantastic manifestations of the unknown. People have always found it difficult to distinguish between mysticism and madness. Sufism, like mysticism, has at times been associated with bizarre phenomena. Westerners in the nineteenth century who went to the East on quests for the exotic were naturally attracted to Sufi groups that displayed psychic powers. Many of the early orientalists were no less interested in the exotic and found marvelous examples of it in various forms of Sufi practice and experience. What has not always been recognized is that Sufism, like any widescale phenomenon, has its peripheral areas. I myself have witnessed Kurdish dervishes of the Qādirī order skewering themselves and crunching down stainless steel razor blades as if they were potato chips, but neither I nor the dervishes themselves—as I found out by asking them—thought that this was anything more than a sideshow.

Much more central to Sufism's concerns are discipline, training, control of the instinctive urges of the self, achievement of a balanced psyche, overcoming mental and moral weakness, virtue, piety, devotion, avoidance of sin, and so on. The last few terms have gained a negative and sentimental color in English because of the break with traditional religiosity. The first two terms—*discipline* and *training*—have kept a certain positive ring to them—so long as they stem from the individual's own initiatives and not from the influence of organized religion.

In order to gain some idea of Sufism's basic concerns, it may be useful to look at the word *discipline*. I have in mind the Arabic term *riyāḍa*, which plays an important role in Sufi teachings. The classical Sufi meaning of the word has largely been lost in modern Arabic, in which the word usually means "exercise, sports, gymnastics." This reflects a change in our own view of discipline in the West. Discipline is fine for the body, as long as we have in view a healthy and normal goal, such as being a soccer player. We do not think it strange that Olympic athletes should undergo years of grueling discipline. Likewise, everyone understands why musicians need to follow a rigorous course of discipline in order to become masters of their art. Discipline might even be praiseworthy for scholars, and certainly so for scientists.

In Arabic, the classical and modern word *riyāḍiyyāt* (mathematics) derives from the same word *riyāḍa*. *Riyāḍiyyāt* means literally "things related to discipline"—that is, discipline of the mental faculty. Mathematics was a branch of philosophy, and the Muslim philosophers called it "the intermediate things" (*al-mutawassiṭāt*), because it represents the halfway point between knowledge of the external world and metaphysics. Numbers and geometrical figures do not exist as such in the outside world, only in the mind. By training the mind to think mathematically, people gain a certain disengagement (*tajarrud*) from material things. This, in turn, prepares them for moving beyond concepts and imagination into the world of pure intelligibles, which have no direct relationship with the outside world. Hence, those who cultivated mathematics in its pure form—as opposed to those who made use of it for practical purposes—understood that one of its functions was to discipline the soul so that it might ascend to perception of the first and highest things.

One of the most common applications of the word *riyāḍa* in classical Arabic was to the types of discipline connected with keeping the soul under control and bringing it into harmony with works, faith, and god-wariness. The tool for this task is *'aql* (intelligence), the same tool that is employed for disciplining the mind in order to learn mathematics. However, here the word *'aql* is understood more in its linguistic and Koranic sense and with less input from Greek philosophy. In this meaning, *'aql* is what "binds" appetite and caprice. Intelligence holds back and controls the willful and headstrong impulses of the soul.

What type of discipline can control the soul? This is a question which Ghazālī sets out to answer in his monumental *Iḥyā' 'ulūm al-dīn* (The Revival of the Sciences of Religion). In brief, his answer, like the answer of so many other Muslim authorities, is that a person must have faith in Islam and practice it with a view toward achieving perfection. In other words, one must bring one's body, soul, and heart into harmony with the Real on the basis of the Sunnah of the Prophet. One must put the Shariah in its fullest sense into effect, so that *tawḥīd* is not simply a verbal statement, but rather the mold of the human substance. Considering the sort of prescriptions that are given for disciplining the soul, it is not surprising that *riyāḍa* is sometimes translated as "asceticism." However, asceticism nowadays calls to mind ridiculous practices such as hair shirts and beds of nails. It cannot be taken seriously as a prescription for human life. Yet, in terms of ascetic discipline, our great athletes put many of the medieval "mystics" to shame.

Ghazālī and many others employ the term *riyāḍa* as a synonym for *mujāhada. Mujāhada*, in turn, is grammatically equivalent to the well-known term jihad (*jihād*), which is commonly and misleadingly translated as "holy war." The meaning of the word is "struggle," and the Koranic context allows us to say that jihad and *mujāhada* both mean "struggle in the path of God." To the extent that jihad is a community struggle *in the path of God*, it can rightly be translated as "holy war." But in fact, the term is normally used for any war, and many—if not most—Muslims might claim that a given war has nothing to do with the path of God.

In a hadith often cited by the Sufis and other authorities, the Prophet is reported to have said, "I have returned from the lesser jihad to the greater jihad." He then explains that the lesser jihad is struggle against the enemies of Islam while the greater jihad is struggle against the limitations and ignorance of one's own soul. In later texts, the word *mujāhada* is usually employed in the context of this greater struggle in the path of God, while *jihad* is employed in reference to the outer struggle—that is, the war against the enemies of the king.

In short, the word *mujāhada*, like the word *riyāḍa*, refers to the efforts that people exert to overcome their own limitations for God's sake. By this definition, the five pillars of Islam are all parts of discipline and struggle, but they are taken for granted, because it is obvious to any Muslim that struggle in the path of God begins with observance of the prescriptions laid down by the Shariah. Hence, the words normally refer to a concerted and sincere effort to do everything that is pleasing to God, not simply what He has commanded. Both terms lead into the domain of *ikhlāṣ* and *taqwā*.

The point of this brief examination of the word *riyāḍa* is to suggest that Sufism is not primarily involved with mystical experience. Although "unveiling of the mysteries" is indeed one possible fruit of Sufi practice, it cannot be taken for granted and should not even be made a goal, at least not in any exclusive sense. Many Sufi masters would maintain that the attempt to achieve unveiling is a dangerous enterprise, because it turns the seeker away from God and puts experience in His place. Hence, it is a form of *shirk* (associating others with God)—certainly a far worse form than that of seeking after paradise instead of God Himself, a form mentioned in Part One.

The goal of Sufism, then, is to reach God, and this does not necessarily involve "direct or intimate knowledge of or communion with God" in this world. By this definition, mysticism is not the central concern of Sufism. Sufis are satisfied to put off direct knowledge of God until the next world, where, in any case, it is promised to everyone. In the meantime, what is absolutely essential is observance of the requirements of the present moment, because, as the well-known Sufi saying goes, "The Sufi is the child of the moment." The Sufi lives with what God wants now, not with anything that has gone by, nor with anything that he or she hopes for in the future. One of the primary themes of love poetry in Islam—and Islamic literature is permeated with love poetry—is separation from the beloved. Yes, the lover wants union—but more than union, the lover wants what the Beloved wants. The following Arabic verse, often quoted in Sufi texts, is typical:

> I want union with Him
> but He wants separation from me—
> I abandon what I want
> for what He wants.[8]

How does one know what God wants if one does not have "direct and intimate knowledge of God"? Muslims reply that the Shariah tells you what God wants. Sufi Muslims add that God also wants people to follow the Tariqah, but in His mercy, He does not place a burden on them that they cannot bear. *God charges a soul only to its capacity* (2:286). The Shariah is the general road that all Muslims must follow. Its fruit is the felicitous encounter with God in the next world. The Tariqah is the narrow path down the middle of the general road. It is much more demanding, since it does not make the same allowances for human weakness. It differs from the Shariah in that it is designed to bring about the encounter with God in this world.

If one wants to summarize the Tariqah in a nutshell, one can say that the Sufi lives with God in the present moment through remembrance (*dhikr*). To remember God is to put God at the center and everything else at the periphery. All Islamic ritual is performed for the sake of remembrance. The Koran calls the ritual prayer (*ṣalāt*) itself "remembrance."[9] But in Sufism, this remembrance tends to be focused on the silent and continuous repetition of one of God's names. This practice derives from numerous Koranic commandments and prophetic injunctions. Moreover, it is a struggle and a discipline, because God's name is eminently elusive, especially when the soul is weak and easily distracted by daily concerns.

All this discussion of discipline and practice is simply to bring out that, according to the classical texts, every moment of the Sufi's existence should be taken up with concentration on God. This is a continuous struggle. There is no passivity in this mysticism, if we can call it that. In most cases, Sufi life and practice have nothing to do with mysticism, because there is no direct knowledge of God involved, nor are there strange psychic phenomena. There is merely the attempt to achieve one-pointed concentration on God's name, or to be aware of God's presence in every moment and every situation in life.

Outwardly, Sufis tend to be ordinary human beings, like the rest of us. Anyone who has lived in Islamic countries and investigated the functioning of the Sufi orders knows that the vast majority of people affiliated with the orders are completely ordinary. Many Westerners go to Islamic countries looking for something mystical, bizarre, exotic. While they find it without too much difficulty in some groups claiming Sufi affiliation, it is not common among the Sufi orders. Most Sufis are different from other Muslims only in their inward occupation (*shughl*), not their outward appearance.

TOWARD A NARROWER DEFINITION OF SUFISM

In looking for a narrower definition of Sufism, we should keep in mind the thrust of the traditional definitions provided by the recognized Sufi authorities—definitions that are always normative. In other words, one should not apply the term to everything that claims to be Sufism or is called Sufism without first investigating its nature according to certain criteria.

I would make Islam's three dimensions the fundamental criteria for discerning whether an individual or an institution deserves to be ascribed to Sufism. I have already suggested that Sufism stresses the third dimension, that of perfection. Almost all the institutions and figures within Islam that make the achievement of perfection an important concern are associated with Sufism. However, Sufism also stresses the second dimension. Many Sufis have written books explaining the contents of faith in ways that can usually be differentiated from treatises on Kalām and philosophy. Sufis also emphasize the importance of the first dimension, which is included in faith. As Annemarie Schimmel rightly remarks,

> Westerners have often regarded the Sufis as representatives of a movement that has freed itself from the legal prescriptions of Islam. . . .That is, however, not correct. One should not forget that the *sharīʿa*, as proclaimed in the Koran and exemplified by the Prophet, together with a firm belief in the Day of Judgment, was the soil out of which their piety grew.[10]

Not only was the Shariah the soil out of which their "piety"—that is, their *iḥsān*, sincerity, and god-wariness—grew, it was also the soil in which the tree of their piety remained firmly rooted. The tree does not start walking around once it has grown. It might be better to compare Sufism to a house built on a foundation, which is the Shariah. No one imagines that the foundation disappears once the rest of the house is built. Without the foundation, the house will be washed away in the first storm.

Most Sufi authorities who were concerned with theoretical Sufism were also masters of applied and practical Sufism. It was only after having achieved a deepened understanding of faith and works—after having advanced on the path toward perfection—that these authors felt competent enough to assume a teaching function and to explain the nature of faith and works to others. However, it is not true that every master of applied Sufism was also a master of theoretical Sufism. As Ibn al-ʿArabī puts it, *kashf al-ʿibāra* (the unveiling of the expression of things) was a special gift and a vocation, and not every Sufi master is given it.

In *Clarifications* (91–92), our author distinguishes between two types of Sufi masters. Both have achieved perfection, but only one teaches. Moreover, many great teaching shaykhs had no particular concern with exposition of Sufi theories, because "doing" and "being" were far more important to them. Here, one is reminded of a certain Zen approach to things. In addition, many shaykhs wrote works on practice, but not on faith, especially in the period before Ibn al-ʿArabī.

If one wants to describe Sufism without direct reference to Islam's three dimensions, one can say that the term refers to the efforts of Muslims to establish an inner and personal relationship with God on the basis of the Koran, the Sunnah, and the example of the great figures who followed the Prophet.[11] Seeking nearness to God according to these criteria is a universal phenomenon in Islam. Wherever there are Muslims, there are Sufis, although they may not go by this name.

Such a definition does not allow the term *Sufism* to be applied to everything that is called by the name, whether by supporters or detractors. One needs to differentiate between "true Sufism" and "false Sufism," or between "authentic Sufism" and "deviated Sufism." Moreover, having drawn this distinction, one must also recognize that there are numerous intermediate forms of Sufism—in fact, most Sufism fits somewhere in between the two extremes.[12] Ideal Sufism—if it has ever been embodied in human beings—must be attributed to the Prophet and the great shaykhs of the past. For others, it remains a goal to be achieved. Where to draw the line between the great shaykhs and the others is one of the many issues that need discussion.

Some will object that this definition is far too broad because it includes most Muslims or, should we say, most committed and engaged Muslims. To this I can only reply by referring to Islam's three dimensions. From that perspective, Islam without the third dimension is not full and integral Islam.

Attempts to define Sufism always involve questions of degree and stress. There are no clear criteria, nor are there black-and-white differentiations. One should always ask to what extent the individuals in question are aware of the relevance and priority of Islam's third dimension. My understanding here is that, if someone stresses either of the other two dimensions over the third, that person belongs in another camp. As the Arabic proverb puts it, "People have the religion of their kings" (*al-nās ʿalā dīn mulūkihim*). Who are the authorities to which appeal is made—not only explicitly, but also implicitly?[13]

Everyone appeals to the Koran and the Hadith, but how are these understood? On this level, it is possible to differentiate between a Sufi understanding of Islam and other understandings. Thus, the Sufis stress the third dimension over the other two, or they strive to maintain a balance among all three dimensions while taking their fundamental orientation from the third dimension.

People will complain that there are no clear lines in this definition, but that is precisely the point. When it comes to actual, living embodiments of qualities—submission, faith, god-wariness, and perfection—we are dealing with an eminently gray area. As Ibn al-ʿArabī would say, the true situation is always "He/not He" (*huwa lā huwa*), it/not it, this/not this. All things are barzakhs or intermediary realms. There are no absolutes in the created world, least of all among human beings.

Leaving aside the fact that this definition might be read as including practically everyone's Islam, one can also object that such a broad definition of Sufism includes many philosophers and Shi'ites who are not Sufis. However, if they are not Sufis, this depends on a different definition of Sufism that needs to be made explicit.

In defense of including many philosophers in the ranks of the Sufis, I would say that to speak of philosophy in Islam is to speak of an intellectual pursuit that studies realities falling within the domain of Islam's three principles. To the extent that philosophy is an applied, practical discipline—and most Muslim philosophers stressed that it was—it necessarily coincides with putting Islam into practice, although not necessarily in the exact way that jurist "X" or jurist "Y" would condone. If not, then we are not speaking about *Islamic* philosophy.

Hence, the deepening of the knowledge that is acquired through Islamic philosophy—so long as it is rooted in Islam's first dimension—should indeed be considered a form of Sufism. Moreover, it is easy to cite authorities usually listed among philosophers who had an eminently Sufi approach, such as the Ikhwān al-Ṣafā', Bābā Afḍal Kāshānī, or Suhrawardī al-Maqtūl. As for Avicenna, the "chief shaykh" of the Peripatetics, his visionary recitals point to a Sufi perspective, and the ninth section of his *al-Ishārāt wa'l-tanbīhāt* speaks explicitly about the levels of human perfection achieved by the gnostics (*al-ʿurafāʾ*), who are apparently the Sufi shaykhs. In philosophy, as in many other areas, there are no "yes" or "no" answers when it comes to the question of Sufism's presence. It all depends on our definition of Sufism and also on the varying degrees in which individuals manifest the qualities associated with Sufism.

As for Shi'ism, it needs to be defined vis-a-vis Sunnism, in which case the differences between Shi'ism and Sunnism appear on the level of the details of the Shariah and the contents of faith, where, simply to begin with, Shi'ism speaks of five principles rather than three. Concerning the question of attempting to achieve human perfection, Shi'ites are similar to Sunnis—some do, and some don't. To the extent that they do, they are Sufis according to my description, whether or not they would approve of this name. Inasmuch as the "Shi'ite esotericism" discussed in great detail by Henry Corbin involves active involvement in perfecting works and faith, it deserves to be called a form of Sufism.

In classic Sufi texts such as *al-Lumaʿ* of Abū Naṣr al-Sarrāj (d. 378/988), *Ḥilyat al-awliyāʾ* of Abū Nuʿaym Iṣfahānī (d. 430/1037), or *ʿAwārif al-maʿārif* of Abū Hafṣ ʿUmar Suhrawardī (d. 632/1234), the word Sufism is used to refer to a high ideal that is rarely realized. To call people "Sufis" is to praise them in no uncertain terms. Many other authors, at various times and places, use the term as a curse. If one pays careful attention to the manner in which all these authors understand the term, it is easy to grasp that supporters and detractors do not have the same thing in mind. In both cases, certain ideals and qualities are viewed as being essential to the religion of Islam. Very often, these are the same ideals and qualities. In one case, the Sufis are seen as the embodiment of these qualities. In the other, they are understood to be those who have rejected them. In both cases, there is a normative understanding of what Islam is all about. As for why Sufism has been perceived in many different ways, this stems from exceedingly complex factors that vary according to time, place, and circumstance and cannot be dealt with here.

In attempting to define Sufism, I would rather stick to those definitions and norms that are provided by figures who considered themselves to be representatives of the Sufi tradition, and who therefore evaluate it positively. There is no doubt, however, that many people calling themselves "Sufis" over the centuries have not lived up to the normative understanding of Islam provided either by Sufism's supporters or detractors. Sufi authorities themselves have not considered such people as "real Sufis."

Of the three translated treatises, only *Clarifications* mentions the term *Sufi* (63.12), in a passage in which the author identifies the Sufis with the friends of God. He says that he has followed their example by not entering into detail concerning the principles and branches of faith and by discussing them in terms of "allusions" (*ishārāt*). The fact that the author mentions the term *Sufi* only once suggests that he may not have been completely happy with the word. Perhaps this was because, at his time, there were already too many charlatans who had appropriated the name to themselves. His contemporary Rūmī often complains of false Sufis, as in his verse, "The vile man steals the words of the dervishes in order to cast a spell on simple minds."[14]

For his part, Ibn al-ʿArabī respects those whom he calls "Sufis," but he does not consider them to have reached the highest stage of human perfection. One reason may be that the term *Sufism* suggests a stress on the innermost dimension of things, virtue and spirituality, and, therefore, it may imply that the more outwardly oriented dimensions of Islam are not given their due. Ibn al-ʿArabī can define Sufism as "assuming the character traits of the divine names," thereby calling attention to *iḥsān* and its connection to the most beautiful names of God.[15] But in his view, the highest human quality is to give everything its due, including the dimensions of works and faith. Perhaps this is why he—like the author of these treatises—frequently refers to those human beings who live up fully to the ideals of Islam as the "verifiers" or *muḥaqqiqūn* (the present participle of the verbal noun *taḥqīq*, itself coming from the root *ḥ.q.q.*). The verifiers are those who have verified the truth (*ḥaqq*) of the Islamic teachings by having realized (*taḥaqquq*) the reality (*ḥaqīqa*) that lies beyond them—a reality that is called the Real, the Truth (*ḥaqq*), God. In Ibn al-ʿArabī's terminology, the Sufis in the strict sense of the term belong on a lower level of human perfection. They are God's friends, but they have not reached the full flowering of human nature.[16]

The word *taḥqīq* (verification) is highly significant if we want to understand the presuppositions of the Sufi authors as well as those of our own times. In modern Islamic languages, it is commonly used to translate the English word *research*, especially scientific research. One of the great virtues of the scientific method is that it verifies the truth of its findings to the satisfaction of scientists, although certainly not to the satisfaction of those philosophers and social critics who question science's assumptions about reality. In any case, most people today tell us that they respect science because of its ability to prove its findings, to verify them, and to demonstrate their objective validity, whereas mysticism is unverifiable and subjective. Yet, the criticisms which the Sufi verifiers direct at the common people—who follow authority (*taqlīd*)—also applies to most scientists, and certainly to the popular reception of science.

Most people accept science's truth because they believe the authorities who speak for it. Some may object that science is verifiable by others as well. However, most serious science is not in fact verifiable by me or you. We simply accept the scientists' opinion that others can verify it. The Sufi verifiers also claim that what they know is verifiable. They know it to be true because they have experienced and established its truth. We can verify it, too—but first, we must dedicate ourselves to the preliminaries. Just as not every one of us has enough mathematical ability to become a frontier physicist, so also not all of us have the ability to learn everything necessary to verify other forms of truth. All of this should be self-evident, but people like to forget it, because it is much more comforting to think that our verification is true, while their verification is "just mysticism."

The goal of Islam, as understood by the authorities who speak for Sufism, is to be fully human. The Sufis feel that they alone have grasped the breadth, depth, and import of the Islamic teachings because they alone perceive Islam in its total, three-dimensional manifestation. In other words, their concerns are directed toward full submission (*islām*) to God on the three levels of works, faith, and perfection. They try to make all their acts, all their ideas and concepts, and all their psychic and spiritual states conform to the Real. *Tawḥīd*, taken to its fullest expression, means that nothing in the human being stands outside a relationship with God. The Sufi is the person who is fully aware of this and draws every necessary conclusion. The verifier is the person who lives this as his or her own personal and objective reality.

Sufism, from this point of view, is simply full and complete actualization of the faith and practice of Islam. The verified Sufi is the perfect Muslim. To become a Sufi in the true sense is to become a *muwaḥḥid*, one who establishes *tawḥīd* or asserts the unity of God, not simply with the tongue (which is the domain of works), but also with the understanding (faith) and the whole being (perfection). By this definition, Islam without Sufism is an aberration from the Koranic norm. The present texts can be called "Sufi treatises" in this broad sense.

In a slightly narrower sense, Sufism refers to those Muslims who have self-consciously set themselves apart from the majority by stressing the overriding importance of the innermost dimension of Islam—god-wariness, sincerity, and achieving perfection. Such representatives of Sufism have often contrasted the Tariqah with the Shariah and devoted most of their attention to bringing out the special characteristics of the Tariqah. Here Sufism becomes a category set up in opposition to jurisprudence, Kalām, and philosophy in order to show that the Sufis are those who have preserved the most essential teachings of Islam. I have in mind such books as Qushayrī's *Risāla*, Hujwīrī's *Kashf al-maḥjūb*, or Suhrawardī's *'Awārif al-ma'ārif*, which set down a specific, Sufi way of practicing Islam, and which are especially concerned with bringing out the exemplary behavior and sayings of the great Muslims of the past or the special technical terms that Sufis have employed to express their own perception of Islam. It should be clear that the three treatises translated here attempt to explain Sufism in the broader rather than the narrower sense of the term.

NOTES

1. One could object that certain other religions—such as Christianity—do not have a Shariah, but this simply means that these religions approach the question of setting down the rules for right conduct in different ways from Islam.

2. For one of the most recent scholarly critiques of the use of this term, see J. Baldick's pointed remarks in *Mystical Islam* 7–8.

3. Smith, *Faith and Belief* 182–184. Smith employs the term *faith* in a broader sense than *īmān* as understood by most Muslims. He uses it to refer to every authentic expression of religion, so he seems to be implying here that Islam finds expression through what I have called its "three dimensions," but he pays no attention to some of the subtleties that must be addressed before this becomes a relatively satisfactory way of accounting for the different approaches. If he were to employ the actual Islamic categories, he would have to show the distinction between the moral (which has an inner side connected to Sufism) and the legal (works), as well as the different expressions of the dimension of faith, including philosophy and theoretical Sufism as opposed to applied Sufism (the third dimension). In any case, I quote him because of his recognition that Kalām has remained relatively peripheral to Muslim concerns.

4. For a good anthropological argument supporting the presence of several currents in Islam from the beginning, see Mark Woodward, *Islam in Java* 60–66.

5. For a detailed sampling, see Javad Nurbakhsh, *Sufism* 1:16–41.

6. See Schimmel, *Mystical Dimensions of Islam*; Baldick, *Mystical Islam*; Awn, "Sufism" in *Encyclopedia of Religion.*

7. See Ghazālī's remarks on the "sciences of unveiling" quoted in Part 1 (18–19).

8. Maybudī, *Kashf al-asrār* 3:734; Farghānī, *Mashāriq al-darārī* 160; ʿIrāqī, *Fakhruddin 'Iraqi* 115.

9. The various meanings and nuances of the word *dhikr* itself are highly instructive for those interested in understanding the intimate connection between Islam and Sufism. See Chittick, "Dhikr" in *Encyclopedia of Religion.*

10. Schimmel, *Mystical Dimensions* 106.

11. That the Prophet's followers should play a role is critical, because this assures a line of transmitted teachings and practices going back to Muhammad himself. This is what is implied by the Sufi term *silsila* (chain of transmission).

12. I again refer the reader to my article, "Spectrums of Islamic Thought."

13. "Implicitly" here is important because the question of how the authorities are interpreted is of primary importance. For example, Ghazālī—who clearly deals with all three dimensions of the religion—might be seen primarily as a jurist, or a Kalām authority, or a Sufi.

14. Rūmī, *Mathnawī* I 319 (quoted in SPL 146).

15. *Futūḥāt* II 42.3 (quoted in SPK 283).

16. See SPK 373–374.

Annotations

My aim in the annotations is to provide background material for nonspecialists, to pinpoint sources for the many quotations, and to illustrate the connections between the author's views and those of other Sufis, especially Ghazālī and Ibn al-ʿArabī. Throughout the annotations, I refer to the three treatises as *Rising Places, Clarifications*, and *Easy Roads*.

In tracking down sources for hadiths, I have referred first to Wensinck's *Concordance*, which indexes nine sources—Bukhārī, Muslim, Tirmidhī, Ibn Māja, Nasā'ī, Abū Dāwūd, Dārimī, Aḥmad ibn Ḥanbal, and Mālik. When I say "standard sources," I have these nine in mind. I have also checked Suyūṭī's *al-Jāmiʿ al-ṣaghīr*. If the hadith is not found in any of these, I have tried to find it in earlier works that the author may have used or had access to. The hadith references are by no means meant to be exhaustive. The purpose is simply to indicate the types of sources that were used.

THE RISING PLACES OF FAITH

35.4 *Discipline* (*riyāḍa*), that is, training the soul to bring it into conformity with the Shariah, the Tariqah (the Sufi path), and the Haqiqah (the Reality, God Himself). See the discussion of this term in Part Four (170–172).

35.6 *Unveiling* (*kashf*). As mentioned in Part One, unveiling is direct knowledge of the realities of things bestowed by God, who "lifts the veils" standing between the human being and the realities. As will become obvious in the texts, "possessors of unveiling" is one of several terms that the author employs to refer to the friends of God (*awliyā'*), those who have actualized Islam's three dimensions.

35.8 *Encounter* (*liqā'*). The encounter with God is mentioned in several Koranic verses and, as the author makes clear in all three treatises, is the goal of the spiritual quest.

35.10 *The dominion* (*malakūt*) is the unseen or spiritual world, usually contrasted with "the kingdom" (*mulk*), the material world, the world of water and clay. *The invincibility* (*jabarūt*) refers to the domain of the highest angels, the "enraptured ones," who will be mentioned in due course.

35.12 *Two Bows' Length* (*qāb-i qawsayn*). This Koranic term is taken as an allusion to the station of divine nearness that the Prophet experienced in his *mi'rāj* (his ascent to God, or "night journey"). The relevant verses read, *He stood poised, being on the higher horizon, then drew near and suspended hung, two bows' length away, or nearer, then revealed to His servant what He revealed* (53:6–10). Sufi poets such as Sanā'ī and 'Aṭṭār often employ the term Two Bows' Length in this sense, as do Sufi prose works (such as Sam'ānī, *Rawḥ al-arwāḥ* 76, 151, 271, 273, 307, 314, 329, 544, 545, 596). In the teachings of Qūnawī and his followers, the term refers to the highest station of spiritual perfection achieved by the prophets and perfect human beings other than the Prophet Muhammad. It correlates with what Ibn al-'Arabī usually calls the "nearness of supererogatory works." The Prophet's own station is that of "Or Nearer" (a term derived from the same Koranic verses), which correlates with the "nearness of obligatory works." See 'Irāqī, *Fakhruddin* 147–148; SPK 325–331.

35.13 *Mustafa*, literally "the Chosen," is one of the most common titles of the Prophet.

35.16 *To come to the point*. The author provides here a rationale for writing the treatise that has many precedents in Sufi works. Qushayrī (d. 465/1073) begins his famous *Risāla* by complaining about contemporary society: "Respect for the Shariah has departed from hearts, people consider unconcern for religion the surest means to reach their goals, and they reject the distinction between the lawful and the unlawful. . . ." (28). Ghazālī, at the beginning of the *Iḥyā'*, excuses himself for writing the book by referring to the sad situation of the contemporary Muslim community, especially those who should be teaching Islam in its fullness, the ulama (1:2–3; *Book of Knowledge* 1–2).

35.19 *Islam began as an exile*. . . . The hadith is found in Muslim (Īmān 232), Tirmidhī (Īmān 13), Ibn Māja (Fitan 15) and other sources (see also Jām, *Uns* 245–248).

35.25 *If you want enemies, Mahdī*. . . . Sanā'ī, *Dīwān* 184. The Mahdī is a descendant of the Prophet who, along with Christ, will fill the earth with justice at the end of time.

35.30 *A group among my community will never cease to support the Truth*. . . . Several versions of this hadith have come in the standard sources. Versions only slightly different from that given here are found in Bukhārī, I'tiṣām 10; Muslim, Īmān 247, Imāra 170, 173; Abū Dāwūd, Fitan 1, Jihād 4; Tirmidhī, Fitan 51.

35.32 *Those with living hearts and Jesus' breath*. The living heart embraces God's self-disclosure, in accordance with the often quoted hadith, "My heaven embraces Me not, nor My earth, but the heart of My believing servant does embrace Me." The author brings out the importance of the heart in the conclusion to this work (54). The Breath of Jesus is the mark of the great shaykhs, who bring to life those who are spiritually dead by guiding them to a new birth.

35.34 *They are God's vicegerents in the earth.* This sentence is taken from a famous saying of ʿAlī (*Nahj al-balāgha* 496) directed at Kumayl ibn Ziyād. The author quotes another passage from this same saying in *Clarifications* 92.31.

36.4 *Primordial religion* (*dīn-i ḥanīfī*), that is, Islam. The Koranic term *ḥanīf* is associated both with *islām* and with the religion of Abraham (see 2:135, 3:67, 4:125, etc.).

36.12 *There is no power and no strength*. . . . This sentence is found in numerous hadiths.

36.26 *I wandered in all those places*. . . . Well-known Arabic verses whose authorship is not known for certain. See Meier's note in Kubrā, *Fawā'iḥ* 93–94.

36.30 *Let your natural reason go*. . . . Sanā'ī, *Dīwān* 460. The author also quotes this poem in *Clarifications* 71.10, with a textual difference—"learning" (*ʿilm*) instead of "reason" (*ʿaql*). Sanā'ī's *Dīwān* has a third reading: "soul" (*nafs*).

36.34 *How evil a steed*. . . . This is an Arabic proverb that is also quoted by Hamadānī, *Tamhīdāt* 13.

36.36 *Imitation* (*taqlīd*), or following the authority of others in matters of faith. It is the opposite of verification (*taḥqīq*). See Part Four, 177–178.

37.1 *If you want to fly to Mount Sinai*. . . . The verses are by Afḍal al-Dīn Badīl ibn ʿAlī (d. 582/1186 or 595/1199), known as Khāqānī (*Tuḥfat al-ʿIrāqayn* 65–66). Khāqānī often refers to himself as the "Son of ʿAlī" (Ibn ʿAlī). The "Father of ʿAlī" (Bū ʿAlī) is Ibn Sīnā or Avicenna (d. 428/1037), the foremost Muslim Peripatetic philosopher. In Sufi writings, Avicenna is pictured as a rational thinker who wastes his life and abilities by following conjecture and surmise without reaching the Truth. Compare Rūmī's verse, "He that has a vision of that Light—how could the Father of ʿAlī ever explain his state?" (*Mathnawī* 4:506). The Prophet was a member of the Arab tribe of Quraysh, while Ibn Sīnā was a native of Bukhara.

37.10 *Which has abrogated the other Shariahs*. Some Muslims would understand this abrogation (*naskh*) to mean that Islam is the only valid religion left on the face of the earth, but this is an open issue, because the only certain knowledge that Muslims have here is the repeated Koranic injunction that they must accept all of God's messages as true. In other words, the position a Muslim takes on this issue—which pertains to the three principles of faith—depends upon interpretation of the texts, and opinions differ. As in most other issues of faith, there is room for discussion. Although the Kalām authorities tend in the direction of exclusivism, many Sufis stress universality. For example, Ibn al-ʿArabī reminds his readers that Muslims are required to have faith in the "messengers and the scriptures"—that is, all the messengers and scriptures from Adam down to Muhammad. Muhammad, as he has told us in a sound hadith, was sent with "the all-comprehensive words," so his religion includes within itself the fundamental teachings of all religions. This all-inclusiveness of Islam proves that other religions have not been abrogated. If they were, how could they be part of Islam? He writes,

> All the revealed religions [*sharā'i'*] are lights. Among these religions, the revealed religion of Muhammad is like the light of the sun among the lights of the stars. When the sun appears, the lights of the stars are hidden, and their lights are included in the light of the sun. Their being hidden is like the abrogation of other revealed religions that takes place through Muhammad's revealed religion. Nevertheless, they do in fact exist, just as the existence of the light of the stars is actualized. This explains why we have been required in our all-inclusive religion to have faith in the truth of all the messengers and all the revealed religions. They are not rendered null [*bāṭil*] by abrogration—that is the opinion of the ignorant. (*Futūḥāt* 3:153.12)

37.33 *Friends of God* (*awliyā'*). This term (singular, *walī*) has often been translated as "saints" and plays an important role in the Sufis' explanations of their aspirations and achievements. In general, they employ the term to refer to those human beings whom God has taken into His own proximity and who are fulfilling the proper function of human existence. In other words, they have perfected their faith and practice. Many authors consider the friends more or less synonymous with the Koranic *al-muqarrabūn* (those brought near to God), especially since nearness is one of the root meanings of the term. The *locus classicus* for the high regard accorded to the friends is the Koranic verse, *Surely God's friends—no fear shall be upon them, neither shall they grieve* (10:62). The author discusses the quality of friendship (*walāya*) in some detail (81–88) in terms reminiscent of Ibn al-'Arabī's teachings. For a good summary of the role of the concept of *walāya* in Sufism and Shi'ism, see H. Landolt, "Walāya," *Encyclopedia of Religion*.

37.34 *Alast*. This term refers to the covenant made between God and the children of Adam before their entrance into this world. It is derived from the following Koranic verse: *And when your Lord took from the children of Adam, from their loins, their seed, and made them testify touching themselves: "Am I not* [alast] *your Lord?" They said, "Yes, we testify"—lest you should say on the Day of Resurrection, "As for us, we were heedless of this"* (7:172). The covenant is a standard theme in Sufi works. See Schimmel, *Mystical Dimensions*, passim.

37.34 *Then He sprinkled*. . . . This is the second half of a hadith which begins, "God created the creatures in darkness." Aḥmad (2:176) and Tirmidhī

(Īmān 18) have "threw" (*alqā*) instead of "sprinkled" (*rashsha*). It is found with "sprinkled" in Suhrawardī, *Majmū'a* 221, and Qūnawī, *Fukūk* 255.

37.36 *We came from the Ruins of Love*.... 'Aṭṭār, *Dīwān* 495. In other words, from the moment God said, "Am I not your Lord?", this third group became so intoxicated with His beauty that they did not possess enough self-awareness to answer, "Yes, we testify." The ruins (*kharābāt*) are where people go to drink, because wine is illegal and cannot be sold in the city. In Sufi terminology, the term *ruins* sometimes refers, as here, to the "nonexistence" that is the source of all existence (see Rūmī's discussions of nonexistence in this sense, SPL 175–178), or it refers to the station of annihilation (*fanā'*), where the spiritual traveler's own attributes are destroyed in order to be replaced by those of God (see SPL 315–316).

38.1 *I think the soul forgot covenants*.... This Arabic verse is from Avicenna's famous "Ode on the Soul," *al-Qaṣīdat al-'ayniyya*. See the loose translation of this ode in Browne, *Literary History* 2:110–111. The verse here corresponds to Browne 111, lines 3–4.

38.11 *Original disposition* (*fiṭrat*). The word *fiṭra* is used in the Koran to refer to the way things are as created by God. In the tradition, it is looked upon as the innate knowledge of *tawḥīd* possessed by every human being—a knowledge, however, that needs to be reawakened by revelation.

38.14 *Solomon has found*.... According to a well-known story, Solomon controlled all creatures through the power of his ring, upon which certain divine names were inscribed. When he went to the washroom one day, a jinni assumed the form of the faithful servant to whom he always entrusted the ring. Upon acquiring the ring, the jinni took Solomon's form and sat upon the throne. Solomon himself was not able to claim to be the rightful king. He wandered in the desert for many days and finally went to the sea, where he would fish by day and worship by night. Āṣaf, Solomon's faithful vizier, realized that the actions of the king were not in keeping with Solomon's wisdom. When he confronted the jinni, it became frightened and fled. It threw the ring into the sea, and a fish swallowed it. The fish was caught by a fisherman, who took pity on Solomon, since he had not caught any fish that day. The fisherman gave Solomon the fish, and when he cut it open to clean it, he found his lost ring and realized that God had returned his authority to him after forty days of trial (Gawharīn, *Farhang* 4:190–192; for another version of the story, see Kisā'ī, *Tales* 317–319). In the Sufi interpretation, Solomon represents the soul that is trapped in this world, while the ring is the soul's true nature, the heart upon which is inscribed God's greatest name. Compare Rūmī, "Knowledge is the ring of Solomon's sovereignty; the whole world is form, and knowledge is spirit" (*Mathnawī* 1:1030).

As for Joseph, Sufi poets frequently refer to his return to Jacob as an image of the soul returning to its eternal abode. The most famous example is the following two lines of Ḥāfiẓ (*Dīwān* 172; see also *Diwan of Hafiz* 499):

Lost Joseph will return to Canaan, grieve not!
Sorrow's home will bloom with roses, grieve not!
O grief-stricken heart, your state will improve, fear not!
This frantic head will regain its calm, grieve not!

38.17 *The pain that we heard about*.... Sanā'ī, *Dīwān* 335.

38.24 *Khizr*. The story of Moses and Khizr (Khiḍr, Khaḍir) is told in the Koran (18:66–83). In the usual Sufi interpretation, Khizr represents direct spiritual knowledge given by God (*knowledge from Us*), while Moses represents the law-bound perspective of the Shariah.

38.28 *We are the sun*.... The second verse of this quatrain is attributed to Rūmī (*Rubāʿiyyāt*, n. 1365). In that version, the first verse reads,

We are the hidden treasure in the world of clay,
we are the keeper of the everlasting kingdom.

38.29 *"Be, and it was!"* Allusion to several Koranic verses that refer to God's creation of the universe, such as *His command, when He desires a thing, is to say to it "Be!" and it is* (36:82).

39.9 *Nondelimited Being* (*wujūd-i muṭlaq*). On God as nondelimited Being in Ibn al-ʿArabī's teachings, see SPK, especially chapter 3 and 109–112.

39.10 *He was, and no one was with Him*.... These sentences paraphrase a hadith often quoted by Ibn al-ʿArabī and his followers. "God was [or is], and nothing was [or is] with Him." In the standard sources, the nearest text to this is "God was, and there was nothing other than He" (Bukhārī, Bad' al-Khalq 1). In the language of Islamic philosophy, this perception of God follows upon the definition of God and the cosmos. God is the Necessary Being who cannot not be, while everything in the cosmos is a possible thing that has no intrinsic claim to existence. If it exists in a certain respect, its existence is on loan from God. Hence, its existence is not really worthy of the name. Ibn al-ʿArabī frequently discusses this point. See SPK, especially part 3.

39.18 *Glory be to Him who discloses Himself from every direction*.... This short prayer is probably based on the saying of al-Ḥallāj quoted in *Clarifications* 83.1.

39.27 *Possible existence* (*imkān*). This technical term of the philosophers and theologians juxtaposes the ambiguous nature of created existence with the absolute reality and necessity of God's Being. For its significance in the context of Ibn al-ʿArabī's teachings, see SPK, index, under *possibility*.

39.34 *Glory be to Him who has set down no path*.... This saying is attributed to Abū Bakr in many sources, such as Sarrāj, *Lumaʿ* 36, 124; Makkī, *Qūt* 2:174.

40.3 *No heart has a way to His inmost center*.... Sanā'ī, *Ḥadīqa* 61.

40.7 *What is true knowledge?* "True knowledge" renders *ma'rifa*, which I also translate as "knowledge" and, on occasion, "gnosis." Authors sometimes differentiate between *ma'rifa* and *'ilm* (knowledge), and sometimes do not (see Part One, 17–18; for Ibn al-'Arabī's discussion of this point, see SPK 148–149). In the present context, *ma'rifa* can probably be contrasted with *'ilm*, which can be understood to mean "received learning." The answer to the question employs two important terms in Kalām—*tashbīh* (declaring God similar) and *ta'ṭīl* (declaring Him disconnected). The Kalām authorities situate the two positions at opposite extremes and consider both of them heretical. They commonly criticize their opponents for believing in one or the other, although no one would claim to hold either of the positions. Since everyone rejects both, this definition of true knowledge should be acceptable to all concerned. See the article "Tashbīh" in the *Encyclopedia of Islam* (old edition). The Ash'arite theologians took the term *tanzīh* (God's incomparability with all things) as denoting the middle position (Wensinck, *Muslim Creed* 207–208), but Ibn al-'Arabī held that *tanzīh* itself, given the way it was being interpreted by the theologians, was an extreme. Note that his position, referred to in the next sentence, differs from most of his predecessors by affirming *tashbīh*, although he also negates it by affirming *tanzīh*. In any case, the middle position which he occupies is normative, in the sense that most theologians and Sufis were trying to achieve a balance between two extremes.

40.9 *The people of witnessing* (*ahl-i shuhūd*), that is, the people of unveiling. Concerning the balance that Ibn al-'Arabī establishes between the declaration of similarity and incomparability and his recourse to the contrary divine names—such as Manifest (*ẓāhir*) and Nonmanifest (*bāṭin*)—in expressing this, see SPK 68–76 and passim; Murata, *Tao*, chapters 2–3.

40.14 *If I speak. . . .* Sanā'ī, *Ḥadīqa* 82.

40.19 *Because of hiddenness. . . .* 'Aṭṭār, *Dīwān* 65.

40.26 *I saw my Lord in the most beautiful form.* Qushayrī gives this hadith with the addition "on the night of the *mi'rāj*" (*Risāla* 204). See Corbin's remarks on the importance of this saying in Ibn al-'Arabī's teachings (*Creative Imagination* 272–277).

40.28 *Glory be to God. . . .* Compare the following prayer of Ibn al-'Arabī: "Glory be to Him who is incomparable with incomparability through similarity and with similarity through incomparability!" (*Futūḥāt* 1:751.35).

40.29 *Since you call Him manifest and hidden. . . .* 'Aṭṭār, *Dīwān* 66.

40.32 *See Him with the eyes of their head.* As mentioned in Part One, the Kalām authorities consider seeing God to be impossible in this world, while the Sufis maintain that He can be seen. But again, they do not claim to see God in Himself, or God as Nonmanifest, but God as He discloses Himself, or God as Manifest. The quatrain quoted next makes this point clearly.

40.36 *If love makes your heart want to see....* This is a quatrain by Awḥad al-Dīn Kirmānī (*Dīwān*, n. 1023).

41.8 *The heart knows only the temporal....* Sanā'ī, *Dīwān* 105.

41.16 *Giving True Knowledge of the Attributes.* Ibn al-ʿArabī and his followers often call the attributes discussed here the "seven leaders."

41.24 *What is tawḥīd?* Note that the definition of *tawḥīd* offered here is parallel to the definition of true knowledge offered earlier (40.8). Both involve maintaining a balance between *tashbīh* and *taʿṭīl*.

41.27 *Majesty and beauty* (*jalāl wa jamāl*). These are the two basic categories of names, also called the names of "justice [*ʿadl*] and bounty [*faḍl*]," or "mercy [*raḥma*] and wrath [*ghaḍab*]," or "gentleness [*luṭf*] and severity [*qahr*]." As Ibn al-ʿArabī likes to point out, these are the "two hands of God" through which He creates and maintains the universe. The names of majesty correlate with incomparability—God as Nonmanifest, Inaccessible, Holy, Far, and King. The names of beauty correlate with similarity—God as Manifest, Loving, Forgiving, and Near. See Murata, *Tao*, especially chapter 3.

42.4 *None repels His decree, None holds back His judgment.* These two sentences are often cited together, for example, in Ghazālī, *Iḥyā'* 1:83 (1.2.3.3), 3:36 (3.1.14).

42.7 *Desire is different from good-pleasure.* In other words, God envisaged as the Desiring is different from God envisaged as He who is pleased with His servants. This type of recourse to the divine names is common in Ibn al-ʿArabī's teachings. The rationale is that each divine name denotes a specific kind of relationship between God and the cosmos, and the relationships are different (see SPK, chapters 2–3). For example, God is Knowing, which is to say that He has knowledge of all things. He is Desiring, which is to say that He desires to bring some of what He knows into existence in any given circumstance. His desire depends upon His knowledge, because He cannot desire what He does not know. However, His knowledge does not depend on His desire, because He can know something that He does not desire to bring into existence. On the third level, God is Powerful, which is to say that He has the absolute ability to bring into existence what He desires. But until He desires something, He does not bring it into existence, and His power cannot overrule His desire. First He desires, then He exercises power and creates. As for "good-pleasure" (*riḍā*), it is the opposite of the divine attribute "anger" (*sakhṭ*). Thus the Prophet said that the people of paradise ask God what could be greater than the Garden, and He replies, "My good-pleasure, for I will never again be angry with you" (Bukhārī, Tawḥīd 37; Muslim, Īmān 302). The point being alluded to in the text is that God exercises His power to bring a universe into existence on the basis of desire, but He is not pleased with everything that happens in the universe. Quite the contrary.

He is angry with some of it. If a person objects that He should not then have brought it into existence, the answer is simply that desire is different from good-pleasure. God is the Possessor of Wrath and of Anger, the Severe in Punishment, the Avenger—all these are divine attributes that denote the Essence Itself, that is, God's very nature. In other terms, God has "two hands," and He cannot create a whole cosmos employing only one hand, because a cosmos demands variety and difference, which, in turn, demand conflict. Both names of majesty and names of beauty must have loci of manifestation. In the last analysis, however, since God is One, all multiplicity is harmonized by Unity—which is to say that all evil is neutralized by a greater good. "God's mercy precedes His wrath," so mercy wins out in the end. God's good-pleasure is more real than His anger, so all anger eventually turns into good-pleasure. The author points this out in his own way in several passages.

In the context of the contrast between desire and good-pleasure, Ibn al-ʿArabī has the following to say, although he is employing the term "decree" (*qaḍāʾ*) instead of desire.

> The seeker should desire to be pleased with God's decree in what He makes happen, but not with everything that is decreed [*maqḍī*]. It is not proper to be pleased with everything decreed, even if you see the Face of the Real within it, for, if you have a sound vision, you will see that the Real's Face within it is not pleased with it, even if you do not see with the divine eye. Otherwise, if you are pleased with it, you have not seen Him, for *He is not pleased with the truth-concealing of His servants* [39.7]. (*Futūḥāt* 2:213.32)

42.9 *The mystery of the measuring out* (*sirr-i qadar*). For sample explanations of this mystery, see the note on 79.39.

42.11 *When the fire takes*. . . . Sanāʾī, *Dīwān* 192. The verse alludes to the accounts of the Prophet's *miʿrāj* according to which Gabriel could not guide the Prophet beyond a certain point because, if he went any further, his wings would burn. The implication is that the mystery of the measuring out can only be grasped in the station in which the gnostic attains to oneness with God, beyond the angelic hierarchy.

42.14 *Measuring out is God's mystery*. . . . This saying is often quoted as a hadith (Hamadānī, *Nāmahā* 2:197, 221, 272; Suhrawardī, *Majmūʿa* 327). But Ghazālī, as does the author here, refers to it simply as a saying of those who know. Ghazālī tells us why this mystery should not be divulged after explaining that knowledge is necessarily divided into outward or "exoteric" (*ẓāhir*), or that which is related to the Shariah, and inward or "esoteric" (*bāṭin*), or that which is related to the Reality (*ḥaqīqa*). This does not imply that the two types of knowledge contradict each other, for "He who says that the Reality opposes the Shariah, or the inward contradicts the outward, is nearer to truth-concealing than to faith." However, certain truths "are singled out for the perception of those brought near to God," so most people do not share in them. Then Ghazālī enumerates five reasons for keeping these truths hidden. The first is that they are beyond the comprehension of most people and hence would only confuse them. In discussing the second type, Ghazālī mentions the mystery of the measuring out. "The understanding is not too weak to grasp [the second type], but mentioning it would be harmful to most listeners, although it does not harm the prophets and the sincere devotees. The mystery of the measuring out—the divulgence of which has been forbidden by the learned—is of this type" (*Iḥyā'* 1:75 [1.2.2]; for the discussion in its context, see Ghazālī, *Foundations* 38–53).

42.18 *What Thou willest, will be*. . . . The poem is by Imam Shāfi'ī, the founder of the Shāfi'i school of the Shariah (Anṣārī, *Ṭabaqāt al-ṣūfiyya* 38; Sam'ānī, *Rawḥ al-arwāḥ* 161–162).

42.40 *The Furqān*. The "Discernment," the best known name of the Koran after "Koran" itself.

43.3 *Personified* (*tashakhkhuṣ*), *locus of manifestation* (*maẓhar*). Both are technical terms in Ibn al-'Arabī's school. "Personification," often used as a synonym for "imaginalization" (*tamaththul*), refers to the appearance of intelligible meanings, which have no forms, within the world of imagination or sense perception. The standard example is provided by a hadith in which the Prophet says that he was given milk to drink in a dream, and that the milk was knowledge. Hence, knowledge had been personified or imaginalized as milk.

The term *locus of manifestation* has two basic meanings. In a broader sense, it refers to each existent thing, since each is a place within which the names and attributes of God become manifest, displaying their effects and properties. In the narrower sense, as employed here, the term refers to something that becomes manifest within the imaginal world in a form appropriate to its intelligible reality, such as an angel or, as here, a scripture. Compare Ibn al-'Arabī's use of the term in SPK 251, column 1, line 17.

Ibn al-'Arabī frequently discusses the relationship between revelation and the world of imagination. He defines revelation as God's "sending down disengaged, intelligible meanings within delimited, sensory forms in the Presence of Imagination. . . . It is perceived by the senses in a sensory domain" (*Futūḥāt* 2:58.8), because the world of imagination combines by definition the attributes of the spiritual and the sensory. Elsewhere, he writes,

> Revelation begins with dream-visions, not the sensory world, since intelligible meanings [*al-ma'ānī al-ma'qūla*] are closer to imagination than they are to sense perception. The reason for this is that the sensory realm is the lower side, while meaning is the higher and subtler domain, and imagination stands between the two. Revelation

is a meaning. When God sends down a meaning to the sensory world, it has to pass through the Presence of Imagination before it reaches the sensory world. And one of imagination's characteristics is that it gives sensory form to everything actualized within it—there is no escape from this. (*Futūḥāt* 2:375.32)

43.5 *My Lord taught me courtesy*. The word *courtesy* (*adab*) is rich in connotations in Islamic thought in general and Sufism in particular. In the Sufi context, to observe courtesy is to do things exactly in the way that pleases God as set down in the Sunnah of the Prophet and the example of God's friends. It is to act with full awareness of God's presence, or "to worship God as if you see Him." In other words, it is to observe the necessities of the situation as defined by the Real. A famous early definition of Sufism has it that "Sufism, all of it, is acts of courtesy (*ādāb*)" (Hujwīrī, *Kashf al-maḥjūb* 47; trans. Nicholson, 41–42). See also Nurbakhsh, *Sufism* 4:139–154; SPK 174–179 and passim. Suyūṭī gives the text of the hadith as, "God taught me courtesy, so He made my courtesy beautiful" (*Fayḍ* 1:224). Sufis frequently quote it (such as Hujwīrī, *Kashf* 432, trans. Nicholson, 334; Hamadānī, *Tamhīdāt* 66, 174; Rūzbihān, *Mashrab* 141).

43.9 *The Koran-bride*. . . . Sanā'ī, *Dīwān* 52. Rūmī develops Sanā'ī's image of the Koran as a bride (*Discourses* 236–237; SPL 273).

43.13 *The Koran is memorized by hearts, recited by tongues, and written on pages*. Similar formulae are standard in the theological creeds. Compare Abū Ḥanīfa (Wensinck, *Muslim Creed* 127, 189), Nasafī (Elder, *Commentary*, 58), Ghazālī (*Iḥyā'* 1:82 [1.2.3.2.6]; *Qawā'id* 151).

43.26 *[Those names Thou hast] kept for Thyself*. . . . Aḥmad 1:391, 452. The whole text of the hadith is quoted on 62.1.

43.28 *Four types* (of names). The first three types are explained in *Clarifications* 72.16–25. The fourth type, report-derived (*khabarī*), probably refers to names such as Allāh (or analogous personal names in other religions) that cannot be rationally deduced but must be provided by revelation.

44.11 *Surely in that are signs*. . . . This Arabic sentence is based on several Koranic verses, the closest being 3:190: *Surely in the creation of the heavens and the earth and the alternation of the night and day are signs for the possessors of minds*.

44.13 *If you don't want reason to laugh*. . . . Sanā'ī, *Dīwān* 201.

44.17 *Supraformal reality* (*ma'nā*). The term *ma'nā*, which I usually translate as "meaning," is invariably employed in Sufi writings as the opposite of *ṣūra* (form). To translate it as "meaning" here would be to suggest an abstract, unreal, or mental sort of operation when, in fact, the author has in view an ontological transformation.

44.20 *In the world of reason and faith*. . . . Sanā'ī, *Ḥadīqa* 425.

44.22 *None will enter the dominion*. . . . An Arabic translation of John 3:3.

44.29 *Cherubim* (*karrūbiyyūn*). Ibn al-ʿArabī devotes a good deal of attention to describing these angels in the *Futūḥāt*, although he more commonly refers to them as the "enraptured spirits" (*al-arwāḥ al-muhayyama*). See Ibn al-ʿArabī, *Futūḥāt* 1:93.5, 148.13, 199–202, 240.3, 252.1, 294.32; 2:19.13, 53.20, 174.18, 310.28, 488.33, 675.4; 3:31.10, 137.2, 294.16, 390.16, 430.4; Ḥakīm, *Muʿjam* 876–878.

45.2 *An angel comes down with every drop of rain.* ʿAyn al-Quḍāt gives a similar hadith (Hamadānī, *Nāmahā* 2:208).

45.12 *Their mastery over human beings*. Sharaf al-Dīn Qayṣarī (d. 751/1350) provides an explanation for this mystery in his commentary on Ibn al-ʿArabī's *Fuṣūṣ al-ḥikam*. Although he is speaking about Adam, it is taken for granted (and made explicit by Ibn al-ʿArabī in any case), that the word *Adam* refers to human beings in general. He is in the midst of discussing the fact that human beings are vicegerents of God because they are made in His form.

> Satan also is a vassal of Adam's reality, even if he took Adam out of the Garden and misguided him through whispering. For Adam's reality gives aid from the world of the unseen to the loci of manifestation for all God's names, just as his Lord gives aid to all the names. Hence, in reality, Adam himself misguided himself in order that all his individuals might reach their appropriate perfection and enter into the abode that seeks them, whether the Garden or the Fire. Were it not for the aid that Satan takes from Adam, he would not have had any authority over him. From here one comes to know the secret of Satan's words, *Do not blame me, but blame yourselves* [14:22]. That is sufficient proof against them, for their own immutable entities demanded that. Hence Satan's misguidance of Adam and his taking him out of the Garden does not detract from Adam's vicegerency and lordship. (*Sharḥ fuṣūṣ al-ḥikam* 90–91)

See also the passages on the mystery of the measuring out quoted in the note to 79.39.

45.13 *None knows it but God*. . . . A reference to Koran 3:7. *None knows its interpretation save God and those firmly rooted in knowledge*.

45.14 *Until God brings opening*. Note that the author understands the term *opening* (*fatḥ*) in the technical sense in which the Sufis employ it, as in the title of Ibn al-ʿArabī's magnum opus, *al-Futūḥāt al-makkiyya* (The Meccan Openings). In this sense, the word is synonymous with unveiling and witnessing. More specifically, it refers to the "opening of the door" (*fatḥ al-bāb*)—that is, as Qūnawī's disciple Jandī puts it, the "opening of the heart's door" (*gushāyish-i dar-i dil*; *Nafḥa* 154), or the initial experience of unveiling—for the authenticity of which Jandī is careful to provide criteria.

Another of Qūnawī's disciples, Farghānī, defines opening as the "manifestation of the ontological mystery" (*ẓuhūr-i sirr-i wujūdī*)—that is, the unveiling of the hidden essence of the human being that is concealed by immersion in the lower world (*Mashāriq* 70). Compare Qūnawī's discussion of various levels of divine, cosmic, and human opening in *I'jāz al-bayān* 152–158/263–268.

45.33 *Images and semblances* (*muthul wa ashbāḥ*). These two terms may be taken from the philosopher Suhrawardī, who employs them, although not in this exact form, in his *Ḥikmat al-ishrāq*. In the parallel passage in *Clarifications* 81.11, the author remarks that the "world of images" is the terminology of "a group of those learned in wisdom"—that is, a group of philosophers. Ibn al-ʿArabī and his followers rarely employ these particular terms, preferring instead *imagination* (*khayāl*) or *image* (*mithāl*, the singular of *muthul*).

45.34 *Barzakh*. The literal meaning of the term is "isthmus." It is mentioned three times in the Koran, twice in the context of an isthmus that keeps the sweet and bitter seas from mixing (25:53, 55:20). These two seas are frequently interpreted as the corporeal and spiritual worlds; then the isthmus is understood as the world of imagination, which is neither purely corporeal nor purely spiritual but combines the attributes of both and keeps the two worlds separate. The third Koranic mention of the term (23:100) refers to the experience of the soul after death, and the tradition identifies this barzakh with the grave, which is the isthmus between this life and the resurrection. The author will have more to say about the barzakh in this sense in the sections on the Return. Ibn al-ʿArabī and his followers consider the barzakh after this world as one of the many worlds embraced by the first barzakh. See SPK, chapter 7 and passim.

45.34 *Insight* (*baṣīra*). For the Sufis, this is more or less synonymous with unveiling and witnessing. It is a God-given vision of the intelligence, as contrasted with *baṣar* (sight), the natural vision of the eyes. Insight sees into the unseen world, while sight sees only the visible world.

46.13 *A man is needed*. . . A Persian verse that has the color of a proverb in Sufi texts. Maybudī, for example, frequently quotes it (*Kashf al-asrār* 1:129, 442; 4:302, 346; 5:244, 6:492). On the use of the term *man*, see the note on 51.21.

46.30 *Every day*. . . . By citing this verse, the author shows that he has in mind Ibn al-ʿArabī's teachings on the renewal of creation at each instant, the "instant" being the "day" of the Essence. See SPK 18 and index of Koranic verses, 55:29.

46.33 *Though the act is not mine*. . . . This is the first line of a quatrain by Kirmānī (*Dīwān*, n. 352). The second line reads,

In the body's darkness,
  the soul needs a lamp.
Though the intellect is a lamp,
  it does not shine by itself.

46.42 *The perfect* (*kummal*). In Ibn al-ʿArabī's technical vocabulary, this term functions as the plural of *al-insān al-kāmil*, the perfect human being, who is a prophet or a great friend of God. See SPK, index, under *perfect.*

47.5 *In Him refuge is taken from Him.* Reference to the prophetic saying quoted in *Clarifications* 109.20.

47.5 *What He wills will be*.... A hadith found in Abū Dāwūd (Adab 101).

47.27 *You should know that it is impossible for the embryo*.... The author may have in view a similar but more detailed discussion by Ghazālī. Part of that passage reads as follows:

> Just as an infant in the cradle finds it difficult to understand the reality of discrimination, and the discriminating child finds it difficult to understand the reality of reason and the wonders that become unveiled in reason's stage before he reaches it, so also the stage of reason finds it difficult to understand the stages of friendship and prophecy. For friendship is a stage of perfection beyond the plane of reason, just as reason is a stage of perfection beyond the plane of discrimination, and discrimination is a stage beyond the plane of the senses.
>
> It is human nature for people to deny what they have not reached and attained. Thus each person denies what he does not witness and has not reached, and he has no faith in what remains unseen for him. Hence, it is people's nature to deny friendship and its wonders as well as prophecy and its marvels. Or rather, it is their nature to deny the second configuration and the next life, because they have not yet reached it. If the stage of reason and its world along with all the wonders that become manifest within it were to be presented to the discriminating child, he would deny it, reject it, and declare its existence impossible. Hence, he who has faith in something that he has not yet reached has had faith in the Unseen, and that is the key to every felicity. (*al-Maqṣad al-asnā* 135–136)

47.32 *Mujassima*. The Mujassima, as indicated by their name, are those who maintain that God has a body. Whether anyone really held this belief or not is unclear, but many were accused of it. The author connects them to "fancy and imagination" (*wahm wa khayāl*) because imagination, as Ibn al-ʿArabī points out, is limited by the fact that it cannot understand anything whatsoever except through embodiment as a form; in contrast, pure reason understands things disengaged from forms. Compare SPK 115ff., especially 122.

48.1 *When the dust clears you will know. . . .* Tha'ālibī (*Tamthīl* 345) cites this Arabic verse as proverbial. Sufi texts often quote it (for example, Maybudī, *Kashf al-asrār* 10:310; Aḥmad Ghazālī, *Majmū'a* 381; 'Ayn al-Quḍāt, *Nāmahā* 1:183).

48.13 *Only declaring similarity and coining likenesses can tell of these objects.* This explanation of the rationale for the imaginal and mythic language found in scripture is probably derived from the teachings of Ibn al-'Arabī, who devotes a great deal of attention to it. Reason, he tells us, can grasp only half the truth, that of God's incomparability. Imagination alone can understand God's similarity. See SPK 186–187 and index, under *imagination, reason.*

48.20 *"Faith in the unseen"* (*īmān bi ghayb*). This is a standard Koranic expression. For example, it is found at the very beginning of Sura 2 in verses that allude to Islam's three dimensions. *This is the Book within which is no doubt, a guide for the god-wary, those who have faith in the unseen and perform the ritual prayer. . .* (2:2–3).

48.24 *Deduction* (*qiyās*). Rūmī often criticizes deductions of this type. One of the more entertaining examples is the story he tells at the beginning of the *Mathnawī* about the parrot who becomes bald after being hit by his master for spilling some rose oil. After that, the parrot refuses to speak, until one day a bald dervish walks by, and the parrot says to him, "Did you spill your master's oil"? Rūmī concludes (*Mathnawī* 1:263–267):

> Do not deduce the business of the pure from yourself,
>   even if *shēr* [lion] is written like *shīr* [milk].
> This has caused the whole world to go astray—
>   few indeed have become aware of God's saints.
> People claim equality with the prophets,
>   they think the friends are like themselves.
> "We're human," they say, "and they're human—
>   both of us need to sleep and eat."
> In their blindness they do not know
>   that the difference between them is infinite.

48.28 *The blind man knows he has a mother. . . .* Sanā'ī, *Ḥadīqa* 82.

48.37 *Heart, how long. . . .* Sanā'ī, *Dīwān* 704.

49.1 *The final stages of the friends are the beginning stages of the prophets.* Ibn al-'Arabī calls this statement a "principle of the way" (*Futūḥāt* 2:51.28; quoted in SPK 222).

49.5 *Ibn 'Abbās* (d. 68/687–688). A relative and companion of the Prophet through whom numerous hadiths were transmitted and who is considered a great authority in Koran commentary.

49.30 *Gnostic sciences* (*ma'ārif*), that is, the sciences of unveiling. The term *gnostic* (*'ārif*) is employed by most Sufis and many philosophers to refer to a person who has achieved direct and authentic knowledge of God, if not to a friend of God or a perfect human being. For Ibn al-ʿArabī's views, see SPK, index, under *gnostic*.

49.37 *Praiseworthy station*. That this station (usually identified with the right to intercede with God) is promised to the Prophet is mentioned in the hadith literature (Aḥmad 1:398, 3:456) and in the Koran commentaries on this verse.

50.5 *Ever since being's*.... Sanā'ī, *Ḥadīqa* 190, 207.

50.19 *On Faith in Human Subsistence*.... The author provides more detailed accounts in *Clarifications* 93–104. Cf. Ghazālī, *The Remembrance of Death*; idem, *The Precious Pearl*; Smith and Haddad, *The Islamic Understanding of Death and Resurrection.*

50.31 *You were created for eternity without end*.... Although often cited as a hadith, this well-known saying is not considered to be sound by specialists such as Suyūṭī, in *al-La'ālī al-maṣnūʿa* (cited by the editor of *Easy Roads* in the notes to the text, Juwaynī, *Manāhij* 108).

50.32 *The grave is one of the plots*.... A hadith found in Tirmidhī, Qiyāma 26.

51.5 *On the day of resurrection death will be brought*.... Several versions of this sound hadith are found in the standard sources, for example, Bukhārī, Tafsīr Sūra 19, 1.

51.11 *We would have opened upon them blessings*.... Here again, the author has in mind the technical sense of the term opening (see the note on 45.14). He quotes this verse in a similar context in all three treatises.

51.21 *Men*. Persian *mard*—like Arabic *rajul*—is commonly employed to refer to a friend of God or a shaykh. The expression has in view the quality of discipline and self-mastery that is necessary to move forward on the path to perfection. The term is applied to both men and women. As the well-known Sufi saying has it, "The seeker of the Lord is male, and the seeker of this world female." For Rūmī's use of the term *mard*, which is typical for Persian Sufi poetry, see Chittick, *Sufi Path of Love* 163–169. For a much broader investigation of the term's use in Islamic thought, see Murata, *Tao of Islam*, especially chapter 10.

51.38 *Munkar and Nakīr*. The names of two angels. See *Easy Roads* 126.29, where a few details are supplied.

52.1 *Bodily form*. Note that the author uses the term *jasadī* for "bodily." Ibn al-ʿArabī frequently employs this term to refer to subtle bodies, as opposed to *jismānī*, which refers to gross, physical bodies. Elsewhere (SPK) I have distinguished the two terms by translating the first as "corporeous" and the second as "corporeal."

52.9 *The greater resurrection*. The author contrasts this with the "lesser" and the "greatest" resurrections (101.41).

52.22 *Each according to his own belief.* The idea that people see God only in accordance with their own beliefs is frequently discussed by Ibn al-ʿArabī and his followers and is supported by a number of hadiths. The point is self-evident as soon as one understands the doctrine of God's incomparability, which demands that God in Himself be beyond forms, whereas all created things are limited by forms. Whenever people "see God," this means that God has disclosed Himself (*tajallī*) to them within the context of their limitations. In other words, finite eyes cannot perceive the infinite light as it is in itself, although they can perceive it to the extent of their capacity. See Ibn al-ʿArabī's teachings on the "gods of belief" (SPK, chapter 19).

52.24 *When they gaze on your beautiful face....* Anwarī, *Dīwān* 2:769.

52.28 *Bounty will judge among the servants.* As noted earlier, theologians frequently employ the terms bounty (*faḍl*) and justice (*ʿadl*) to refer to two contrasting categories of God's names, also called the names of beauty and majesty, or mercy and wrath. Here, the author alludes to the idea that mercy will precede wrath at the resurrection, and hence bounty rather than justice will judge (*qaḍā*') over the servants.

52.31 *Scales appropriate for this task....* This sentence alludes to the "imaginal" nature of experience in the next world, since images always accord with the state of the viewer, as in dreams. Compare the following passage from Qūnawī's Persian *Risāla dar ʿarsh*:

> Tomorrow on the day of resurrection, the four divine attributes that maintain the Throne will become embodied [*tajassud*] within imaginal forms, as will the other meanings that become manifest there. For example, justice, which is a meaning here, will be personified as scales; in the same way, character traits and attributes are meanings here, but they become forms of beauty and ugliness there. The sentence "There is no god but God" will be placed in the scales. The meaning "ownership" will become materialized and will torture the greedy hoarder. Such things will be numerous, without doubt, according to the words of God and all the messengers. The four attributes that maintain the meaning of the Throne are also of this kind. The embodiment of disengaged meanings is one of the characteristics of that day. All the great verifiers have constant knowledge of this right now in the way that the prophets have reported and explained it—or rather, they also see it.

53.11 *Will last forever.* This is the common belief, but even most Kalām authorities had to admit that it is not quite accurate. In *Clarifications* (77.30), the author alludes to a different understanding. Ibn al-ʿArabī provides many arguments to prove that the idea of the eternity of hell is not supported by the Koran, the Hadith, reason, or unveiling. For some of these, see Chittick, "Death and the World of Imagination."

53.24 *When you showed us your beauty*. . . . Sanā'ī, *Dīwān* 902.

53.30 *O seeker of this world*. . . . A quatrain that has been attributed to Rūmī (*Rubāʿiyyāt*, n. 1788). It is also quoted in the other two treatises.

54.26 *My heaven embraces Me not*. . . . Makkī (*Qūt* 1:240) quotes this as a "report transmitted from God" (*al-khabar al-ma'thūr ʿan Allāh*) and Ghazālī simply as a report (*Iḥyā'* 3:12). Sufi authors, such as Hamadānī (*Zubda* 78), usually consider it a *ḥadīth qudsī* (words of God as quoted by the Prophet).

54.30 *Tariqah*, that is, the Sufi path.

55.8 *Abū Sulaymān Dārānī* (d. 205/820–821 or 215/830). He was a well known early Sufi from Syria. A slightly different version of this saying is given in the biographies of Dārānī by Sulamī (*Ṭabaqāt* 78) and Qushayrī (*Risāla* 108).

55.11 *The signs on the horizons and in the souls.* Here there is reference to the Koran: *We shall show them Our signs on the horizons and in their souls, till it is clear to them that He is the Real* (41:53). On some of the dangers of the Sufi path, see SPK, chapter 17.

55.16 *He who has no shaykh*. . . . This well-known saying has been attributed to the Prophet (see Furūzānfar, *Aḥādīth* 30), but it is far more likely that the author is correct in ascribing it to Abū Yazīd, the famous early Sufi (d. 261/874 or 264/877). On him, see A.J. Arberry, *Muslim Saints*, 100–123; Schimmel, *Mystical Dimensions*, index, under *Bāyezīd*.

55.19 *He who has no moon-like face*. . . . Hamadānī quotes this verse, in the same sort of context, as the first half of a quatrain (*Tamhīdāt* 28; *Nāmahā* 1:475). The second half is as follows: "Coming from self to Self is no short road—no path is found outside the tips of the Witness's two tresses." In *Tamhīdāt* he goes on to explain the meaning of the second half in rather allusive fashion. What he seems to be saying is that the two tresses of the Witness (who is God as witnessed in the heart, the Beloved) are the roads of guidance and error. Without a guide, it is impossible to tell the difference between them.

55.25 *Old man* (*pīr*). Both *pīr* in Persian and *shaykh* in Arabic mean literally "old man," secondarily "wise man," and by extension "teacher" or "spiritual master." Rūmī sometimes alludes to the double meaning of the term. "O son! The *pīr* is an 'old man' through intelligence, not through white hair in the beard or on the head" (*Mathnawī* 4:2163).

55.28 *The shaykh among his people*. . . . A hadith often cited by Sufis such as Hujwīrī, *Kashf* 62 (trans. Nicholson, 55); Ghazālī, *Iḥyā'* 1:73. It is found in a slightly different form in Suyūṭī, *Jāmiʿ al-ṣaghīr* (*Fayḍ* 4:185). For a detailed discussion of sources, see Fāḍil's notes to Jām, *Rawḍa* 338–340.

56.9 *Caprice* (*hawā*). In *Easy Roads* (119.18), the author describes caprice as every motive and desire not deriving from the command of God. Generally, the Sufis view this Koranic term as summing up the ignorance and shortcomings of the soul. Caprice (*hawā*) is a wind (*hawā'*) that blows this way and that on the basis of the whims of the moment. The term is often used interchangeably with *shahwa* (passion or appetite). The Koran describes caprice as the worst of the false gods that people worship. *Have you seen him who takes his own caprice to be his god?* (25:43). *Who is more misguided than he who follows his own caprice without guidance from God?* (28:50). A person who follows his own caprice is no less guilty of associating other gods with God (*shirk*) than a person who worships idols, for, as the Prophet's companion Ibn ʿAbbās put it, "Caprice is a worshiped god" (Thaʿālibī, *Tamthīl* 30). Rūmī expresses the idea poetically. "The idol that is your own soul [*nafs*] is the mother of all idols, for that [outward] idol is a snake, but this idol a dragon" (*Mathnawī* 1:772). The author will mention caprice often in what follows.

56.9 *Remembrance* (*dhikr*). Sometimes translated as "invocation," this term plays an important role in the Koran and in Sufi teachings. It means keeping God constantly in mind, most often by the repeated mention of divine names or certain formulae. The author dedicates a section of *Easy Roads* to it (146–148). As mentioned in Part Four, it is the quintessence of Sufi practice. See Chittick, "Dhikr."

56.13 *To empty the locus* (*tafrīgh-i maḥall*). The *locus* is the heart, that is, the place to which God descends in order to disclose Himself to the servant. Ibn al-ʿArabī often employs this expression or its synonym "emptying the heart." For example,

> We empty our hearts of reflective consideration and sit in remembrance [*dhikr*] with the Real on the carpet of courtesy, self-examination, presence, and readiness to receive whatever comes to us from the Real. . . . *Be wary of God, and God will teach you* [2:282]. (*Futūḥāt* 1:89.26)

> When the aspiring traveler clings to the retreat and remembrance, when he empties the locus of reflective thought, and when he sits in poverty, having nothing, at the door of his Lord, then God will bestow upon him and give him something of knowledge of Him, the divine mysteries, and the lordly gnostic sciences. . . . *Be wary of God, and God will teach you* [2:282]. (*Futūḥāt* 1:31.4)

> You will never gain this knowledge unless God acquaints you with it from yourself and lets you witness it in your own essence. . . . But there is no way to gain this except through a beginningless solicitude that gives you a complete preparedness to accept it; [and this preparedness will show itself] in discipline of the soul. . . , and emptying the locus of all "others." (*Futūḥāt* 3:257.16)

Qūnawī often employs the expression. In his *Risālat al-hādiyyat al-murshidiyya,* which explains to his disciples how to perfect the practice of remembrance, he writes, "In this treatise I will explain, God willing, the secret of remembrance, presence, and emptying the locus in order to face the Real." In *I'jāz al-bayān,* he writes,

> Reaching knowledge through genuine tasting by way of perfect and sound unveiling depends first upon divine solicitude and then upon detaching the particular faculties. . . and emptying the locus of every knowledge and belief, or rather, of everything other than the Sought, the Real. (34/136)

In *Miftāḥ al-ghayb* Qūnawī uses the time-honored comparison of the heart to a rusty mirror to explain the meaning of the expression:

> When engendered forms leave impressions in the human spirit and heart, this is like the bumps, pittings, and blotches in a mirror that bring about distortion and prevent the reflection of that which should be disclosed. To empty the locus of every form is to polish and prepare the mirror so that it allows and demands the reflection of everything that faces it. (266)

56.18 *Disengagement* (*tajrīd*). A technical Sufi term that signifies detachment from everything in the cosmos through concentration upon God. Spiritual beings such as angels are said to be disengaged (*mujarrad*) by nature from the external world, but human beings need to achieve disengagement through discipline and god-wariness.

56.19 *If caprice makes you want*. . . . Allusion to a story about Jesus often mentioned in Persian poetry. When the angels took him to the heavens, he had a needle along with him. When they reached the fourth sphere, they were told by a voice from the Unseen to see if Jesus had brought anything. When they found the needle, they were told to keep him in the fourth heaven. Alhough in a sense Jesus is belittled through this story, notice that the fourth heaven is the abode of the sun. Hence, the story recognizes what has been called Jesus's "solar" nature. In the Islamic context, this connection with the sun is understood as illustrating his elevated spirituality (because of the intervention of the Holy Spirit in his conception), for the sun is the most manifest exemplar of the spirit's qualities (light, life-giving, and so on) in the corporeal world.

56.35 *Put up with pain*. . . . This is the first half of a quatrain, with some textual difference, that has been attributed to Rūmī (*Rubā'iyyāt,* n. 1255). The second line sounds very much like an authentic line from Rūmī, and it may be that he took over the first line from an earlier source, modified it, and added a second. The whole quatrain, in Rūmī's version, reads as follows:

Put up with pain,
for I am your medicine;
look at no one,
for I am your intimate.
If you are killed,
don't say, "I've been killed."
Give thanks,
for I am your blood-price.

57.6 *All these deceptive tints....* Sanā'ī, *Ḥadīqa* 166.

57.21 *What has not been allotted....* This is the second half of a quatrain by Awḥad al-Dīn Kirmānī (*Dīwān*, n. 431); the whole quatrain is quoted in *Easy Roads* 125.10.

57.27 *My mercy precedes My wrath.* A sound *ḥadīth qudsī* found in several sources, including Bukhārī (Tawḥīd 22, 28, 55) and Muslim (Tawba 15).

57.27 *Having a good opinion of the Lord....* This is an allusion to a sound *ḥadīth qudsī* found in the standard sources: "I am with my servant's opinion of Me" (Bukhārī, Tawḥīd 15, 35; Muslim, Tawba 1, etc.). In some sources the following is added: "So let him have any opinion of Me that he wants" (Dārimī, Riqāq 22; Aḥmad 3:491, 4:106); or, "If he has a good opinion, that belongs to him, and if he has a bad opinion, that belongs to him" (Aḥmad 2:391); or, "So let him have a good opinion of Me" (Ibn al-ʿArabī, *Futūḥāt* 1:708.3).

CLARIFICATIONS FOR BEGINNERS AND REMINDERS FOR THE ADVANCED

60.2 *I was a Hidden Treasure....* Frequently cited in Sufi sources (for example, Hamadānī, *Zubda* 19), it is not found in the books on hadith. Ibn al-ʿArabī claims that its truth has been verified through unveiling (SPK 391 n. 14), and even the *muḥaddith* Muḥammad al-Qāwuqjī, while rejecting its authenticity, says, "Its meaning is correct and clear" (*al-Lu'lu' al-marṣūʿ* 61, cited in Furūzānfar, *Aḥādīth* 29).

60.7 *Moses asked his Lord....* Muslim, Īmān 312.

60.23 *No eye has seen it....* This sentence represents one of many versions of a well-known *ḥadith qudsī* found in most of the standard sources (with Biblical parallels in Isa. 64.4 and I Cor. 2.9). See Graham, *Divine Word* 117–119.

60.34 *You think this emerald field....* Sanā'ī, *Dīwān* 56.

61.4 *God warns you...* Ibn al-ʿArabī frequently quotes this verse in the same sort of context. See SPK, index of Koranic verses.

61.6 *Glory be to Him*.... A saying of Abū Bakr, as indicated by the author in 39.34.

61.8 *Intellect of intellect*.... Sanā'ī, *Ḥadīqa* 62.

61.15 *You will see your Lord*.... The hadith is found in Bukhārī (Mawāqīt 16, 26; Tafsīr Sūra 50, 2; Tawḥīd 24) and other standard sources.

61.16 *I saw my Lord in the most beautiful form.* See the note on 40.26.

61.19 *Look! Everything marked*.... This is the second half of a quatrain that is most likely by Awḥad al-Dīn Kirmānī (*Dīwān,* n. 1796; Weischer, *Heart's Witness* 170), although it has also been attributed, with textual differences, to Bābā Afḍal Kāshānī (*Dīwān* 159). The printed text of *Clarifications* includes the first half as well, but none of my manuscripts do. The first half reads, "Look! The heart is the kernel of reality, the body the shell. Look at the form of the Friend in the clothing of skin."

61.23 *There is nothing in existence but God.* This is a common saying, often quoted by Ibn al-ʿArabī. A slightly different saying is attributed to Maʿrūf al-Karkhī (Hamadānī, *Tamhīdāt* 256).

61.23 *None other than God*.... Nasafī (*Maqṣad-i aqṣā* 277) attributes a different version of the saying (with "other than He" instead of "other than God") to the Sufi Abu'l-ʿAbbās Qaṣṣāb (second/eighth century).

61.25 *No one's in the village*.... Khāqānī, *Dīwān* 852.

62.1 *I ask Thee by every name*.... Aḥmad 1:391, 452.

62.27 *Not lately has meaning's kingdom*.... Sanā'ī, *Dīwān* 210, with some textual discrepancy.

62.33 *Hold back your tongue*.... Sanā'ī, *Dīwān* 706.

62.37 *Whoever entrusts himself sincerely*.... This hadith is often cited in Sufi texts (such as Rāzī, *Mirṣād al-ʿibād* 29; trans. Algar, 52). Abū Nuʿaym Iṣfahānī (*Ḥilya* 5:189) transmits it through Abū ʿAbdallāh Makḥūl al-Shāmī (d. 118/736).

63.1 *Enter God's school*.... This is a quatrain by Awḥad al-Dīn Kirmānī (*Dīwān,* n. 464).

63.16 *When someone knows God*.... A well-known saying sometimes attributed to the Prophet (Furūzānfar, *Aḥādīth* 67; Hamadānī, *Tamhīdāt* 332).

64.14 *Bewilderment is of two types.* Hujwīrī already refers to these two. He writes,

> Bewilderment is of two types: Bewilderment in His "is-ness," and bewilderment in His "what-ness" [these two correspond to the philosophers' categories of existence (*wujūd*) and quiddity or essence (*māhiyya*)]. Bewilderment in His is-ness is to associate others with Him and conceal the truth, but bewilderment in His what-ness is true knowledge. For the knower has no doubt about His existence,

but reason has no way to grasp His whatness. Hence, the knower is left with the certainty of His existence, but bewilderment as to how He exists. (*Kashf al-Maḥjūb* 353)

Nicholson's translation of this passage (*Kashf* 275) is misleading. Ibn al-ʿArabī frequently discusses bewilderment as one of the highest stages of spiritual attainment (see SPK, index, under *bewilderment*; Chodkiewicz, *Illuminations*, index, under *ḥayra*). He contrasts "the bewilderment of the Folk of Allah" with that of the "considerative thinkers" in *Futūḥāt* 1:270–272. Qūnawī provides a long description of three degrees of bewilderment in *Iʿjāz al-bayān* 360-362/ 487-490 (quoted with deletions by Jāmī in *Naqd al-nuṣūṣ* 278-280, which is translated by Chittick in "Ibn ʿArabī's own Summary" 91-93).

64.18 *Whoever seeks Him....* Compare Ḥallāj, *Dīwān* 120.

64.26 *Seek not....* Sanāʾī, *Dīwān* 201. Both "but God" and "No" refer to "the sentence that expresses *tawḥīd*," that is, "There is no god but God." The poet means to say that reason is a false god destroyed by *tawḥīd*. True knowledge of God can come only through God's bestowal, not the servant's rational attempts to understand.

64.37 *My Lord, increase my bewilderment....* This is probably a variation on the saying, "O Guide of the bewildered, increase my bewilderment!", which has been ascribed to Shiblī (Hujwīrī, *Kashf* 488; trans. Nicholson, 374; Hamadānī, *Tamhīdāt* 241) as well as to the Prophet (Rāzī, *Mirṣād al-ʿibād* 326; trans. Algar, 321).

64.39 *I am bewildered in Thee....* This Arabic verse is frequently quoted in Sufi sources (Sarrāj, *Lumaʿ* 345; Anṣārī, *Ṭabaqāt* 129; Samʿānī, *Rawḥ* 183).

65.1 *Why, O tress, do you assume....* In Sufi poetry, the tress symbolizes the world's multiplicity. God's never-ending self-disclosures in the cosmos veil His face or Essence and throw the seeker into bewilderment. See Nurbakhsh, *Sufi Symbolism* 1:75–79. David is considered to be a chain mail maker because of the Koran. *We gave David bounty from Us.... We softened for him iron: "Fashion wide coats of mail, and measure well the links"* (34:10–11). Harut, along with Marut, is an angel who came down to Babylon and taught the inhabitants sorcery (Koran 2:102; see also al-Kisāʾī, *Tales* 47–48).

65.10 *Empty the locus.* See the note on 56.13.

65.10 *Attentiveness (tawajjuh).* Like "emptying the locus," this term is frequently employed by Qūnawī to refer to a type of spiritual practice. His *Risālat al-hādiya,* which discusses emptying the locus in detail, is sometimes called "The treatise on attentiveness" (*al-Risālat al-tawajjuhiyya*) and "The treatise on the most complete attentiveness" (*Risālat al-tawajjuh al-atamm*). The plaque over the door of the mosque that was built next to his tomb in the year of his death (673/1274) refers to his disciples as "those who turn the attentiveness of their hearts and frames to God."

65.26 *Those taken at Alast*. . . . The term *Alast* is derived from the Koranic verse just quoted, *Am I not* [alast] *your Lord*? (See the note on 37.34.) Rūmī quotes these five lines plus three more from the same ghazal in *Majālis-i sab'a* 20 (a work written before he started composing poetry).

66.1 *Thy Face has lit up my night*. . . . Qushayrī quotes these Arabic verses twice (*Risāla* 280, 732).

66.10 *Love cures the heart*. . . . In a slightly different form, the quatrain has been attributed to Najm al-Dīn Rāzī, a contemporary and acquaintance of Qūnawī. See Rāzī, *Mirṣād* 581.

66.24 *Where is a heart*. . . . The earliest manuscript ascription of this quatrain is to Awḥad al-Dīn Kirmānī (*Dīwān*, n. 203), although it is also ascribed in later manuscripts to other poets, including 'Aṭṭār and Afḍal al-Dīn Kāshānī. See the remarks of the editor of Kirmānī's *Dīwān* (329).

66.34 *Junayd was asked*. . . . This is Junayd of Baghdad (d. 298/910), one of the most famous of the early Sufis (see Schimmel, *Mystical Dimensions*, passim).

67.1 *Shaykh al-Islām Anṣārī said*. . . . 'Abdallāh Anṣārī (d. 481/1088) was a Sufi from Herat famous for his "Intimate Conversations" in Persian and his "Waystations of the Travelers" in Arabic. Though this saying is in Arabic, it is reminiscent of his Persian prayers. 'Ayn al-Quḍāt Hamadānī quotes it (*Zubda* 85), but without mentioning its author. See Anṣārī, *Intimate Conversations*.

67.19 *With God*. . . . This is also quoted in *Rising Places* 39.14.

67.25 *All these deceptive tints*. . . . See the note on 57.6.

67.29 *Is it Thou or I, this entity in the eye*. . . . The poem is by al-Ḥallāj, but the text here differs in several places from that established by Massignon (Ḥallāj, *Dīwān* 103–104).

67.33 *Don't think this thread*. . . . The quatrain is by Awḥad al-Dīn Kirmānī (*Dīwān*, n. 374; Weischer, *Heart's Witness* 134). 'Irāqī quotes it in *Lama'āt* 59 (*Fakhruddin* 79).

68.1 *I have killed two thousand lovers*. . . . The line is also quoted by Sam'ānī (*Rawḥ al-arwāḥ* 203) and Hamadānī (*Nāmahā* 1:284, 403).

68.7 *Incarnationism* (*ḥulūl*), *unificationism* (*ittiḥād*). See the criticism of these ideas by Qūnawī's disciple 'Irāqī, *Fakhruddin* 93–94.

68.9 *The science of annihilation and subsistence*. The saying is by Ibrāhīm ibn Shaybān (d. 377/948–949). Sulamī, *Ṭabaqāt* 404.

68.14 *The light is not cut off*. . . . Sanā'ī, *Ḥadīqa* 68.

68.18 *No one meddles in this question*. . . . Sanā'ī, *Ḥadīqa* 69. The poet is alluding to the Sufi teaching that, through self-disclosure (*tajallī*), God reveals Himself to the creatures such that the creature is annihilated and only God remains. The *locus classicus* for the term self-disclosure is the Koran: *When his Lord disclosed Himself to the mountain, He made it crumble to dust, and Moses fell down swooning* (7:143). In contrast, incarnation (*ḥulūl*), which has invariably been criticized by Muslim thinkers, implies that God enters into the human being. Hence, self-disclosure demands the affirmation of the unique reality of God, while incarnation requires the duality of God and creature.

68.22 *God discloses Himself to people*. . . . Hamadānī also quotes this saying, without attribution (*Tamhīdāt* 307, *Nāmahā* 2:209).

68.24 *Immutable entities* (*a'yān-i thābita*). This is a technical term connected specifically with Ibn al-'Arabī and his followers. On the nonexistence of the entities and their identity with the creatures, see SPK 83–88 and passim.

68.27 *Majesty and generous giving* (*jalāl wa ikrām*). These two terms, mentioned in the Koranic divine name "Possessor of majesty and generous giving" (55:27, 55:78), are often, as here, taken as allusions to the contrasting names of majesty and beauty, which, in turn, point to nonmanifestation and incomparability on the one hand, and manifestation and similarity on the other. Hence, the author now turns to explaining God's incomparability and similarity, mentioning in the process some of the divine names with which the two sides are associated.

68.33 *The higher plenum* (*mala'-i a'lā*), that is, the angels. The term is sometimes contrasted with the "lower plenum," or the things of this world.

69.5 *Nothing stands between the creatures*. . . . A sound hadith found in the standard sources with slight textual variations (e.g., Muslim, Īmān 296; Tirmidhī, Janna 3; Bukhārī, Tafsīr Sūra 55, 1,2).

69.8 *My head's eye gazed*. . . . The quatrain is by Awḥad al-Dīn Kirmānī. The text here differs from that found in his *Dīwān* (n. 1144). A third version is given in Weischer, *Heart's Witness* 166.

69.13 *I have never seen anything*. . . . The saying is by Muhammad ibn Wāsi' (Kalābādhī, *Ta'arruf* 64; trans. Arberry, 53). A saying to the same effect is attributed to 'Alī (Hamadānī, *Tamhīdāt* 279–280).

69.22 *He is a light, how should I see Him*. The hadith is found in Muslim, Īmān 291; Aḥmad 5:157.

69.24 *If love makes*. . . . See the note on 40.36.

69.31 *What does dust*. . . . An often quoted Arabic proverb (as in Hamadānī, *Tamhīdāt* 276).

69.33 *Do not boldly fly so high*. . . . Sanā'ī, *Dīwān* 191. The poet refers to the Shahadah, "There is no god but God," and to the accounts of the Prophet's *mi'rāj* according to which Gabriel could fly no further than the Lote Tree of the Far Boundary. Beyond that point, implies the poet, there is only God, and everything else is naughted.

69.39 *Glory be to Thee—we have not truly known Thee!* This prayer is often quoted (Sanā'ī, *Sayr al-'ibād* 216; Suhrawardī, *Majmū'a* 376).

70.1 *When Eternity's magnificence*.... This is the second half of a quatrain by Awḥad al-Dīn Kirmānī (*Dīwān*, n. 3).

70.32 *The mysteries of the path*.... Kirmānī, *Dīwān*, 337. On Kirmānī's importance for the author, see Appendix 1 in this volume. This quatrain has been wrongly attributed to Rūmī (*Rubā'iyyāt*, n. 1085). "States" (*ḥāl*) here is a technical Sufi term, referring to temporary divine gifts of higher awareness. States are achieved by Sufis, while "words" (*qāl*) are the business of jurists and theologians.

71.10 *Let your natural learning*.... Sanā'ī, *Dīwān* 460 (see the note on 36.30).

71.19 *Sahl Tustarī* (d. 282/896). A famous Sufi from Shushtar in southwest Iran, he is the author of a number of works, including a short commentary on some of the verses of the Quran. See Böwering, *Mystical Vision*; Arberry, *Muslim Saints* 153–160. 'Aṭṭār gives a Persian translation of this Arabic saying in *Tadhkira* 313.

71.26 *Dastān* is one of heroes of Firdawsī's *Shāhnāma*, the Iranian national epic. The point of the second half of the poem depends on a pun. "Old man" renders *zāl*, which is also the name by which Dastān is usually called, because he was born with white hair. He is the father of Rustam, the greatest hero of the *Shāhnāma*.

72.4 *High indeed is God exalted*.... This is almost a direct quotation from Koran 17:43.

72.6 *But the masters of the path*.... After summarizing and rejecting a number of positions that have been proposed in the history of Kalām, the author turns to the ambiguous status given to the names by the Ash'arite theologians. But he has in mind the explanation of this position offered by Ibn al-'Arabī (see SPK, chapters 2–4; Chodkiewicz, *Illuminations* 108–116).

72.18 *The names of the names*. This is one of Ibn al-'Arabī's technical terms. See SPK 34–35.

72.20 *The four pillars of the Divinity*. Ibn al-'Arabī provides detailed discussions of the role of these four names in establishing quaternity (*tarbī'*) throughout existence. For a table of correspondences, see Chittick, "Ibn 'Arabī and His School" 72.

72.30 *Most of the ulama hold that this name is not derived*.... Qūnawī does not agree with this opinion, although one could argue that, if he is the author of this work, he prefers to follow the majority rather then enter into a theological debate. In *I'jāz al-bayān* he offers several arguments to show that this name should not be considered as God's proper name (169–176/ 279–286). He indicates his preference for the view that the name is derived from a root, though he does not choose from the several possibilities (ibid. 177–178/ 287–289).

72.32 *Merciful is a name*. . . . Ibn al-ʿArabī often speaks of the identity of *raḥma* (mercy) with *wujūd* (existence, Being, finding; see SPK 130–132). Qūnawī gives this teaching a philosophical slant that is highly reminiscent of this paragraph. He writes,

> The Merciful is a name of the Real inasmuch as He is identical with Being. . . . The name "God" comprehends all levels and existent things, while the name "Merciful" is more specific, since it denotes Being alone. (*Iʿjāz al-bayān* 201/315)

> The Real is named "God" inasmuch as He becomes entified within the task [*sha'n*] through which He rules over all the tasks that receive His properties and effects. He is named "Merciful" inasmuch as His nondelimited Being becomes deployed among the states that become manifest through His manifestation. Mercy is Being Itself, and the "Merciful" is the Real inasmuch as He is a Being deployed over everything that becomes manifest through Him and, in addition, inasmuch as He—in respect of His Being—possesses the perfection of receiving every property that rules over every state in every time and in every level. (From Qūnawī's glosses to *Iʿjāz al-bayān*, as quoted by Jāmī, *Naqd al-nuṣūṣ* 74; see also Fanārī, *Miṣbāḥ al-ins* 90)

> In respect of the Real's nondelimited Being, He is called "Merciful," but in respect of the level and quality that comprehends all qualities, He is called "God." (Qūnawī, *Nafaḥāt* 73)

73.3 *The mystery of the Throne*. The Throne is the outermost limit of the corporeal world and encompasses the whole sensory universe. Both Ibn al-ʿArabī and Qūnawī connect God's sitting upon the Throne with the precedence of His mercy over His wrath. Since the Throne—the locus of sheer mercy—embraces the whole created universe, all things will return to mercy in the end. See Chittick, "Death and the World of Imagination" 73ff.

73.6 *The angels*. Ibn al-ʿArabī refers to the mysteries of these two names in the third and fourth chapters of the *Fuṣūṣ*. In brief, the angels or spirits are the locus of manifestation for the divine names that demand God's incomparability. Hence they praise Him with the names "Glorified" (*subbūḥ*) and "Holy" (*quddūs*), both of which are "negative" names. This explains why the angels were unable to grasp Adam's all-comprehensive perfection (which includes positive names) and protested to God when He created him (compare *Fuṣūṣ*, chapter 1).

73.10 *The mystery of Iblis*. On the basis of Koranic references, such as 28:15, Satan is said to be a locus of manifestation for the name "Misguider" (*al-muḍill*), which is one of the names of majesty and wrath. As the author points out in *Rising Places* 57.10, as long as manyness remains, God in His inaccessibility will not reveal His beauty. What is "other" than sheer oneness dwells in multiplicity and disequilibrium. God's inaccessibility, majesty, and jealousy keep His beauty hidden from the view of multiplicity and disequilibrium. Whatever is veiled from Him is to some extent under the sway of Satan, who manifests misguidance, dispersion, and disequilibrium. God's inaccessibility has caused the veiling, so Satan's power may be said to derive from it.

Aḥmad Ghazālī draws slightly different conclusions from this correlation between Iblis and inaccessibility. Along with Ḥallāj and others, he interprets Iblis's activities as manifesting the properties of true love, which refuses to pay attention to anything but the real Beloved (see Awn, *Satan's Tragedy*, chapter 3). Since the Beloved lies infinitely beyond any created thing, the lover refuses to look at anything to which he can gain access. Ghazālī writes as follows:

> Love has an aspiration. The lover desires a beloved whose attributes are transcendent. He will not accept as beloved any beloved that falls into the snare of union. That is why, when it was said to Iblis, *Upon you is My curse* [38:79], Iblis replied, *By Thy inaccessibility*. In other words: I love this expression of inaccessibility on Your part, since You have need of no one, and no one is worthy of You. If someone were worthy of You, then You would not have perfect inaccessibility. (*Sawāniḥ* 49; see also *Sawāniḥ: Inspirations* 75)

The editor and translator of *Sawāniḥ* cites this passage in *Clarifications* to prove that its author was somewhat influenced by Aḥmad Ghazālī (Pourjavady, *Sulṭān-i ṭarīqat* 79). However, it is more likely that the author of the treatise has in view Ibn al-ʿArabī's teachings on the meaning of the divine attribute of "inaccessibility," especially because the author, Qūnawī, and Ibn al-ʿArabī never defend Iblis's position as does Ghazālī.

Ibn al-ʿArabī writes that everything in existence shares in the attribute of inaccessibility. This attribute gives each thing its specific identity that makes it different from every other thing. Each thing, by being itself and nothing else, is a servant of God's inaccessibility. "Hence everything worships itself. From here becomes manifest everyone whose self dominates over him so that he follows his own caprice" (*Futūḥāt* 4:206.28). This is precisely the attribute of Iblis, who worships himself by saying, *I am better than he* (7:12).

Ibn al-ʿArabī has a great deal more to say about the characteristics of inaccessibility, much of which applies directly to Iblis. For example, he writes, "When the servant achieves the presence of the name Inaccessible through direct tasting, the mark it leaves upon him is that nothing other than himself has any effect upon him in that which he does not desire or crave" (ibid. 207.2).

73.12 *The configuration of the human being*. . . . As a microcosm, the human being comprehends all the realities in the cosmos and reflects God as such, not God inasmuch as He is called by one name or another. Only human beings can truly love God because, as Ibn al-ʿArabī puts it, only they coincide with Him fully (*Futūḥāt* 2:325.25). When a human being loves anything less than a full image of himself, he loves that thing with the part of himself that corresponds with it. Hence the rest of his reality remains unaffected (see Chittick, "Ebn al-ʿArabi as Lover"). In any case, the fact that love is a divine quality shared by no one except human beings is a common theme in Sufi literature. Perhaps the most eloquent spokesman for this position, although he has remained unknown to modern scholarship until recently, is Aḥmad Samʿānī (d. 534/1140). He writes, "God created every creature in accordance with the demand of power, but He created Adam and his children in accordance with the demand of love. He created other things inasmuch as He is Powerful, but He created you inasmuch as He is Lover" (*Rawḥ al-arwāḥ* 223).

73.18 *Love's dew made clay*. . . . The poem is found among the quatrains of Afḍal al-Dīn Kāshānī (*Dīwān* 62), and has also been attributed, probably wrongly, to Majd al-Dīn Baghdādī. See Rāzī, *Mirṣād* 581.

73.22 *It has been reported that the ready cash (naqd) of each heaven*. . . . The author may have in view here the following passage by Hamadānī, although others have surely made the same point.

> All the names of the Eternal are gathered together only in the heart of Adam and his descendants. Each of the angels knows one name. The ready cash of each of their hearts is the reality of a single specific name. *None of us there is, but has a known station* [37:164]. The angel that knows the Subtle does not know the Intensely Severe, and the one that says "All-compeller" does not say "Merciful." The attributes that instill fear and incite hope are brought together in the human being. After all, He says in the Koran, *He taught Adam the names, all of them. Then He presented them to the angels and said, "Now tell Me the names of these"* [2:31]. They did not know all the names, so they said, *We know not save what Thou hast taught us* [2:32]. In other words, each angel possesses a known station and remembers God through a specific name. The angel of the earth has a specific name through which it takes care of the earth, and a similar thing can be said about the angel of heaven. The angel of life has a specific name through which it breathes spirits into human bodies. The angel of death has another name through which it slays. Thus, it has been reported that the angel of death and the angel of life had an argument. The one said, "I give life." The other said, "I slay." They appealed for a decision to God. He said to

them, "Be as I have entrusted to you, for I am the Life-giver and the Slayer." The angel of fire knows the name through which it causes burning. The angel of air has a name, the angel of water a name, and so also the angels of wind, thunder, lightning, and rain. *None knows the hosts of your Lord but He* [74:31]. *To God belong the hosts of the heavens and the earth* [48:4]. (*Nāmahā* 2:207–208)

73.26 *The locus of manifestation for the name of Divinity*. . . . The name of Divinity (*ulūhiyyat*) is the all-comprehensive name "God" (*Allāh*). That Adam is the locus of manifestation for this name is the central theme of the first chapter of Ibn al-ʿArabī's *Fuṣūṣ*. Since human beings alone were created in God's form, they alone can know Him as God, not as He who possesses one name or another. In the language of Islamic philosophy, this is to say that human beings alone manifest God as sheer, nondelimited *wujūd*. Their quiddity, in the last analysis, is that they have no quiddity. Thus Qūnawī writes at the end of his *Nafaḥāt* (305) that he reached a station of witnessing in which God showed him that he had no immutable entity, "for such is the situation of him who is upon God's form" (Qūnawī makes explicit the identification between quiddity and immutable entity in *Nuṣūṣ* 74/295; *Miftāḥ* 67). Ibn al-ʿArabī refers to this station of human perfection in which no specific name rules over the human being as the "station of no station" (see SPK, chapter 20). Qūnawī employs the term *equilibrium* (*iʿtidāl*) in the same meaning (see Murata, *Tao*, index, under *equilibrium*).

73.28 *When We sent Adam out*. . . . ʿAṭṭār, *Dīwān* 493. Another line from the same ghazal is quoted on 77.15.

74.8 *[Those names Thou hast] kept*. . . . The full text of the hadith is on 62.1.

74.32 *None will enter*. . . . See note on 44.22.

74.37 *Opening* (*fatḥ*). See note on 45.14.

75.3 *We have another tongue*. . . . This is the first line of a quatrain that is attributed to Abū Saʿīd Abi'l-Khayr (Nafīsī, *Sukhanān-i manẓūm* 12) and to Rūmī (*Rubāʿiyyāt*, n. 230). For details on other sources and versions, see Rāzī, *Mirṣād* 610–611, or Rāzī, *Marmūzāt* 177.

75.9 *Having passed*. . . . See the notes on 38.24, 38.28.

75.12 *Reports are not*. . . . Suyūṭī gives this proverbial saying as a hadith in *al-Jāmiʿ al-ṣaghīr* (*Fayḍ* 5:357).

75.13 *The pain*. . . . Sanā'ī, *Dīwān* 335.

75.30 *God has a white earth*. . . . This saying is not found in the standard hadith collections. A similar saying is attributed to the Prophet in *Sirr al-ʿālamayn* 179 (chapter 30, *faṣl* 2), a work with a rather Hermetic orientation that is ascribed to Ghazālī but is most likely apocryphal.

75.39 *The first thing God created was the Pen*. Sufis often quote this saying, and they universally identify the Pen with the First Intellect, especially on the basis of the next saying. Thus the Pen that writes upon the Tablet is identical with the First Intellect that marries the Universal Soul and gives birth to the visible universe. See Murata, *Tao* 153ff.

76.1 *The first thing God created was the Intellect....* This hadith is found in several early Shi'ite hadith collections, but among Sunnis it is mainly the Sufis who quote it (for example, Iṣfahānī, *Ḥilya* 7:318; Rāghib, *Dharī'a* 73; Ghazālī, *Mīzān al-'amal* 331). See also Jām, *Uns* 330–333.

76.17 *Everything has an angel.* Suhrawardī calls this saying one of the proverbs (*amthāl*) of the prophets (*Alwāḥ* 162; *al-Alwāḥ* 51).

76.18 *An angel comes down....* See the note on 45.2.

76.19 *The people of unveiling say that unless there are seven angels....* Hamadānī says something to this effect in *Nāmahā* 2:208. Jāmī quotes this passage from *Clarifications* and adds a gloss stating that the philosophers call these seven angels the "seven corporeal faculties" that are necessary for any growing thing to grow: nutrition, augmentation, generation, attraction, digestion, retention, and expulsion (*Naqd al-nuṣūṣ* 50).

77.6 *The higher plenum brought near to God.* These are the cherubim, the enraptured spirits. According to Ibn al-'Arabī, they were not asked to prostrate themselves before Adam along with the other angels when he was created. This would indicate that they were not dependent upon his existence for their existence. The Koran seems to be alluding to this in the words that God addresses to Iblis. *What prevented you from prostrating yourself before him whom I created with My own two hands? Have you waxed proud, or are you one of the high ones?* (38:75) Ibn al-'Arabī writes, "God may mean by the 'high ones' the angels enraptured in God's majesty, those who were not included in the command to prostrate themselves" (*Futūḥāt* 3:294.16).

77.6 *But for you....* This *ḥadīth qudsī* is commonly quoted by Sufis such as Rūmī and is found in the writings of Hamadānī (*Nāmahā* 2:248). It is probably based on more detailed versions found in earlier sources, such as the following cited by the Sufi Abū Ibrāhīm Bukhārī: "But for Muhammad, I would not have created this world or the next world, the heavens or the earth, the Throne or the Footstool, the Pen or the Tablet, the Garden or the Fire. But for Muhammad, I would not have created you, O Adam" (*Sharḥ-i ta'arruf* 2:46). The author's words—"has been verified for the possessors of eyes and verification"—allude to the fact that the saying is not considered sound by the hadith specialists.

77.15 *Know for certain....* 'Aṭṭār, *Dīwān* 493.

77.17 *O David, I created Muhammad for Myself....* Makkī (*Qūt* 1:495) quotes this saying from "one of our ulama."

77.22 *You were brought up from the two worlds....* Firdawsī, *Shāhnāma* 1:14–16.

77.30 *God created Gehenna from an excess of mercy. . . .* The saying until the word "mercy" is quoted in Hamadānī, *Nāmahā* 2:226.

77.34 *Measuring out is God's mystery. . . .* See the note on 42.14.

77.35 *When the saints seize the mystery. . . .* The quatrain is by Awḥad al-Dīn Kirmānī (*Dīwān*, n. 218). "Saints" here translates the word *abdāl* (the "substitutes"). The term is often used synonymously with "friend," although in a more specific sense it denotes one of the higher categories of the Men of the Unseen (*rijāl al-ghayb*). See Ibn al-ʿArabī's description of the *abdāl* in SPK 370. See also Landolt, "Walāya" 321.

78.6 *The good, all of it, is in Thy hands. . . .* Muslim, Musāfirīn 201; Nasā'ī, Iftitāḥ 17.

78.14 *Why have the pillars of wisdom said that no evil occurs in existence. . . .* The pillars of wisdom are the masters of philosophy and the great authorities of theoretical Sufism. For some of Avicenna's views here, see A. L. Ivry, "Avicenna's Concept of Determinism" and the sources cited there. For Ibn al-ʿArabī's view, see SPK 290ff. Jāmī refers to this understanding of the philosophers' position in *Lawā'iḥ* 37–38.

78.16 *Idris*. These words of Idris—usually identified with Enoch and Elias—are quoted by Hamadānī, *Nāmahā* 2:225.

78.29 *A time will come. . . .* Most Muslim theologians hold that hell cannot be eternal, because that would make it a partner in God's eternity. For Ibn al-ʿArabī and his followers, the fact that "God's mercy precedes His wrath" is sufficient indication that no one will suffer chastisement forever. See Chittick, "Death and the World of Imagination" 77–80.

78.35 *The wrath of a generous man. . . .* This Arabic verse is also quoted by Hamadānī, *Nāmahā* 2:226.

79.12 *You are the instrument of an act, nothing else. . . .* The quatrain is by Awḥad al-Dīn Kirmānī (*Dīwān*, n. 743).

79.20 *However, since the human being. . . .* In this paragraph the author summarizes Ibn al-ʿArabī's doctrine of "He/not He" along with its relevance to the debates of the theologians. See SPK, chapter 7 and 205–211.

79.25 *Though the act. . . .* See the note on 46.33.

79.32 *Those who believe in free will. . . (al-qadariyya majūs hādhihi'l-umma).* This is a much debated hadith found in Abū Dāwūd, Sunna 16. During the early theological controversies, this saying was employed to attack the Muʿtazilites, who emphasized free will. Two other hadiths make the same point with slightly different language. "Every community has its fire worshipers, and the fire worshipers of this community are those who say there is no measuring out (*lā qadar*)" (Abū Dāwūd, Sunna 16; Aḥmad 2:86, 5:407). "The fire worshipers of this community are those who deny God's measuring out" (Ibn Māja, Muqaddima 10). On the use of the term *qadar* in two opposing senses, see the article "Ḳadar" in the *Encyclopedia of Islam* (new edition).

79.36 *Perform works, for everyone*. . . . This hadith is found in most of the standard sources in various versions. The complete text helps clarify the meaning. The Prophet said, "The seat of each of you in the Fire or the Garden has been written down." The people asked him, "O Messenger of God, then should we not trust in what has been written for us and leave aside our works?" He answered, "Perform works, for everyone will be eased to that for which he was created. As for him who is one of the people of felicity, he will be eased to the works of the people of felicity; but as for him who is one of the people of wretchedness, he will be eased to the works of the people of wretchedness." Then he recited the verse, *As for him who gives and is god-wary and recognizes the most beautiful, We shall surely ease him to the Easing. But as for him who is a miser, and self-sufficient, and cries lies to the most beautiful, We shall surely ease him to the Hardship. His wealth shall not avail him when he perishes* (92:5–11). (Bukhārī, Tafsīr Sūra 92, 3; see also Bukhārī, Adab 120, Qadar 4, Tawḥīd 54; Muslim, Qadar 6–8, etc.)

79.39 *Immutable entities*. Ibn al-ʿArabī and his followers frequently discuss the relationship between the immutable entities and the mystery of the measuring out. In the *Futūḥāt* (2:63.34), Ibn al-ʿArabī distinguishes clearly between knowledge of the measuring out and knowledge of its mystery. He says that no one but God knows the first, while the second can be known by human beings. In the second chapter of the *Fuṣūṣ al-ḥikam*, he describes the ascending degrees of the knowledge of God's friends. He writes,

> Among them are those who know that God's knowledge of them in all their states corresponds to what they are in the state of their entity's immutability before the entity comes into existence. They know God's knowledge of them from the place where He knows it. No group of the Folk of Allah is higher and more complete in unveiling than this group. They are the ones who are aware of the mystery of the measuring out. (*Fuṣūṣ* 60; *Bezels* 64; compare *Futūḥāt* 2:64.20, 65.16; 3:182.11)

Ibn al-ʿArabī then goes on to describe two degrees within this group—those who know their own immutable entities in a general and undifferentiated mode, and those who know them in a specific and differentiated mode. The second group is the higher of the two.

Ibn al-ʿArabī's followers go into more detail on this mystery (for example, Qūnawī, *Nafaḥāt* 43ff.), especially in their commentaries on chapter 14 of the *Fuṣūṣ*, which Ibn al-ʿArabī dedicates to measuring out and in which he alludes to its mystery. In discussing measuring out, Qūnawī's disciple Jandī first differentiates it from the decree (*qaḍā'*), a term that is usually discussed along with it. In short, the decree is God's general determination of the existent things, while the measuring out is the specific form that the decree takes in specific times and places. Jandī continues,

> No one can say—as the ignorant wrongdoers say in judging about God—that He measures out truth-concealing, disobedience, and ignorance for the truth-concealers, the disobedient, and the ignorant, and then takes them to task for that and demands from them what is not in their capacity and scope. On the contrary, God writes, decrees, and measures out only that which is required by the thing that receives His ruling through its beginningless, specific preparedness, which is not made by God. This preparedness demands that God rule that the thing become manifest according to what it is in itself and that He make manifest what is latent within it through giving it existence. (*Sharḥ fuṣūṣ al-ḥikam* 483–484)

In other words, the thing's immutable entity—which is nothing other than the thing as known by God for all eternity—demands that the thing be as it is. God does not "make" (*ja'l*) it the way it is, because it has been that way for all eternity. Thus, Jandī writes,

> It is impossible for any created entity to become manifest in existence in its essence, attributes, descriptions, character, acts, and so on, except in the measure of the specific characteristic of its own essential receptivity. This is the mystery of the measuring out. The mystery of this mystery is that these immutable entities—which, depending on a person's tasting or perspective are also called the "realities of the things," the "forms taken by the objects of the Real's knowledge in eternity without beginning," the "quiddities," or the "ipseities"—are nothing outside the Real. He has known them from eternity without beginning, and they are entities in His knowledge as they are in themselves. Or rather, they are the relationships of the Real's Essence and Entity, or the tasks or the names of the Essence.... They cannot possibly change from what they are in their own realities, because they are the realities of God's own Essence. Things pertaining to God's Essence do not accept making, change, alteration, increase, or decrease. (*Sharḥ fuṣūṣ al-ḥikam* 487–488)

Discussion of this mystery was not limited to Sufis. Avicenna, for example, has a treatise on the subject. See Hourani, "Ibn Sīnā's 'Essay on the Secret of Destiny'" and Ivry, "Avicenna's Concept."

80.2 *Surely in that there is a reminder....* Ibn al-'Arabī frequently cites this Koranic verse to show that understanding the Koran requires knowledge through the heart, which sees God in both His incomparability and His similarity (see SPK 106–109).

80.4 *How can the partial intellect....* Sanā'ī, *Dīwān* 190. The contrast between the partial intellect and the universal, prophetic intellect is a recurrent theme in Rūmī's works. See SPL 35–37 and passim.

80.7 *To say or write more than this....* The author is alluding here to the types of dangers to which Ghazālī and others refer in explaining why the sciences of unveiling should not be divulged to those who are not ready for them (see the note on 42.14). Typical is the following passage from the fifth/eleventh-century scholar al-Rāghib al-Iṣfahānī (Ghazālī covers some of the same ground, perhaps with this passage in mind [*Iḥyā'* 27–28; *Book of Knowledge* 93–94]):

> The knowing and erudite sage must follow the Prophet in his saying, "We prophets have been commanded to come down to people's levels and speak to them in the measure of their intelligence."...It has been related that the Prophet said, "Speak to people about what they recognize and leave aside what they do not know. Do you want them to deny God and His Messenger?" He also said, "No one speaks to a people about a knowledge that their intelligence does not reach without causing a trial for some of them." Jesus said, "Impart no wisdom to those unworthy of it, lest they wrong it; and withhold it not from those worthy of it, lest you wrong them. Be like a skillful physician, who applies the medicine where he knows it will profit."...It was said to one of the sages, "Why is it that you do not inform people about wisdom when they seek it from you?" He replied, "I am following God, who said, *If God had known of any good in them, He would have made them hear; but if He had made them hear, they would have turned away, swerving aside* [8:23]." (Rāghib, *Dharī'a* 121).

80.8 *But let evil pass.* This is an Arabic proverb that Hamadānī also cites (*Nāmahā* 2:12, 425).

80.13 *How many the pearls of knowledge!....* In the *Futūḥāt* (1:32.18) and elsewhere, Ibn al-'Arabī identifies the author of these lines as "al-Sharīf al-Raḍī, the descendant of 'Alī ibn Abī Ṭālib." Kamāl al-Shaybī (*Ṣila* 155) claims that Ibn al-'Arabī means 'Alī ibn al-Ḥusayn, 'Alī's grandson, not the Sharīf al-Raḍī who is the compiler of 'Alī's *Nahj al-balāgha*. He provides evidence that others have attributed the verses to 'Alī ibn al-Ḥusayn, and one can add to the sources he cites Ibn al-Dabbāgh (*Mashāriq* 82). The style and content, however, make this attribution unlikely, as al-Shaybī points out.

80.27 *The mystery of their mastery over mankind.* See the note on 45.12.

80.29 *Just as the true religion has mentioned.* This is an allusion to Koran 72:1ff.

80.34 *O God, show us things as they are....* The first clause of this prayer is often quoted from the Prophet (for example, by Maybudī, *Kashf al-asrār*

1:35, 5:42), but it is not found in the hadith collections (see Furūzānfar, *Aḥādīth* 45; Bukhārī, *Manāhij* 387–388).

81.12 *World of images*. See the note on 45.33.

81.13 *Contiguous imagination* (*khayāl-i muttaṣil*).... *discontiguous imagination* (*khayāl-i munfaṣil*). These are Ibn al-ʿArabī's technical terms. See SPK 117.

81.20 *Diḥya Kalbī*. Dihya was a companion of the Prophet and known for his great beauty. According to another companion, "Gabriel used to come to the Prophet in the form of Diḥya" (Aḥmad 2:107). Ibn al-ʿArabī frequently refers to Gabriel's appearance in Diḥya's form in this sort of context. See SPK, index, under *Diḥya*.

81.22 *Khizr is also seen in this world*. Jāmī quotes this passage in *Naqd al-nuṣūṣ* (53), but he points out in a gloss that the Sufi shaykhs do not all agree on this point. Many of them, such as ʿAlāʾ al-Dawla Simnānī, have held that Khizr appears in his elemental (not imaginal) body. In the *Futūḥāt* (2:5.32) Ibn al-ʿArabī seems to say that Khizr lives in this world in his corporeal body, although the passage is not completely explicit.

81.38 *Folk of Allah*. This term, often employed by Ibn al-ʿArabī, is derived from the hadith, "God has folk among the people—the Folk of the Koran, who are the Folk of God and His elect" (SPK 388 n. 20). The Folk of Allah "guard the mysteries of the psalms of love" because only those perfect human beings who have actualized the form of the all-comprehensive name "Allah" can truly love God. As already pointed out, all other beings—even the angels—know God through certain specific names, not through all names.

82.6 *Right Side of the Valley*. This image is taken from the Koranic story of Moses. *When he came to it, a voice cried from the right side of the valley, in the sacred hollow, coming from the tree: "Moses, I am God, the Lord of the Worlds"* (28:30).

82.11 *When light enters the heart*.... This hadith is found with some variation in many Sufi sources, such as Makkī, *Qūt* 1:509; Ghazālī, *Iḥyāʾ* 1:58. For other sources, see Jām, *Rawḍa* 250–252.

82.15 *When greed leaves you*.... Sanāʾī, *Dīwān* 487.

82.21 *Fancy* (*wahm*). In Islamic psychology, *wahm* is a faculty shared by all animals. It stands above the five senses but below reason. Scholars have not come to any consensus as to how to translate the term into English.

82.22 *Reason the tailor*.... ʿAṭṭār, *Dīwān* 368.

82.29 *The concept of nearness has four levels*. Hamadānī has a similar discussion in *Zubda* 77–78, and the author may have had it in view.

82.34 *Abū Yazīd* and *Abu'l-Ḥasan* (d. 425/1034) are famous Sufis, while ʿ*Utba* ibn Rabīʿa ibn ʿAbd Shams and *Shayba* ibn Rabīʿa were two of the important opponents of the Prophet killed at the Battle of Badr.

82.41 *Ḥallāj*. Massignon gives the text in *Akhbar al-Hallaj* 8.

83.9 *Lote Tree*. This is the "lote tree of the far boundary" (Koran 53:14). It is said to mark the outer edge of the created world. As mentioned earlier, Gabriel is said to have taken the Prophet only as far as the Lote Tree on the *miʿrāj*, and from there on he had to go alone.

83.10 *This is the meaning of*. . . . This interpretation of the Koranic verse derives from the understanding of the name Merciful as denoting God as Being, as discussed in the note on 72.32. Qūnawī makes this clear in *Iʿjāz al-bayān* 290–291/407–408. He explains that, although all paths lead to God, this does not necessarily yield benefit, since God is both Forgiving and Vengeful (compare SPK 301–303). He writes,

> God says, *Surely [O Muhammad] you guide upon a straight path, the path of God, to whom belongs whatsoever is in the heavens and whatsoever is in the earth. Surely to God all things come home* [42:52]. Hence, God points out that each thing goes home to Him, and each thing walks upon a suprasensory or sensory path, depending on the walker, and that God is the goal. *Unto God is the homecoming* [3:28]. God informed His Prophet in order that he would inform us. He says, *Surely you guide upon a straight path* in relation to all the other paths. Hence, God is the goal of the travelers, just as He is the guide of the bewildered. However, there is no excellence in things that are unconditioned such that disparity is removed—as, for example, His unconditioned addressing [all human beings], His unconditioned withness [indicated in the Koranic verse, *He is with you wherever you are* (57:4)], His unconditioned companionship [with all things], and the unconditioned ending of all paths with Him. These are all unconditioned in respect of the fact that He encompasses all things and He turns the unconditioned attention of His Essence and His attributes toward bringing all things into existence. For there is no difference, in respect of the unity of His Essence and the attention, between His attention toward creating the Throne or the Supreme Pen and an ant. . . . *You see no disparity in the creation of the Merciful* [67:3].

Suhrawardī the Illuminationist reads this same Koranic verse differently, because he understands it as confirming the idea that the cosmos is the best of all possible worlds. He writes,

> Existence cannot possibly be more complete and more perfect than it is, as is indicated by the revelation: *God's handiwork, who has made all things very well* [27:88], alluding to the secure and solid order. In another verse He says, *You see no disparity in the creation of the Merciful*. This alludes to the well-guarded interrelationship and the well-preserved order. Nothing is left to its own devices or kept empty of the effects of God's solicitude. Everything reaches the perfection appropriate to it. (*al-Alwāḥ* 39; *Alwāḥ* 150)

83.14 *His Face in every direction*. . . . This Arabic verse is also quoted by Hamadānī (*Zubda* 7), a fact that supports the suggestion that the author had this work in view in discussing the levels of nearness.

83.16 *By day I praised Thee*. . . . A quatrain by Awḥad al-Dīn Kirmānī (*Dīwān*, n. 184), 'Irāqī quotes it in *Lama'āt* (*Fakhruddin* 124). It has also been attributed to Rūmī, but not in the old manuscripts used by Furūzānfar in editing his *Dīwān*.

83.24 *Everyone drawn to a beloved*. . . . Also quoted by 'Irāqī (*Fakhruddin* 85).

83.32 *With your Lord is neither*. . . . Hamadānī (*Tamhīdāt* 83) gives the text as "my Lord" rather than "your Lord," suggesting that it is a hadith.

84.9 *The second configuration*. As is indicated later in this work (99.15), this is the world of the barzakh, while the first configuration is the present world.

84.15 *Reason can find no way*. . . . Sanā'ī, *Dīwān* 201.

84.19 *It has been reported*. . . . So also says Hamadānī (*Nāmahā* 2:256).

84.21 *This path cannot be walked with reason's feet*. . . . A quatrain by Kirmānī (*Dīwān*, n. 1226).

84.32 *No created thing*. . . . Sanā'ī, *Ḥadīqa* 326.

84.34 *The journey is two: a journey to God*. . . . Compare 'Irāqī's discussion of these two journeys (*Fakhruddin* 94–95). Ibn al-'Arabī gives a different formulation. "There are three journeys established by the Real, without a fourth: A journey from Him, a journey to Him, and a journey in Him. The journey in Him is a journey of perplexity and bewilderment. . . . The first two journeys have ends where people put down their baggage, but perplexity's journey has no end" (*Asfār* 3).

85.7 *Keep traveling this road*. . . . The quatrain is most likely by Awḥad al-Dīn Kirmānī (*Dīwān*, n. 320; see the editor's note on 331), although it has also been attributed in late manuscripts to Afḍal al-Dīn Kāshānī (*Dīwān* 76) and 'Umar Khayyām.

86.11 *Certain objects of perception are related to the stage*. . . . Compare the similar discussion in Hamadānī, *Zubda* 93.

86.16 *A single attraction of God*. . . . A well-known Sufi saying, frequently quoted, for example, by Hamadānī (*Tamhīdāt* 47, 75, 156, 243, 299) and Najm al-Dīn Rāzī (*Mirṣād* 212, etc., trans. Algar, 222). Sulamī (*Ṭabaqāt* 488) attributes a slightly different version to Abu'l-Qāsim Ibrāhīm ibn Muḥammad Naṣrābādī (d. 367/977–978).

86.24 *Thy beauty is greater than my sight*. . . . The verse is found in Aḥmad Ghazālī, *Sawāniḥ* 7; and Maybudī, *Kashf al-asrār* 6:463.

86.29 *Voicing Sanā'ī's subtleties and symbols* . . . . Sanā'ī, *Dīwān* 193.

86.33 *If someone hears of it*. . . . Ibn Sīnā, *Ishārāt* 3:235.

86.36 *Caress each one....* Also quoted by Hamadānī, with another line and with the two half-lines reversed (*Nāmahā* 2: 130; see also 1:91, 2:188; idem, *Tamhīdāt* 223).

87.2 *Then there happened....* Samʻānī (*Rawḥ al-arwāḥ* 213) quotes this Arabic verse as the second of two. The first reads, "He came to me concealed in the shirt of night, stepping lightly because of my eagerness and caution."

87.7 *A man is needed....* See note on 46.13.

87.14 *Nothing can be found....* Sanā'ī, *Dīwān* 614.

87.27 *Sometimes the ear falls in love....* This is the second hemistich of an often quoted Arabic verse. The first hemistich reads, "O my people, my ear has fallen in love with one of the tribe." Naṣrallāh, *Kalīla* 179; Ibn al-ʻArabī, *Futūḥāt* 2:21.1.

88.4 *And I, when people spoke of love....* These Arabic verses are also quoted by Hamadānī (*Nāmahā* 1:209).

88.26 *Question me not....* These are Khizr's words when Moses asked permission to accompany him. See the note on 38.24.

88.29 *Your master is love....* This is the second verse of a quatrain that is quoted by Shihāb al-Dīn Suhrawardī (*Majmūʻa* 285–286). The first verse reads, "Clear your head of empty melancholy, decrease your indifference and increase your need."

88.33 *God have mercy on my brother Moses....* Hadiths with similar wording are found in Muslim (Faḍā'il 172) and Abū Dāwūd (Ḥurūf 1). The same wording is found in Hamadānī (*Zubda* 68), who remarks that the Prophet said something to this effect, although the words may be different. It is likely that the author took the hadith from this source.

88.35 *When serving kings....* These two Arabic verses are attributed to Aḥmad Ghazālī by Subkī in *Ṭabaqāt al-Shāfiʻiyya* and are quoted without ascription by his brother Abū Ḥāmid Ghazālī in *Naṣīḥat al-mulūk* 144 (see the footnote on that page).

89.10 *The angels are His daughters....* These are all allusions to Koranic verses.

89.22 *Splitting the moon....* These miracles of Muhammad, Christ, and Moses respectively are all mentioned in the Koran.

89.27 *Three characteristics.* The three characteristics, whose division is made clear by the parallel passage in *Rising Places* (49.12), are indicated by the numbers in brackets.

89.32 *There is no power...to the Garden.* The hadith is found in exactly these words in Aḥmad (5:156) and in slightly different versions in most sources, such as Bukhārī (Daʻawāt 51, 68) and Muslim (Dhikr 44–46).

89.33 *The sin of him who says. . . .* The author probably has the following hadith in mind: "When someone says 'Glory be to God and His is the praise' one hundred times in a day, his faults will be taken away, even if they are like the foam of the ocean" (Bukhārī, Da'awāt 66).

89.37 *Half a dinar.* See the article "Zakāt," *Encyclopedia of Islam* (old edition); and Ghazālī, *Mysteries of Almsgiving* 10–11.

89.39 *Eight classes.* These are mentioned in Koran 9:60. See Ghazālī, *Mysteries of Almsgiving* 22–23 and passim.

89.40 *Fasting on the Day of 'Arafa.* Muslim (Ṣiyām 196, 197) and other sources give a hadith that says fasting on the Day of 'Arafa expiates the sins of both the past year and the coming year.

90.2 *In the Garden is a barren plain. . . .* In the standard sources, the closest hadiths to this are the following: Abū Hurayra relates that the Prophet passed him while he was working in his garden. The Prophet said, "O Abū Hurayra, what are you planting?" He replied, "It is one of my plants." The Prophet said, "Should I point you to a planting better for you than this?" He replied that he should. The Prophet said, "Say, 'Glory be to God, praise belongs to God, there is no god but God, and God is greater.' For each of them a tree will be planted for you in the Garden" (Ibn Māja, Adab 56). "On the night I was taken on my journey [to God], I met Abraham, and he said to me, 'O Muhammad, give my greetings of peace to your community and tell them that the Garden has good earth, sweet water, and plains, and that its seedlings are 'Glory be to God, praise belongs to God, there is no god but God, and God is greater' " (Tirmidhī, Da'awāt 58).

90.7 *In his grave the person of faith dwells in a luxuriant garden. . . .* Ghazālī gives the text of this hadith, with slight differences (*Arba'īn* 281–282; *Iḥyā'* 4:358–359; *Remembrance of Death* 138 and note). The ninety-nine *tinnīn*s are mentioned with a similar description in Dārimī (Riqāq 94) and Aḥmad (3:38).

90.17 *They are only your works. . . .* Ghazālī quotes this saying in a similar discussion in *Arba'īn* 283 (compare Hamadānī, *Tamhīdāt* 289; Ibn al-'Arabī, *Futūḥāt* 1:175.20). The closest hadith to it in the standard sources is a sentence in a long *ḥadīth qudsī* in which God says, "O My servants, they are only your works that I have kept track of for you. I will give you over to them fully. If someone finds good, let him praise God, and if he finds something else, let him blame only himself" (Muslim, Birr 55).

90.34 *The Garden has a market. . . .* Tirmidhī, Janna 15. Ibn al-'Arabī often discusses the nature of this market and its relationship with the infinitely varied self-disclosures of God (see *Futūḥāt* 2:183.22, 628.3; 3:518.22). Qūnawī has this to say about it:

> As for the Market of the Garden—which contains beautiful human forms that the people of the Garden choose to wear as they like—it derives from certain streams stemming from the World of Nondelimited Imagination, which is the source and origin of the Market's loci of manifestation. This Market is the channel for the aid that arrives from the world of imagination to the loci of manifestation of the people of the Garden. It is the source of their food, drink, clothing and everything that they enjoy in the "earths," which are the levels of their works, beliefs, character traits, and attributes. (*Nuṣūṣ* 64–65/ 292)

For more on the Market of the Garden, see the note on 99.8.

90.40 *What do you know*. . . . Sanā'ī, *Sayr al-'ibād* 229. Solomon's knowledge of the birds' speech is referred to in the Koran. *Solomon said, "People, we have been taught the speech of the birds"* (27:16). Sufis understand "birds" as alluding to spirits, which fly in God's neighborhood. Knowledge of their speech is knowledge of the goings-on in the spiritual world. Translating this expression as "Conference of the Birds," as has been done in the case of the title of 'Aṭṭār's famous poem, obscures its significance.

91.3 *You need a star-consuming sun*. . . . Sanā'ī, *Ḥadīqa* 339.

91.8 *Mustafa in the world*. . . . Sanā'ī, *Dīwān* 43. Alcor is a faint star next to Mizar, the middle star of the Big Dipper's handle.

91.14 *Prophets among the friends* (*anbiyā'-i awliyā'*). This is a technical term specific to Ibn al-'Arabī. According to his teachings, the prophets among the friends share in the Prophet's message by witnessing, through unveiling, Gabriel's revelations to him (see SPK 250–252). They are the people of general (*'āmm*) or nondelimited (*muṭlaq*) prophecy as opposed to the people of a law-giving (*tashrī'ī*) prophecy—that is, a prophecy that sets down a shariah or modifies a previous shariah. See *Futūḥāt* 2:58.11, 90.19, 90.27, 91.1. See also Chodkiewicz's remarks on Ibn al-'Arabī's distinction between indeterminate or free (*muṭlaq*) and law-giving prophecy (*Sceau* 69–74, 142).

91.15 *Oh, the yearning*. . . . This saying is common in Sufi works (such as Maybudī, *Kashf al-asrār* 3:545). It is also found imbedded in a long saying of the Prophet transmitted through his companion Abū Dharr and cited by Hamadānī (*Tamhīdāt* 334–335). 'Alī (*Nahj al-balāgha* 497) has a parallel description of God's friends, ending with the sentence, "Oh, oh, the yearning to see them!" In a similar long saying describing God's friends attributed to Sahl al-Tustarī, God says to Adam, "Their yearning for the encounter with Me has become drawn out, but My yearning for them is more intense" (Iṣfahānī, *Ḥilya* 10:193).

91.16 *The ulama of my community are like the prophets of the Children of Israel*. A saying often quoted in Sufi works (for example, Hamadānī, *Tamhīdāt* 5; for other sources, see Jām, *Uns* 339). The second version, "like the prophets of the other communities,'' is more difficult to find. Ibn al-ʿArabī sometimes quotes the two sayings together (*Futūḥāt* 1:223.4, 546.8). In the second of these two instances, he apologizes for mentioning a hadith that has no sound chain of transmission and says, ''but I mention it to accustom my listeners to the idea that the ulama of this community have joined the prophets in rank.''

91.21 *The friends are of two types*. The distinction between the sober and the intoxicated is common (see Hujwīrī, *Kashf*, trans. Nicholson, 184–188; Kalābādhī, *Doctrine* 121–123; Nurbakhsh, *Sufism* 2:65–84; Schimmel, *Mystical Dimensions*, passim; SPK 197–199 and passim; SPL, passim). I have not found a precise source for the contrast between ''restored [*mardūd*] and perfected [*mukammal*]'' and ''consumed [*mustahlak*] and perfect [*kāmil*],'' but Ibn al-ʿArabī employs most, if not all, of these terms in ways that support their usage here. Concerning the ''perfected'' he writes, ''In our view the perfected is he toward whom things stand in the same relation as they do toward God. It is he who sees the face of the Real in every affair'' (*Futūḥāt* 1:699.21; compare 2:208.5, 233.3, 529.20). As for ''restoration,'' he writes concerning the friends of God who are the perfect inheritors of Muhammad, ''God restores them to the creatures in order to guide the creatures to the wholesomeness of their hearts with God, to distinguish for them between praiseworthy and blameworthy thoughts, and to clarify for them the goals of the Shariah'' (1:251.6). The term *to be consumed* (*istihlāk*) is roughly equivalent to annihilation (*fanā'*), that is, the annihilation of human attributes, which implies the ''subsistence'' (*baqā'*) of divine attributes in their place. Ibn al-ʿArabī tells us that God has servants whom He does not restore to creation, so their creaturely dimension is ''consumed'' by their divine dimension:

> When the Real comes to them suddenly, He takes them to Himself and does not restore them to the cosmos. He keeps them busy with Himself. This often happens. But the perfection of inheritance from the prophets and messengers is to be returned to the creatures. . . . The ones who are not restored have no face turned toward the cosmos, so they stay there [with God]. . . Among them are those who are consumed by what they witness there. There are quite a few of them. This state lasted for some time for Abū Yazīd Basṭāmī. It was also the state of Abū ʿIqāl al-Maghribī and others. (*Futūḥāt* 1:251.18)

On the divine madness of Abū ʿIqāl al-Maghribī, see SPK 266. I have not yet found a text by Ibn al-ʿArabī for the contrast between ''perfect'' and ''perfected.'' For one of his discussions of two kinds of shaykhs that parallels the passage here, see SPK 270–273.

Possibly, the term *perfected* should be read as ''perfecting'' (*mukammil*). In some passages, Qūnawī's disciple Farghānī employs the gerund form, *takmīl* (to perfect), as a synonym for giving guidance (*irshād*) and training (*tarbiya; Mashāriq* 309, 393, 494). In this meaning, "perfecting" is equivalent to *murshid* (guiding or guide), a term synonymous with shaykh.

91.34 *Love for Thee....* Sanā'ī, *Dīwān* 697.

92.6 *When the face....* Sanā'ī, *Dīwān* 930–931.

92.15 *Affirmation after obliteration (ithbāt ba'd al-maḥw).* Hujwīrī (*Kashf*, trans. Nicholson, 379–380) and Qushayrī (*Risāla* 273–276) discuss the relationship between these two concepts, and other Sufis frequently employ them.

92.19 *We are the radiance....* A rather common pattern for quatrains. Compare the following, attributed to Rūmī (*Rubā'iyyāt*, n. 1366):

> We are the treasury of divine mysteries,
> we are the sea of uncounted pearls,
> We have filled the space between moon and Fish,
> we have mounted the throne of kingship.

(The "Fish" is a mythical being upon which the earth is said to rest).

92.25 *I am Jesus and my miracle....* This is the second half of a quatrain by Kirmānī (*Dīwān*, n. 1058).

92.31 *'Alī ...in a long sermon.* The text is found in 'Alī's *Nahj al-balāgha* (496–497), although with a number of variants, including a difference in sentence order.

93.1 *Except the prophecy of law-giving....* This is Ibn al-'Arabī's position. See the note on 91.14.

93.4 *O Abū Bakr....* This is apparently a hadith, but it is not found in the standard sources.

93.5 *O 'Umar....* A hadith to this effect is recorded in Tirmidhī (Manāqib 17). "If there were to be a prophet after me, it would be 'Umar ibn al-Khaṭṭāb."

93.21 *The pleasures of this world have three aspects.* This discussion may be inspired by Ghazālī's *Iḥyā'* (3:155 [3.6.5]), in which the same points are made but in great detail. See also idem, *Kīmiyā* 1:75.

94.5 *I think the soul....* See the note on 38.1.

94.18 *Before you is a road....* The quatrain is attributed to Afḍal al-Dīn Kāshānī, *Dīwān* 109.

94.29 *Love for this world....* A hadith found in Suyūṭī, *al-Jāmi' al-ṣaghīr* (*Fayḍ* 3:368). For sources in literature, see Jām, *Uns* 336.

94.32 *Intelligence takes this one....* Sanā'ī, *Ḥadīqa* 306, with the two hemistiches reversed.

95.4 *How good is honest wealth....* Ghazālī and others attribute this saying to the Prophet (Furūzānfar, *Aḥādīth* 11; Rāghib, *Dharī'a* 207).

95.6 *Whatever you have*. . . . Sanā'ī, *Ḥadīqa* 127.

95.12 *A world where every heart*. . . . Sanā'ī, *Dīwān* 705.

95.18 *The soul that commands to evil* (*al-nafs al-ammāra [bi'l-sū']*). This is the lower soul, which is dominated by everything that turns human beings away from God. The term is Koranic (12:53) and is contrasted with the "blaming soul," which wavers between good and evil and criticizes itself for its own shortcomings, and the "soul at peace with God," which has reached perfection. See Schimmel, *Mystical Dimensions* 112 and passim; Murata, *Tao of Islam*, chapter 9.

95.21 *Should I abandon the pleasure of wine*. . . . Hamadānī quotes these two Arabic verses at the end of the following passage, in which he is explaining that the expression *human being* (*ādamī*) refers not to the bodily frame (*qālib*), but to the spirit (*jān*), for which the body is simply the mount.

> Here some people say that the revealed law has no genuine root. *What, when we are dust, shall we indeed be raised up again in a new creation?* [13:5]. Poets have made fun of this idea.
>
> The Prophet tells us that we shall be revived—
> How can bones and dust come to life?
>
> But this was not specific to the people of the Age of Ignorance. Even Muslims have said this. (*Nāmaha* 2:37)

95.28 *Crushers*. This is an allusion to Koran 104:4–9: *No indeed; he shall be thrust into the Crusher; and what shall teach thee what the Crusher is? The kindled Fire of God, rising up over the hearts, closing in upon them, extended in columns.*

95.30 *Look at Jesus' renunciation*. . . . Sanā'ī, *Ḥadīqa* 443.

96.2 *The rich* (*ghanī*). The term is employed as the opposite of the poor (*faqīr, darwīsh*), which is synonymous with Sufi.

96.14 *Fear this world*. . . . Suyūṭī, *al-Jāmiʿ al-ṣaghīr* (*Fayḍ* 1:187); Ghazālī, *Kīmiyā* 1:75. For other sources, see Jām, *Uns* 314–315. On Harut and Marut, see the note on 65.1.

96.16 *My advice to you*. . . . Sanā'ī, *Ḥadīqa* 431. Rūmī quotes this verse approvingly and expands on its meaning in a section of his *Mathnawī* (4:2562–567) called, "How human beings are deluded by their cleverness and by the forms configured by their own nature, and how they fail to seek the knowledge of the unseen, which is the knowledge of the prophets." He has just explained that the hidden treasure of divine knowledge can only be reached by demolishing the house of attachment to this world.

> I saw in my house paintings and pictures;
> I was overcome by love for the house.
> I was unaware of the hidden treasure,
> or else I would have sought comfort in the ax.

Oh, if I had only given the ax its due,
I would now be quit of heartache!
I used to look at the paintings—like children,
I had many things I loved.
How well has that great sage spoken—"You are a child,
and the house is full of paintings and pictures."
In the *Ilāhī-nāma*, he gave a great deal of advice:
"Raise dust from your own house!"

96.23 *Whoever wants to look at a dead man walking*.... The hadith is not found in the standard collections, but Hamadānī quotes it (*Tamhīdāt* 14, 52, 287). Both here and in the *Tamhīdāt*, the text calls Abū Bakr by the name "Ibn Abī Quḥāfa."

96.26 *One of the great companions*. ʿAyn al-Quḍāt Hamadānī quotes the saying from the companion Ibn Masʿūd with an extra clause after "steeds": "that lead the servant to God's neighborhood" (*Nāmahā* 2:220).

96.29 *Aḥmad Ghazālī* (d. 520/1126). Younger brother of the famous Abū Ḥāmid Muḥammad Ghazālī, he was an important Sufi in his own right. See the English translation of his *Sawāniḥ*. This passage seems to be the earliest source for this story (Ghazālī, *Majmūʿa* 104–105).

96.32 *God looks not at your forms*.... See the note on 132.37.

97.18 *You were created for eternity*.... See the note on 50.31.

97.22 *The spirits of the martyrs*.... Muslim, Imāra 122, and several other standard sources.

97.27 *O Abū Jahl*.... Muslim, Janna 77, and other standard sources.

97.38 *In that house*.... Also quoted in *Rising Places* 51.1.

98.1 *People were created*.... Arabic verses by Abu'l-ʿAlā' al-Maʿarrī (d. 449/1057; *Dīwān* 112).

98.11 *For the spirit is qualified*.... Ghazālī makes a similar statement in *Kīmiyā* 1:88.

99.8 *After the abode of Alast*.... On the covenant that human beings made on the Day of Alast, see the note on 37.34. Ibn al-ʿArabī frequently describes the many stages of human becoming. In one passage, he calls each transferal from one stage to the next a "mustering" (*ḥashr*), employing one of the terms which the Koran uses for the bodily resurrection.

> When God brings the human spirit into existence, He brings it into existence governing a natural, sensory form that belongs to it. This is true in this world, in the barzakh, in the abode of the hereafter, and wherever it might be. The first form the human spirit put on was the form in which God made the Covenant with it through its acknowledgment of God's Lordship [on the Day of Alast]. Then it was mustered from that form into the bodily, this-worldly form

and imprisoned there, beginning in the fourth month of the engendering of its body's form in its mother's womb and lasting until the hour of its death. When it dies, it is mustered into another form that lasts from the time of its death to the time of its questioning [by Munkar and Nakīr in the grave]. When the time of its questioning comes, the spirit is mustered from that form into its dead body. Then the body is revived through it. But people's ears and eyes are blocked from perceiving the body's life through the spirit, except for those prophets and friends among the humans and the jinn whom God has singled out for the unveiling of this. However, other living things witness objectively the body's life and what it undergoes.

After the questioning, the spirit is mustered into another form in the barzakh to which it clings; or rather, that form is the barzakh itself. Here sleep and death are exactly the same. It stays in this form until the Trumpet is blown at the Uprising. It rises up from that form and is mustered into the form from which it parted in this world, if it still must be questioned. If it does not belong to that group, then it is mustered into the form in which it will enter the Garden. After being questioned, those who are questioned on the Day of Resurrection are mustered into the forms in which they will enter the Garden or the Fire. The People of the Fire are all questioned.

Those who enter the Garden settle down there. Then they are summoned to the Vision and set out for it. They are mustered into a form that is only suitable for the Vision. When they return, they are mustered into a form suitable for the Garden.

In each form, the spirit forgets the form that it used to have. Its ruling property takes over the form into which it has passed and into which it has been mustered. When it enters the Market of the Garden and sees the forms within it, it is mustered into whichever form it sees and considers beautiful. In the Garden, it never ceases being mustered from one form to another ad infinitum. Thus, it comes to know the Divine Expanse [*al-ittisāʿ al-ilāhī*]. Just as God never repeats the forms of His self-disclosure, so also the spirit to which He discloses Himself needs a new form for every form that is disclosed to it so that it can gaze upon Him in His self-disclosure. Hence, the spirit never ceases being mustered into forms, forms that it takes from the Market of the Garden. It does not take or consider beautiful any of the forms in the Market unless that form corresponds with the coming self-disclosure, since the form is like the specific preparedness for the next self-disclosure. (*Futūḥāt* 2: 627.27)

99.15 *The barzakh.* On the barzakh as the place where the inward becomes outward and vice versa, see Chittick, "Eschatology" and idem, "Death and the World of Imagination." Qūnawī has a section in one of his Arabic works that parallels this discussion. He writes,

> Every configuration into which human beings pass after death is born from this elemental configuration. Within this configuration [that is, the elemental configuration of this world] there are things that remain and subsist, even if their manifestation changes and their qualities and compositions become diverse. There are other things that disappear at death and still others that accompany the spirit in the barzakh. The latter include natural faculties and imaginal and mental concepts, both the good and the evil. Here by "evil" I mean corrupt beliefs, base concepts, and ugly goals. . . . The configuration of the Mustering is the inward dimension of the present world's outward dimension. What is now outward becomes inward there, and what is now inward becomes outward, in a way that comprehends all the properties of what is now inward and outward and of what results from the present inwardness, outwardness, comprehensiveness, and composition. . . . So here [in the present world] the inward is unconditioned [*muṭlaq*], whereas the outward is conditioned [*muqayyad*]. But there [at the Mustering] the situation is the contrary. The property of being unconditioned pertains to the outward dimension of the paradisial plane, whereas the property of being conditioned pertains to its inward dimension. The dominating property and influence in what is outward there belongs to what is inward here, and vice versa.
>
> The human configurations are four. First is this elemental configuration, which is like the seed of the remaining configurations. . . .
>
> Second is the barzakh configuration. It is configured from some of the forms of people's states, and some of their works, opinions, concepts, character traits, and attributes. Certain things come together from all of these, and hence a specific condition is actualized. . . . Then this condition requires that the soul become manifest in the form actualized from this condition and this coming together. The attributes of this form will accord with the attribute that dominated over the person when he left the first, lower configuration. Therefore in the barzakh—or rather, a short time before the Mustering—some people appear in the form of lions, wolves, and birds, as the Shariah has mentioned, and as unveiling and divine instruction have given witness.
>
> But this does not happen by means of the metempsychosis [*maskh*] or transmigration [*tanāsukh*] that is denied, for people who

believe in such things hold that it occurs in this world. But what we are speaking about occurs in the barzakh after death. The souls of those people over whom spiritual attributes held sway and who greatly shunned the present world—such as martyrs killed in the Path of God with pure hearts and correct faith—will appear in the forms of spiritual birds, as the Prophet reported. . . .

The third human configuration is the Mustering, and the fourth is the plane of being established within one of the two Abodes [paradise or hell]. (*Nafaḥāt* 114–117)

99.27 *When they take off the mask*. . . . Sanā'ī, *Dīwān* 708.

99.34 *Will appear in the form of a leopard.* Already in the Koran and the Hadith, imperfect human personality types are represented by animals and reference is made to the appearance of human beings in animal form (for example, Koran 2:65, 5:60, 7:166). Authorities who discuss eschatology make use of this imagery from early times. See Murata, *Tao* 277–283.

99.35 *Appetite* (*shahwa*), *anger* (*ghaḍab*). In Islamic psychology, these represent the two basic tendencies of the animal soul, which human beings share with all animals. The first dominates in the make-up of animals such as pigs and cows, which are included in the beasts (*bahā'im*), while the second dominates in predators (*sibā'*). Through the first (such as hunger and the sexual drive), the soul draws things to itself. Through the second, it fends off dangers. Both faculties are necessary for life, but if either becomes the predominant characteristic of the soul, the human being will remain at the animal level. In texts on philosophy, the terms are often translated as "concupiscence" and "irascibility." See the note on 104.31. For a detailed discussion of their significance in Islamic psychology, see Murata, *Tao* 258–259 and passim.

100.9 *Through the properties of dreams*. . . . For a relatively detailed explanation of Ghazālī's views on the connection between dreams and the barzakh, see his *Remembrance of Death* 149–169 (*Iḥyā'* 4.10.1.8).

100.15 *Sleep is the brother of death.* The text of this hadith is given by Suyūṭī (*Fayḍ* 6:300) and Tabrīzī (*Mishkāt al-maṣābīḥ* 500, trans. Robson, 1205) as "Sleep is the brother of death, and the people of the Garden do not die." Some sources give a longer text. Jābir asked the Prophet, "O Messenger of God, do the people of the Garden sleep?" He replied, "No. Sleep is the brother of death, and the people of the Garden neither sleep nor die" (cited in Nasafī, *Kashf* 323). See also Furūzānfar, *Aḥādīth* 5; Hujwīrī, *Kashf* 457, trans. Nicholson, 351.

100.22 *As you sleep*. . . . I have not found a source for this hadith. Bahā' Walad, Rūmī's father, quotes a hadith similar in structure but significantly different in meaning. "As you live, so you shall die and so you shall be raised up" (*Ma'ārif* 105; also Rāzī, *Mirṣād* 343, 354). Sanā'ī gives a similar report, without attributing it to the Prophet. "As people live, so they die, and as they die, so they are raised up" (*Ḥadīqa* 379).

100.24 *Ibn Sīrīn* (d. 110/728–729). He is the most famous dream interpreter in Islam, and a number of works are attributed to him. The anecdote is most likely taken from Ghazālī (*Iḥyā'* 4:362; *Remembrance of Death* 153). For biographical notes, see the latter work, 295.

100.34 *By Him whose hand holds Muhammad's soul. . . .* Bukhārī (Riqāq 29) and Aḥmad (1:287, 413, 442) give the text of this hadith as follows: "The Garden is nearer to each of you than his shoelace, and the Fire is the same."

100.37 *Your paradise and hell. . . .* Sanā'ī, *Dīwān* 708.

101.8 *When morning comes. . . .* Also quoted in *Rising Places* 48.5.

101.12 *Nakīr and Munkar.* See the note on 51.38.

101.12 *The pit and the garden plot.* Reference to the hadith quoted on 50.32.

101.15 *Elemental configuration.* In other words, it is made of the four elements—earth, water, air, and fire. In contrast, the barzakh is natural, but not elemental. Hence, the barzakh is governed by the four natures—heat, cold, wetness, and dryness—but not by the four elements. See Chittick, "Death and the World of Imagination" 75.

101.36 *Khizr.* I am not sure about the meaning here, and I have translated the passage in a way that makes sense of it. The author seems to be saying that some people have objected to the idea that Khizr could have drunk the water of life and lived on earth ever since. But for Khizr, this long period of time is very short. This interpretation is supported by the fact that the author has already told us that Khizr is seen in the world of imagination, and the worlds after death all pertain to the imaginal or intermediate realms.

102.2 *When someone dies. . . .* Ghazālī quotes this hadith in *Arba'īn* 280 and *Iḥyā'* 4:46 (4.2.1), expanding on its meaning in the latter (see Chittick, "Eschatology" 398). It is found as part of a longer hadith in some collections, such as 'Ajlūnī's *Kashf al-khifā'* and Sakhāwī's *al-Maqāṣid al-ḥasana* (cited in Nasafī, *Kashf al-ḥaqā'iq* 324). Also quoted in Suhrawardī, *Alwāḥ* 181; idem, *al-Alwāḥ* 66; Hamadānī, *Tamhīdāt* 52, 78, etc.

102.23 *O heart, how long. . . .* Sanā'ī, *Dīwān* 704.

102.27 *When the people of the Garden. . . .* Muslim, Janna 22.

102.32 *High up in His sky. . . .* Sanā'ī, *Dīwān* 705.

102.36 *The felicitous are of two types.* As mentioned in the introduction, this division of the people of the next world into three groups—the companions of the left, the companions of the right, and those brought near to God (or the foremost)—is discussed in some detail in Sura 56 of the Koran. Among the many passages one could quote in early works to illustrate the distinction between the two types of felicitous, I choose part of Maybudī's commentary on Sura 56. He has just been explaining the nature of the beautiful black-eyed virgins—the houris—who will be the reward of the pious. He continues:

> This is the reward for the works of the faithful and the recompense for their acts of obedience and worship. It is the attribute of hirelings who do a job and then want to be paid. But God has friends who do not bow their heads to the paradise of His good pleasure, nor do they hunt the houris, the castles, the rivers, and the trees. They are the servants of the tent of the sultan of *tawḥīd*, the residents of the world of love, the sultans of the universe of true knowledge, those who yearn for the drink of nothingness.
>
> The Paradise of Everlastingness presents its adornment and beauty to them, and they disclose their certainty and true knowledge to it. Paradise presents its rivers of wine, milk, and honey to them, and they disclose the springs of *tawḥīd* and the oceans of detachment to it. Paradise presents its trees full of fruits with their blossoms and lights to them, and they disclose the green shoots of pain and bewilderment to it. Paradise presents to them the black-eyed beauties, decorated and adorned, and they disclose to it the veiled virgins of true knowledge and the secrets of witnessing. Finally, paradise turns away from them in shame, and they pass on, as far as *a sitting place of strength, with a Powerful King* [54:55]. They do not open the eyes of their aspiration toward anyone else. (*Kashf al-asrār* 9:455–456)

102.39 *Most of the people of the Garden are simpletons.* A different version of the first half of this saying is found in Suyūṭī's *Jāmiʿ al-ṣaghīr* (Fayḍ 3:522, under *dakhaltu*). Rāghib discusses the meaning of the first half of the saying, which he does not attribute explicitly to the Prophet, while talking about acquired intelligence (*al-ʿaql al-muktasab*).

> Acquired intelligence is of two types. One is experience of this world and acquired sciences, while the other is the sciences of the next world and the divine sciences. ʿAlī coined three similitudes here. He said, "The likeness of this world and the next is like the two pans of a balance. One does not go down without the other coming up. Or it is like the East and the West. The closer you get to one, the further you move from the other. Or it is like two wives. If you please one, you anger the other." That is why you will see that some people are clever in taking care of this world but simpletons in taking care of the next, while others are clever in taking care of the next world but simpletons in the affairs of this world. Hence, the Prophet said, "The clever person is he who abases his own soul and works for what comes after death." And it was said to someone who called one of the upright a simpleton, "Most of the people of the Garden are simpletons." (*Dharīʿa* 76)

103.1 *In the paradise of the spheres....* Sanā'ī, *Ḥadīqa* 152. In the conclusion to *Easy Reads* the author offers an explanation for "hell-drinker" (164). He also quotes this line along with another (148.14).

103.35 *If you drive nature's rabble....* Sanā'ī, *Dīwān* 706.

103.39 *O Children of Israel! Do not say....* Compare Deuteronomy 30:11–14. Ghazālī quotes this saying with some textual differences in *Iḥyā'* 1:54 (1.1.6). Sayyid Ḥaydar Āmulī tells us that the saying is by Jesus (*Jāmi' al-asrār* 513).

104.21 *In value you are greater than the two worlds....* Sanā'ī, *Ḥadīqa* 500.

104.29 *Justice.* The word *'adālat* (justice) is from the same root as *'adl* (equity) and is often used synonymously with it. In philosophical and Sufi discussions of ethics, which continue the Greek tradition, justice is usually given the highest rank of all the virtues (*faḍā'il*). Naṣīr al-Dīn Ṭūsī, who corresponded with Qūnawī on philosophical matters, provides a good example of this type of approach in his classic *Nasirean Ethics.* In typical fashion for Muslim thinkers, he begins by showing the ontological grounding of justice in God, who alone is truly One. Thus, the root of justice is not found in social or human considerations. On the contrary, social and human considerations must be grounded in the divine reality in order for justice to be established. And this has nothing to do with abstract notions of good, but rather with the nature of *wujūd* itself, which is the ultimate reality. Justice is good in human affairs because it is the direct effusion of the Real. It is the proper equilibrium (*i'tidāl,* from the same root as *'adl* and *'adālat*) among the qualities of existence—the names of God. Ṭūsī writes,

> In its denotation, the word *justice* gives news of equality [*musāwāt*]. Conceiving of equality is impossible without taking oneness [*waḥdat*] into account. Among the levels and degrees of perfection and nobility, oneness is singled out for the furthest level and the highest degree. Beginning from the First Source—which is the True One—the effects of oneness permeate all things that partake of number, just as the lights of *wujūd* radiate out from the First Cause—which is the Nondelimited Existent [*mawjūd-i muṭlaq*]—onto all existent things. Hence, when something is nearer to oneness, its existence is more noble.... Among virtues, none is more perfect than justice, as becomes obvious in the art of ethics. The reason for this is that the true middle point belongs to justice. Relative to justice, all other qualities are off to one side or the other, and all of them are referred back to it.
>
> Just as oneness demands nobility, or rather, requires the permanence and stability of existent things, so also manyness demands meanness, or rather, calls for the corruption and unreality of existent things. Equilibrium [*i'tidāl*] is the shadow of oneness. It removes the stamp of quantity, manyness, and increase and

> decrease from the diverse kinds of things. By means of the quality of oneness it takes them from the depths of decrease and the lowliness of corruption to the pinnacle of perfection and the virtue of permanence. Without equilibrium, the circle of existence would not hold together, since the birth of the three kingdoms from the four elements depends upon mixing through equilibrium. (*Akhlāq-i Nāṣirī* 131)

This work has a careful but almost impenetrable English translation by Wickens. For this passage, see Ṭūsī, *Nasirean Ethics* 95.

104.31 *Justice..., temperance, courage, and wisdom.* These four virtues, which go back to Greek sources, are standard in Muslim discussions of ethics. For Ghazālī's views, see Sherif, *Ghazali's Theory* 38ff. For a more philosophical approach, see Ṭūsī, *Nasirean Ethics* 79ff. The discussion here parallels the introduction to *Easy Roads,* which concerns the perfecting of character, and the author's statement at the beginning of that treatise (117.31): "So that I may advance from the *lowest of the low* [95:5]—which is the station of beasts, predators, and satans—to the highest of the high—which is the station of the angels brought near to God." As pointed out in the note to that passage, these four types of being represent the four principle characteristics of the soul—appetite, anger, satanity, and angelic intelligence. Satanity can be interpreted as a misapplication of practical intelligence. Ṭūsī writes,

> The soul has two faculties: first, perceiving through its very essence, and second, acting through instruments. Each of these in turn has two branches. The faculty of perception is divided into the theoretical and practical faculties, while the faculty of action is divided into the faculty of repulsion, that is, anger, and the faculty of attraction, that is, appetite. From this point of view, the faculties are four. When all four act upon their own objects in a mode of equilibrium—in the way and to the extent that is appropriate while avoiding the two extremes—then a virtue comes into existence. Hence, the virtues are four. One derives from the purification of the theoretical faculty. This is wisdom. The second derives from the purification of the practical faculty. This is justice. The third derives from the purification of anger. This is courage. The fourth derives from the purification of appetite. This is temperance. (*Akhlāq-i Nāṣirī* 109–110; see also *Nasirean Ethics* 80)

105.3 *Love for this world....* See the note on 94.29.

105.12 *My heaven embraces Me not....* See the note on 54.26.

105.17 *Within it is what no eye has seen....* Bukhārī, Tafsīr Sūra 32. Variations on this hadith are common in the standard sources (see Graham, *Divine Word* 117-119).

105.20 *In the dominion's garden....* Sanā'ī, *Ḥadīqa* 428.

105.22 *God has a Garden*. . . . The text as far as "honey" is found in the works of Aḥmad Ghazālī (*Majmū'a* 481). That "God discloses Himself to them laughing" (*yatajallā lahum ḍāḥik* or *yaḍḥak*) is mentioned in a hadith about the day of resurrection that has come in Muslim (Īmān 316) and Aḥmad (3:383, 4:407).

105.24 *If I can seize your tress*. . . . This quatrain has been ascribed to Rūmī (*Rubā'iyyāt,* n. 821).

105.28 *The person who considers it proper*. . . . Ibn Sīnā, *al-Ishārāt* 3:227. Avicenna's words leading up to this passage clarify its meaning.

> The gnostic desires the Real—the First—only for His sake, not for the sake of anything else. He prefers nothing over true knowledge of Him. His worship is directed only to Him, since He is worthy of worship and because worship is a noble relationship with Him. But the gnostic has neither desire nor fear. Were he to have them, the object of his desire or fear would be his motive, and it would be his goal. Then the Real would not be his goal but rather the means to something else, less than the Real, which would be the goal and the object.

105.32 *O seeker of this world*. . . . See the note on 53.30.

106.25 *In my whole life*. . . . The quatrain is also found in Maybudī, *Kashf al-asrār* 3:717. This makes the ascription to Awḥad al-Dīn Kirmānī (*Dīwān,* n. 709) highly unlikely.

107.12 *Before this excuse-offering soul*. . . . Sanā'ī, *Dīwān* 182.

107.37 *Strive—if you can take advice*. . . . This quatrain is most likely by Awḥad al-Dīn Kirmānī (*Dīwān,* n. 809). It has also been ascribed to Abū Sa'īd Abi'l-Khayr (Nafīsī, *Sukhanān* 49, n. 339), with no early sources to support the ascription, and to Rūmī (*Rubā'iyyāt,* n. 959).

108.5 *Be in the world like a stranger or like a traveler*. . . . A hadith found in Tirmidhī, Zuhd 25.

108.30 *Seize the words of God*. . . . Sanā'ī, *Dīwān* 309. *Bas* in Persian is written *bs,* without the vowel.

109.4 *I was seated on a camel*. . . . The hadith is given in almost identical words by Aḥmad (1:307–308). Other versions are found in Tirmidhī, Qiyāma 59; Aḥmad 1:293, 303.

109.20 *I seek refuge in Thy pardon*. . . . A sound hadith found in most sources, including Muslim (Ṣalāt 222), Abū Dāwūd (Ṣalāt 148), and Tirmidhī (Da'awāt 75, 112).

109.24 *Belong to Him, so that you may be considered blessed*. . . . A quatrain by Kirmānī (*Dīwān,* n. 292), although there are important textual differences in both lines. *Yā Sīn* and *Tabārak* are the names of Suras 36 and 67 of the Koran.

THE EASY ROADS OF SAYF AL-DĪN

117.16 *The stars of the heaven of guidance.* This is an allusion to the hadith that is quoted on 126.17.

117.20 *Spirits are assembled troops....* This is a hadith found in Bukhārī (Anbiyā' 2), Muslim (Birr 159, 160), and other standard sources.

117.26 *Ṭughril.* See the introduction (xi).

117.32 *Beasts, predators...satans...angels.* As already suggested in the note to 104.31, these four terms were not chosen arbitrarily. They are standard symbols for the tendencies that make up the human soul. In the thirty-first book of the *Iḥyā'*, "On the Wonders of the Heart," Ghazālī says that a human being is made up of four basic qualities which he calls "pig, dog, devil, and wise man." The pig is appetite, the dog is anger, and the devil is perverted intelligence or cleverness—the negative, dispersive tendency that draws people away from God. All three qualities are necessary for the subsistence of the human being, but they are negative inasmuch as they are not governed by the fourth quality—the "wise man," who is pure intelligence (*'aql*). By nature, intelligence is luminous, spiritual, and angelic. It draws people toward God, while the other three qualities pull in other directions. Viewed in terms of spiritual psychology, the goal of the path of perfection is to establish equilibrium (*i'tidāl*) among these four qualities, with intelligence in command. As suggested here, all this has a direct bearing on the destiny of the soul because, as we saw in the two treatises on faith, the soul takes on an appropriate form in the barzakh. Thus Mullā Ṣadrā (d. 1050/1641) tells us that, after death, human beings become four main genera, corresponding to these four qualities—appetite, anger, satanity, and angelic wisdom (*Wisdom of the Throne* 144–146; see also Chittick, "Eschatology" 401–404; Murata, *Tao of Islam,* chapters 8–10).

118.26 *An hour's reflection....* Often quoted as a hadith by the Sufis (for example, Hujwīrī, *Kashf al-maḥjūb* 135; trans. Nicholson, 108), the saying is found in Suyūṭī's *al-Jāmi' al-ṣaghīr* (4:443) in a slightly different form, but the same author tells us elsewhere that it is not sound. Some have considered it to be a saying of the Sufi Sarī Saqaṭī. See Nasafī, *Kashf* 323.

119.15 *The search for knowledge....* Tirmidhī, Muqaddima 17.

119.17 *Caprice (hawā).* See the note on 56.9.

119.23 *Sciences of practice.* As pointed out in Part One (17), Ghazālī surveys the differences of opinion among the ulama on the meaning of the hadith, "The search for knowledge is incumbent upon every Muslim," and concludes that the Prophet meant knowledge of practice.

119.30 *When someone acts in accordance with what he knows....* Sufis such as Hamadānī (*Tamhīdāt* 6) and Ibn al-'Arabī (*Futūḥāt* 1:506.12) cite this as a hadith, but the text is not found in the standard sources.

120.4 *Those learned in wisdom and the leaders in the principles ('ulamā-yi ḥikmat wa a'imma-yi uṣūl).* In other words, the philosophers and the Kalām authorities.

120.10 *The remedy of those who have corrupt constitutions.* Compare Ghazālī's remarks on Kalām. "The proofs of the Koran are like food—they benefit all human beings. But the proofs of the Kalām scholars are like medicine—they benefit a few individuals, but harm most people" (*Iljām al-'awāmm* 88). Rāghib makes a similar point.

> Intellectual concepts play a role parallel to medicines that bring about health, while the revealed teachings play a role parallel to foods that preserve health. When a person's body is ill, he takes no benefit from food; on the contrary, he is harmed by it. In the same way, when a person's soul is ill—as God says, *In their hearts is a sickness* [2:10]—he takes no benefit from listening to the Koran, within which are deposited the revealed teachings. On the contrary, it harms him, like food that harms a sick person. That is why God says, *Whenever a sura is sent down, some of them say, "Which of you has this increased in faith?"* [9:124]. (*Dharī'a* 99)

120.20 *One of the great possessors of knowledge.* This probably refers to the saying of Junayd quoted on 66.35.

120.25 *The God of highness and lowness is Thou....* This oft-quoted verse is found in a slightly different version in most editions of the *Shāhnāma* of Firdawsī (d. 411/1020). See Firdawsī, *Shāhnāma* 4:254.

120.27 *In each thing is found a sign....* This is a frequently cited Arabic verse by Abu'l-'Atāhiya (d. ca. 211/826). See Fayṣal, *Abu'l-'Atāhiya* 104.

121.1 *Ponder the plants....* These two Arabic verses, along with a third, are quoted in Maybudī, *Kashf al-asrār* 7:477.

121.9 *O you who are unable to know yourself!...* Sanā'ī, *Ḥadīqa* 63.

121.15 *Glory be to Thee wherever Thou art....* Hamadānī quotes these words from the Greatest Spirit (*rūḥ-i a'ẓam*) in *Nāmahā 1:197.*

121.18 *Glory be to Thee—we....* See the note on 69.39.

121.20 *Intellect of intellect....* Sanā'ī, *Ḥadīqa* 62; also quoted in *Clarifications* 61.8.

121.24 *He is nearer to the servants than the jugular vein.* This is a Persian paraphrase of Koran 50:16.

121.39 *But the view of intelligence lets us see....* This statement alludes to the view of many Muslim authors—including Ghazālī, Suhrawardī al-Maqtūl (see the note on 83.10), and Ibn al-'Arabī—that the cosmos is the best of all possible worlds (see Ormsby, *Theodicy in Islamic Thought*). Theologically, this idea is rooted in seeing God's mercy as the determining quality of His relationship with the world, because His mercy precedes His wrath. The evils that exist are seen as part of a greater good that frequently escapes human understanding. For some of Ibn al-ʿArabī's views, see SPK 290–296.

122.21 *He was, and the creatures were not. . . .* See the note on the similar passage in *Rising Places* 39.10.

122.25 *What God wills will be. . . .* See the note on 47.5.

123.12 *Ladders of holiness.* These ladders (*maʿārij*), which are frequently discussed by Ibn al-ʿArabī, are alluded to in the Koran. *A questioner asked. . .from God, the Possessor of the Ladders. To Him the angels and the Spirit climb up* [*yaʿrujūn,* from the same root as *maʿārij*] *in a day whose measure is fifty thousand years* (70:1-4).

123.21 *The Koran is memorized by hearts. . . .* See the note on 43.13.

123.38 *Nothing more perfect. . . .* This is another allusion to the best of all possible worlds. See the note on 121.39.

124.7 *Worthy of giving decrees. . . .* Awḥad al-Dīn Kirmānī, *Dīwān,* n. 146.

124.35 *Acquisition and free choice (kasb wa ikhtiyār).* These are favorite terms of the Kalām authorities, and the debates over their exact definition and significance are well-known.

125.10 *You will not find. . . .* Awḥad al-Dīn Kirmānī, *Dīwān,* n. 431.

126.6 *The moon's being split. . . .* The splitting of the moon is mentioned in the Koran (54:1). That this refers to a prophetic miracle is attested to by hadiths found in Bukhārī, Muslim, and other standard sources. The incident of the poisoned lamb is mentioned in the hadith literature and in biographies of the Prophet. Dārimī quotes the Prophet as saying that the lamb "informs me [*ikhbār*] that it is poisoned" (Muqaddima 6). Ibn al-ʿArabī says that "The hearing of the Messenger of God and those of his companions who were with him was opened to the perception of the glorification of the pebbles in his pure and good hand" (*Futūḥāt* 1:139.33; Yahya edition, 2:314; Yahya [ibid. 508] traces the hadith to Ghazālī's *Iḥyā'* and Bayhaqī's *Dalā'il al-nubuwwa*). Although some scholars—especially nineteenth-and twentieth-century Muslim apologists—have claimed that Muhammad was a completely ordinary mortal, the classical sources recognize dozens of miracles. See, for example, Ghazālī's *Iḥyā'* 2:256 (2.10.13), translated by Zolondek in Ghazālī, *Book XX.* See also Schimmel, *Muhammad,* chapter 4.

126.17 *My companions are like stars. . . .* Thaʿālibī cites this as a hadith in *Tamthīl* 23. For other sources, see Furūzānfar, *Aḥādīth* 19.

126.38 *Whose measure is fifty thousand years.* A day of fifty thousand years is mentioned in Koran 70:4 in reference to the time it takes the angels and spirits to rise up to God. Ghazālī cites a hadith that gives this as the length of the resurrection day (*Iḥyā'* 4:369 [4.10.2.4]; *Remembrance* 182). Ibn al-ʿArabī quotes a lengthy hadith with a line of transmission going back through ʿAlī that mentions fifty stations (*mawqif*) on the day of resurrection, each lasting one thousand years. See *Futūḥāt* 1:309.20–311.19 (Yahya 4,436.6–447.7), 320.21-321.12 (Yahya 5,78.12–82.10).

127.34 *The religion is built....* Ghazālī cites this as a hadith (*Iḥyā'* 1:37, 94 [1.1.5, 1.3.1]).

127.34 *The key to the ritual prayer....* Aḥmad 3:340, with the two clauses reversed.

128.10 *Wait till God lifts....* Sanā'ī, *Dīwān* 487.

128.15 *Purity has five levels.* Ghazālī (*Iḥyā'* 1:94 [1.3.1]) provides a similar discussion, but lists only four—body, members, heart, and inmost mystery (*sirr*). See also his *Kīmiyā-yi sa'ādat* 1:139–140.

128.24 *The wisdom that is well-known.* The term *wisdom* (*ḥikmat*) is commonly applied to both philosophy and medicine. According to Ghazālī, "The word *wise man* (*ḥakīm*) has come to be used for the physician, the poet, and the astronomer" (*Iḥyā'* 1:28 [1.1.3]). See Ibn al-'Arabī's defense of philosophy inasmuch as it deals with true wisdom (SPK 203).

128.38 *Whatever holds you back from the way....* Sanā'ī, *Dīwān* 51. For Rūmī's commentary on this verse, see his *Mathnawī* 1:1763ff.

129.12 *On the Rules of Relieving and Cleaning Oneself.* Ghazālī provides a more detailed explanation that may be the main source for this section (*Iḥyā'* 1:98–99; see also idem, *Kīmiyā* 1:147–148; Watt, *Faith* 92–93).

129.13 *If a person wants to sit and relieve himself....* One does not "stand" and relieve oneself. As Ghazālī says, "One should not urinate while standing without a good excuse" (*Kīmiyā* 1:147). He provides more details in *Iḥyā'* 1:98, including the saying of 'Ā'ishā, "If someone says that the Prophet used to urinate while standing, do not accept that as true." The reason for this is basically that urine is impure. If one stands and urinates, one's clothing will be splashed and will then need to be purified. That this is the issue is made clear in the books on hadith and jurisprudence. Reference is also made to this point in what follows.

129.19 *The chastisement of the grave....* Hadiths more or less to this effect are common. "Most of the chastisement of the grave is from urine" (Ibn Māja, Ṭahāra 26). Another hadith tells us that two men saw the Prophet urinating, and one said to the other, "Look at him, he urinates like a woman." The Prophet heard him and replied, "Woe upon you! Do you not know what happened to the companion of the Children of Israel? When [their clothing] was struck by urine, they used to cut it away with scissors. He forbade them from doing that, and he was chastised in his grave" (ibid.).

129.24 *O God, I seek refuge....* This sentence is found in many hadiths, for example, Bukhārī, Wuḍū' 9, Da'awāt 14.

129.26 *Cough lightly* (*tanaḥnuḥ*). This is done to help dislodge any urine left in the urinary tract. Ghazālī does not mention this in the relevant section of the *Iḥyā'* but, perhaps because he felt his Persian readers might not be as familiar with the rules and therefore needed a more complete explanation, he does provide some detail in *Kīmiyā* (1:148).

129.27 *Clean himself with the wall.* Perhaps it needs to be pointed out that the toilet in view here is an outhouse made from sun-dried bricks, which absorb moisture quickly and are always in the process of disintegrating. As Ghazālī says, if the person rubs his penis against the wall, he does so "until he sees no more sign of moisture" (*Iḥyā'* 1:99).

129.36 *He who cleans himself with stones....* Bukhārī, Wuḍū' 25, 26, etc.

130.6 *The mosque of Qubā.* This hadith is found in Ghazālī, *Iḥyā'* 1:99. Qubā is a place outside of Medina where a mosque was built before the Prophet left Mecca. This mosque is also called the "Mosque of God-wariness" because of the beginning of the verse. *A mosque that was founded upon god-wariness from the first day is worthier for thee to stand in; therein are men....* Some sources for relevant hadith mention only water (Ibn Māja, Ṭahāra 28; Aḥmad 3:422). What the Koran commentators have to say suggests that cleaning oneself with stones was taken for granted. Fakhr al-Dīn Rāzī tells us that most of them agree that the verse refers to using water after stones (*Tafsīr* 4:742). Thus, Maybudī remarks that the Companions answered the Prophet by saying, "We use water after the stones, and that washes away the trace of excrement and urine" (*Kashf al-asrār* 4:213).

130.13 *On the Rules of the Minor Ablution (wuḍū').* Ghazālī provides a parallel account, including some of the same supplications, in *Iḥyā'* 1:99–101 (1.2.3). See also Ghazālī, *Kīmiyā* 1:148–151; Watt, *Faith* 93–97; Makkī, *Qūt al-qulūb* 2:184–185.

130.31 *I will now cease speaking....* This sentence is in Persian, not Arabic. Intentions, if articulated, are normally made in one's own language.

130.38 *O God, whiten my face....* This prayer incorporates part of Koran 3:105. English parallelism would normally demand that "light" and "darknesses" in this supplication be rendered either as both singular or both plural, but I follow the text, which is based on Koranic usage and alludes to the important theological point that light is one, while the darknesses are many. All that pertains to the divine side is close to unity, whereas all that is far from God is dispersed and scattered. The Koran juxtaposes light and darknesses in twelve verses, such as, *Praise belongs to God, who created the heaven and the earth and appointed the darknesses and the light* (6:1) and *God is the friend of those who have faith; He brings them out of the darknesses into the light* (2:257).

131.4 *O God, I seek refuge....* There are references here to two sets of Koranic verses. *Then as for him who is given his book in his right hand..., he shall be in a pleasing life in a lofty Garden....But as for him who is given his book in his left hand..., "Take him, and fetter him, and roast him in Hell"* (69:19–37). *Then as for him who is given his book in his right hand, he will be called to account with an easy accounting....But as for him who is given his book behind his back, he shall call for destruction and he shall roast in a Blaze* (84:7–12).

131.6 *On the day of resurrection, the hands and feet*. . . . The text here is in Persian. The original Arabic text is quoted three paragraphs later in the text.

131.17 *O God, allow me to hear*. . . . There is an allusion here to the Koran. *Our Lord, we have heard a caller calling to faith*. . .(3:193).

131.18 *O God, I seek refuge in Thee from the chains*. . . . The prayer alludes to several Koranic verses, such as the following: *When the fetters and chains are on their necks, and they are dragged into the boiling water*. . .(40:71).

131.21 *He begins with the small toe on the right foot*. . . . Makkī says that the reason for the order here is that the small toe is on the right side of the right foot, while it is on the left side of the left foot (*Qūt* 2:184). His readers know that right is the side of blessedness and purity, while left is the side of impurity. The Koran and many hadiths point to the superiority of right over left and the fact that actions connected with goodness and purity should begin with the right hand or right foot. Thus, for example, one enters the toilet with the left foot and leaves it with the right foot.

131.27 *On the day of resurrection my community*. . . . Bukhārī (Wuḍū' 3), Muslim (Ṭahāra 35, 38, 39). See also Lane, *Lexicon*, under *muhajjal*.

131.30 *O God, I bear witness that*. . . . The text of this supplication as given by Ghazālī is shorter (*Iḥyā'* 1:100; Watt, *Faith* 96–97). The sentence, "In His hand is the good, and He is powerful over everything," is almost a direct quotation of Koran 3:26.

132.14 *A seal will be placed*. . . . The details about the seal are also related by Makkī (*Qūt* 2:185) and Ghazālī (*Iḥyā'* 100; Watt, *Faith* 97). Notice that the ablution itself will glorify God. Ibn al-ʿArabī combines such accounts with his own visionary experience of the angelic realm and tells us that all human acts give birth to angels. Good deeds produce angels that glorify God in the name of their producer and accept him into their arms when he dies, then taking him to felicity. Evil deeds produce angels that become disoriented and, although they glorify God, they cannot find the person who was their source. However, if the person should repent and have his repentance accepted by God, the angel reestablishes its connection with him and aids him in the next world. See Ibn al-ʿArabī, *Futūḥāt* 2:448.17, 639.25; 3:14.14.

132.24 *This last is reprehensible medically—and God knows best.* By saying "God knows best," the author shows that he is skeptical about the medical reason, which is given by Ghazālī without such a qualification (*Iḥyā'* 1:100).

132.28 *He should make his heart present*. . . . The heart, as pointed out in the introduction, is the center of knowledge and awareness. Hence "presence of heart" (*ḥuḍūr al-qalb*) might be translated as "mindfulness." Ghazālī defines it in the context of ritual prayer as follows:

> By this we mean that the heart is empty of everything other than that which the person has undertaken and concerning which he is

speaking. Awareness must be joined with word and deed, and thoughts must not wander in other than these two. When the person's thought leaves aside everything but what he is busy with, when his heart remembers [*dhikr*] what he is concerned with, and when he is heedless of everything else, then he has actualized presence of heart. (*Iḥyā'* 1:118 [1.4.3.2])

132.34 *He is like someone*. . . . Ghazālī provides a similar explanation (*Iḥyā'* 1:100).

132.37 *God looks not at your forms*. . . . Hamadānī cites the hadith in this form (*Tamhīdāt* 146). Muslim gives it as "God looks not at your bodies or your forms, but He looks at your hearts" (Birr 32). Ibn Māja (Zuhd 9) and Aḥmad (2:285, 539) give it as "God looks not at your forms or your possessions, but He looks only at your works and your hearts."

133.2 *On the Rules and Method*. . . . This account of the major ablution (*ghusl*) is similar to that of Ghazālī (*Iḥyā'* 1:101; Watt, *Faith* 97–98).

133.17 *Sunnah*. That is, it is recommended, but not required. In the parallel passage in the *Iḥyā'*, Ghazālī uses the word *mustaḥabb* (recommended) (1:101).

133.19 *On the Tayammum and the Masḥ*. The *tayammum* is an ablution with earth or sand when water is unavailable. *Masḥ* means wiping the boots with water, instead of removing them and washing the feet. The word *boots* means footwear that is used in work or traveling and is difficult to take off. In this section, the author follows Ghazālī's *Iḥyā'* almost word for word, except for the paragraph on *masḥ*, which is not found there (1:101–102). See also *Kīmiyā* 1:152–153; Watt, *Faith* 98–99.

134.19 *The ritual prayer is the foundation of religion*. . . . Ghazālī provides this text in *Iḥyā'* 1:108 (1.4.1), but it is not found in the standard sources. Aḥmad gives the following hadith: "The beginning of the whole affair is submission [*al-islām*], for he who submits has gained safety. Its foundation is the ritual prayer, and its highest peak is struggle [*jihād*] in the path of God" (5:237. See also Tirmidhī, Īmān 8; Aḥmad 5:231.)

134.21 *The first act of the servants*. . . . The author gives a Persian text here. The following hadith is found in several of the standard collections with slight variations:

> The first act for which the servant will be called to account on the Day of Resurrection is the prescribed ritual prayer. If he has completed it, it will be written for him completely. If he has not completed it, God will say, "Look and see if My servant has performed any supererogatory prayers to complete for him what is missing from his obligatory prayers." Then the same thing will be done for the alms, then the other works. (Tirmidhī, Ṣalāt 188; Abū Dāwūd, Ṣalāt 145; Nasā'ī, Ṣalāt 9; etc.)

The author may have in view another hadith. "When a person encounters God having wasted the ritual prayer, God will pay no attention to any of his good deeds" (*Iḥyā'* 1:108).

134.27 *It has been reported that God has made obligatory for His servants. . . .* Makkī (*Qūt* 2:200) and Ghazālī (*Iḥyā'* 1:108) give the text of this hadith, as well as the argument that follows it. Makkī's more detailed explanation provides an early example of the idea that the superiority of human beings over most of the angels lies in their all-comprehensive nature. He writes,

> When the person of faith prays two cycles of the ritual prayer, ten rows of angels are amazed at him, each row having ten thousand angels. God makes him vie in excellence with one hundred thousand angels. The reason for this is that God brings together in the servant the four pillars of the ritual prayer—the standing, the sitting, the bowing, and the prostrating. But He divides that among forty thousand angels. The angels who stand do not bow until the day of resurrection, those who prostrate themselves do not lift their heads until the day of resurrection, and so also is the case with the bowers and the sitters. Then God brings together in the servant the six pillars of the ritual prayer, such as the recitation, the praise, the asking forgiveness, the supplication, and the blessing on the Prophet, while He divided that among sixty thousand angels, since each row of angels worships God through one of the six formulae of remembrance. Hence, when the angels see how the human being brings together the four pillars and the six formulae of remembrance in two cycles, they are amazed at him and how God makes him vie with them, for He has divided those acts and pillars among one hundred thousand angels. It is here that the person of faith is more excellent than the angels. (*Qūt* 2:200)

135.6 *The five times for the ritual prayer.* Bayḍāwī ascribes this interpretation of this Koranic verse to Ibn ʿAbbās, who said that *When you enter the night* refers to both the evening and the night prayer, while the other three times are stated explicitly—morning, afternoon, and noon.

135.21 *The two cycles of the dawn. . . .* Muslim (Musāfirīn 96, 97), Tirmidhī (Ṣalāt 190), Ghazālī (*Iḥyā'* 1:139 [1.4.7.1]). This hadith refers to the voluntary two cycles.

135.26 *When someone performs four cycles. . . .* The text is Persian. Ghazālī provides the Arabic in *Iḥyā'* 1:140.

135.32 *God have mercy on a servant. . . .* Ghazālī, *Iḥyā'* 1:141. The hadith is found in a slightly different version in Tirmidhī (Mawāqīt 201), Abū Dāwūd (Taṭawwuʿ 8), and Aḥmad (2:117).

135.36 *Ibn ʿAbbās.* He relates this explanation from the Prophet (Tirmidhī, Tafsīr Sūra 52).

136.1 *Witr* (literally, odd). The *witr* is a prayer said after the night prayer. It consists of an odd number of cycles, varying from one to eleven, but most commonly three or five. See *Encyclopedia of Islam* (old edition), s.v.; Ghazālī, *Iḥyā'* 1:141–142.

136.2 *Mustafa counselled me....* This hadith is found in most standard sources, such as Muslim, Musāfirīn 85, 86. See Wensinck, *Concordance* 7:225, lines 45–51.

136.2 *Anas ibn Mālik relates that Mustafa....* Ghazālī, *Iḥyā'* 1:141. This saying is transmitted from ʿĀ'isha by Tirmidhī (Witr 9) and Abū Dāwūd (Witr 4).

136.9 *The duty (waẓīfa) of tahajjud. Tahajjud* is voluntary ritual prayer or other devotional practices performed in the middle of the night after a period of sleep. The term occurs once in the Koran. *And as for the night, do* tahajjud *for part of it, as a work of supererogation for thee* (17:79). In the earliest part of the Prophet's career, it seems to have been required, but later it became a supererogatory act. See the article "Tahadjdjud" in *Encyclopedia of Islam* (old edition).

136.18 *On How to Perform the Outward Acts.* Again, much of what the author says paraphrases or translates parts of Ghazālī's *Iḥyā'* (1:112–113 [1.4.2]). See also Watt, *Faith* 118–123.

136.24 *People of abstinence (ahl-i waraʿ)*. This refers to those who are especially careful in observing the Sunnah of the Prophet, or those who abstain even from certain permitted acts in order to protect themselves from being drawn into forbidden acts. For definitions of abstinence from classical Sufi sources, see Nurbakhsh, *Sufism* 4:35–46.

136.32 *Thus he will have combined all the different reports,* that is, all the hadiths on how to hold the hands while making the *takbīr*.

137.7 *I seek refuge in God....* This phrase is required before recitation from the Koran. Three of the four *madhhabs* consider it to be recommended at this point in the ritual prayer, while the Mālikīs consider it to be reprehensible (Jazīrī, *Fiqh* 1:256).

137.17 *Mufaṣṣal chapters.* The most generally held opinion is that the *mufaṣṣal* or "much divided" chapters are those from 49 to the end. See Lane, *Lexicon,* under *mufaṣṣal.*

137.19 *The Footstool Verse.* This verse is commonly called the "Throne Verse," but Muslim cosmologists—especially Ibn al-ʿArabī and his followers—draw a sharp distinction between the Throne (*ʿarsh*) and the Footstool (*kursī*). Nor is the translation of the terms indifferent, because the Footstool is precisely the location where God places His "two feet." See Murata, *Tao of Islam,* chapter 3; SPK 359–360.

137.25 *God hears the one who praises Him....* For the source of these sentences in the hadith literature, see Muslim, Ṣalāt 202–206, etc.

137.31 *He keeps his elbows away from his sides.* This is one of several places in which we are reminded that the author is writing for Sayf al-Dīn Ṭughril, a man, since Ghazālī adds here, "but a woman should not do that." That is, a woman should keep her elbows close to her sides (*Iḥyā'* 1:113; Watt, *Faith* 121).

137.39 *He sits and makes the witnessing (tashahhud).* The witnessing—also called the greetings (*taḥiyyāt*) because of the first word of the formula—is one of the pillars of the ritual prayer. The exact wording varies slightly in keeping with the different juridical schools. According to the Shāfiʿīs, it goes as follows:

> The greetings, the benedictions, the good things, the blessings belong to God. Peace be upon thee, O Prophet, and God's mercy and benedictions. Peace be upon us, and upon God's upright servants. I bear witness that there is no god but God, and I bear witness that our master Muhammad is God's messenger. (Jazīrī, *Fiqh* 1:236)

138.1 *If his juridical school is Ḥanafī. . . .* In the corresponding passage in the *Iḥyā'*, Ghazālī does not mention the difference between the Shāfiʿī and Ḥanafī views because, as usual, he is providing only the Shāfiʿī position.

138.4 *The formula, "Bless Muhammad."* The formula of blessings on the Prophet is added at the end of the greetings. The normal formula is "O God, bless Muhammad and the household of Muhammad."

138.5 *During the second recitation of the greetings.* The author has left out many details that can be summarized as follows: All five daily prayers have at least two cycles that are brought to a close in a sitting position while making the witnessing and the greetings. The morning prayer consists of two cycles and hence is completed with these first greetings. Therefore, what the author says here about the "second recitation" applies to the first greetings in the morning prayer. The other prayers have more than two cycles. The extra cycles resemble the first and second cycles except that in the standing position only the Fatiha is recited, without a second Koranic chapter or verse. The sunset prayer has three cycles, so the "second witnessing and greetings" is made after the third cycle. The other three prayers (noon, afternoon, and night) have four cycles, so the second witnessing and greetings are made after the fourth cycle.

138.6 *He blesses Muhammad and his household.* In other words, in this second recitation, he recites the formula, "O God, bless Muhammad and the household of Muhammad," then he adds the words, "just as . . .".

138.14 *O God, I have wronged myself with much wrong . . . .* Bukhārī (Daʿawāt 89) and other standard sources.

138.28 *The Messenger of God forbade* ṣafd *and* ṣafn. Makkī, *Qūt* 2:191; Ghazālī, *Iḥyā'* 1:112.

138.32 *Courtesy.* See the note on 43.5.

138.39 *He is protected from the sword.* In other words, this is enough for him to be considered a Muslim according to Islamic law, which, generally speaking, maintains that if a person living under Islamic rule is not one of the "People of the Book" or a Muslim, his blood can be shed unless he converts to Islam. While discussing the limitations of the jurist's authority, Ghazālī remarks as follows:

> The jurist rules that becoming a Muslim under the shadow of the sword is valid, even though he knows that the sword does not unveil for him the person's intention, nor does it expel from the person's heart the covering of ignorance and perplexity. But he is the advisor of the possessor of the sword, for the sword is extended toward the person's neck and the hand [of its owner] toward the person's property. But this word with the tongue protects the person's neck and property as long as he has a neck and property, that is, in this world. That is why the Prophet said, "I was commanded to war against the people until they say, 'There is no god but God.' When they say it, their blood and property are protected from me." (*Iḥyā'* 1:14; see also *Book of Knowledge* 42)

139.1 *They hold that a correct ritual prayer must be acceptable to the Presence of Divinity.* Ghazālī provides a more detailed treatment of these points that helps place this discussion in its context:

> You may object as follows: You have ruled that. . .presence of heart is a condition for the ritual prayer's correctness. But this opposes the consensus of the jurists, because they have not made presence of heart a condition except in saying the *takbīr*. [My answer is that] You should know that it has already been explained in the *Book of Knowledge* that the jurists have nothing to say about the inward domain [*al-bāṭin*], and that they do not open the heart or look into the next world. On the contrary, they base the outward rulings of religion on the outward acts of the limbs. The outward acts are sufficient to prevent being killed or punished by the king. But the fact that the ritual prayer has benefits in the next world is not within the domain of jurisprudence, which is to say that consensus cannot be cited concerning it. Abū Ṭālib Makkī mentions that Bishr ibn al-Ḥārith quotes Sufyān al-Thawrī as saying, "If someone has no humility, his ritual prayer is ruined." Ḥasan al-Baṣrī said, "When the heart is not present in a ritual prayer, that prayer is closer to hastening punishment [than to yielding reward]." Mu'ādh ibn Jabal said, "When someone knows intentionally who is standing on his right and left sides during the ritual prayer, he has no ritual prayer." It has been related that the Prophet said, "The servant performs

a ritual prayer of which not even one-sixth or one-tenth is written for him. As much of the servant's prayer is written down for him as he understands." If this had been related from anyone else, it would have been made into a juridical position. How should one not have recourse to it? ʿAbd al-Wāḥid ibn Zayd said, "The ulama have reached consensus that the servant has of his ritual prayer only what he understands of it." So he makes it a consensus.

In this connection more has been related from the upright jurists and those who have knowledge of the next world than it is possible to reckon. The right thing to do is to go back to the proofs provided by the Shariah. The reports and sayings clearly make this condition. However, the station of giving pronouncements [*fatwā,* that is, the business of the jurists] concerning the outward prescriptions of the Shariah is limited by the measure of the creatures' inadequacies. Hence, it is impossible to make it a condition for people that their hearts be present in the whole ritual prayer, for human beings are incapable of that except for a few. It is clearly impossible to make full presence a condition, so there is no recourse but to make as much of it a condition as can be called by the name, even if that be a single instant. The best instant for this is the instant of making the *takbīr.* Hence, we have limited ourselves to prescribing that. Nevertheless, we hope that the person who is negligent in the whole of his prayer is not like the person who abandons it completely. For, in short, he has set out to perform the ritual prayer outwardly and made his heart present for an instant. . . .With all this, no one should oppose the jurists in their pronouncements concerning the correctness of the heedless prayer, since this is one of the necessities of giving pronouncements, as was pointed out. But whoever knows the secret of the ritual prayer knows that heedlessness is opposed to it. . . .The conclusion of this discussion is that presence of heart is the spirit of the ritual prayer. (*Iḥyā'* 1:117; compare Ghazālī, *Kīmiyā* 1:166–167)

139.16 *If a heart is not present. . . .* The Persian text conforms to Ghazālī's translation of the same hadith in *Kīmiyā* 1:166. The Arabic text, provided by Ghazālī in the *Iḥyā'*, reads, "God does not look at a ritual prayer in which a man does not make his heart present with his body" (1:110). Tirmidhī provides the hadith, "Know that God does not answer a supplication from a heart that is heedless and distracted" (Daʿawāt 65).

139.17 *Many are the servants who. . . .* The text is Persian (compare Ghazālī, *Kīmiyā* 1:166). Ghazālī provides the Arabic in *Iḥyā'* 1:117, which is translated in the note on 139.1. See also Makkī, *Qūt* 2:205.

139.20 *When the heart is not present. . . .* Ḥasan al-Baṣrī (d. 110/728) is a famous authority on Islam's spiritual dimension. The saying is given by Ghazālī (*Iḥyā'* 1:117, translated in the note on 139.1), and Makkī (*Qūt* 2:205).

139.26 *To be personified as a luminous condition (bi hay'atī nūrānī mushakhkhaṣ gardad).* Here again, the author alludes to the idea that every work produces an angel in the unseen world. See the note on 132.14.

139.30 *Self-examination (murāqaba).* This is an important part of Sufi discipline that is defined in various ways by different teachers. See Sarrāj, *Luma'* 54–56; Qushayrī, *Risāla* 519–524; Ghazālī, *Iḥyā'* 4:281–303 [4:8]; SPK 348–349. For most Sufis, self-examination concerns the passing thoughts (*khāṭir*) that enter the heart. Coming from one of four directions, these thoughts are called "divine" or "merciful" (*raḥmānī*), "angelic" or "spiritual" (*malakī, rūḥānī*), "soul-derived" (*nafsānī*), and "satanic" (*shayṭānī*). Qūnawī's student Jandī has this to say about the importance of *murāqaba.*

> Self-examination is one of the highest stations of the masters of the path and the noblest adornment of the possessors of verification. Every station and perfection that exists in all the levels of friendship, prophecy, and so on can be reached through the blessing of presence and self-examination. Whenever the Men of God find anything, they find it through self-examination and self-accounting [*muḥāsaba*]. Self-examination is that the Sufi. . .looks at his heart constantly at every moment to see what passing thought enters in. If a passing thought pertains to the soul or satan, he forbids it and considers it necessary to negate it. If it is angelic and spiritual, he puts it into practice. If it is merciful, he thanks God and acts upon it. (*Nafḥa* 103–104)

139.31 *As soon as a person hears the call to prayer. . . .* From here on, this section is similar to the *Iḥyā'* (1:121–124), and some of the explanations are basically the same.

140.23 *With two kiblahs. . . .* Sanā'ī, *Dīwān* 488.

141.1 *O you whose caprices. . . .* Sanā'ī, *Dīwān* 197.

142.4 *Like Jews, Christians, and other truth-concealers.* This interpretation of this verse is, of course, aimed at beginners who live within the Islamic context and for whom there is no necessity to explain the fine points of the discussion. To find a more subtle interpretation, we do not even have to look at Sufi explanations. For example, the famous Kalām master Fakhr al-Dīn Rāzī has this to say about this verse.

> The well-known interpretation is that *those against whom Thou art wrathful* are the Jews, because of God's words *Whomsoever God has cursed, and with whom He is wrathful*. . . [5:60], while *those who are astray* refers to the Christians, because of God's words, *a people who went astray before, and led astray many, and now again have gone astray from the right way* [5:77]. However, the following has been said: This is weak, because those who deny the Creator and

associate others with Him are far worse in their religion than the Jews and the Christians, so it is much more appropriate to avoid their religion. Or rather, it is much more appropriate to understand *those against whom Thou art wrathful* as referring to anyone who does wrong in outward works, and these are the ungodly [*fussāq*]. Then *those who are astray* can be understood as referring to everyone who has wrong beliefs. The reason for this is that the words are of general import. To make them specific is to go against the original sense. It is also possible to say that *those against whom Thou art wrathful* are the truth-concealers, and *those who are astray* are the hypocrites [*al-munāfiqūn*]. (*al-Tafsīr al-kabīr* 1:203–204)

142.14 *The key to the Garden is the ritual prayer.* See the note on 127.34.

142.24 *Every good deed will be rewarded. . . .* Ibn Māja, Adab 58; Aḥmad 1:446, 2:465; Ghazālī, *Iḥyā'* 1:166; Watt, *Faith* 130. For similar hadiths, see Wensinck, *Concordance* 4:216, lines 9–14.

142.26 *By that God in whose. . . .* The text is Persian. The Arabic original is found in all the standard hadith collections (Wensinck, *Concordance* 3:456, lines 38–44). See also Ghazālī, *Iḥyā'* 1:166; Watt, *Faith* 130.

142.29 *The fasting person has two joys. . . .* The hadith is found in most collections. See Wensinck, *Concordance* 3:457, lines 3–6.

142.33 *O seeker of good, hurry. . . .* This is a Persian translation of a hadith given by Tirmidhī (Ṣawm 1), Nasā'ī (Ṣiyām 5), Ibn Māja (Ṣiyām 2), Aḥmad (2:312, 5:411), Ghazālī (*Iḥyā'* 1:166).

143.4 *Appetite and anger.* On the significance of these two terms, see the note on 99.35.

143.10 *If the satans did not swarm. . . . Iḥyā'* 1:166. A similar saying is found in one of the Prophet's accounts of his *mi'rāj*. He looked down from the first sphere and saw this world full of dust, smoke, and noise. Having asked Gabriel about this, he was told, "Those are the satans. They swarm around the eyes of the children of Adam lest they reflect upon the dominion of the heavens and the earth. Were it not for that, they would see wonders" (Aḥmad 2:353).

143.13 *Could Adam have been brought. . . .* Sanā'ī, *Dīwān* 188.

143.25 *Satan runs in the child of Adam. . . .* Ghazālī (*Iḥyā'* 3:60 [3.3.1]); Hamadānī (*Nāmahā* 2:373). In the standard sources, only the first clause is found (see Wensinck, *Concordance* 3:129, lines 32–35).

143.27 *Keep your bellies. . . .* Ghazālī quotes a different version of this saying from Jesus (*Iḥyā'* 3:60 [3.3.1]). Hamadānī gives a third version (*Nāmahā* 2:107, 383), and Hujwīrī gives a fourth and longer version, attributing the saying to the Prophet Muhammad (*Kashf* 427, trans. Nicholson, 329).

143.35 *The best of affairs is their middlemost.* Ghazālī considers this to be a hadith (*Iḥyā'* 3:71 [3.3.4]).

143.36 *Both sides of moderation*.... Ghazālī quotes this without attribution (*Iḥyā'* 3:70 [3.3.4]). His Persian translator puts it in the mouth of the Prophet (*Iḥyā'*, trans. Khwārazmī, 3:264).

143.38 *Fasting has three degrees*.... Ghazālī also gives three degrees, but explains them differently (*Iḥyā'* 1:168–170).

144.7 *Five things break the fast*.... Ghazālī, *Iḥyā'* 1:168; Makkī, *Qūt* 1:229; Watt, *Faith* 129.

144.12 *Poverty (faqr)*. This term is commonly employed as a synonym for Sufism. Or, as Schimmel puts it, "The central attitude in Sufi life is that of *faqr*" (*Mystical Dimensions* 120; see 120–124 and passim). The Sufi understanding of the term goes back to such Koranic verses as *O people, you are the poor toward God, and God—He is the Rich, the Praiseworthy* (35:15). Rūmī brings out the contrast between God's Being and human nothingness (*nīstī, 'adam*) in a way that is typical for many Sufis. God alone truly is, so human beings must "become nothing," which is to give up every claim to existence. Intimately connected with poverty and nothingness is the concept of annihilation (*fanā'*), which the author will mention shortly. When the Sufi's false self is annihilated, he subsists (*baqā'*) through the true Self, which is God. The *locus classicus* for the pairing of annihilation and subsistence is the Koran. *Everything upon the earth is annihilated, and there subsists the Face of thy Lord, the Possessor of majesty and generosity* (55:26). Sufis read this verse as referring to the actual situation, which simply needs to be recognized. The goal of the path is to verify one's own nonexistence and annihilation, and thus to subsist through God's subsistence. For Rūmī's views, see SPL 186–191. Ibn al-'Arabī makes the same points while employing more technical language and stressing the roots of poverty in ontology. See SPK, index, under *poverty*.

144.19 *I have sold myself*.... The Arabic sentence "I don't care" (*lā ubālī*) is often employed as an adjective in Persian and is frequently applied to the lover who has given up thought of his own life for the sake of his beloved. It is also applied to God, on the basis of a hadith in which God says,

> God created Adam and struck his right shoulder, bringing out white seed as if they were pearls. He struck his left shoulder and brought out black seed as if they were coals. He said to those in His right hand, "To the Garden, and I don't care." He said to those in His left hand, "To the Fire, and I don't care." (Aḥmad 6:441)

In Sufi poetry, the true Beloved says "I don't care" because He has no care for the worldly concerns of His lovers. Instead, he kills them indiscriminately—that is, He takes them away from themselves and replaces their attributes with His own attributes. 'Aṭṭār provides a good example of the ascription of the attribute to God. "Your love, saying 'I don't care,' has filled the world—see how it has hung the masters of the path from the gallows"

(*Dīwān* 598). Rūmī uses the term frequently, especially in his story about the "I-don't-care lover" who went traveling for the sake of his beloved (*Mathnawī* 3:3810ff.). In one passage the lover is blamed for his recklessness in love and replies (3:3948),

> I'm not a vagabond who goes in search of bread,
> I'm an I-don't-care vagabond, seeking death.

144.22 *A man of perfection....* This quatrain, with some textual difference, has been attributed to Rūmī (*Rubā'iyyāt,* n. 811), and, in a relatively late manuscript, to Awḥad al-Dīn Kirmānī (*Dīwān,* n. 1768 and the note on 356).

144.31 *When the poor man is complete....* This saying is more often seen in the form, "When poverty is complete..." (Hamadānī, *Tamhīdāt* 20, 130, 142, etc.; see also Schimmel, *Mystical Dimensions* 123).

144.34 *The Third Road-Clearing.* Except for the last three paragraphs and some of the hadiths, this section follows Ghazālī's *Iḥyā'* rather closely (1:166–168). See also Ghazālī, *Kīmiyā* 1:208–210.

145.1 *Fast, having seen....* The text is found with slight variations in Bukhārī, Ṣawm 11; Tirmidhī, Ṣawm 2; Nasā'ī, Ṣiyām 9. Many other hadiths in these and other sources say basically the same thing.

145.13 *Is there anything for me to eat?...* The text here is Persian. For a hadith to this effect, see Muslim, Ṣiyām 170. Ghazālī quotes this hadith in *Iḥyā'* 3:71 (3.3.4).

145.22 *He has to make up for the fast.* In other words, he has to repeat the fast for that day, at a day of his choice after Ramadan has finished.

145.30 *The soul that commands to evil.* See the note on 95.18.

145.38 *The Night of Power (laylat al-qadr).* This is the night of the year on which the Koran was revealed and which, according to Sura 97, is better than a thousand months. Muslims traditionally try to busy themselves with prayer during this night so that they will not miss its blessing.

146.5 *The noble days of the year.* Ghazālī gives the same list, with more details (*Iḥyā'* 1:170; *Kīmiyā* 1:215–216; Watt, *Faith* 128–129).

146.6 *'Arafa* is the ninth day of Dhu'l-Hijja, when the pilgrims gather at the hill named 'Arafa to the east of Mecca for part of the hajj ceremonies.

146.6 *'Āshūrā.* The tenth day of Muharram, which seems to have originally corresponded with Yom Kippur.

146.7 *The white days* are the thirteenth, fourteenth, and fifteenth days of the lunar calendar, when the moon is full or practically so.

146.21 *The best that I....* Mālik, Qur'ān 32, Ḥajj 246 (as cited in Wensinck, *Concordance*); Ghazālī, *Iḥyā'* 1:211.

146.23 *"There is no god but God" is My fortress....* Hamadānī quotes this as a hadith (*Tamhīdāt* 73).

146.33 *I am the city of knowledge*. . . . Suyūṭī, *al-Jāmiʿ al-ṣaghīr* (*Fayḍ* 3:46). For a discussion of various versions of this saying, see Raḍawī, *Taʿlīqāt* 369–370.

146.35 *One day the Commander of the Faithful, ʿAlī ibn Abī Ṭālib, came before Mustafa*. . . . This hadith is not found in the standard sources (which may help explain the author's defensiveness), but it is well known in Sufi circles. It provides the model for the imparting of the remembrance of God (*talqīn al-dhikr*) that is part of the initiation ceremony in most Sufi orders (see Schimmel, *Mystical Dimensions* 169; Trimingham, *Sufi Orders* 182, 188–190).

147.7 *The Hour will not come . . . "Allah, Allah."* This sentence (in a slightly different form) is a sound hadith related through Anas (Muslim, Īmān 234; Tirmidhī, Fitan 35; Aḥmad 3:107, 201, 259). Qūnawī cites it in one of his works to support Ibn al-ʿArabī's teaching that the maintenance of the universe depends upon the perfect human being, the true vicegerent of God made in the form of the name Allah (*Fukūk* 244–246; translated in Chittick, "Ibn al-ʿArabī's Own Summary" 39–40).

147.15 *Exercises governing control.* In other words, the shaykh becomes the means whereby a certain divine influence takes control of the soul of the disciple. The word *taṣarruf* (to exercise governing control) is often used by Sufi authors to refer to an immaterial force that takes control of something lower in the hierarchy of existence. Qūnawī's disciple Jandī employs the term to explain how his master taught him the meaning of the whole *Fuṣūṣ al-ḥikam* in a single instant, and how Qūnawī himself had learned its meaning from Ibn al-ʿArabī in the same manner.

> [Qūnawī] explained to me the meaning of the preface to the book. While he did this, the influx from the unseen world manifested its signs within him and the Merciful Breath blew into him with its blowing. Its refreshing breezes overcame my outer and inner self. . . . He exercised a marvelous governing control through his noble inner self over my inner self. . . . Through that, God gave me to understand the meaning of the entire book during the explanation of the preface. . . . When the Shaykh learned about this from me . . . , he said to me, "Our shaykh, the author, began to explain to me the meaning of this book. He explained to me in the preface the kernel of what is in it in the view of the possessors of minds. He exercised a marvelous governing control within me, through which I came to know the meaning of the whole book." (*Sharḥ Fuṣūṣ al-ḥikam* 9–10)

147.34 *The good deeds of the pious*. . . . This well-known Sufi saying is most likely by Abū Saʿīd al-Kharrāz (see Furūzānfar, *Aḥādīth* 65). It is also quoted by Qushayrī (*Risāla* 238), Maybudī (*Kashf* 2:495), and Najm al-Dīn Kubrā (*al-Uṣūl al-ʿashara* 75).

147.42 *Folk of Allah.* See the note on 81.38.

147.43 *God has a Garden....* See the note on 105.22

148.1 *O seeker....* See the note on 53.30.

148.11 *Most of the people of the Garden are simpletons....* See the note on 102.39.

148.14 *In the paradise of the spheres.* See the note on 103.1.

148.24 *The Second Road-Clearing.* All except two of these supplications (both noted) are also found in Ghazālī, *Iḥyā'* 1:220–222; *Invocations* 57–70.

148.30 *O God, I ask Thee for a mercy from Thee....* This supplication is found with a great deal of difference in sentence order and a few minor differences in phrasing in Tirmidhī (Daʿawāt 30). The text follows Ghazālī's *Iḥyā'* rather closely, with some discrepancies (1:220–221).

149.32 *The call for destruction.* This is a reference to the Koran. *When they are cast, coupled in fetters, into a narrow place of the Fire, they will call out there for destruction. "Call not out today for one destruction, but call for many destructions!"* (25:13–14; compare 84:11).

151.19 *O God, I supplicate Thee with Thy concealed, hidden name....* This supplication, not found in Ghazālī, is provided in a somewhat longer version by Hamadānī (*Tamhīdāt* 38), who apparently put great stock in it. It is the only long supplication he provides in his *Tamhīdāt,* and he tells us that it has proven effective in all situations. He says that it has been transmitted by the "great leaders" (*a'imma-yi kibār*), presumably the Sufi shaykhs. He also writes, "Alas, O friend, I wonder whether or not you have understood the worth of this supplication. Understand that this supplication is written at the top of the Guarded Tablet [*lawḥ-i maḥfūẓ*], and that no one recites it but Muhammad himself. The others are his parasites" (ibid.).

151.33 *Ihyā ashar ihyā.* This is the Arabic pronunciation of the Hebrew words *'ehyeh 'asher 'ehyeh* ("I am that I am," Exodus 3.14). The Arab lexicographers explain it to mean "The existing from eternity" (see Lane, *Lexicon,* under *sh.r.h.*). In commenting on Koran 27:40, Maybudī tells us that it was these words that were pronounced by Solomon's vizier, Āṣaf, in order to bring the throne of the queen of Sheba into Solomon's presence before he could blink his eyes (*Kashf al-asrār* 7:223).

151.34 *Adūnay ṣabā'ūth.* This is the Arabic pronunciation of the common Biblical expression *'adhōnāy sebhā'ōth* (Lord of hosts).

152.10 *O God, I ask Thee by Muhammad, Thy prophet....* This supplication is not indexed in Wensinck's *Concordance.*

153.14 *It should be recited...,* that is, after the two verses cited earlier (137.3) that begin with this sentence, and before the Fatiha.

153.17 *O God, Thou art the King and other than Thou there is no god....* Most of the standard hadith collections give this supplication, although none of them has the clause "The guided is he whom Thou hast guided." See Abū Dāwūd, Ṣalāt 119; Tirmidhī, Daʿawāt 32; Nasāʾī, Iftitāḥ 17; Aḥmad 1:102; Muslim, Musāfirīn 201.

153.36 *O ʿĀʾisha, you should recite the all-comprehensive words....* The supplication is found in Aḥmad 4:147 (see ibid. 134). In place of "all-comprehensive words" (*jawāmiʿ al-kalim*), both Ghazālī and Aḥmad have "the perfect all-comprehensive things" (*al-jawāmiʿ al-kawāmil*). The discrepancy here may have something to do with the importance which Ibn al-ʿArabī gives to "all-comprehensive words" in his teachings. See SPK, index, under *all-comprehensive.*

154.24 *O Alive, O Self-subsistent....* Abū Dāwūd (Adab 101) and Aḥmad (5:42) cite a similar prophetic supplication related from Abū Bukra.

155.36 *ʿUtbat al-Ghulām.* A second/eighth-century ascetic from Basra. See Iṣfahānī, *Ḥilya* 6:226–238.

156.8 *The supplication of the bird.* This is not found in Ghazālī.

157.35 *On Traditional Supplications.* Except where noted, these supplications are found in Ghazālī, *Iḥyāʾ* 1:226–227; *Invocations* 81–91. See also Ghazālī, *Kīmiyā* 1:262–267.

157.36 *In morning upon waking up.* Implicit to this supplication is the Muslim perception of the close connection between sleep and death, discussed by the author in *Clarifications* (100.15). Compare the last supplication of this section, on going to sleep.

159.30 *Which is related from the Commander of the Faithful, ʿAlī.* This supplication is not found in Ghazālī. Although the author says that it is by ʿAlī, it is more likely by ʿAlī's grandson, ʿAlī ibn al-Ḥusayn. Another version of it, with some major differences, is found in the latter's *al-Ṣaḥīfat al-sajjādiyya* (140–141).

161.21 *In Thy name, my Lord, I put down my side....* This is not found in Ghazālī's *Iḥyāʾ*, but he provides a similar text in *Kīmiyā* 1:266. The supplication responds to Koran 39:42: *God takes the souls at the time of death, and that which has not died, in its sleep. He withholds that against which He has decreed death, but sends back the other till a stated term.*

161.34 *The origin of his journey....* The author probably has in mind a saying of ʿAlī quoted by Rāghib at the beginning of the first chapter of *al-Dharīʿa.* "The human being is on a journey, and this world is an abode of passage, not an abode of rest. His mother's womb is the beginning of his journey, and the next world is his goal. His lifetime is the journey's distance, his years its waystations, his months its parasangs, his days its miles, his breaths its steps" (14). See also Ghazālī, *Kīmiyā* 1:74, where part of this same saying is translated into Persian.

162.4 *Take an example from the house of delusion....* Sanāʾī, *Ḥadīqa* 419.

162.15 *In this world's delusion*. . . . Sanā'ī, *Ḥadīqa* 431.

162.23 *My advice to you is only this*. . . . See the note on 96.16.

162.28 *Your love for a thing makes you blind and deaf.* A hadith found in Abū Dāwūd, Adab 116; Aḥmad 5:194, 6:45.

162.29 *Why be kind to that unkind companion*. . . . Sanā'ī, *Dīwān* 53.

162.35 *For the present moment is*. . . . This is an Arabic verse.

163.14 *In my whole life*. . . . See the note on 106.25.

163.24 *Men.* On the use of this term, see the note on 51.21.

163.26 *Whose sitting companion will never be wretched*. . . . This clause is part of a long hadith describing a conversation between God and various angels who travel in the earth looking for sessions of remembrance. Toward the end of the hadith, God says, "I bear witness that I have forgiven them." One of the angels objects, "But among them is so-and-so who is not one of them. He has only come on some business." God replies, "They are sitting companions whose sitting companion will never be wretched" (Bukhārī, Da'awāt 66; see also Tirmidhī, Da'awāt 129; Robson, *Mishkat* 477–478).

163.27 *He who has no moon-like face*. . . . See the note on 55.19.

163.29 *He who has no shaykh has no religion.* This is a well-known Sufi saying. Hamadānī quotes it in a slightly different form (*Tamhīdāt* 11, 28; *Nāmahā* 1:475).

163.37 *In this path, observe*. . . . Sanā'ī, *Dīwān* 656.

164.6 *Alms in secret extinguish*. . . . Ghazālī, *Iḥyā'* 1:162 (1.5.4); Tha'ālibī, *Tamthīl* 24. Tirmidhī (Zakāt 28) gives the text without the words "in secret."

Appendix 1—The Author

When I prepared editions and translations of two of these treatises in the late 1970s, I was convinced that they were by Ṣadr al-Dīn Qūnawī, the stepson of Ibn al-ʿArabī and the major conduit for the spread of his teachings in Turkey and the eastern lands of Islam. Since then, a good deal of evidence has come to light that throws doubt on this ascription. My opinion now is simply that Qūnawī is possibly the author, but the three treatises are more likely by another Sufi master called Naṣīr (or Nāṣir) al-Dīn, who may have been a member of Qūnawī's circle. What is certain is that the three works were written before 660/1262, when they were copied together by one Salmān ibn Yūnus from Konya.

With the exception of Sayf al-Dīn Ṭughril, for which *Easy Roads* was written, the only contemporary mentioned by name in any of the works is Awḥad al-Dīn Kirmānī. In *Easy Roads*, his name is accompanied by a prayer formula indicating that he is dead. The editor of the text claims that this means that it was composed after Kirmānī's death in 635/1238, but it could also mean that the copyist, knowing that Kirmānī had died, had changed the formula. However, *Clarifications* also mentions Kirmānī by name, in a sentence built on a formula indicating his death, and this sentence could not easily have been altered by a copyist. This makes it practically certain that the work was written after Kirmānī's death and supports the judgment that *Easy Roads* was also written in the same period. *Rising Places of Faith* was presumably written at about the same time.

The similarities in content and style have convinced me that the three treatises were written by the same author. *Clarifications* is usually attributed to Qūnawī, whereas *Easy Roads* has never, to my knowledge, been attributed to him. I know of only one old source for the ascription of *Rising Places* to Qūnawī. In what follows, I summarize the evidence for the attribution of the works to Qūnawī and others.

Clarifications is ascribed to Qūnawī in some later manuscripts and many later sources. Most early manuscripts do not mention the author's name. The earliest ascription to Qūnawī that I know of is by his contemporary, ʿAzīz al-Dīn Nasafī (d. before 700/1300), a disciple of Saʿd al-Dīn Ḥammūya (d. 649/1252). Ḥammūya corresponded with Ibn al-ʿArabī and can be considered to have been a peripheral member of his school. He was also a friend of Qūnawī, who mentions him with high praise in an Arabic work.[1] Nasafī helped popularize Ibn al-ʿArabī's teachings through his writings, all of which are in Persian. He must have known of Qūnawī through his master, and he may have met him. On two occasions in his *Maqṣad-i aqṣā* he quotes from *Clarifications*, ascribing the passage to "Ṣadr al-Dīn Rūmī." The *nisba* Rūmī was often given to people from Konya, as in the case of the most famous of its inhabitants, Jalāl al-Dīn Rūmī. On three other occasions in the same work, Nasafī copies passages from *Clarifications* without mentioning his source (a common practice that was not considered plagiarism).[2] Another relatively early author who attributes the work to Ṣadr al-Dīn Rūmī is Shams al-Dīn Abarqūhī in *Majma' al-baḥrayn*, written between 711/1311 and 714/1315.[3]

Internal evidence for the ascription of *Clarifications* to Qūnawī includes references to certain of Ibn al-'Arabī's technical terms and the style. Both the logical structure and the fluency of the language are strongly reminiscent of Qūnawī's Arabic writings. The simplicity and profundity of the discussions of faith demonstrate the author's great mastery of the subject matter. When I edited this text in the late 1970s, I was engrossed at the same time in studying Qūnawī's Arabic works, and I was also familiar with the writings of most of Ibn al-'Arabī's major followers in the seventh/thirteenth and eighth/fourteenth centuries. At that time—and probably still today—I would immediately recognize a passage from Qūnawī's Arabic writings because of certain stylistic peculiarities that are difficult to put into words. I had no doubt then that *Clarifications* was Qūnawī's work, but the evidence to the contrary is now strong.

As for the second work, *Rising Places of Faith*, it is attributed to Qūnawī by such modern scholars as Ülken and Ruspoli.[4] I published it in 1978 in Qūnawī's name, being convinced at the time that he was the author. The only relatively early attribution to Qūnawī that I know of is by Sayyid Muḥammad Nūrbakhsh (d. 869/1464) in *Silsilat al-awliyā'*.[5]

The evidence for the ascription of the third work, *Easy Roads*, to Qūnawī is simply that the style and approach of the sections on faith are identical with the first two works. Moreover, the already mentioned manuscript that was copied in 660/1262 provides the oldest text for all three works in a manner suggesting that they are by the same author.[6]

As for evidence against the ascription to Qūnawī, we can begin with the bibliographer Ḥājjī Khalīfa (d. 1067/1656) in *Kashf al-ẓunūn*. Although he attributes *Clarifications* to Qūnawī, he adds, "but on the back of one (*ba'ḍ*) manuscript it is said that its author is Shaykh Nāṣir al-Dīn al-Muḥaddith." Shams al-Dīn Aflākī, author of the famous *Manāqib al-'ārifīn*, a history of Rūmī and his circle begun in 728/1328, mentions one Shaykh Nāṣir al-Dīn, "who was the author of the *Clarifications* and a rival of Shaykh Ṣadr al-Dīn in gathering sciences, and who had many reputable disciples."[7] On the basis of these two passages, the well-known authority on Rūmī, Abdulbâki Gölpınarlı, attributed *Clarifications* to Shaykh Nāṣir al-Dīn. However, as N. Māyil Hirawī points out in discussing Gölpınarlı's conclusion, one might also read Aflākī's passage as supporting the attribution to Qūnawī. If Shaykh Nāṣir al-Dīn was Qūnawī's rival, he may have written his *Clarifications* as an answer to Qūnawī's *Clarifications*.[8]

Mikâil Bayram complicates the issue somewhat in a doctoral dissertation written for Istanbul University.[9] According to him, *Clarifications* along with the two other treatises is by Shaykh Naṣīr (not Nāṣir) al-Dīn Khū'ī, whose full name is Abu'l-Ḥaqā'iq Naṣīr al-Dīn Maḥmūd ibn Aḥmad al-Khū'ī al-Qūnawī. He points out rightly that the three treatises must be by the same hand because of the similarities in style and content. However, he tells us, this Shaykh Naṣīr al-Dīn was soon forgotten, so only Aflākī mentions him. Then he cites the passage already quoted from Aflākī, where the name is mentioned as *Nāṣir* al-Dīn and not *Naṣīr* al-Dīn. The difference may seem slight in transliteration, whether into English or modern Turkish, but one cannot confuse the two spellings in the Arabic alphabet. Bayram's argument is weakened by the fact that he attributes a number of other books of diverse style and content to the same Shaykh Naṣīr al-Dīn, although the authors of some of them are known.

As previously mentioned, the earliest manuscript of *Clarifications* is found along with the other two treatises translated here. Of the three works in that codex, only the first, *Easy Roads*, is attributed to an author. Māyil Hirawī, who edited and published *Easy Roads*, reads the author's name as Abu'l-Ḥaqā'iq Muḥammad ibn Aḥmad al-Juwaynī. However, the manuscript gives his name as *Naṣīr al-Dīn* Abu'l-Ḥaqā'iq *Maḥmūd* (not Muḥammad) ibn Aḥmad al-Juwaynī (or perhaps al-Khū'ī, as the text is not clear at this point). Hence, this is the same Naṣīr al-Dīn Khū'ī to whom Bayram dedicates his dissertation. Māyil Hirawī may have been led to record Muḥammad in place of Maḥmūd because of his desire to identify the author with a Sufi shaykh mentioned by Yāfi'ī in *Mir'āt al-jinān:*

> In the year 658 [1260] occurred the death of the shaykh, the jurist, the imam, Muḥammad ibn Aḥmad al-Juwaynī. He put on the dervish frock [*khirqa*] at the hands of Shaykh 'Abdallāh al-Baṭā'iḥī, who took it from Shaykh 'Abd al-Qādir [al-Jīlānī]. He was elegized by Shaykh 'Abdallāh al-Juwaynī. He was learned, ascetic, humble, pious to God, awe-inspiring, beautiful of face, good in voice and dignity.[10]

As for *Rising Places of Faith*, a manuscript dated 663/1265 (Yusuf Agha 4866) attributes the work to "Sayyid al-Muḥaqqiqīn Shaykh Nāṣir al-Milla wa'l-Dīn. . . [illegible], one of the disciples of the Shaykh of the Shaykhs, the Pole of the Pegs [*quṭb al-awtād*], Awḥad al-Dīn. . . [illegible]." This Awḥad al-Dīn is of course Awḥad al-Dīn Kirmānī, who is mentioned by name in the other two treatises. Hence we see that two of the three treatises have been attributed to Shaykh *Naṣīr* al-Dīn, while the third has been attributed to Shaykh *Nāṣir* al-Dīn, who may indeed be the Shaykh Nāṣir al-Dīn mentioned by Aflākī. Moreover, the editor of Awḥad al-Dīn Kirmānī's poetry provides a list of Kirmānī's direct and indirect disciples. Among the latter he lists "*Naṣīr* al-Dīn Muḥammad ibn Aḥmad Khū'ī, the author of *Rising Places of Faith.*"[11] Unfortunately he does not provide his source for this information.

All of this points rather strongly to one Naṣīr (or Nāṣir) al-Dīn Juwaynī (or Khū'ī) as the author of the three works, especially since Qūnawī was famous, and famous authors quickly have books ascribed to them, while Naṣīr al-Dīn was not well-known and soon, no doubt, was forgotten.[12] Nevertheless, the fact that *Clarifications* is attributed to Qūnawī by Nasafī is strong evidence in his favor.

The author's close connection with Awḥad al-Dīn Kirmānī—as shown by the frequent quotations of Kirmānī's poetry, the mention of his name in *Clarifications* and *Easy Roads*, and the remarks of the copyist of the Yusuf Agha manuscript of *Rising Places*—may also be taken as supporting Qūnawī's authorship, since he underwent a period of discipleship at Kirmānī's hands. It is well known that Qūnawī was Ibn al-ʿArabī's disciple, and that Ibn al-ʿArabī and Kirmānī were close friends. It is less well known that Ibn al-ʿArabī entrusted Qūnawī to Kirmānī for a period of training. Qūnawī tells us that he spent two years in Kirmānī's company.[13] If Qūnawī did not write the three works, their author certainly had a relationship with Kirmānī, and this would help explain why many of the teachings are similar to Qūnawī's.

Although I have adduced the style of the work as evidence for Qūnawī's authorship, it can also be argued that this rules against him. The only unquestionable examples that we have of Qūnawī's Persian prose are a number of letters, the preface written for a disciple's work, and a brief *Risāla dar ʿarsh* (Treatise on the Throne of God) written for another disciple. Neither the letters nor the preface provide a good basis for comparison, because they are short and belong to different genres. But *Risāla dar ʿarsh*, like the three treatises here, is expository and written in straightforward Persian, although it does not have the same sweetness and fluency. The presence of a relatively large number of technical terms makes it more reminiscent of Qūnawī's Arabic writings than the three treatises. But, in short, Qūnawī's known Persian works provide no real evidence for or against the ascription.

Further evidence can be sought from *Mashāriq al-darārī*, a Persian commentary by Saʿīd al-Dīn Farghānī (d. 695/1296), one of Qūnawī's most important disciples, on the 750-verse "Poem of the Way" by the great Egyptian poet Ibn al-Fāriḍ (d. 632/1235). It is this work for which Qūnawī wrote his Persian preface. Here Qūnawī tells us that, in 643/1245-1246, he traveled to Egypt, where he began teaching Ibn al-Fāriḍ's poem to a group of scholars and possessors of tasting (*dhawq*). He continued teaching on the return journey through Syria and then back in Anatolia. Several of his listeners took notes with the aim of putting together studies of the work, but only Farghānī succeeded in this task.[15] Qūnawī's remarks suggest that he traveled to Egypt with a large group of disciples. This would not have been surprising, considering that he was the heir apparent of the Greatest Master, Ibn al-ʿArabī, who had died only five years earlier.

According to an account transmitted from one of Qūnawī's students by ʿAbd al-Raḥmān Jāmī (d. 898/1492), Qūnawī used to teach Hadith in Arabic. Then, at the end of the session, he would comment in Persian on one line of Ibn al-Fāriḍ's poem.[15] If this report is true, Farghānī probably would have taken several years to compile notes on the 750 lines of the poem. In any case, it is certain that Qūnawī lectured on the poem in Persian, since Farghānī wrote his book in Persian, which is why Qūnawī's introduction is in Persian. Moreover, Farghānī did not write in Persian because of any lack of knowledge of Arabic. After finishing the Persian text, he rewrote it in Arabic in much more detail, with the title *Muntaha'l-madārik*, and left out Qūnawī's introduction. The Arabic version was being taught in Cairo as early as 670/1271, three years before Qūnawī's death.[16] Both versions have played important roles in disseminating Qūnawī's teachings.

What is interesting in the present context is that Farghānī's Persian work is notoriously difficult, especially because of the plethora of technical terminology pertaining to the teachings of Ibn al-ʿArabī and Qūnawī. There is little resemblance between Farghānī's prose and that of the three translated texts. But all this does not necessarily mean that Qūnawī could only express himself by employing technical terms and philosophical arguments. When writing for beginners, he may well have changed his style to fit the audience. Some of his letters are written with little reference to technical terms, although not with the crafted fluency of the three treatises.

Mention of the fact that Qūnawī taught Hadith brings up another piece of evidence that works against both Qūnawī's authorship and Ḥājjī Khalīfa's ascription of *Clarifications* to Nāṣir al-Dīn al-Muḥaddith. A *muḥaddith* is a specialist in the science of Hadith, and Qūnawī fits into this category. However, the author of these treatises had no concern for the standards by which authentic hadiths are differentiated from questionable or inauthentic hadiths. As remarked earlier, he quotes many hadiths that have no reliable source. This indiscriminate citation suggests that the author was not a *muḥaddith*, although it is possible that he left aside the standards of the science of Hadith because of the genre.

In short, there are two basic candidates for the authorship of these treatises. One is the well-known disciple of Ibn al-ʿArabī, Ṣadr al-Dīn Qūnawī; the other, the unknown Naṣīr (or Nāṣir) al-Dīn. One possible explanation for the confusion may be that Naṣīr al-Dīn was one of Qūnawī's companions or disciples (although Aflākī's remark that Shaykh Nāṣir al-Dīn was Qūnawī's rival does not support this suggestion). This would explain the references and allusions to teachings pertaining to the school of Ibn al-ʿArabī. Aflākī mentions a Naṣīr al-Dīn Qūnawī as being one of Qūnawī's most important disciples, along with Mu'ayyid al-Dīn Jandī, Shams al-Dīn Īkī, Fakhr al-Dīn ʿIrāqī, Sharaf al-Dīn Mawṣilī, and Saʿīd al-Dīn Farghānī.[17] Like Farghānī, Mu'ayyid al-Dīn Jandī and Fakhr al-Dīn ʿIrāqi wrote important and influential books, while Īkī, whose name is Shams al-Dīn Muḥammad ibn Abī Bakr, was appointed chief shaykh of Cairo in 670/1271.[18] I have found nothing on Sharaf al-Dīn Mawṣilī or Naṣīr al-Dīn Qūnawī, but the latter cannot be ruled out as a possible author of the three works.

NOTES

1. Qūnawī refers to Ḥammūya as having reached one of the highest stages of unveiling, whereby he witnessed the objects of God's knowledge within the world of Nondelimited Imagination (*al-khayāl al-muṭlaq*). He tells us that he had seen others who had this vision as well but, unlike Ḥammūya, "most of them did not know that the immutable entities which they were seeing were objects entified in God's knowledge from eternity without beginning to eternity without end" (*Fukūk* 232). According to Qūnawī's disciple Jandī, Qūnawī and Ḥammūya attended a session of music and remembrance of God (*samā'*) together in Damascus along with Ibn al-'Arabī's companion Ibn Sawdakīn. Ḥammūya went into a state of ecstasy and, having come back to normal consciousness, called Qūnawī and Ibn Sawdakīn to his side. Then he opened his eyes and said to them, "The Prophet of God was present, and I was before him just as you see me now. When he left, I wanted to open my eyes upon your faces" (*Sharḥ fuṣūṣ al-ḥikam* 107). Another early source tells the same story, but mentions Awḥad al-Dīn Kirmānī as the second person rather than Ibn Sawdakīn (Furūzānfar, *Manāqib* 98–99).

2. Nasafī mentions Qūnawī's name and quotes or rewrites passages from *Clarifications* in *Maqṣad-i aqṣā* 236 and 237. Unacknowledged borrowings are on 230–231 (from *Clarifications* 2.1), 238–240 (1.3), and 279 (2.1).

3. Abarqūhī, *Majma' al-baḥrayn* 327.

4. Ülken, *Le pensée* de l'Islam, Istanbul, 1953; cited in Ruspoli, *Clef* 19.

5. See Karbalā'ī, *Rawḍāt al-jinān* 2:606.

6. The stylistic similarities may not be immediately obvious in the English translation, especially if one focuses on the main body of *Easy Roads*, which is concerned with the details of the Shariah. The Persian texts leave less room for doubt. Even in English, the similarities with the other two treatises are clear in sections I.1–5, V.1, and the conclusion. Sections I.1–5 reproduce the structure of the first two treatises in abbreviated form, and some passages are almost identical in wording. One could argue that the author had seen one or both of those works and is borrowing from them, but I would counter that the text shows all the signs of a fresh reexpression of the same ideas, not quotations or rewordings. Moreover, the stylistic similarity is just as plain where there is no model in the other two treatises. The best place to see the identical style with different phraseology is in the three conclusions, which make the same basic points, each in its own way.

7. Aflākī, *Manāqib* 188.

8. Māyil Hirawī, introduction to Abarqūhī, *Majma' al-baḥrayn* 37.

9. Bayram, "Anadolu Selçuklulari Devri Bilginlerinden Sayḫ Nasīr al-Dīn al-Ḫoyī." My thanks to Professor Cornell Fleischer for providing me with details on the content of this work.

10. Quoted by Māyil Hirawī in the introduction to Juwaynī [?], *Manāhij-i sayfī* 16–17.

11. A. Abū Maḥbūb, in the introduction to Kirmānī, *Dīwān* 49.

12. A short Arabic work, *Mir'āt al-'ārifīn fī multamas Zayn al-'Ābidīn*, has also been attributed both to Qūnawī and *Nāṣir* al-Dīn. In *Histoire et classification de l'oeuvre d'Ibn 'Arabī* (388–389), Osman Yahia points out that the work must be by one of Ibn al-'Arabī's followers, since he is mentioned in the text. Of the thirteen manuscripts that Yahia saw, two of them attribute it to Shaykh Nāṣir al-Dīn, while others attribute it to other authors. Yahia also mentions that Brockelmann refers to a Paris manuscript that cites Qūnawī as the author. S.H. Askari published the text with translation as *Reflection of the Awakened*, attributing it to Qūnawī but suggesting in the introduction that it might be by Imam Ḥusayn, the Prophet's grandson. This is an utter impossibility, even if certain later Sufis in India did write commentaries on the text making the assumption of Imam Ḥusayn's authorship. The style and content of the work are consonant with Qūnawī's Arabic writings, and my own opinion is that he is the most likely author. I have seen twenty-nine Istanbul manuscripts of the work, in addition to those mentioned by Yahia, and in none of them are Shaykh Nāṣir al-Dīn or Qūnawī mentioned. The most commonly cited author after Ibn al-'Arabī is the Persian poet Ibn Shīrīn Maghribī.

13. In his last will and testament, Qūnawī asks to be buried in the clothing of Ibn al-'Arabī and on the prayer carpet of Awḥad al-Dīn (see Chittick, "The Last Will and Testament" 53). In a Persian letter to one of his disciples in which he is discussing the difficulties that arise for those not yet firmly established on the Sufi path, Qūnawī says that even an accomplished master like Awḥad al-Dīn called out at the end of his life for his shaykh, Rukn al-Dīn Sajāsī (who had died twenty-five or thirty years earlier), saying, "O Shaykh, where are you? I have a mountain of difficulties." Parenthetically, Qūnawī remarks that Awḥad al-Dīn had been his shaykh "for a time" (*muddatī*), "in certain respects" (*min ba'ḍ al-wujūh*). He adds, "For two years in Shiraz—both traveling and remaining in one place—I was able to be his companion and to serve him" (ms. Konya Müsesi 1637, folio 108 reverse). This information supports what is said in a biography of Awḥad al-Dīn written, according to its editor, in the second half of the seventh/thirteenth century. Its author tells us that Ibn al-'Arabī entrusted Qūnawī to Awḥad al-Dīn for a period of training, and that Qūnawī remained his companion for fifteen or sixteen years, no doubt meaning from about 620 to Kirmānī's death in 635. Qūnawī used to say, "I drank milk from the breasts of two mothers," meaning Ibn al-'Arabī and Kirmānī (Furūzānfar, *Manāqib* 84–87). That Qūnawī was Awḥad al-Dīn's companion for that period may mean no more than that they had a master-disciple affiliation. It is unlikely that he actually lived in Kirmānī's company for more than the two years that he himself mentions.

14. Farghānī, *Mashāriq al-darārī* 5–6.

15. Jāmī, *Nafaḥāt al-uns* 542.

16. Massignon, *Passion* 1:44.

17. Aflākī, *Manāqib al-'ārifīn* 360.

18. On 'Irāqi, see 'Irāqī, *Fakhruddin 'Iraqi: Divine Flashes*. Jandī is the author of the earliest major commentary on Ibn al-'Arabī's *Fuṣūṣ al-ḥikam*, while Farghānī is the author of the two commentaries on Ibn al-Fāriḍ's poetry already mentioned. Massignon provides a few details on Īkī in *Passion* 1:44, although he is mistaken about Qūnawī's role in Farghānī's commentary (see also Jāmī, *Nafaḥāt al-uns* 542).

Appendix 2—Corrections to the Printed Persian Texts

TABṢIRAT AL-MUBTADĪ (CLARIFICATIONS FOR BEGINNERS)

I prepared an edition of the text in about 1977 on the basis of more than ten Istanbul manuscripts, one of which was the oldest manuscript employed by the editor of the printed edition (Halet Efendi Ilavesi 92, dated 660). The Istanbul manuscripts I used included Nuruosmaniye 2286 (dated 689); Ayasofya 1691, 1692, 1711, and 1419; Şehid Ali Paşa 1394; Asad Efendi 3781; and Raşid Efendi 333. I also looked at a Tehran manuscript, Malik 6309/11. In almost all cases where my edition differs from the printed edition, either my manuscripts are practically unanimous, or the editor's error is obvious. I record places where I have followed my own edition and where a careful reader would note that I have deviated from the printed text. In a few instances I record discrepancies that would be important for the reader of the Persian text but have no effect on the English translation. I have ignored many minor textual differences. Pagination follows the printed text (ascribed to Qūnawī and edited by Najaf'alī Ḥabībī, *Ma'ārif* 1 [1364/1985] 69–128).

73.3	*khazīna*→*khazana*
73.9	*walāyat*→*wa ṭālib*
74.9	*jahl*→—
74.13	*al-janna al-janna*→*al-janna al-janna, fayuqāl lahu'dkhul al-janna*
74.17	*ṣif lī yā rabbi mā 'alāhum*→—
74.18	*'alayhim bismī mā lam*→*'alayhā falam*
75.17	*dil*. . . . This line of poetry is found in none of my mss.
76.-6	*wāfiq shawad*→*muwaffaq buwad*
76.-2	*ḥikmat*→*maktab*
77.5	*wa waqafa 'aqluhu wa'ntahā khāṭiruh*→—
77.13	*jumūdihi wa'l-i'āna minhu subḥānahu*→*junūdihi*
78.3	*ahl-i naẓar*→*ahl-i baḥth wa naẓar*
78.7	*fayḍ-i nūr*→*nūr-i fayḍ*
78.10	Manṣūr→Manṣūr Ḥallāj
78.17	*būd wa*→*būd*
79.4	Hārūn→Hārūt

79.7 *and*→*chahār*
79.14 *alast*→*alastu birabbikum*
79.14 *wa yuḥibbūnahu*→—
79.15 *dar ḥaqq-i īshān*→—
79.17–20 The order of the verses in all my manuscripts is as in the translation.
80.6 *nuḍūl*→*fuṣūl*
80.13–14 The order of the lines in the translation follows the manuscripts.
80.18 *sakhkhafaka*→*ashaqaka*
80.19 ʿAbd Allāh→—
80.23 *admat* [?]→awmat
80.24 *ijmāl*→*ijmāl biniwīsam*
81.2 *az maẓhar-i waḥdāniyyat*→—
81.3 *nihand*→*nihad*
81.5 *bigūyand*→*bigūyad*
81.9 *ḥāshāya ḥāshāya*→*ḥāshāka ḥāshāya*
81.13 *āmanū*→*āmanū bi'l-qawl al-thābit*
81.13 *dalīlī*→*mudārā'ī*
81.20 *alladhī*→—
82.4 *īnjā*→*inna Allāh yatajallā li'l-nās ʿāmmatan wa li-Abī Bakr khāṣṣatan īnjā*. This sentence (my translation, 68.22) is found in all except the Tehran manuscript, where the second half (from *ʿāmmatan*) is changed to *ʿalā ṣūra muʿtaqadātihim*. Clearly, the Shi'ite editor thought the sentence was too sensitive to include in the text, although he does mention its presence in footnote number 71 and tells us that the variant reading is to be preferred.
83.7 *mīgūyad*→*mīguyand*
83.11 *wa gūyand*→—
83.13 *kibriyā bā quds*→*kibriyā-yi qidam*
83.16 *gūyadī*→*gūyad ay*
83.20 *mawrid*→*maʿrifat*
84.8 *manṣab*→*ḥishmat*
85.4 *khajālat*→*jahālat*
85.5–6 *wa khwud rā fuqahā gūyand*→—
85.12 *rā*→—
85.13 *wa az*→*wa ān az*
85.16 *ʿalīm*→*ʿālim*
85.17 *asmā'-i ān asmā'*→*asmā'-i asmā'*
86.12 *wa chūn*→*wa hamchunīn chūn*
86.14 *shayṭāniyyat*→*shayṭanat*
86.21 *bi quds*→*naqd*
87.1 *tāmm*→*nām*
87.20 *khalq ʿālamī*→*ʿālam-i khalq ʿālamī*
88.2 *ʿibārat*→*ʿibārāt*
88.4 *kitāb*→*kitāb-i qadīm*
88.8 *ilā*→*illā*
88.10 *qufl*→*wa qufl*
89.2 *tamayyuz*→*tamyīz*

89.9	*sina→marra*
89.-1	*wa dar→wa hamchunīn dar*
89.-1	*malak al-ra'd wa malak al-rīḥ→malak al-rīḥ wa malak al-ra'd*
90.15	*ḥakāya 'an Allāh ta'ālā→—*
91.7	*wa ma'lūm→wa īnjā ma'lūm*
91.16	*gufta ast→gūyad*
91.22-23	*qāl al-nabī. . .jahannam→—*
92.2	*sawāduh→sawād*
92.3	*ay→ay 'alā*
92.7	*amr→ū*
93.7	*sirrī→sirrat*
94.1	*wa aṣnāf→wa anwā' wa aṣnāf*
94.4	*ḥikmat→ḥikmat ān rā*
94.6	*maqāmāt→manāmāt*
94.10	*dīd→dīdī*
94.-1	*nūr→zabūr*
95.1	*ṭā'ifa→ahl*
95.7	*farmāyad→gūyad*
95.8	*wa ju'ila→hal*
95.8-9	*min 'alāmatih→—*
96.1	*bi awṣāf→awṣāf*
96.4	*'alā→min*
96.5	*ḥaqq→bi ḥaqq*
96.11	*qābalahu→qābaltahu*
96.21	*nihād→ārad*
97.9	*khafīh* [?]*→yukhfīh*
97.18	*daw'ī→ū'ī-yi ū*
97.22	*ṭālibān→ghāliban*
98.1	*rahī raft→sulūkī kunad*
98.1	*maqṣad →maqṣūd*
98.3	*awhālan→wiṣālan*
98.7	*ayyuhā al-sāmi'→—*
98.11	*bā ṭab'→bi'l-ṭab'*
98.13	*ishārāt→—*
98.14	*ūst→ū nīst*
98.22	*wajadū mā→wajadū wa mā*
99.4	*īn ma'ānī→īn jins ma'ānī*
99.7	*sami'a→sami'ahu*
99.9	*dih nawā→dar nawā*
99.18	*al-ghayr→al-'īr*
99.18	*al-sharā min sharāha→al-surā 'an surāhā*
99.20	*gūsh→wa gūsh*
100.1	*mutabassim→mutayyam*
100.15	*ajall→a'azz*
101.4	*quwwatī→qudratī*
101.4	*āmad→—*
101.13	*yak→du*

101.14 *jawalān*→*ḥawalān*
101.15 *ṣifat*→*ṣinf*
101.17 *aḥwāl*→*aʿmāl*
101.19 *khabar*→*chunīn khabar*
102.2 *yanhishūnahu*→*yanhishūnahu wa yalḥasūnahu*
102.2 *al-qiyāma*→*yubʿathūn*
102.13 *shawq* [twice]→*sūq*
102.15 *bi ṣuwar*→*al-ṣuwar*
102.21 *chirāghī*→*chirāgh-i tu*
102.26 *Muḥammad ṣallā Allāh ʿalayhi wa ālihi az adhwāq-i ṭawr-i ū*→*Muḥammadī az adhwāq-i ṭawr-i ū ṣallā Allāh ʿalayhi wa sallam*
103.1 *anbiyāʾ wa awliyāʾ*→*anbiyāʾ-i awliyāʾ*
103.2 *lihādhā gūyad*→—
103.2 *ikhwānī*→*ikhwānī min baʿdī*
103.2 *ʿulamāʾ*→*wa ʿulamāʾ*
103.3 *Isrāʾīl wa*→*Isrāʾīl aw ka anbiyāʾ sāʾir al-umam*
103.3 *mimman*→*wa mimman*
103.8 *kay*→*kay tawānad*
103.9 *ishghaltanī*→*ashghalnī*
103.13 *nakunad*→*nakunand*
103.17 *cha bāsham man cha bāsham man*→*ka bāsham man ka man bāsham*
103.21 *dānand*→*khwānand*
103.23 *yakī*→*ka yakī*
104.6 *wa ayn*→*wa kam wa ayn*
104.8 *bi*→*bā*
104.9 *mukāshafāt wa adhwāq*→*adhwāq wa mukāshafāt*
104.10 *bāshand*→*bāshand. Yā Abā Bakr, laysa baynī wa baynaka farq illā annī buʿithtu; yā ʿUmar law lam ubʿath, labuʾithta*. Found in all manuscripts. The editor has seen fit to relegate these two sayings to a footnote, suggesting that they must have been added by a Sunni copyist.
105.4 *wa dar*→*dar*
105.7 *qawānīn*→*afānīn*
105.15 *tā*→*wa*
105.19 *nāyad bāyad*→*nāyad*
106.2 *barad ān*→*barad īn*
106.14 *ʿālamī*→*ʿālam-i dīgar*
106.16 *anṣabahā* [?]→*al-ṣahbā*
106.17 *nashr*→*ḥashr*
106.17 *ṣarāfa*→*khurāfa*
106.18 *maʿālīq*→*maghālīq*
106.19 *asaf al-sāfilīn*→*asfal*
107.1 *miqdārī*→*miqdārī muʿayyan*
107.1 *bun*→*bun-i ū*
107.2 *qawāʿid*→*qawāʿid-i ṭibbī*
107.3 *ḥālat*→*ḥāl*
107.4 *afʿī*→*afʿī kūshad*

107.5	*pas*→—
107.7	*and*→*and bīshtar-i khalq rā ka*
107.18	*wa niyyātikum*→—
108.2	*iftiqār*→*iftiqār-i ū*
108.3	*nasha'āt*→*nash'at*
108.7	*anbiyā' ṣalawāt Allāh 'alayhim ajma'īn wa awliyā' wa ḥukama' wa 'ulamā'*→*anbiyā' wa awliyā' wa 'ulamā' wa ḥukama' ṣalawāt Allāh 'alayhim ajma'īn*
108.12	*aḥwāl-i īshān*→*farīqayn*
108.14	*mu'allaq*→*mu'allaqa*
108.14	*malik*→*tilka*
108.15	*badr ka*→*badr chūn*
108.17	*ḥaqqan*→*ḥaqqan fa innī wajadtu mā wa'ada rabbī ḥaqqan*
108.17	*qawlahu 'alayhi al-salām*→—
108.21	*ḥaqq*→*khudāy*
108.22	*nafs-i nafas*→*nafs wa nafas*
109.1	*khalaqnā al-insān*→*khuliqa al-nās*
109.1	*li'l-fanā'*→*li'l-nafād*
109.1	*shaqwa wa*→*shaqwa aw*
109.6	*wa mawjūdī*→*mawjūdī*
109.13	*būd*→*bāyad*
109.14	*natawān*→*nigah namītawān*
109.17	*maẓhar*→*maẓharash*
109.18	*īn*→—
109.21	*fa'l-jism*→*fi'l-jism*
110.2	*ba'ḍī az*→*ba'ḍī*
110.6	*af'āl*→*aḥwāl*
110.13	*jāhil*→*gabrī*
110.15	*ān ṣifat*→*ū rā*
110.21	*'amal*→*'alam*
111.11	*dar khidmat*→*bi khidmat*
111.13	*māh-i ramaḍān waqt-i subḥ*→*waqt-i subḥ-i māh-i ramaḍān*
111.14	*ḥadīth*→*ḥadīth chūn*
112.9	*qidda* [twice]→*qudhdha*
112.12	*idrāk-i īn*→*idrāk-i akthar-i ān*
112.13	*tawān idrāk*→*idrāk tawān*
112.13	*wa 'iyān*→—
112.18	*sirr*→—
112.22	*bidīn*→*bar īn*
112.22	*ān rā*→*ān rā qiyāmat-i kubrā mīgūyand wa bi rūz-i marg-i ṭabī'ī iṭlāq mīkunand wa ān rā*
113.3	*maqṣūd*→*ḥālā maqṣūd*
113.6	*qarābat*→*gharāyib*
113.6	*asrār*→*asrār wa sharḥ-i ladhdhāt-i ān dar makāyīl wa mawāzīn-i 'uqūl wa awhām nagunjad*
113.8	*qarīb*→*farīb*

113.11	*tasqamū*→*tasqamū abadan*
113.12	*ta'sū*→*ta'basū*
113.16	*tajallī*→*tajallī wa*
113.19	*dīgar dūzakh*→*dūzakh*
113.20	*mīshawad*→*mīshawand*
113.22	*iqtibās*→*ṭalab-i iqtibās*
113.27	*jūd*→*jūd wa luṭf*
113.27	*malakūt*→*malakūtī*
114.1	*bīsh*→*bīsh az īn*
114.6	*adnās*→*awbāsh*
114.10	*'alā alsinatikum*→—
114.17	*quds*→*qudsī*
114.24	*'adl tawānī*→*'adl nagāh tawānī*
115.10	*'izz*→*'izzat*
115.11	*manzil*→*tanazzul*
115.16	*bal mā aṭla'tuhum*→*balha mā aṭla'tukum*
116.2	*ka*→*ka kasī*
116.2	*wujūd*→*khwud*
116.7	*bī*→*bas*
116.12	*luṭf*→*luṭf-i azal*
116.25	*sang*→*gasht*
117.6	*dunyāka*→*dunyāka 'ala'l-jumla*
117.7	*taswīf*→*sawf sawf*
117.10	*ghaflat*→*ghaflat wa ghurūr*
117.19	*muzakhraf*→*muzakhrafāt*
118.4	*'amīq*→*bī 'umq*
118.5	*Muḥammad*→—
118.9	*sa'ādāt*→*sa'ādat*
118.11	*junūd-i ẓulmat*→*ẓulmat-i Iblīs*
118.14	*jaffat*→*jaffa*
118.15	*ilā yawm al-qiyāma*→—
118.15	*al-khalā'iq*→*al-khalā'iq jamī'an*
118.15	*lan yanfa'ūka illā bimā qaddara Allāh laka*→*lam yaqḍihi Allāh laka lam yaqdirū 'alayhi*
118.16	*lam yaḍurrūka illā bimā qaḍā Allāh 'alayk*→*lam yaqḍihi Allāh laka lam yaqdirū 'alayhi*
118.17	*faraḥ*→*faraj*
118.17	*fa inna*→*inna*
118.19	*zabān*→*zabān-i jān*
118.21	*yāsīn*→*yāsīn u*
118.23	*mubdi'*→*mubdi'*
118.24	*wa ṣaḥbihi wa 'itratihi al-ṭāhirīn 'ayn al-wujūd wa'l-mawjūd*→*ajma'īn*

MANĀHIJ-I SAYFĪ (EASY ROADS OF SAYF AL-DĪN)

The following corrections are based on the older of the two manuscripts used by the editor for his edition (Halet Efendi Ilavesi 92). In some cases, the editor did not read the text correctly, whereas in other cases it is simply a matter of a printing error. These corrections are indicated by "MS." In a number of other cases, the editor's text follows the manuscript, but the manuscript itself is clearly incorrect for one reason or another. I have made the necessary corrections based on the meaning demanded by the text. These corrections are indicated by "CR" for "corrected." Pagination follows the printed edition (ascribed to Juwaynī and edited by N. Māyil Hirawī, Tehran: Mawlā, 1363/1984).

30.-1	*ḥaddī*→*jiddī* (MS)
32.-5	*daw qism*→*qism* (CR)
34.7	*barakat*→*tarkīb* (MS)
34.14	*bifarmūd*→*nafarmūd* (CR). The meaning demands a negative verb.
34.15	*tanabbuhī*→*tanbīhī* (MS)
38.-2-3	*ū bāshad wa khalq nabāshad*→— (MS)
47.-4	*yawma'idhin*→*yawma'idhin lamaḥjūbūn. Wa hamchunīn dar bihisht darajāt wa ladhdhāt ast wa ʿaẓīmtar ladhdhatī ahl-i bihisht rā liqā-yi ḥaqq jalla jalāluhu khwāhad būd. Wujūhun yawma'idhin* (MS)
55.3	*dhikr*→*al-dhikr* (MS)
55.5	*naʿūdhu bika*→— (CR). These two words are written in the margin of the manuscript and, if added to the text, ruin the grammar.
55.6	*tubāʿidnī*→*fabāʿidnī* (MS)
57.5	*biḥamd laka*→*biḥamdika* (MS)
58.5	*mutaṣarrif*→*munṣarif* (MS)
60.2	*nahār*→*namāz* (MS)
60.6	*nīst*. At this point there is a lacuna in the text, as is indicated by the incomplete meaning and the parallel passages in *Iḥyā'* (1:102) and *Kīmiyā'* (1:152). The least that the missing portion has to say is indicated in my translation by the sentence, "Then he wipes his whole face once with both hands."
60.12	*musāʿid*→*sāʿid* (CR)
60.12	*bugdharānad tā bi*. . . . There is another lacuna here. Again, I have guessed at the original on the basis of the *Iḥyā'* (1:102) and *Kīmiyā'* (1:152): "to the elbow. Then he passes the front of his left hand along the front of his forearm."
63.3	*taʿyīn wa*→*taʿyīn* (CR)
63.-5	*ṣādiq*. There is a lacuna here. The context demands, at the minimum, the passage, "and this is the earliest time for the morning prayer. Its latest time is when the sun." For the juridical ruling on this point, see Jazīrī, *Fiqh* 1:183–185.
66.12	*yād nadānad*→*ziyād nadārad* (MS ??). The text here—and probably in the surrounding words—is corrupt, but the meaning is clear from the parallel passage in *Iḥyā'* 1:112.
69.3	*bar ān*→*bar āl* (MS). In addition, there must be a lacuna. I read *bar Muḥammad wa āl*.
70.8	*mū-yi maḥāsin*→*mūy wa maḥāsin* (MS)
74.-2	*yataʿammaduhu*→*yataʿahhaduhu* (MS)
75.6	*pas*→*bas* (MS)
75.11	*ham*→*fahm* (MS)
76.10	*bar*→*tar* (MS)

76.13, 15 *murāqabat*→*murāfaqat* (CR). Compare 89.13.
76.16 *isti'ādat*→*isti'ādhat* (MS)
76.18 *pas az*→*pas dar* (CR)
77.6 *hay'at*→*hay'āt* (CR)
81.-3 *binumūd*→*paymūd* (CR)
81.-2 *nār* [twice]→*tār* (MS)
82.8 *fasūmū*→*fa'iddū* (as in the author's alternative reading and in the hadith collections)
86.8 *mā'alat* [?]→*mā naltu* (CR)
88.-6 *rūḥ*→*dūzakh* (MS)
90.-6 *'iẓāmī*→*'iẓāmī wa nūran min bayna yadayya wa nūran min khalfī wa nūran 'an yamīnī* (MS)
90.-5 *wa'j'al*→*wa'j'al lī* (MS)
91.1 *al-muṭhir*→*al-ṭahir* (MS)
91.2 *yā huwa*→*yā huwa yā huwa yā lā ilāha* (MS)
91.2 *illā huwa*→*illā huwa, yā man lā ya'lamu mā huwa illā huwa, yā man lā ya'lamu ayn huwa illā huwa* (MS)
91.3 *mukawwinan*→*mukawwin* (MS)
92.9 *anta rabbī*→*anta anta rabbī* (MS)
92.-5 *tabārak*→*tabārakta* (MS)
94.-2 *al-shuhadā'*→*al-shuhadā' wa* (MS)
96.4 *munqidh*→*yā munqidh* (MS)
98.6 *ja'ala*→*ja'alaka* (MS)
98.11 *al-ayyām*→*al-āthām* (MS)
99.7 *ḥasīnihā*→*ḥassinhā* (MS)
101.2 *kaj*→*ganj* (MS)

Bibliography

Abarqūhī, Shams al-Dīn Ibrāhīm. *Majma' al-baḥrayn*. Edited by N. Māyil Hirawī. Tehran: Mawlā, 1364/1985.

Abū Dāwūd. *al-Sunan*. Edited by A.S. 'Alī. Cairo: Muṣṭafā al-Bābī al-Ḥalabī, 1952.

Aflākī. *Manāqib al-'ārifīn*. Edited by T. Yazıcı. Ankara: Türk Tarih Kurumu Basımevi, 1959–1961.

Aḥmad (ibn Ḥanbal). *al-Musnad*. Beirut: Dār Ṣādir, n.d.

'Alī (ibn Abī Ṭālib). *Nahj al-balāgha*. Edited by Ṣubḥī al-Ṣāliḥ. Beirut: 1967.

'Alī ibn al-Ḥusayn. *Al-Ṣaḥīfat al-sajjādiyya: The Psalms of Islam*. Translated by W. C. Chittick. Oxford: Oxford University Press, 1988.

Āmulī, Sayyid Ḥaydar. *Jāmi' al-asrār*. Edited by H. Corbin and Osman Yahia. Tehran: Institut Franco-Iranien, 1969.

Anṣārī, 'Abdallāh. *Ṭabaqāt al-ṣūfiyya*. Edited by 'A. Ḥabībī. Kabul: Wizārat-i Ma'ārif, 1341/1962.

———. *Intimate Conversations*. Translated by W. Thackston. New York: Paulist Press, 1978.

Anwarī. *Dīwān*. Edited M. T. Mudarris Raḍawī. Tehran: Bungāh-i Tarjama wa Nashr-i Kitāb, 1958–1961.

Arberry, A. J. *Muslim Saints and Mystics*. Chicago: University of Chicago Press, 1966.

Asad, M. *The Message of the Qur'ān*. London: E. J. Brill, 1980.

'Aṭṭār, Farīd al-Dīn. *The Conference of the Birds*. Translated by A. Darbandi and D. Davis. New York: Penguin, 1984.

———. *Dīwān*. Edited by T. Tafaḍḍulī. Tehran: Bungāh-i Tarjama wa Nashr-i Kitāb, 1967.

———. *Tadhkirat al-awliyā'*. Edited by M. Isti'lāmī. Tehran: Zuwwār, 1346/1967.

Awn, Peter. *Satan's Tragedy and Redemption: Iblīs in Sufi Psychology*. Leiden: Brill, 1983.

———. "Sufism." *The Encyclopedia of Religion*. New York: MacMillan, 1987. 14:104–123.

Bahā' Walad. *Ma'ārif*. Edited by B. Furūzānfar. Tehran: Majlis, 1333/1954.

Baldick, J. *Mystical Islam: An Introduction to Sufism*. New York: New York University Press, 1989.

Bayḍāwī, al-. *Anwār al-tanzīl wa asrār al-ta'wīl.* N.p.: al-Maṭba'at al-'Uthmāniyya, 1329/1911.

Bayram, Mikâil. "Anadolu Selçuklulari Devri Bilginlerinden Sayḫ Nasīr al-Dīn al-Ḫoyī (Hayati, Çevresi ve Eserleri)." Istanbul: Edebiyat Fakültesi Arap-Fars Filolojisi Doktora Tezi, 1975

Böwering, G. *The Mystical Vision of Existence in Classical Islam: The Quranic Hermeneutics of the Ṣūfī Sahl At-Tustarī (d. 283/896).* New York: de Gruyter, 1980.

Browne, E. G. *A Literary History of Persia.* 4 vols. Cambridge, England: Cambridge University Press, 1902–1921.

Bukhārī. *al-Ṣaḥīḥ.* N.p.: Maṭābi' al-Shu'ab, 1378/1958-1959.

Bukhārī, Abū Ibrāhīm Mustamlī. *Sharḥ-i ta'arruf.* Lucknow, India: 1328/1910.

Bukhārī, Sayyid Muḥammad. *Manāhij al-ṭālibīn.* Edited by N. Māyil Hirawī. Tehran: Mawlā, 1364/1985

Chittick, W. C. "Death and the World of Imagination: Ibn al-'Arabī's Eschatology." *The Muslim World,* 1988. 78:51–82.

———. "Dhikr." *Encyclopedia of Religion.* New York: MacMillan, 1987. 4:341–344.

———. "Ebn al-'Arabi as Lover." *Sufi,* 1991. 9:6–9.

———. "Eschatology." *Islamic Spirituality: Foundations.* Edited by S. H. Nasr. New York: Crossroad, 1987. 378–409.

———. "Ibn 'Arabī and His School." *Islamic Spirituality: Manifestations.* Edited by S. H. Nasr. New York: Crossroad, 1991. 49–79.

———. "Ibn 'Arabī's Own Summary of the *Fuṣūṣ*: The 'Imprint of the Bezels of Wisdom.'" *Journal of the Muhyiddin Ibn 'Arabi Society,* 1982. 1:31–93.

———. "Mysticism vs. Philosophy in Earlier Islamic History: The al-Ṭūsī, al-Qūnawī Correspondence." *Religious Studies,* 1981. 17:87–104.

———. "The Last Will and Testament of Ibn 'Arabī's Foremost Disciple and Some Notes on its Author." *Sophia Perennis,* 1978. 4.1:43–58.

———. "Rūmī and *Waḥdat al-wujūd.*" *The Heritage of Rumi.* Edited by Amin Banani and Georges Sabagh. Cambridge, England: Cambridge University Press, in press.

———. "Spectrums of Islamic Thought: Sa'īd al-Dīn Farghānī on the Implications of Oneness and Manyness." *The Legacy of Medieval Persian Sufism.* Edited by L. Lewisohn. London: Khaniqahi Nimatullahi Publications, 1992. 203–217.

———. *The Sufi Path of Knowledge: Ibn al-'Arabī's Metaphysics of Imagination.* Albany: State University of New York Press, 1989.

———. *The Sufi Path of Love: The Spiritual Teachings of Rumi.* Albany: State University of New York Press, 1983.

Chodkiewicz. M. *Le Sceau des saints: Prophétie et sainteté dans le doctrine d'Ibn Arabî.* Paris: Gallimard, 1986.

Chodkiewicz. M. (ed.) *Les Illuminations de La Mecque/The Meccan Illuminations: Textes choisies/Selected Texts.* Paris: Sindbad, 1988.

Corbin, Henry. *Creative Imagination in the Ṣūfism of Ibn 'Arabī*. Princeton: Princeton University Press, 1969.
Dārimī, al-. *al-Sunan*. N.p.: Dār Iḥyā' al-Sunnat al-Nabawiyya, n.d.
Elder, E. E. *A Commentary on the Creed of Islam: Sa'd al-Dīn al-Taftāzānī on the Creed of Najm al-Dīn al-Nasafī*. New York: Columbia University Press, 1950.
Fanārī. *Miftāḥ al-ins*. Tehran: 1323/1905.
Farghānī, Sa'īd al-Dīn. *Mashāriq al-darārī*. Edited by S. J. Āshtiyānī. Mashhad: Dānishgāh-i Firdawsī, 1398/1978.
———. *Muntaha 'l-madārik*. Cairo: 1293/1876.
Fayṣal, Shukrī. *Abu'l-'Atāhiya: Ash'āruhu wa akhbāruhu*. Damascus: Maṭba'a Jāmi'a, 1965.
Firdawsī. *Shāhnāma*. Moscow: Academy of Science, 1963–1970.
Furūzānfar, Badī' al-Zamān. *Aḥādīth-i Mathnawī*. Tehran: Amīr Kabīr, 1347/1968.
———. *Manāqib-i Awḥad al-Dīn Abi 'l-Fakhr Kirmānī*. Tehran: Bungāh-i Tarjama wa Nashr-i Kitāb, 1347/1968.
Gardet, L. "Īmān." *Encyclopedia of Islam* (new edition). 3:1170–174.
Gawharīn, S. S. *Farhang-e lughāt wa ta'bīrāt-i Mathnawī*. Tehran: Dānishgāh, 1337-1354/1958-1975.
Ghazālī, Abū Ḥāmid Muḥammad. *Al-Arba'īn fī uṣūl al-dīn*. Edited by M. M. Abu'l-'Allā. Cairo: Maktabat al-Jundī, 1970.
———. *Bidāyat al-hidāya*. Cairo: 'Īsā al-Bābī al-Ḥalabī, n.d. Translated in Watt, *The Faith and Practice of al-Ghazālī*. 86–152.
———. *Book XX of al-Ghazālī's Iḥyā 'Ulūm al-Dīn*. Translated by L. Zolondek. Leiden: Brill, 1963.
———. *The Book of Knowledge*. Translated by N. A. Faris. Lahore: Sh. Muhammad Ashraf, 1962.
———. *The Foundations of the Articles of Faith*. Translated by N. A. Faris. Lahore: Sh. Muhammad Ashraf, 1963.
———. *Iḥyā' 'ulūm al-dīn*. Cairo: Maṭba'at al-'Āmirat al-Sharafiyya, 1326–1327/1908-1909. Persian translation by Mu'ayyid al-Dīn Muḥammad Khwārazmī. Edited by H. Khadīw-jam. Tehran: Intishārāt-i 'Ilmī wa Farhangī, 1351–1352/1972–1973.
———. *Iljām al-'awāmm 'an 'ilm al-kalām*. In Ghazālī, *al-Quṣūr al-'awālī*. 3:61–123.
———. *Invocations and Supplications*. Translated by K. Nakamura. Cambridge, England: The Islamic Texts Society, 1990.
———. *Kīmiyā-yi sa'ādat*. Edited by H. Khadīw-jam. Tehran: Jībī, 1354/1975.
———. *al-Maqṣad al-asnā fī sharḥ ma'ānī asmā' Allāh al-ḥusnā*. Edited by Fadlou A. Shehadi. Beirut: Dar el-Machreq, 1971.
———. *Mīzān al-'amal*. Edited by S. Dunyā. Cairo: Dār al-Ma'ārif, 1965.

———. *The Mysteries of Almsgiving*. Translated by N. A. Faris. Beirut: American University, 1966.

———. *Naṣīḥat al-mulūk*. Edited by J. Humā'ī. Tehran: Anjuman-i Āthār-i Millī, 1351/1972.

———. *The Precious Pearl: Al-Durra Al-Fakhira*. Translated by J.I. Smith. Missoula: Scholar's Press, 1979.

———. *Qawā'id al-'aqā'id*. In Ghazālī, *al-Quṣūr al-'awālī*. 4:148–154.

———. *al-Quṣūr al-'awālī min rasā'il al-Imām al-Ghazālī*. 4 vols. Edited by M. M. Abu'l-'Allā. Cairo: Maktabat al-Jundī, 1970–1973.

———. *The Remembrance of Death and the Afterlife. . . . Book XL of The Revival of the Religious Sciences*. Translated by T. J. Winter. Cambridge, England: Islamic Texts Society, 1989.

———. [ascribed]. *Sirr al-'ālamayn wa kashf mā fi'l-dārayn*. Najaf: Maṭābi' al-Nu'mān, 1965.

Ghazālī, Aḥmad. *Majmū'a-yi āthār-i fārsī*. Edited by A. Mujāhid. Tehran: Dānishgāh, 1358/1979.

———. *Sawāniḥ*. Edited by N. Pourjavady. Tehran: Bunyād-i Farhang, 1359/1980. Translated by Pourjavady as *Sawāniḥ: Inspirations from the World of Pure Spirits*. London: KPI, 1986.

Graham, William. *Divine Word and Prophetic Word in Early Islam*. The Hague: Mouton, 1977.

Ḥāfiẓ. *Dīwān*. Edited by M. Qazwīnī and Q. Ghanī. Tehran: Zuwwār, 1320/1941. Translated by H. Wilberforce Clarke as *The Diwan of Hafiz*. India, 1891. Reprinted New York: Samuel Weiser, 1970.

Ḥakīm, Su'ād al-. *al-Mu'jam al-ṣūfī*. Beirut: Dandara, 1981.

Ḥallāj, Ḥusayn Manṣūr. *Dīwān*. Translated by Louis Massignon. Paris: Cahiers du Sud, 1955.

Hamadānī, 'Ayn al-Quḍāt. *Nāmahā*. 2 vols. Edited by 'A. Munzawī and 'A. 'Usayrān. Tehran: Bunyād-i Farhang, 1969–1972.

———. *Tamhīdāt*. Edited by 'A. 'Usayrān. Tehran: Dānishgāh, 1341/1962.

———. *Zubdat al-ḥaqā'iq*. Edited by 'A. 'Usayrān. Tehran: Dānishgāh, 1341/1962.

Hourani, G.F. "Ibn Sīnā's 'Essay on the Secret of Destiny.' " *Bulletin of the School of Oriental and African Studies*, 1966. 2.1:25–48.

Hujwīrī. *Kashf al-maḥjūb*. Edited by V. Zhukovsky. Tehran: Amīr Kabīr, 1336/1957. Translated by R. J. Nicholson as *The Kashf al-Mahjūb: The Oldest Persian Treatise on Sufism*. London: Luzac, 1970.

Ibn al-'Arabī. *Asfār, Kitāb al-*. In *Rasā'il Ibn al-'Arabī*. Hyderabad-Deccan: The Dāiratu'l-Ma'ārifi'l-Osmania, 1948.

———. *Fuṣūṣ al-ḥikam*. Edited by A. 'Afīfī. Beirut: Dār al-Kutub al-'Arabī, 1946. Translated by R.W.J. Austin as *Ibn Al'Arabī: The Bezels of Wisdom*. Ramsey, N.J.: Paulist Press, 1981.

———. *al-Futūḥāt al-makkiyya.* Cairo: 1911. Reprinted Beirut: Dār Ṣādir, n.d. Also edited by O. Yahia. Cairo: Al-Hay'at al-Miṣriyyat al-ʿĀmma li'l-Kitāb, 1972–.

Ibn al-Dabbāgh. *Mashāriq anwār al-qulūb.* Edited by H. Ritter. Beirut: Dār Ṣādir, 1959.

Ibn Māja. *al-Sunan.* Edited by M. F. ʿAbd al-Bāqī. Cairo: Dār Iḥyā' al-Kutub al-ʿArabiyya, 1952.

Ibn Sīnā. *Al-Ishārāt wa'l-tanbīhāt.* 3 vols. Edited by S. Dunyā. Cairo: Muṣṭafā al-Bābī al-Ḥalabī, 1947.

ʿIrāqī, Fakhr al-Dīn. *Lamaʿāt.* Edited by M. Khwājawī. Tehran: Mawlā, 1363/1984. Translated by W. C. Chittick and P. L. Wilson as *Fakhruddin ʿIraqi: Divine Flashes.* New York: Paulist Press, 1982.

Iṣfahānī, Abū Nuʿaym al-. *Ḥilyat al-awliyā'.* 10 vols. Cairo: Maṭbaʿat al-Saʿāda, 1971–1979.

Ivry, Alfred L. "Avicenna's Concept of Determinism." In *Islamic Theology and Philosophy.* Edited by M. E. Marmura. Albany: State University of New York Press, 1984. 160–171.

Jām, Aḥmad. *Rawḍat al-Mudhnibīn.* Edited by ʿA. Fāḍil. Tehran: Bunyād-i Farhang, 1355/1976.

———. *Uns al-ṭālibīn.* Edited by ʿA. Fāḍil. Tehran: Bunyād-i Farhang, 1350/1971.

Jāmī, ʿAbd al-Raḥmān. *Lawā'iḥ. A Treatise on Sufism.* Edited and translated by E. H. Whinfield and M. M. Ḳazvīnī. London: Theosophical Publishing House, 1978.

———. *Nafaḥāt al-uns.* Edited by M. Tawḥīdīpūr. Tehran: Saʿdī, 1333/1954.

———. *Naqd al-nuṣūṣ fī sharḥ naqsh al-fuṣūṣ.* Edited by W. C. Chittick. Tehran: Imperial Iranian Academy of Philosophy, 1977.

Jandī, Mu'ayyid al-Dīn. *Nafḥat al-rūḥ wa tuḥfat al-futūḥ.* Edited by N. Māyil Hirawī. Tehran: Mawlā, 1362/1983.

———. *Sharḥ fuṣūṣ al-ḥikam.* Edited by S. J. Āshtiyānī. Mashhad: Dānishgāh-i Mashhad, 1361/1982.

Jazīrī, ʿAbd al-Raḥmān al-. *Al-Fiqh ʿalā madhāhib al-arbaʿa.* Second edition. Cairo: Maṭbaʿat al-Istiqāma, n.d.

Juwaynī, Abū'l-Ḥaqā'iq Muḥammad [ascribed]. *Manāhij al-sayfiyya.* Edited by N. Māyil Hirawī. Tehran: Mawlā, 1363/1984.

Kalābādhī, Abū Bakr al-. *Al-Taʿarruf li madhhab ahl al-taṣawwuf.* Edited by ʿA. H. Maḥmūd and T. ʿA. Surūr. Cairo, 1960. Translated by A. J. Arberry as *The Doctrine of the Sufis.* Lahore: Sh. Muhammad Ashraf, 1966.

Karbalā'ī, Ḥāfiẓ Ḥusayn. *Rawḍāt al-jinān wa jannāt al-janān.* Edited by J. Sulṭān al-Qurrā'ī. Vol. 2. Tehran: Bungāh-i Tarjama wa Nashr-i Kitāb, 1349/1970.

Kāshānī, Afḍal al-Dīn. *Dīwān.* Edited by Muṣṭafā Fayḍī et al. Kāshān: Idāra-yi Farhang wa Hunar, 1351/1972.

Khalīfa, Ḥājjī (Kâtib Çelebi). *Kashf al-ẓunūn*. Istanbul: Milli Eğitim Basımevi, 1971.

Khāqānī. *Dīwān*. Edited by ʿA. ʿAbd al-Rasūlī. Tehran: Khayyām, 2537/1978.

———. *Tuḥfat al-ʿirāqayn*. Edited by Y. Qarīb. Tehran: 1333/1954.

Kirmānī, Awḥad al-Dīn. *Dīwān-i rubāʿiyyāt*. Edited by A. Abū Maḥbūb. Tehran: Surūsh, 1366/1987.

Kisā'ī, al-. *The Tales of the Prophets of al-Kisa'i*. Translated by W. M. Thackston. Boston: Twayne, 1975.

Kubrā, Najm al-Dīn. *Fawā'iḥ al-jamāl*. Edited by F. Meier as *Die Fawā'iḥ al-Ǧamāl wa-Fawātiḥ al-Ǧalāl*. Wiesbaden: Franz Steiner, 1957.

———. *Al-Uṣūl al-ʿashara*. Edited by N. Māyil Hirawī. Tehran: Mawlā, 1363/1984.

Landolt, H. "Walāya." *Encyclopedia of Religion*, New York: MacMillan, 1987. 15:316–23.

Lane, E. W. *Arabic-English Lexicon*. Cambridge, England: Islamic Texts Society, 1984.

Lings, Martin. *A Moslem Saint of the Twentieth Century*. London: George Allen & Unwin, 1961.

Maʿarrī, Abu'l-ʿAlā' al-. *Dīwān saqṭ al-zand*. Edited by N. Riḍā. Beirut: Dār Maktabat al-Ḥayāt, 1965.

Makkī, Abū Ṭālib al-. *Qūt al-qulūb*. Cairo: Muṣṭafā al-Bābī al-Ḥalabī, 1961.

Massignon, L. *Akhbar al-Hallaj*. Paris: 1975.

———. *The Passion of al-Ḥallāj: Mystic and Martyr of Islam*. 4 vols. Princeton: Princeton University Press, 1982.

Maybudī, Rashīd al-Dīn. *Kashf al-asrār wa ʿuddat al-abrār*. 10 volumes. Edited by ʿA. A. Ḥikmat. Tehran: Dānishgāh, 1331–1339/1952–1960.

Mullā Ṣadrā. *The Wisdom of the Throne*. Translated by J. W. Morris. Princeton: Princeton University Press, 1981.

Murata, Sachiko. *The Tao of Islam: A Sourcebook on Gender Relationships in Islamic Thought*. Albany: State University of New York Press, 1992.

Muslim. *al-Ṣaḥīḥ*. Cairo: Maṭbaʿa Muḥammad ʿAlī Ṣabīḥ, 1334/1915–1916.

Nafīsī, Saʿīd. *Sukhanān-i manẓūm-i Abū Saʿīd-i Abu'l-Khayr*. 2d. ed. Tehran: Sanā'ī, 1350/1971.

Nasafī, ʿAzīz al-Dīn. *Kashf al-ḥaqā'iq*. Edited by A. Mahdawī-yi Dāmghānī. Tehran: Bungāh-i Tarjama wa Nashr-i Kitāb, 1344/1965.

———. *Maqṣad-i aqṣā*. Appended to Jāmī's *Ashiʿʿat al-lamaʿāt*. Edited by Ḥ. Rabbānī. Tehran: Kitābkhāna-yi ʿIlmiyya-yi Ḥāmidī, 1352/1973.

Nasā'ī, al-. *al-Sunan*. Beirut: Dār Iḥyā' al-Turāth al-ʿArabī, 1348/1929–1930.

Naṣrallāh Munshī, Abu'l-Maʿālī. *Kalīla wa Dimna*. Edited by M. Mīnuwī. Tehran: Dānishgāh, 1345/1966.

Nawawī, al-Ḥāfiẓ Muḥyī al-Dīn al-. *Bustān al-ʿārifīn*. Edited by Muḥammad al-Ḥajjār. Aleppo: Dār al-Daʿwa, n.d.

Nurbakhsh, Javad. *Sufi Symbolism*. 5 vols. London: Khaniqahi Nimatullahi, 1984–1991.

———. *Sufism*. 4 vols. New York and London: Khaniqahi Nimatullahi, 1981–1988.

Ormsby, Eric L. *Theodicy in Islamic Thought: The Dispute over al-Ghazālī's "Best of All Possible Worlds"*. Princeton: Princeton University Press, 1984.

Pourjavady, Nasrollah. *Sulṭān-i ṭarīqat*. Tehran: Āgāh, 1358/1979.

Qayṣarī, Sharaf al-Dīn al-. *Sharḥ fuṣūṣ al-ḥikam*. Tehran: Dār al-Funūn, 1299/1882.

Qūnawī, Ṣadr al-Dīn. *Al-Fukūk*. On the margin of ʿAbd al-Razzāq Kāshānī's *Sharḥ manāzil al-sā'irīn*. Tehran: Ibrāhīm Lārījānī, 1315/1897–1898.

———. *Iʿjāz al-bayān fī tafsīr umm al-Qurʾān*. Hyderabad-Deccan: Osmania Oriental Publications Bureau, 1949. Also printed as *Al-Tafsīr al-ṣūfī li'l-Qur'ān*. Edited by ʿA. Aḥmad ʿAṭā'. Cairo: Dār al-Kutub al-Ḥadītha, 1969.

——— [ascribed]. *Maṭāliʿ-i īmān*. Edited by W. C. Chittick. *Sophia Perennis*, 1978. 4.1:57–80.

———. *Miftāḥ al-ghayb*. On the margin of Fanārī's *Miṣbāḥ al-ins*. See Fanārī.

——— [ascribed]. *Mir'āt al-ʿārifīn*. Text edited and translated by S. H. Askari. *Reflection of the Awakened*. London: Zahra Trust, 1983.

———. *Al-Nafaḥāt al-ilāhiyya*. Tehran: Aḥmad Shīrāzī, 1316/1898.

———. *Al-Nuṣūṣ*. Edited by S.J. Āshtiyānī. Tehran: Markaz-i Nashr-i Dānishgāhī, 1362/1983. Also, appended to Kāshānī's *Sharḥ manāzil al-sā'irīn*. Tehran: Ibrāhīm Lārījānī, 1315/1897–1898.

———. *Risāla dar ʿarsh*. Konya Museum, ms. 1637, folios 114r–115r; ms. 5020, folios 15r–17r.

———. *Risālat al-hādiyat al-murshidiyya*. Istanbul mss. Bağdatlı Vehbi Efendi 2087/1; Şehid Ali Paşa 1342m/9; Nuruosmaniye 5101/2; Ayasofya 1691/1; Istanbul University 3158/2, 3239/7, 3318/5.

——— [ascribed]. *Tabṣirat al-mubtadī*. Edited by Najafʿalī Ḥabībī. *Maʿārif*, 1364/1985. 1:69–128.

———. *Taḥrīr al-bayān fī taqrīr shuʿab al-īmān wa rutab al-iḥsān*. Istanbul mss. Crh. 1001/4, 2054/9; Fatih 1394/2, 2630/1; Feyzullah 2163/13; Halet Efendi ilavesi 66/6; Şehid Ali Paşa 1340/2, 1382/7; Topkapı E. H. 546/3.

Qushayrī, Abū'l-Qāsim. *al-Risāla*. Edited by ʿA. Maḥmūd and M. ibn al-Sharīf. Cairo: Dār al-Kutub al-Ḥadītha, 1972–1974.

Raḍawī, Mudarris. *Taʿlīqāt-i Ḥadīqat al-ḥaqīqa*. Tehran: ʿIlmī, 1344/1965.

Rāghib al-Iṣfahānī, al-. *al-Dharīʿa ilā makārim al-sharīʿa*. Edited by T. ʿA. Saʿd. Cairo: Maktabat al-Kulliyyāt al-Azhariyya, 1973.

Rāzī, Fakhr al-Dīn. *al-Tafsīr al-kabīr*. 8 vols. Istanbul: Dār al-Ṭibāʿat al-ʿĀmira, 1307–1308/1889–1891.

Rāzī, Najm al-Dīn. *Marmūzāt-i asadī dar mazmūrāt-i dāwūdī*. Edited by M. R. Shafīʿī Kadkanī. Tehran: McGill Institute of Islamic Studies, 1973.

———. *Mirṣād al-ʿibād min al-mabdaʾ ilaʾl-maʿād*. Edited by M. A. Riyāḥī. Tehran: Bungāh-i Tarjama wa Nashr-i Kitāb, 1352/1973. Translated by H. Algar as *The Path of God's Bondsmen from the Origin to the Return*. New York: Caravan, 1982.

Rūmī, Jalāl al-Dīn. *Dīwān-i Shams-i Tabrīzī*. Edited by B. Furūzānfar as *Kulliyyāt-i Shams yā dīwān-i kabīr*. 10 vols. Tehran: Dānishgāh, 1336–1346/1957–1967.

———. *Fīhi mā fīhi*. Edited by B. Furūzānfar. Tehran: Amīr Kabīr, 1348/1969. Translated by A. J. Arberry as *Discourses of Rumi*. London: John Murray, 1961.

———. *Majālis-i sabʿa*. In the introduction to *Mathnawī-yi maʿnawī*. Edited by M. Ramaḍānī. Tehran: Kulāla-yi Khāwar, 1315–1319/1926–1930.

———. *The Mathnawī*. 8 vols. Edited, translated, and annotated by R. A. Nicholson. London: Luzac, 1925–1940.

———. *Rubāʿiyyāt*. Published as volume 8 of his *Dīwān*.

Ruspoli, S. "La clef du monde suprasensible" (thèse). Paris: Sorbonne, Ve section, sciences religieuses, n.d. [1976?].

Rūzbihān Baqlī. *Mashrab al-arwāḥ*. Edited by N. M. Hoca. Istanbul: Edebiyat Fakültesi Matbaası, 1974.

Samʿānī, Aḥmad. *Rawḥ al-arwāḥ fī sharḥ asmāʾ al-malik al-fattāḥ*. Edited by N. Māyil Hirawī. Tehran: Intishārāt-i ʿIlmī wa Farhangī, 1368/1989.

Sanāʾī. *Dīwān*. Edited by Mudarris Raḍawī. Tehran: Ibn Sīnā, 1341/1962.

———. *Ḥadīqat al-ḥaqīqa*. Edited by Mudarris Raḍawī. Tehran: Sipihr, 1329/1950.

———. *Sayr al-ʿibād*. Edited by M. T. Mudarris Raḍawī in *Mathnawīhā-yi Ḥakīm Sanāʾī*. Tehran: Dānishgāh, 1348/1969. 181–233.

Sarrāj, Abū Naṣr al-. *Kitāb al-lumaʿ*. Edited by R.A. Nicholson. Leiden: Brill, 1914.

Schimmel, Annemarie. *And Muhammad Is His Messenger: The Veneration of the Prophet in Islamic Piety*. Chapel Hill: The University of North Carolina Press, 1985.

———. *Mystical Dimensions of Islam*. Chapel Hill: The University of North Carolina Press, 1975.

Shaybī, Kamāl al-. *Al-Ṣila bayn al-taṣawwuf waʾl-tashayyuʿ*. Cairo: Dār al-Maʿārif, 1969.

Sherif, M.A. *Ghazali's Theory of Virtue*. Albany: State University of New York Press, 1975.

Smith, Jane I., and Y. Y. Haddad. *The Islamic Understanding of Death and Resurrection*. Albany: State University of New York Press, 1981.

Smith, Wilfred Cantwell. *Faith and Belief*. Princeton: Princeton University Press, 1979.

———. "Faith as *Taṣdīq*." In *Islamic Philosophical Theology*. Edited by P. Morewedge. Albany: State University of New York Press, 1979. 96–119.

SPK. See Chittick, *Sufi Path of Knowledge.*

SPL. See Chittick, *Sufi Path of Love.*

Suhrawardī, Shihāb al-Dīn Abū Ḥafṣ. *'Awārif al-ma'ārif.* Beirut: Dār al-Kitāb al-'Arabī, 1966. Persian translation by Abū Manṣūr Iṣfahānī. Edited by Q. Anṣārī. Tehran: Shirkat-i Intishārāt-i 'Ilmī wa Farhangī, 1364/1985.

Suhrawardī al-Maqtūl, Shihāb al-Dīn Yaḥyā. *Al-Alwāḥ al-'imādiyya.* In *Sa Risāla az Shaykh-i Ishrāq.* Edited by N. Ḥabībī. Tehran: Imperial Iranian Academy of Philosophy, 1977. Suhrawardī's own Persian translation as *Alwāḥ-i 'imādiyya,* in his *Majmū'a-yi āthār-i fārsī.*

———. *Ḥikmat al-ishrāq.* Edited by Henry Corbin. In *Majmū'a-yi Muṣannafāt-i Shaykh-i Ishrāq.* Tehran: Imperial Iranian Academy of Philosophy, 1977.

———. *Majmū'a-yi āthār-i fārsī.* Edited by S. H. Nasr. Tehran: Imperial Iranian Academy of Philosophy, 1977.

Sulamī, Abū 'Abd al-Raḥmān. *Ṭabaqāt al-ṣūfiyya.* Edited by N. Shurayba. 2d ed. Cairo: Maktabat al-Khānjī, 1969.

Suyūṭī, Jalāl al-Dīn al-. *Al-Jāmi' al-ṣaghīr.* In al-Munāwī. *Fayḍ al-qadīr fī sharḥ al-jāmi' al-ṣaghīr.* Beirut: Dār al-Ma'rifa, 1972.

Ṭabarī, al-. *The History of al-Ṭabarī.* Vol. 3. Translated by W. M. Brinner. Albany: State University of New York Press, 1991.

Tabrīzī. *Mishkāt al-maṣābīḥ.* Translated by J. Robson. Lahore: Sh. Muhammad Ashraf, 1963–1965.

Tha'ālibī. *Al-Tamthīl wa'l-muḥāḍara.* Edited by 'A. M. al-Ḥuluw. Cairo: 'Īsā al-Bābī al-Ḥalabī, 1961.

Tirmidhī, al-. *Al-Jāmi' al-ṣaḥīḥ, wa huwa sunan al-Tirmidhī.* Edited by A. M. Shākir. Cairo: al-Maktabat al-Islāmiyya, 1938.

Trimingham, J. S. *The Sufi Orders in Islam.* Oxford: Oxford University Press, 1971.

Ṭūsī, Naṣīr al-Dīn. *Akhlāq-i Nāṣirī.* Edited by M. Mīnuwī and 'A. Ḥaydarī. 2d. ed. Tehran: Khwārazmī, 1360/1981. English translation by G. M. Wickens as *The Nasirean Ethics.* London: George Allen and Unwin, 1964.

Watt, W. Montgomery. *The Faith and Practice of al-Ghazālī.* Lahore: Sh. Muhammad Ashraf, 1963.

Weischer, B., and P. L. Wilson. *Heart's Witness: The Sufi Quatrains of Awḥaduddīn Kirmānī.* Tehran: Imperial Iranian Academy of Philosophy, 1978.

Wensinck, A. J. *The Muslim Creed.* London: Frank Cass, 1965.

Wensinck, A. J., et al. *Concordance et indices de la tradition musulmane.* Leiden: Brill, 1936–1969.

Woodward, Mark. *Islam in Java: Normative Piety and Mysticism in the Sultanate of Yogyakarta.* Tucson: The University of Arizona Press, 1989.

Yahia, Osman. *Histoire et classification de l'oeuvre d'Ibn 'Arabī.* Damascus: Institut Français de Damas, 1964.

Index of Koranic Verses

Index of Hadiths and Sayings

Index of Names and Terms